BEYOND THE FIELDS

The publisher gratefully acknowledges
the generous support of the Anne G. Lipow
Endowment Fund for Social Justice and Human
Rights of the University of California Press
Foundation, which was established by
Stephen M. Silberstein.

BEYOND THE FIELDS

CESAR CHAVEZ, THE UFW, AND THE STRUGGLE FOR JUSTICE IN THE 21ST CENTURY

Randy Shaw

UNIVERSITY OF CALIFORNIA PRESS

BERKELEY   LOS ANGELES   LONDON

University of California Press, one of the most distinguished university presses in the United States, enriches lives around the world by advancing scholarship in the humanities, social sciences, and natural sciences. Its activities are supported by the UC Press Foundation and by philanthropic contributions from individuals and institutions. For more information, visit www.ucpress.edu.

University of California Press
Berkeley and Los Angeles, California

University of California Press, Ltd.
London, England

Library of Congress Cataloging-in-Publication Data

Shaw, Randy, 1956–
  Beyond the fields : Cesar Chavez, the UFW, and the struggle for justice in the twenty-first century / Randy Shaw.
    p. cm.
  Includes bibliographical references and index.
  ISBN: 978-0-520-25107-6 (cloth : alk. paper)
    1. United Farm Workers of America.   2. Chavez, Cesar, 1927–1993.   3. Social action—United States.   4. Social justice—United States.   I. Title.
  HD6515.A292U548   2008
  331.88'13092—dc22
  [B]   2008031252

Manufactured in the United States of America

17 16 15 14 13 12 11 10 09 08
10 9 8 7 6 5 4 3 2 1

This book is printed on Natures Book, which contains 50% post-consumer waste and meets the minimum requirements of ANSI/NISO Z39.48–1992 (R 1997) (*Permanence of Paper*).

CONTENTS

ILLUSTRATIONS

PREFACE

When I attended UC Berkeley in the mid-1970s, United Farm Workers volunteers were everywhere. The UFW had tables on campus, on Telegraph Avenue, and in front of the local Co-op supermarkets. The volunteers would always have clipboards, donation cans, and literature and were as animated as carnival barkers in trying to get people's attention. My future wife signed up to volunteer, and through her I got to know some of the full-time boycott staffers. I was incredibly impressed by their dedication and wondered then—and ever since—why other causes or movements could not also attract a huge cadre of idealistic young activists.

As I followed the careers of many UFW alumni over the years, it seemed that their experience with the farmworkers had changed their lives, leading them to a lifetime of working for social justice, often in strategically critical roles. But the link between the UFW of the 1960s and 1970s and later progressive struggles has remained largely unexplored. This link involves both the activists themselves and the way in which the UFW's strategies and tactics still bring success to a wide variety of progressive campaigns. I wrote this book to tell that story.

My own activism emerged from my work in San Francisco's Tenderloin neighborhood. In 1980, I joined with other law students in founding the Tenderloin Housing Clinic (THC) (http://thclinic.org). Our goal was to assist residents with landlord-tenant problems. Those were exciting years, as the neighborhood waged a historic campaign against three luxury hotels slated for the community's border. The Tenderloin became the nation's first community to require private developers to fund affordable housing as a condition of project approval. We subsequently waged many other successful fights to improve living conditions for the city's low-income residents and to preserve the Tenderloin as an affordable area of the city. Like those whose experience with the UFW led them to dedicate their lives to social justice, my experience with these campaigns in the 1980s instilled a sense of excitement and solidarity that hooked me on a career as an activist.

During the 1980s, I strongly opposed San Francisco's approach to homelessness. When a new mayor took office in 1988, he gave me the chance to put my ideas for housing homeless single adults into practice. THC implemented a program that provided permanent housing in single-room occupancy hotels (SROs) for thousands of formerly homeless tenants. In 1999, we began leasing SROs for homeless persons and became San Francisco's leading provider of permanent housing for homeless single adults. In 1980, most believed that it was only a matter of time before this neighborhood, located between San Francisco City Hall and posh Union Square, was gentrified. But we organized to defeat gentrification, winning passage of several city laws that protected low-income tenants and the SRO housing stock; today, the Tenderloin is the only neighborhood in San Francisco whose long-term future as a low-income community is assured.

As a result of my experiences in San Francisco, I concluded that activists' tactics and strategies were often central to the outcome of social justice struggles. Conversations with participants in a wide range of campaigns across the United States reaffirmed this point. To focus on the tactics and strategies most likely to bring success, I wrote *The Activist's Handbook*, which was first released in 1996 and then updated in 2001. In 1999, I expanded my study of the fight for social change to argue that activists should combine their local work with efforts to influence national policies. The resulting book, *Reclaiming America: Nike, Clean Air, and the New National Activism,* analyzed the anti-sweatshop movement, national environmental campaigns, and strategies that allow community-based groups to participate in the important federal fights that increasingly shape what can be achieved locally.

During the course of both my own activism and the writing of these books, I have gained great insights from working with ACORN (Association of Community Organizations for Reform Now) on local, state, and national campaigns. I have also spent considerable time talking with Public Interest Research Group (PIRG) organizers at campus, regional, and national events. Both of these organizations have effectively recruited young organizers. I ran a program from 2001 to 2003 called JusticeCorps, which sought to place graduating college students into full-time organizing jobs with community organizations across the nation. JusticeCorps gave me great insight into the limited options available to young people seeking careers in social change. Many community groups faced funding cutbacks and were unable to hire qualified young staff. While groups across the country were thrilled that I was trying to get talented young people into organizing jobs, we had to end the program because of a lack of employment opportunities.

This experience made me start thinking about the key role the UFW played during the 1960s and 1970s as an incubator for hundreds of young activists—a role that has not been replicated even today. As stories continued to appear in the press about the UFW's current problems, it struck me that the movement's true legacy was being missed. This legacy should not be based on the size of the UFW's current membership rolls. Rather, it should be evaluated by the impact of its ideas and alumni on current social justice struggles. By this measure, the lasting legacy of Cesar Chavez and the UFW is enormous and has extended well beyond the fields.

Understanding this legacy requires familiarity with the UFW's history. As I started this book, I got a good sense of how little is known about Cesar Chavez and the farmworkers movement. I ran into a young activist from the East Coast who had worked with Justice for Janitors and the Working Families Party before starting law school at Yale. I knew she was very well read on labor and political issues, and I asked her what she knew about Cesar Chavez and the UFW. She replied that while she obviously knew who Chavez was, she knew nothing of the history of the farmworkers movement. Her comments echoed those of a twenty-eight-year-old co-worker who was also politically informed and had grown up in California. It seemed that my attempt to show the connection between the UFW of the 1960s and 1970s and current movements would require informing readers about what Chavez and the union had in fact accomplished.

This book connects the history of the UFW to an analysis of post-1980 and twenty-first-century social movements. The vast majority of books about the UFW were written before 1980 and do not address the movement's decline or its legacy over the past two decades. A 1998 work—*The Fight in the Fields: Cesar Chavez and the Farmworkers Movement,* by Susan Ferriss and Ricardo Sandoval, with an accompanying video—powerfully captures the UFW spirit but does not attempt to link it to ongoing social struggles. My book has a very different focus, particularly emphasizing the role of UFW alumni, ideas, and strategies in post-1998 developments in the immigrant rights movement, the transformation of the labor movement, and the campaign to increase Latino voting. I hope that readers of this book will become interested in learning more about the UFW's history and discover the many important works that were produced during the movement's peak success. This book builds upon, rather than competes with, these earlier histories.

I noted in the introduction to *The Activist's Handbook* that activists spend too much time bemoaning defeats and not enough time celebrating and remembering victories. One reason current challenges appear so daunting is that activists are unaware that prior generations triumphed over even greater odds; those unaware of grassroots activism's history of success are less likely to believe that they can make a difference in the world. As calls for a change in the country's direction reverberate across the United States, there will soon be historic opportunities to further social and economic justice. But the struggles for implementing universal health care, redirecting military spending to human needs, reducing if not reversing the pace of global warming, and establishing a host of other long-overdue policies will not be easy. It is my hope that by learning about the UFW's success and about how those who built the union brought its strategies and tactics into other social justice campaigns, today's activists will have greater confidence in waging, and prevailing in, their own David and Goliath battles. Cesar Chavez always expected the spirit of *"sí se puede!"* to live on in future generations. Continuing the struggle for justice in the twenty-first century is the best testament to his and the UFW's legacy.

ACKNOWLEDGMENTS

I was inspired to write this book by those who worked during the 1960s and 1970s to empower farmworkers. Although the book began more than two decades after the heyday of the United Farm Workers of America, memories of the movement's success lingered with me, and the ongoing work of UFW alumni continued to impress me. I felt that the UFW's role as a training ground for idealistic young activists had not been sufficiently explored, and I hoped that addressing the union's success might remind activists of the importance of creating vehicles for harnessing such talent in the pursuit of social change.

Many UFW alumni either were interviewed for this book or provided essays from which I drew information and insights. I am most greatly indebted to LeRoy Chatfield, who deepened my understanding of Cesar Chavez's 1968 fast and who created the Farmworker Movement Documentation Project, an invaluable archive of essays and other materials by activists. This remarkable website, at www.farmworkermovement.org, also features rare photographs, videos, and even music from the movement. Chatfield's entirely voluntary effort allows the legacy of UFW volunteers and staff members to come to life and supplies archival material that is not easily available elsewhere. Chatfield's labors deserve not only my thanks but also the appreciation of all who care about the UFW's history.

Several other UFW alumni were of particular help in understanding the movement. I have spent years discussing the union with Sandy Nathan, and he provided consistent encouragement during the writing of this book. I got to know Sandy's mentor, former UFW chief legal counsel Jerry Cohen, several years ago. Cohen offered valuable insights and guidance, especially concerning the UFW's anti-pesticide campaign and the important role of the late UFW leader Jessica Govea. Tom Dalzell routinely took time from his own writing and busy life to respond to my inquiries. Gary Guthman was the boycott staffer who introduced me to the UFW in 1977, and his personal journey from the farmworkers to the hotel workers to SEIU has long seemed emblematic to me.

UFW alums Fred Ross Jr., Scott Washburn, and Marshall Ganz graciously shared their thoughts and gave feedback, as did Stephen Lerner. Lerner gave me all the materials I needed to write about SEIU's University of Miami campaign and was always available to answer questions. Other UFW veterans who were interviewed for this book include Chava Bustamante, Elaine Elinson, Mark Pitt (whose photographs of a young Eliseo Medina, taken with a Polaroid camera, are included in the book), David Bacon, Bill Carder, Larry Tramutola, Nick Jones, Nancy Grimley Carleton, Jean Eilers, Alice Sunshine, Gilbert Padilla, Humberto Gomez, Sharon Delugach, Larry Frank, Peter Jones, Eliseo Medina, Wayne "Chris" Hartmire, Susan Sachen, Mark Sharwood, Paul Milne, and Bob Purcell.

I want to thank all of the busy SEIU and UNITE HERE staff who were not UFW alums who took time to be interviewed. This list includes SEIU's Martin Manteca, Ben Monterroso, Lauren Martens, Mark Gomez, Renee Asher, Tracy Zeluff, Blanca Perez, Erik Brakken, and Javier Gonzalez as well as UNITE HERE's Ben Mantle, Mike Casey, Lisa Jaicks, the Reverend Teran Loeppke, Alicia Ortiz, Bishaara Clark, Jim McNeil, and Sam Pullen. UNITE HERE Local 2 attorney Matt Ross contributed insight into legal issues around the boycott. Hotel boycott coordinator Dave Glaser was especially helpful in facilitating my access to organizers, and his analysis of UNITE HERE's boycott strategy was invaluable.

Adrian Pantoja and Ricardo Ramírez, leading scholars of Latino political behavior, both took time to help me understand their studies; and Henry Flores offered perspective on Latino voting patterns. Juan Sepulveda Jr. confirmed for me Cesar Chavez's great influence on William Velasquez's career. Cecilia Barragan, Consuelo Valdez, and Father Pat Murphy all supplied information about the Active Citizenship Campaign. Ron Kaye of the *Los Angeles Daily News* provided clippings that greatly contributed to my account of the ACC.

John Adler, currently with SEIU, played a key role in compiling the list of former Neighbor to Neighbor organizers who went on to advance social justice. Adler also helped to clarify the UFW's influence on Neighbor to Neighbor, a group whose coffee boycott harkened back to the farmworkers' grape campaign.

Others interviewed for this book include Kim Bobo, founder of Interfaith Worker Justice; Gouri Sadhwani, Rodel Rodis; Mary Ann Buckley; Peter Dreier; John Burton; Ruth Milkman; Kent Wong; and Dick Meister, coauthor of *A Long Time Coming: The Struggle to Unionize America's*

Farm Workers. Harold Meyerson was not interviewed, but his *LA Weekly* columns on Miguel Contreras and the rise of Latino labor power in Los Angeles were invaluable. The Reverend C. W. Hawking, a consultant with Interfaith Worker Justice, also contributed to my analysis of the Miami struggle, as did Father Frank Corbishley, Jacob Coker-Dukowitz, Renee Asher, Eric Brakken, and Melewau Hall.

For assistance in securing photos, thanks go to Mary Gutierrez of the Los Angeles County Federation of Labor, legendary UFW photographer Jon Lewis, Hub Segur, Nick Jones, Jeannine Briceno, David Sachs of SEIU, and Margo Feinberg.

Casey Mills, my former *Beyond Chron* colleague, provided invaluable feedback on several chapters and greatly improved the final product. I was also able to benefit from comments by my longtime friend Chris Tiedemann. Mercy Gonzales and Steven Shubert supplied valuable word-processing assistance, and Jesse Nathan assisted with research.

I had the benefit of many earlier histories of Cesar Chavez and the UFW. Two were particularly helpful. *The Fight in the Fields: Cesar Chavez and the Farmworkers Movement,* by Susan Ferriss and Ricardo Sandoval, is likely the single best history of the movement and has an accompanying documentary video that is available in many libraries. Jacques E. Levy's *Cesar Chavez: The Autobiography of La Causa,* recently reissued in paperback, is the leading source for interviews with Chavez. Readers of *Beyond the Fields* are encouraged to learn more about the farmworkers movement, and these and other sources cited in the text are a good place to start.

I would like to thank everyone at the University of California Press who has assisted in this project, particularly my editor, Naomi Schneider, who has now shepherded me through three books.

Finally, special thanks to my daughters, Anita and Ariel Feingold-Shaw, and to my wife, Lainey Feingold, whose editorial assistance and critical support made this project possible.

INTRODUCTION

When Cesar Chavez decided in 1962 to pursue the impossible dream of organizing California's farmworkers, he knew firsthand the difficult plight of those working in the fields. Chavez's family had moved to California and become farmworkers in 1937, after financial difficulties caused them to lose their Arizona ranch. Eleven-year-old Cesar was soon exposed to the sight of farmworkers bathing in and drinking from irrigation ditches and living on riverbanks or under bridges. He saw that a typical farmworker "home" was a shack built of cardboard cartons and linoleum scraps or a tent made of gunny sacks. For farmworkers living in labor camps, plumbing facilities were inadequate or nonexistent; often, fifty to a hundred families shared one faucet. Years later, Chavez recalled that the camps' toilets were "always horrible, so miserable you couldn't go there." Although farmworkers spent their days in fields rich with fruit and vegetables, they lived in constant hunger. Most survived on beans, fried dough, dandelion greens, and potatoes. Working as stoop laborers in 100-degree heat was hard enough, but growers also forced farmworkers to use the short-handle hoe. This backbreaking tool damaged the health of Chavez and generations of farmworkers, leading him to conclude at an early age that growers "don't give a damn" about farmworkers as human beings but instead see them "as implements." The combination of brutal working conditions, unsanitary living conditions, poor diet, and grinding poverty explained why farmworkers had short life expectancies, with many dying before age fifty.[1]

Against this harsh backdrop, Cesar Chavez launched a movement that made history, leaving an indelible mark on the 1960s and 1970s. This book describes how Chavez and the farmworkers movement developed ideas, tactics, and strategies that proved so compelling, so original, and ultimately so successful that they continue to set the course for America's progressive campaigns—and will likely do so for decades to come. Chavez and the United Farm Workers also developed a generation of progressive leaders who are reshaping the American labor movement, building the nation's immigrant rights movement, revitalizing grassroots democracy, and are at the forefront of the struggle to transform national politics in twenty-first-century America.[2]

While tens of thousands attended civil rights and antiwar marches in the 1960s and 1970s, it was the UFW that became the organizational home for a generation of young people eager to devote their lives to a righteous cause. Chavez's charismatic leadership and the long history of injustices perpetrated against farmworkers led many individuals with little or no activist experience to quit jobs, drop out of college, or delay career plans so that they could join others in working hundred-hour weeks for $5 a week plus room and board. Many of those who worked with the UFW from 1965 to 1980 underwent life-changing experiences. Contrary to conventional wisdom about activists from that era later becoming stockbrokers, an astonishing number of UFW alumni went on to devote their lives to winning social and economic justice for working people, particularly Latino immigrants.

The Delano grape strike, launched in the fall of 1965, proved to be a historic turning point for Chavez, California farmworkers, and America's future progressive movements. Before the strike, Chavez himself was largely unknown, and Americans paid little attention to the wages and working conditions of those who picked their fruit and vegetables. But on March 17, 1966, Chavez began a three-hundred-mile march, along with strikers and supporters, from the Central California town of Delano to the state capitol building in Sacramento. News photos of a limping and bleeding Chavez completing his pilgrimage on Easter Sunday captivated the nation. America not only learned about a strike against grape growers but also had its first glimpse of a man who would become the nation's most honored Latino.

Chavez and the farmworkers movement soon transcended their fight for justice in California's fields and came to embody the era's struggles against racism and poverty. Idealistic young activists seeking to work full time for social change flocked to La Causa (the cause) and joined with Latino and Filipino workers in creating a stirring national campaign for economic justice. During its heyday, the UFW was known for its nationwide grape, wine, and vegetable boycotts, for colorful mass marches, for chants of *"huelga!"* (strike!) throughout the fields of rural California, for its black and red Aztec eagle flag, and, most of all, for the determined and uncompromising leadership of Cesar Chavez. His framing of the farmworkers struggle in spiritual rather than simply economic terms, as a new national civil rights movement, fit perfectly with the times. Chavez was unlike any other labor leader of his time, and his personal commitment to voluntary poverty struck a chord among the young clergy and college students rebelling against rampant materialism.

Establishing a farmworkers union seemed to be an impossible dream, but Chavez and the UFW developed a range of new strategies and tactics for its fulfillment. He began by engaging in the most painstaking organizing campaign ever directed at Mexican immigrant farmworkers, seeking supporters one on one and house to house. Knowing that farmworkers could not win this fight on their own, Chavez then broke from labor tradition and recruited young outsiders looking to make a difference in the world. The result was an unlikely alliance of Latino and Filipino farmworkers, migrant ministers and progressive priests, and former college students of various ethnicities. Chavez helped to forge La Causa into the most powerful farmworker movement in American history.

By 1972, the UFW had contracts with 150 growers and an estimated membership of fifty to sixty thousand, of which thirty thousand were year-round workers while others worked only during the harvest season.[3] For the first time in the long, tortured history of California agricultural labor, those who picked the nation's fruits and vegetables had rest breaks, safe drinking water, and toilets; and they earned wages that enabled them to settle down and perhaps even to buy modest homes rather than migrating to follow the crops. In addition to bringing historically high wages, benefits, and improved working conditions, the UFW also heightened farmworkers' self-esteem. A group that had long been looked down on as powerless had forced America's largest growers to the bargaining table and now demanded respect.

In 1975, ten years after the Delano grape strike began, California enacted the Agricultural Labor Relations Act, the first legislation of its kind in the country. After more than seventy years of struggle, the state's farmworkers had finally won a remarkable victory, securing many of the same labor protections that industrial and factory workers had won in the 1930s. Passage of the act was a remarkable victory for Chavez, the farmworkers movement, and the millions of Americans and Canadians who supported the boycotts and La Causa. Following the enactment of this legislation, union elections were quickly scheduled on more than six hundred farms, and the UFW won nearly all of them.

In 1979, the union engaged in a massive lettuce strike, supported by more than twenty-five thousand farmworkers marching for justice, and won another huge victory. By the start of 1980, the fastest UFW lettuce

pickers could earn as much as $20 an hour, a wage close to that of union-
ized manufacturing workers. UFW members had paid vacations, paid overtime, unemployment benefits, and health insurance for their families—
benefits long denied agricultural workers. A group that had begun with
Cesar Chavez holding house meetings and collecting $3.50 in monthly
dues stood poised to become California's most powerful union and a leading statewide vehicle for economic justice and progressive reforms. And
since Chavez had never lost sight of farmworker problems in Florida,
Texas, Arizona, Oregon, and Washington, many saw the success in California spreading to other states, triggering a powerful new national movement for greater social and economic fairness.[4]

But the 1979 victory in the lettuce fields proved to be the high point
of the UFW's success. Instead of sparking a nationwide campaign for a
national farmworkers union, the UFW soon began a steady decline. Most
of the key figures who had built the union left the organization between
1977 and 1981. By 2006, the UFW had no table grape contracts, and
membership had fallen as low as seven thousand, compared to the high
of sixty thousand in 1972. Sadly, some believe that wages and working
conditions for farmworkers today lag farther behind those of other workers than they did in 1965, when the Delano grape strike began.

The UFW's steep decline has not erased the name of Cesar Chavez
from public consciousness. To the contrary, Chavez remains America's
most famous Latino. He holds a permanent place in many U.S. history
books; schools, parks, roads, and community centers across the country
bear his name. California has established a state holiday to celebrate
Chavez, and a campaign is growing to create a national holiday in his
honor. But his accomplishments have become frozen in the past. While
Chavez is credited for inspiring generations of Latinos, he is viewed as
an icon of a bygone era, whose legacy—the building of the UFW—has
been wrongly defined (and limited) by the union's steep membership decline since 1981. But measuring Chavez's ongoing legacy on the basis of
UFW membership is both misleading and inaccurate. This framing ig-
nores the extent to which UFW alumni brought the ideas, tactics, and
strategies of the farmworkers movement to subsequent progressive campaigns. The story of how these ideas are profoundly influencing America's movements for social and economic justice has not been told.

This book seeks to tell that story. I argue that, from the reshaping of
the American labor movement to the building of state and national Latino
political power, from the growing national struggle for immigrant rights
to the transformation of California politics, and ultimately to the push

to improve social conditions and life opportunities for tens of millions of Americans, the imprint of Cesar Chavez and the UFW is inescapable.

In 1960, two years before Chavez's efforts began, the powerful AFL-CIO launched a heavily funded effort to organize farmworkers. This effort relied on conventional union organizing tactics. The campaign went nowhere. In contrast, nearly all of labor's successful organizing campaigns since the 1960s have relied on the grassroots activist–style approach pioneered by the UFW. In fact, Chavez and the UFW originated or revived so many strategies and tactics now utilized by progressive movements and campaigns that it is hard to imagine how activists succeeded without such tools:

- Conducting consumer boycotts and corporate campaigns
- Building alliances between the religious community and labor unions
- Framing issues of economic justice in moral and spiritual terms, and engaging in activities such as spiritual fasts
- Encouraging civic participation among union members
- Emphasizing voter outreach and election day activities
- Building coalitions of labor, community groups, and students
- Generating media attention
- Using innovative forms of communication, such as "human billboards"
- Integrating cultural activities such as street theater into organizing efforts

In detailing the link between the UFW's ideas, tactics, and strategies and current progressive movements, the second major focus of this book will emerge: how UFW alumni have played pivotal roles in building and winning campaigns for social and economic justice for more than four decades. One would be hard-pressed to think of a progressive organization of the 1960s that produced more activists who went on to full-time careers working for social change or that had such a significant impact on America's social justice struggles. If there were a post–World War II Hall of Fame for activists in America, UFW veterans would dominate the inductees.

The long-term impact of the UFW's recruitment, training, and leadership development of a generation of young activists has long been overlooked. Mentors such as Fred Ross Sr., Gilbert Padilla, Marshall Ganz, and Cesar Chavez himself treated organizing as a profession, with a set of skills that had to be correctly implemented. A good heart was not enough; young people required training, on-the-job experience, and intensive feedback to nurture their talents. But the demands of the struggle were intense, and the UFW imposed a "sink or swim" philosophy, granting young organizers a degree of independence and flexibility unheard of in today's labor and social change organizations. These new organizers quickly learned how to build a broad coalition of community support, to recruit volunteers, and to mobilize activists for protests and rallies. Not all succeeded, and some of the best nearly quit before figuring out how to get the job done. But when UFW alumni with this remarkable training moved on to future jobs, they took the skills and strategies that brought unprecedented success to the farmworkers in the 1960s and 1970s with them.

From 1965 to 1979, the United Farm Workers of America was the nation's leading organizer training school. The union drew some activists caught up in the spirit of the '60s, but many joined in the early '70s, when signs of changing times were already evident. The synergy between new and veteran activists built the skill level of the former, enabling the UFW's talent pool to grow almost exponentially. Organizing for the UFW was both physically and mentally exhausting, but this rigor instilled activists with the confidence that they could win progressive campaigns, regardless of the apparent odds.

Cesar Chavez's organizing prowess has been eclipsed by his other accomplishments, but he started the movement by knocking on doors and holding house meetings, where he would ask people to pay $3.50 in monthly membership dues. He understood the frustrations and challenges of grassroots organizing, having walked into houses for meetings only to find the home vacant and the host family missing. His determined spirit infused the farmworkers movement, inspiring others to continue his work.

Today, the ongoing legacy of Cesar Chavez and the UFW has moved from the lettuce fields of rural California to the hospitals, luxury hotels, and office towers of urban America. This is where UFW veterans created the "Justice for Janitors" campaigns, where the UFW's influence is felt in the struggle to unionize hospital and hotel workers. This legacy is found in the massive immigrant rights marches of 2006, in organized labor's effective voter outreach efforts on election day, and in increased civic participation among immigrants and union members in a broad array of progressive movements and campaigns. The UFW grape and vegetable boycotts are long over, but their success spawned similar campaigns against

Salvadoran coffee during El Salvador's bloody civil war, against South African apartheid, against the sale of infant formula in developing nations, and against the global corporations that now own America's luxury hotels.

Although the UFW had always practiced "social movement" unionism, it was not until 1996 that the AFL-CIO officially embraced the idea that labor unions should join with community groups in seeking broader social goals. The Service Employees International Union (SEIU) and UNITE HERE are the two unions most responsible for this shift, and these are also the unions most influenced by UFW alumni.[5] In 2005, these unions broke from the AFL-CIO to form Change to Win, designed to be a more activist-oriented labor federation that would prioritize organizing. In 2006, Change to Win supported UNITE HERE's national Hotel Workers Rising campaign, which began transforming hotel work into the type of well-paid, middle-class jobs long held by unionized autoworkers and steelworkers. UFW president Arturo Rodriguez gave the keynote speech at the campaign's national kickoff, and the fighting spirit of the farmworkers was evoked throughout the event.

Cesar Chavez sought to build a union, rather than remain a community organizer, because he saw unionization as the best strategy for improving living conditions for blue-collar Latino immigrants. The pursuit of this strategy for Latino empowerment did not end with his death or the UFW's decline. Chavez and the farmworkers movement overcame skeptics to prove that Mexican immigrants could be unionized, and organized labor in the twenty-first century continues to build on this tradition.

While Cesar Chavez and the UFW are often credited with bringing national attention to the problems of Mexican Americans, their ongoing impact on rising Latino political empowerment remains underappreciated. This contemporary legacy is evidenced by significantly greater rates of Latino voting in California, a sharp rise in the number of Latino legislators in that state, and the creation of a powerful voter outreach apparatus, which laid the groundwork for the election of Los Angeles's first Latino mayor in 2005. The UFW grassroots electoral model has expanded from California to other states with sizable Latino populations, dramatically increasing Latino voter turnout in both Colorado and Arizona during the 2006 midterm elections.

The millions of immigrant rights protesters who took to the streets in 2006 understood this connection between the farmworkers movement and the ongoing drive for Latino empowerment. These marchers needed no prompting before spontaneously adopting the UFW chant "*sí se puede!*" (yes, we can!) in cities across America. As huge throngs of Latino immigrant parents chanted, sang, and marched with their kids, it was clear that the UFW's tradition of nonviolent protests had helped legitimize the tactic and had bolstered undocumented Mexican immigrants' willingness to take to the streets to assert their rights. When Barack Obama's 2008 presidential campaign adopted the "Yes we can!" rallying cry, it highlighted how the UFW's chant has extended beyond Latinos to become an almost universal call for social and economic justice.

The opening chapter of this book focuses on the consumer boycott, a strategy that brought most of the volunteers into the movement and proved instrumental to the UFW's success. Chavez and the UFW reinvented this nineteenth-century strategy, and the union's grape boycott became the most successful consumer boycott in American history. The building of the boycott is the story of a mass movement, a phenomenon often dreamed of but seldom realized. Running a nationwide boycott with virtually no funds required recruiting a huge influx of volunteers, giving the era's young people, clergy, women, and Latino immigrants an entrée into the labor movement.

Chapter 2 discusses how the UFW's boycott model was subsequently adopted and enhanced by other labor and progressive movements. These range from the high-profile J. P. Stevens textile boycott in the 1970s to the eight-year boycott of Campbell's Soup launched by the UFW-inspired Farm Labor Organizing Committee in 1979 to the 1989 boycott of Salvadoran coffee led by the activist group Neighbor to Neighbor, which helped bring a cease-fire in that nation's civil war. The chapter also illustrates how UNITE HERE's Hotel Workers Rising campaign has developed the UFW boycott model for effective use by social movements in the Internet age.

The building of a clergy-labor alliance and the use of the spiritual fast are the subjects of chapter 3. Photos of farmworker marches and rallies typically show supporters in religious garb, but many forget that when Chavez began organizing farmworkers in 1962, strong relationships between labor and the religious community had not existed for more than two decades. Chavez and the farmworkers had to build this relationship, overcoming indifference and even hostility from local churches. The UFW was the only workers' struggle to secure strong church backing until a coal strike in 1989. Today, many unions create alliances with local clergy as a matter of standard procedure, yet few credit Chavez and the UFW for rebuilding this critical alliance. One reason the UFW eventually won the committed involvement of so many members of the clergy was because the union framed many of its campaigns in religious or spiritual terms. Chapter 3 discusses two critical examples: the three-hundred-mile pilgrimage from Delano to Sacramento in 1966, and Chavez's twenty-five-day spiritual fast in 1968. Both tactics galvanized broad support for La Causa among the religious community in part by fusing traditional Catholic religious symbols with protest activities. While Chavez did not "invent" the spiritual fast—the Bible describes how Jesus fasted for forty days—he engaged in the most prominent American fast of the century and inspired others to use the tactic in future progressive campaigns.

Chapter 4 presents a case study of how the UFW's legacy influenced a 2006 union organizing effort by SEIU's Justice for Janitors in Miami, Florida. The "Yes We Cane" campaign at the University of Miami—its very name was a clever, English-language takeoff on Cesar Chavez's classic "sí se puede!" motto—included almost the full range of innovative UFW strategies. The organizing drive replicated the UFW's model of a clergy-worker-student alliance, included a spiritual fast, and involved such key former UFW figures as Dolores Huerta, SEIU international vice president Eliseo Medina, and the Reverend Wayne "Chris" Hartmire. The campaign's chief architect was Stephen Lerner, the SEIU Building Services leader, who had been trained as an organizer while working on the UFW boycott in New York.

Chapter 5 describes the UFW's leading role in battling the use of pesticides in the fields during the 1960s and its transformation of a local fight over spraying into a national campaign to ban DDT and other hazardous chemicals. The UFW became the first union to address environmental safety through labor contract provisions and pioneered strategies that forced growers to be more safety conscious. The chapter also discusses the UFW's efforts to secure support from mainstream environmental groups, which met with only mixed success. Nonetheless, the UFW's pesticide campaign was an early example of what emerged as the environmental justice movement, which targets the disproportionate health risks imposed on low-income people and communities of color.

Chapter 6 discusses the UFW's approach to political organizing and electoral work. During the 1960s and 1970s, the need to fend off political attacks from growers led the UFW to create a powerful vehicle for outreach to low-income and Latino voters. This grassroots electoral operation relied on door-to-door personal contacts, precinct organization, volunteer recruitment, and leadership development. The UFW brought a community organizing analysis to its electoral and legislative campaigns at a time when other American labor unions bypassed "people power," relying instead on campaign donations to favored politicians. In later years, UFW veterans would apply this electoral model to local and congressional races, including San Francisco mayoral races and the campaign of first-time candidate Nancy Pelosi, who became the first woman Speaker of the U.S. House of Representatives in 2007. In the Pelosi campaign and others, UFW alumni enhanced the UFW grassroots electoral model, paving the way for its widespread future adoption by progressive campaigns.

One of the most positive political stories of the 1990s was the rise in Latino voting and political clout in Los Angeles, and throughout much of California. Chapter 7 explores the role of UFW alumnus Miguel Contreras as the leading architect of this electoral transformation. Contreras had learned how to run grassroots election campaigns from the UFW and through later campaigns that involved former UFW staffers Marshall Ganz and Jessica Govea. After he became head of the Los Angeles County Federation of Labor in 1996, Contreras began to implement the UFW electoral model. Working in concert with UFW veteran Eliseo Medina and others, Contreras built a Latino voter outreach machine that transformed Los Angeles into a union stronghold. He also played a central role in creating the electoral infrastructure that elected Antonio Villaraigosa as Los Angeles's first Latino mayor in 2005, which significantly strengthened the position of the Democratic Party statewide. Although most accounts attribute rising Latino voter turnout to a "hostile political environment" created by California's anti-immigrant Proposition 187 in 1994, this chapter examines statistical data from California and other states with large numbers of Latinos showing that electoral outreach by organized labor deserves far greater credit. Further, as Eliseo Medina and other UFW veterans have helped expand the group's grassroots electoral model to other states such as Arizona and Colorado, it has the potential to alter the future political landscape of the United States.

The ongoing struggle for immigrant rights is the focus of chapter 8. This chapter first addresses the often misunderstood stance of the UFW toward the rights of undocumented immigrants. Chavez and the union opposed strikebreakers of all races and backgrounds, including those who were undocumented; but the UFW's first constitution made no distinction between members who were undocumented and those who were legal immigrants, and Chavez strongly and publicly opposed the growers' exploitation of undocumented workers. The chapter also analyzes the crucial role of UFW alumni in campaigns that helped to build the national immigrant rights movement, including Fred Ross Jr., in the Active Citizenship Campaign, an Industrial Areas Foundation–sponsored effort uniting labor unions and the religious community to help immigrants apply for citizenship, demand expedited processing of citizenship applications, and turn newly naturalized Latino immigrants into registered, active voters. Another UFW veteran, Eliseo Medina, brought SEIU's resources into the ACC and was also a central figure in pressuring the AFL-CIO to shift its longstanding opposition to immigrant rights to a stance favoring legalization for the undocumented. Organized labor's membership and resources greatly expanded the immigrant rights movement, and the labor-sponsored Immigrant Worker Freedom Ride in 2003 proved to be a key stepping-stone to the massive protests of 2006.

Chapter 9 describes this public emergence of a powerful national immigrant rights movement and the dramatic increase in Latino voting in the November 2006 election. The tens of thousands of marchers in more than two hundred American cities chanting the UFW's rally cry *"sí se puede!"* demonstrated the deep connection immigrants felt between their actions and those of Cesar Chavez and the farmworkers movement. Eliseo Medina spent 2006 as the chief congressional negotiator for the immigrant rights movement, and his vision has guided much of the labor movement's approach to immigration reform since the late 1990s.

Chapter 10 examines the decline of the UFW, which began in 1977, just as its fortunes appeared brightest. Chavez's actions played a major role in the exodus of most of the UFW's key organizers, attorneys, and worker leaders between 1977 and 1981. As UFW alumni went on to promote social justice beyond the fields, the UFW began a steady decline that has continued for more than two decades. While most books describing the UFW's current weakness blame hostile Republican politicians, it was the union's loss of the talented activists who had built it that led to its inability to secure contracts in the 1980s and beyond.

Chapter 11 includes a chart of UFW alumni who went on to work for social justice and profiles of several individuals whose life histories collectively offer a broader understanding of the quality of people who worked for the UFW in its heyday. Many UFW veterans stayed in the labor movement, while others organized low-income people in communities across America. Some made important cultural contributions, including Luis Valdez, whose Teatro Campesino brought a mythic brand of Chicano culture to the forefront of the UFW organizing drives and helped to politicize an emerging Chicano art world. This chapter describes people who dropped out of high school, quit their religious orders, left farm labor to become professional organizers, or otherwise redirected their lives to work with the UFW. The chapter also discusses how UFW alumni built the group Neighbor to Neighbor in the 1980s, which itself became an important training ground for young activists who have continued to struggle for justice in the twenty-first century.

The concluding chapter explores a question that underlies this book: Why haven't more incubators for young activist talent emerged since the UFW's peak? To put it another way, what options exist today for training potential activists in organizing, leadership, and developing strategies for social justice movements? Is volunteering full time for the modern equivalent of $5 a week plus room and board no longer viable in an era of increased living costs and crushing debt from student loans? Was there something about Cesar Chavez's charismatic leadership that made the UFW special, an attribute that cannot be replicated in an era where progressive activists seek nonhierarchical leadership and consensus decision-making? I have pondered these questions for many years, regretting that so many idealistic young activists who want to make a difference in the world have never found an organizational home for their talents. This chapter examines the factors that enabled the UFW to attract and retain so many committed young people and to turn them into lifetime activists for social and economic justice.

Today, out of the national spotlight, the struggle for justice in the twenty-first century has been building and is emerging in a new form. It is inspired and enriched by the innovative tradition of the UFW and led in part by a generation of leaders who were trained or influenced by Chavez and the farmworkers movement. It has been nearly half a century since Cesar Chavez and a band of seventy-five supporters began their pilgrimage from Delano, but the UFW's legacy remains a powerful force. In fact, the spirit of *"sí se puede!"* has never been stronger and still provides the clearest roadmap for achieving greater social and economic justice in the United States.

1

CESAR CHAVEZ AND THE UFW:
REVIVAL OF THE CONSUMER BOYCOTT

Of all the personal experiences that inspired Cesar Chavez to undertake
the challenge of building a union of farmworkers, none was more important than his history in the fields. Chavez had done the backbreaking work of picking cantaloupes, and he saw that hardworking farmworker families were poorly compensated and subjected to inhumane
living conditions. Chavez also understood that farmworkers were neither afraid nor reluctant to resist; but he had witnessed enough failed
campaigns to know the importance of picking the right strategy and not
simply settling for such traditional labor tactics as the strike. His experience in the fields convinced him that new strategies and tactics, such as
using a consumer boycott to win a labor dispute, were necessary to overcome the history of grower dominance and farmworker defeat.

CHAVEZ IN THE FIELDS

Farmworkers in the 1930s were called migrants, because they were always moving from town to town in search of work. The Chavez family
was no different. In the spring, they threshed beans and picked walnuts
in the small coastal town of Oxnard, north of Los Angeles, and then drove
a few hundred miles north to earn about thirty cents a day—collectively—
cutting and pitting apricots in San Jose. When Cesar was twelve or thirteen, he picked cantaloupes for eight cents an hour, while adult workers
received twelve cents. Although Congress had enacted a federal minimum
wage of twenty-five cents an hour in 1938, farmworkers were exempted
from this and every other protection afforded by federal labor law.

California's politically powerful growers ensured that the state's primarily Mexican farmworkers would not share in the benefits of President Franklin Roosevelt's New Deal for American workers, a fact typically overlooked in accounts of labor's progress during this era. Nor could
Congress claim ignorance of the farmworkers' plight. John Steinbeck's

classic novel *The Grapes of Wrath* had brought national attention to the issue, and his stirring tale of the Joad family's fight for survival in California's fields won converts to the migrants' cause. But Mexicans made up more than half of the state's farmworkers, and elected officials were not going to anger California's influential agricultural interests in order to bring justice to Mexican workers. After all, a Congress that remained silent as Mexican American citizens were denied the right to vote, to eat in restaurants, to patronize movie theaters, and to attend public schools was hardly going to get worked up about low wages and inhumane working conditions.

The Chavez family made so many trips up and down California that Cesar and his two siblings attended thirty-seven schools before they started high school. Cesar performed some of the most physically demanding work available, including topping sugar beets in the Sacramento Valley, thinning lettuce in Salinas, and picking broccoli in Brawley, where he and other workers had to stand in water and mud up to their necks. He planted onions and carrots in the winter months; the constant stooping required for this activity left workers' backs hurting all day. They were paid $3 a day for planting seedlings over half a mile.[1]

When he was nineteen, Chavez was picking cotton in the town of Corcoran, in the San Joaquin Valley, when a car came by with loudspeakers blaring, urging workers to walk off the job to protest their low pay and to come to a rally downtown. The Chavez family had always stuck by workers who complained of unfair treatment on the job; Cesar once noted that they were probably "one of the strikingest families in California." On this occasion, Cesar and his brother Richard left and joined with several thousand cotton pickers in a downtown park. The recently formed National Farm Labor Union had called the strike, and a union leader started talking to the workers about *"la causa"* (the cause). Chavez later recalled, "I would have died right then if someone had told me how and why to die for our cause. But no one did. There was a crisis, and a mob, but there was no organization, and nothing came of it at all. A week later everyone was back picking cotton in the same field at the same low wages. It was dramatic. People came together. Then it was over. That won't organize farm workers."[2]

Chavez's experience in Corcoran mirrored a long history of failed efforts to organize agricultural laborers. As far back as 1903, Japanese and Mexican farmworkers had tried to organize for better wages and working conditions, but they were rebuffed even by the American Federation of Labor, which refused to help workers who were not white. In 1913, the Industrial Workers of the World organized a rally of two thousand workers at a large ranch in rural Northern California, who were then attacked by national guardsmen. The two lead organizers for the IWW were arrested, wrongly convicted of murder, and sentenced to life imprisonment. Despite such obstacles, the primarily Mexican and Filipino farm workforce, along with poor whites and blacks, consistently fought back. Farmworkers staged more than 140 strikes in the California fields from 1930 to 1939; in 1933 alone, more than fifteen thousand predominantly Mexican cotton workers were on strike. Protesting workers were arrested, violently attacked, or, in many cases, both.

An official from the Roosevelt administration reported that farmworkers lived on as little as fifty-six cents a day in "filth, squalor and entire absence of sanitation" and that local authorities "forbid free speech and assembly, and indiscriminately arrest innocent men and women under fake charges." In rural communities, "so-called peace officers do the bidding of their masters with the able assistance of pistols, machineguns, tear gas bombs, and hard wood sticks." A U.S. Senate committee in 1939 and 1940 found "a shocking degree of human misery among farmworkers" and a pattern of "sheer vigilantism" on the part of growers. But the committee did not issue its report until October 1942, when America's war effort was pushing the plight of farmworkers and other nonmilitary issues to the side.[3]

After the war, attempts to organize farmworkers confronted a new obstacle: the bracero program. This joint U.S. and Mexican government program had begun during World War II to address labor shortages, and it had effectively replaced resident farmworkers with temporary "guest workers" who were forced to return to Mexico once the harvest was over. For the next two decades, 4.5 million braceros came to California to pick crops, taking jobs from the primarily Mexican American residents, who had proved willing to fight for better living conditions and wages. The bracero program represented an insurmountable barrier to labor progress for these farmworkers, and in 1959 the AFL-CIO and the Catholic Rural Life Conference mounted a strong campaign in Congress to end it. Their efforts succeeded when Secretary of Labor James Mitchell, a devout Catholic, imposed reforms that reduced the number of California braceros from five hundred thousand in 1959 to around two hundred thousand in 1962. By 1963, one year after Cesar Chavez began trying to build an organization of farmworkers, Congress had ended the program.[4]

From Chavez's perspective, the timing could not have been better. But other longstanding obstacles to farmworker organizing remained. Grow-

ers still controlled local politicians and law enforcement and had the political clout to prevent changes in federal or state law that would protect
union organizing. The growers included some of California's wealthiest
individuals and corporations, while Cesar Chavez had a name (the National Farm Workers Association), a red and black thunderbird eagle logo,
and a plan to survive by collecting $3.50 in monthly dues from workers.
Chavez had so little money that he and his wife, Helen, picked cotton
from 6:00 A.M. to 2:00 P.M. to support their eight children, and he spent
the balance of the day and late into the night knocking on doors and
meeting with farmworkers. Cesar Chavez's drive to organize farmworkers has been described as a David versus Goliath struggle, but even
this analogy may greatly underestimate the odds he faced.[5]

But Chavez did not begin his organizing drive equipped only with a
big heart and a passion to succeed. A decade earlier, in 1952, he had met
Fred Ross, an organizer for the Community Services Organization, a
group affiliated with Saul Alinsky's Industrial Areas Foundation. The IAF
had empowered previously disenfranchised working-class residents of
Chicago's Back of the Yards neighborhood, through a combination of
grassroots organizing and securing the support of the religious community and labor unions; and the CSO intended to bring this successful
model to California's Mexican American communities. Though he initially expressed reluctance to talk with Ross, Chavez was quickly hooked
on becoming a CSO organizer. Ross trained him in the door-to-door,
house meeting method of organizing that would become the UFW hallmark. Chavez later concluded that Ross was his "hero" and that, while
he had "learned quite a bit from studying Gandhi, Fred Ross Sr. . . .
changed my life."[6]

Chavez and Ross organized twenty-two new CSO chapters in San
Jose's Mexican American neighborhoods during the 1950s, and Chavez
became the CSO's executive director in 1959. The group was making a
name for itself by registering tens of thousands of voters, offering citizenship classes, and promoting Mexican American interests in city affairs.
But Chavez's dream was to organize a union for farmworkers. The IAF's
Alinsky never shared Chavez's passion for this endeavor, arguing in
1967 that organizing farmworkers "was like fighting on a constantly
disintegrating bed of sand." Alinsky even suggested that rural Mexican
American workers should be "retrained for urban living." At the CSO's
March 1962 convention, Chavez offered a proposal for a pilot farmworker organizing project, but the CSO membership voted it down,
preferring to focus the group's energies on urban residents. Chavez re-

Fred Ross Sr. and Cesar Chavez. Photo by Jon Lewis.

sponded by resigning from the organization and launching his own organizing drive.[7]

Chavez did not have a "farmworker organizing master plan" for building power; rather, he compared his approach to picking grapes: you start
by picking a bunch and then go on to the entire vineyard. By the fall of
1965, his person-to-person, house-by-house approach was slowly and
steadily building a strong sense of community among farmworkers. His
fledgling organization, the National Farm Workers Association, was providing assistance to farmworkers who had problems with government
agencies and was also aggressively registering voters. The NFWA had
twelve hundred members, although only two hundred were paying dues.
But Chavez was patient. He knew the long history of organizing failures—
and knew that the workers themselves were aware of this history. The
association was only three years old, and Chavez felt that it was not yet
strong enough to win a labor dispute against the powerful growers. Nevertheless, he lent the group's support to a brief and unsuccessful strike
by workers in the rose industry in the spring of 1965. That fall, when
workers in the grape fields of Delano wanted to call a strike over the grow-

ers' refusal to raise wages from $1.20 to $1.40 an hour (a tactic that had recently won this increase in the Coachella Valley), Chavez again agreed, even though he doubted that they had the strength to prevail.

THE BOYCOTT BEGINS

The Delano strike against grape growers was called by Filipino workers who were affiliated with the AFL-CIO–chartered Agricultural Workers Organizing Committee (AWOC). Filipinos were a minority of the primarily Mexican farm workforce and lacked the capacity to win a strike. Nevertheless, their decision to strike on September 8, 1965, forced Chavez and the NFWA to either join the struggle or appear to be turning their backs on workers. Chavez believed that it should be the workers' decision, and on September 16, Mexican Independence Day, a crowd of more than twelve hundred NFWA supporters and members filled the parish hall of Our Lady of Guadalupe Church to decide whether to join the strike. The revolutionary spirit of the day led to chants of *"Huelga! Huelga! Huelga!"* and the great Delano grape strike—and the impetus for America's first successful national consumer boycott—began.

Despite the excited chants, Chavez knew that the NFWA and AWOC could not win the Delano grape strike through traditional means. Although picketing in the fields was robust, many of the people on strike went elsewhere to work. Marshall Ganz, who became the union's organizing director, estimated that those picketing involved a "hard core of about 150," a relatively small number, which led the union to initiate the "roving picket line" to give the illusion of greater numbers. Chavez was recruiting student, labor, and religious volunteers to support the strikers, but the bottom line was that grape growers harvested a record crop that fall. As grape season drew to a close and all the workers left the fields, activists and strikers were left with nothing to picket. Chavez had to think of something for them to do. He instructed two workers and a student to follow a shipment of grapes from one of the picketed growers as it made its way to the Oakland docks. When Chavez's delegation arrived on the docks, they convinced the longshoremen not to load the fruit. More than a thousand ten-ton cases of grapes were left rotting on the dock. Chavez and the strikers had figured out not only a way to keep members and activists busy but also a strategy that gave the farmworkers movement a real chance of victory.[9]

While Cesar Chavez did not invent the boycott—the term originated in Ireland in 1880, after Captain Charles Boycott evicted tenants from his land and the town stopped doing business with him as a way of pressuring him to allow their return—the farmworkers movement revived and reinvented this strategy. Chavez was so taken with the idea of consumer boycotts of corporations that he even named one of his dogs Boycott (the other was Huelga).[9] Although the initial use of economic pressure was not specifically planned, Chavez had long believed that the only way farmworkers could counter the growers' superior economic power was through public support for an economic boycott.

Chavez accurately described the boycott's beginnings as "helter skelter." The almost inadvertent start of the boycott on the Oakland waterfront was followed by regular picket lines on Bay Area docks, which were honored by the progressive International Longshoremen's and Warehousemen's Union. As ILWU workers refused to load nonunion grapes, Chavez decided to launch a formal boycott of the two largest corporations involved in the Delano grape industry—Schenley Industries and the DiGiorgio Corporation.[10]

Because it was early December 1965, Schenley became the first target—the company's Cutty Sark whiskey and its other liquors were big sellers during the holiday season. This initial attempt at a national consumer boycott was not particularly sophisticated—it has been described as a "rag tag affair"—but it got the job done. Union volunteers and staff spread out to more than one hundred cities, handing out cards that people were asked to sign and send to Schenley's headquarters pledging that the signers would not buy Schenley's products until they were union-made. Supporters in Boston held a "Boston Grape Party" to spread the boycott; sympathetic unions in New York City picketed Schenley headquarters; and student, labor, and church activists picketed and leafleted liquor stores throughout the country, demanding that Schenley products be removed from the shelves. In March 1966, a U.S. Senate subcommittee hearing in Delano led to a high-profile confrontation between Senator Robert F. Kennedy and a local sheriff, which brought increased national publicity for the Schenley boycott. When these actions were followed by a fabricated memo spread by union sympathizer "Blackie" Leavitt, head of the San Francisco Bartenders Union, stating that the city's bartenders would no longer sell Schenley liquor, the company quickly caved. In April 1966, Schenley workers won a union contract that immediately raised wages and established a hiring hall.[11]

This quick victory confirmed Chavez's faith in the power of the boycott. But Schenley was not a typical Delano grower. Its five thousand acres of Delano grapes represented only a tiny part of its holdings, and most of its $250 million in annual sales came from liquor, not grapes. Many of Schenley's diverse operations were unionized, and it viewed itself as having good relations with its unions. Delano's grape growers correctly viewed Schenley as unrepresentative of the industry, and they would not so quickly capitulate to a boycott. This became clear when the union next confronted the giant DiGiorgio Corporation, historically one of California's leading agricultural powers. DiGiorgio's anti-union attitudes and practices had been fictionalized in Steinbeck's *Grapes of Wrath,* and its staff had already used violence against union members. Even though the company's farming operations accounted for only 10 percent of its total business, DiGiorgio would not accept a farmworkers union easily. Chavez called for a boycott of all the company's products, including its well-known TreeSweet brand juices and S&W canned foods. The union quickly commenced picketing and reaching out to consumers at stores, warehouses, and DiGiorgio's San Francisco headquarters.[12]

In May 1967, after nearly a year of encouraging consumers across America to boycott DiGiorgio's products, the UFW increased pressure through a new tactic: blocking grape distribution centers. Boycott staff were convincing shoppers not to buy TreeSweet or S&W products, but reducing sales would be even easier if these products never reached supermarkets and were not available for purchase. The UFW unleashed the new tactic in Chicago, whose S&W distribution center supplied the entire Midwest. Although the union had only sixty people trying to stop distribution, primarily students and labor activists, many Teamster truck drivers refused to cross the UFW picket line at the distribution center. The element of surprise effectively shut the facility down. When the Catholic bishop of Chicago allowed UFW supporters to use his office to coordinate an ongoing blockade, DiGiorgio began to talk settlement.

After extensive negotiations, the first UFW representation election among DiGiorgio's workers was slated for August 30, 1967. The boycott had forced the powerful grower to hold an election, and Chavez felt it essential that the UFW win. In the 1967 DiGiorgio election, the only union competing with the UFW for the workers' loyalty was the Teamsters. The Teamsters had little base among farmworkers but had the advantage of being the grower's preferred choice.

Leaving nothing to chance, Chavez asked Fred Ross, his mentor from the CSO, to take charge of organizing for the election. Ross used the Di-Giorgio campaign to introduce a model for winning elections that would bring the UFW victories in hundreds of representation elections in future years. UFW organizing director Marshall Ganz would later describe

Ross's training of fifty or sixty young organizers for this election as akin to a "school"—and its instructor made sure that his lessons were learned. Ross required organizers to keep a file card on every worker, to record every contact with that worker, to write down any questions the worker had, and to keep going back until the individual agreed to vote for the UFW. Ross expected his staff to update him daily on their progress and "not to leave anything to chance."[13] Ross's meticulous approach applied as readily to identifying voters and getting them to the polls in political elections, a connection not lost on the many UFW alumni who subsequently organized progressive electoral campaigns.

The DiGiorgio election also marked the emergence of Eliseo Medina, a twenty-year-old farmworker whose first exposure to Cesar Chavez had been at the Mexican Independence Day church meeting in 1965, when the Delano strike was approved. Initially, Medina had not been impressed by Chavez, considering him "a little pipsqueak." But Chavez's words inspired Medina, who, after hearing that the poor "shouldn't be taken advantage of" and that "we deserve more," became firmly committed to the strike.[14] As the DiGiorgio campaign was getting under way, Medina had wandered into the UFW hiring hall, inquiring about opportunities to pick wine grapes. He was greeted by Dolores Huerta, who, like Chavez, had been recruited by Fred Ross to be a CSO organizer and had joined the AFL-CIO's campaign to unionize farmworkers before joining the NFWA in 1962. Huerta told Medina that the season had not yet started, and she asked if he would like to help with the election. Medina agreed, having no idea of Ross's no-nonsense expectations.[15]

Medina's chance participation as part of Ross's election team enabled him to learn directly from a master of organizing and was his first step in becoming one of America's most successful labor and immigrant organizers. Though inexperienced, Medina was sufficiently effective to prompt the Teamsters to beat him up badly during the run-up to the election, requiring four stitches in his lip. (The Teamsters of the 1960s and 1970s often resorted to violence to intimidate opponents. Medina was only one of countless UFW members victimized in the next decade by the then corruption-plagued union.) The DiGiorgio election, generated by the boycott, created a long-term model for union and electoral organizing, brought Eliseo Medina into the organizing field, and won the UFW a critical victory, with a 530 to 331 vote.[16]

The boycott had barely started, and the strategy had already garnered two union contracts against major growers. Chavez next targeted the Giumarra Vineyards. This powerful grower had figured out a way to circumvent the boycott by shipping its grapes under more than one hundred different, non-boycotted labels. As a result, pro-UFW shoppers trying to avoid purchasing the Giumarra brand could unknowingly purchase boycotted grapes. Giumarra's tactic posed a dilemma for Chavez. He believed that it was much easier to get consumers to boycott a specific brand of grape than to convince them to forgo grapes entirely. But Huerta, Ross, and others argued that to combat Giumarra's false-labeling strategy, the boycott would have to be expanded to the entire table grape industry. It was an audacious plan, but Giumarra had given Chavez and the union no choice. The industrywide grape boycott began in January 1968 and soon burst into public consciousness as never before.

RECRUITING FOR THE GRAPE BOYCOTT:
STUDENTS, WOMEN, CLERGY, LABOR

Convincing millions of Americans and Canadians to stop buying grapes was quite an ambitious goal. Expanding the boycott in this way required a far greater number of staff and volunteers, more training and coordination, and the creation of extensive alliances with outside groups. With unlimited funds, the UFW could have run slick radio and television commercials urging people not to buy grapes, hired public relations staff to generate sympathetic media coverage, and taken out full-page newspaper ads to spread the word. But the UFW could not afford such advertising. Instead, it was attempting to run a nationwide consumer boycott by recruiting volunteers to work more than a hundred hours a week for weekly stipends of $5 plus room and board.

The sheer number of personnel needed to pull off such a boycott appeared insurmountable. In the forty to fifty cities targeted by the boycott in the United States and Canada, thousands of supermarkets were selling grapes. At least one volunteer had to be present at each supermarket to convince shoppers to stop buying grapes, while others were needed to staff tables at major street corners. Additional help was required to build and maintain community support for the boycott and to work closely with institutional allies in the labor, religious, and student communities. Although the personnel and organizational requirements for operating an effective nationwide boycott were onerous, the UFW was convinced that it was the only way to force growers to the negotiating table.

The immediate challenge was recruitment. When the boycott was first expanded in January 1968, UFW vice president Dolores Huerta headed to New York City with more than fifty farmworker families to direct the operation in one of the nation's key distribution points for grapes. Many of the California boycott directors had formerly been farmworkers; for them, staffing the national boycott often meant leaving California for the first time, traveling to places where they had no friends or family, and then conducting a campaign with little training or experience. But it was also true that shoppers were more easily persuaded by those who had actually labored in the fields and could explain the unfair conditions firsthand.

Eliseo Medina recalled that when Dolores Huerta and Cesar Chavez asked him to go to Chicago to work on the boycott, he was twenty-one years old and had never been outside Delano. "When I was asked to go to Chicago and stop the grapes, I didn't know where Chicago was. I thought it was an hour away driving, so I said, 'What time do I leave?'" He then learned he would have to take a plane. Equipped with "one name and a bag of buttons," Medina was dispatched to Chicago to "go stop the sale of grapes." Volunteers from established allies in labor unions, churches, and civil rights organizations, including the Student Nonviolent Coordinating Committee (SNCC), quickly supplemented this boycott staff. Skilled activists from these groups joined farmworkers-turned-organizers like Medina in anchoring boycott efforts in New York City, Boston, Chicago, Los Angeles, and Detroit. But boycotters were needed in dozens of other cities as well, and the UFW sought them from the new generation of idealistic young people committed to social and economic justice.[17]

America's First Student-Labor Coalition

The UFW attracted students and recent college graduates to join the boycott staff in two ways. First, it gave them the opportunity to work full time in a movement for social change—never mind that the pay was low and the hours were long. Second, boycott volunteers gained entrée into a whole new world of labor and civil rights activism, with many receiving training in organizing and campaign strategy directly from experts such as Fred Ross, Marshall Ganz, and Cesar Chavez. The UFW, through the vehicle of the boycott, became the preeminent home for young activists seeking full-time engagement in a movement for social justice. Volunteers had the opportunity to work with others equally committed to activist work and progressive ideals, creating a deep sense of community that was not easy to find in the often contentious political movements of the era.[18]

Gary Guthman, who introduced me to the world of UFW organizers in 1977, described how he became part of the movement. In September 1976, Guthman was on campus at the University of California at Berkeley, thinking about enrolling there after spending two years attending college in Maine. He observed a UFW organizer "barking" her "rap" and "sweeping" people over to the UFW table. Guthman approached the table and was asked if he would sign up to help the farmworkers. Convinced by the organizer's rap that help for the farmworkers was desperately needed, he signed up and told them to "give me a call." The organizer called Guthman the next night and asked him to come to Telegraph Avenue the next day to register voters. Guthman soon found himself doing his own "barking" and quickly became an expert at juggling clipboards and attracting people to his table.

Still in his first day of work, and only two days after learning about the UFW, Guthman was given a bullhorn and encouraged to really get people's attention. He continued volunteering and received an evening call two weeks later, asking him to help provide all-night security for Cesar Chavez, who was staying in a Berkeley church. Guthman could hardly resist the chance to protect the legendary UFW leader; while on duty, he was personally greeted by Chavez. Imagine working for a well-known group for less than a month and being personally thanked for your service by the head of the national organization, who also happened to be one of America's preeminent labor and civil rights leaders. Chavez had a personal magnetism born from his deep commitment to social justice that often drew talented young activists to join the UFW; after meeting him that night, Guthman was hooked. He decided to become a full-time UFW volunteer, launching his eventual career as a labor organizer less than a month after first being exposed to the movement.[19]

Guthman's experience was far from unique. Hundreds of college students were so attracted to the idea of making a difference in the world that they dropped out of school soon after encountering the farmworkers movement. Lilli Sprintz was a student taking archaeology classes at Temple University in Philadelphia in 1969 when she began questioning why she was not rallying against the Vietnam war, fighting for civil rights, or taking some other action to improve the world. While she was wondering "What could I do?" she walked off campus to a shopping center, where female farmworkers were promoting the boycott in front of the A&P grocery store. One of the women, Carolina Franco, told Sprintz "that people would be picking crops in the fields all day and not be able to use the bathroom" and that "women would have to make a circle around the woman who had to go, so she could have some privacy." Angry at this lack of respect for workers, Sprintz visited the women later at the Philadelphia boycott house. The young woman who had felt herself "floating" through college found her home, and Sprintz worked for the UFW for the next five years.[20]

Harriet Teller was one of many who left college after a summer internship with the movement. A University of Michigan student from a family of union organizers, Teller spent the summer of 1970 working on the Philadelphia boycott and was there when the UFW prevailed in the grape campaign. Noting that "the spirit of victory was contagious," she did not return to classes in Ann Arbor that fall. After leaving Philadelphia in 1971, she spent eighteen months organizing the boycott in St. Louis. In 1987, Teller finally graduated from Michigan, twenty years after she began.[21]

Whereas the UFW offered activists like Guthman and Sprintz immediate entry into an exciting multiracial movement for social and economic justice, other labor unions of the 1960s and 1970s were not interested in recruiting them. As Marshall Ganz observed, "no unions were hiring in the sixties when they were strongest." Ganz first learned about unions in 1965, when SNCC and Students for a Democratic Society (SDS) organized a meeting at the Highlander Center in New Market, Tennessee, the famous training center for civil rights activists. But no mainstream unions attended. Ganz concluded, "While the Peace Corps and the poverty programs were recruiting us, unions were too afraid of communists to talk to us. The unions were so scared of young people, and an organization fearful of the young is a dying organization."[22]

Born in Bakersfield, California, only a short drive from agricultural fields, Ganz was among a group of white students from elite schools who had participated in the Mississippi Freedom Summer campaign in 1964. That same year, he had dropped out of Harvard to work for civil rights in the South. When he returned home from Mississippi, he observed that the plight of California's rural farmworkers involved many of the same injustices he had witnessed being perpetrated against black people in the South. As Ganz came to see the farmworkers with "Mississippi eyes," he decided to join the UFW. From 1965 to 1981, he was among the farmworkers' chief strategists and campaign organizers, playing a major role in building the movement. Like Harriet Teller, Ganz eventually returned to his original college to get his bachelor's degree, in his case twenty-eight years later.[23]

Since SNCC no longer provided white students with year-round ac-

Marshall Ganz directs a question to a union member. Photo by Nick Jones.

tivist jobs, a well-trained cadre of politically committed young organizers found themselves looking for new challenges when the UFW grape strike commenced in September 1965. They were thus available a few months later, when the Schenley boycott was launched. They had already become experts in picketing and other forms of nonviolent protest, and their experience with local police and law enforcement in Mississippi proved invaluable for interactions with sheriffs in Delano. The involvement of these former students from the civil rights movement heightened interest in the UFW among other urban activists, bolstering recruitment. Student recruitment also benefited from Chavez's frequent campus speaking engagements, which introduced many to the farmworkers' cause and invariably ended with people rushing to sign up to volunteer.[24]

Although the role of student activism in the antiwar and civil rights movements is widely recognized, the UFW's success at forging the first labor-student alliance is often overlooked. The UFW did not inherit the allegiance of students; rather, the union actively recruited students and created a culture hospitable to their broader social concerns. Cesar Chavez, like Martin Luther King Jr., spoke out against the Vietnam war, when some believed that he should confine his opinions to issues more narrowly focused on workers in the fields. But Chavez's antiwar stance, as well as his zealous support for the civil rights struggle of African Americans, helped the UFW attract young activists whose concerns extended beyond the labor movement. The UFW's constitutional convention in 1973, for example, adopted a resolution urging the United States to withhold recognition of the military junta the U.S. government had helped to install in Chile, and the delegates stood in memory of that nation's democratically elected and recently assassinated former leader, Salvador Allende. From resolutions on Chile to protests against government crackdowns on progressive groups, the UFW demonstrated that, unlike others in the labor movement, it shared young activists' broader social vision.[25]

In contrast, these young people saw AFL-CIO president George Meany as "epitomizing all that was wrong with the labor movement." Meany and the AFL-CIO staunchly backed the Vietnam war, and in 1970 the longtime labor chief made these comments about youthful antiwar protesters: "There is more venereal disease among them. . . . There are more of them smoking pot and . . . they have long beards and look dirty and smell dirty." Meany's lack of personal commitment to civil rights was seen in his refusal to sanction official AFL-CIO participation in the 1963 March on Washington, where Martin Luther King Jr. gave his famous "I have a dream" speech. While AFL-CIO lobbyists did back all of the era's major civil rights legislation, Meany defended the discriminatory hiring policies of the building trades unions and referred to a new generation of "wild men of the NAACP" and fire-eating "black militants." According to Jim Drake, who began working with Chavez as a migrant minister in 1962 and became a key UFW organizer, the UFW's political and strategic autonomy within the AFL-CIO drove Meany "up the wall."[26]

Meany could not understand the UFW posting signs on college campuses to recruit $5-a-week organizers for the boycott, as labor was accustomed to hiring only well-paid professional organizers. Nor was Meany happy about the UFW's political independence, particularly when the union's grassroots outreach to Latino voters had been instrumental in Robert Kennedy defeating Hubert Humphrey, the candidate backed by the AFL-CIO, in the 1968 California presidential primary. The UFW joined the nation's student movement in strongly backing George McGovern in the 1972 presidential race, whereas Meany's AFL-CIO stayed neutral. And one can only imagine Meany's reaction to Chavez's endorsement of Black Panther Party member Bobby Seale in the 1973 Oakland mayor's race. All in all, Drake concluded that the UFW's dual role as both a union and a social movement of the poor, whose leadership and membership were primarily Latino, gave the AFL-CIO "nothing but headaches."[27]

In contrast to the indifference and even hostility young activists encountered from the nation's leading labor unions, the UFW laid out a welcome mat. Longtime labor activist Kim Fellner, who began working in 1974 with the same SEIU local of Pennsylvania social workers that launched the career of future SEIU president Andy Stern, recalled that "most AFL-CIO unions had been closed communities for more than 15 years. I knew no one active in the labor movement and few who thought well of it." Susan Sachen, who joined the boycott in Boston in 1971, expressed the view of many volunteers in noting that she "would never have gotten involved with another union because working for the UFW was working for the movement." As a result of her UFW experience, Sachen went on to become a lifelong labor organizer. She followed her UFW stint by working on the J. P. Stevens boycott and then was a key organizer in Denver in the first Justice for Janitors campaign. Sachen spent more than twenty years with SEIU and the California Labor Federation and is one of countless skilled and committed young activists for whom the UFW boycott provided the only available entry to the labor movement. If Cesar Chavez and the UFW had never launched a boycott, Sachen and other valuable organizers would have been forever lost to the labor movement.[28]

Students and young people are vital to national campaigns for many reasons, including practical ones such as their capacity to work long hours, their ability to pick up and move on short notice, and the presence of campuses in communities large and small across America. But despite the obvious advantages of labor unions building relationships with students, the UFW was the only one to aggressively recruit these young people from 1965 until 1995, when new leadership in the AFL-CIO finally began encouraging student recruitment. Today, as other chapters describe, labor-student alliances are often formed for economic justice campaigns. But Cesar Chavez and the UFW deserve credit for pioneering this strategy.

Organizing Opportunities for Women

In addition to actively recruiting students for the boycott, the UFW also distinguished itself from other unions that had primarily male membership by empowering women organizers. UFW vice president Dolores Huerta was a top leader in the union, and she served as the union's first contract negotiator. This was an unusually prominent role for a woman of that era in a male-dominated union. Huerta not only negotiated the UFW's first union contract (with Schenley) but also was in charge of

Dolores Huerta in front of Safeway headquarters, 1968. Photo by Jon Lewis.

building the union's negotiating department. She headed the New York City boycott when the grape campaign went industrywide in 1968 and created a model for building broad community support, assisting efforts along the East Coast and throughout the Midwest. One gets a good sense of Huerta's organizing style from a letter she mailed to boycott offices across the country in 1969:

> In those areas that are absolutely clean like Long Island, we are beginning to do saturation type organizing. The students have volunteered to form a speakers bureau and we now have students who will be going to churches to speak on the boycott. After we cover churches and political groups, we hope to pick up enough speakers to approach each, individual union shop. We are doing this by areas though, and as we pick up people to help we refer them to the coordinator in their own town, or neighborhood. We hope to build a community neighborhood machine by this method for the boycott.[29]

Huerta returned to California in February 1969 and assumed leadership of the San Francisco boycott. She had won an agreement from A&P, the nation's and New York City's largest supermarket chain, not to sell grapes; and she soon launched a major campaign against the country's second largest grocery giant, California-based Safeway, for its sale of boycotted grapes. As the UFW became involved in major political struggles in Arizona, Washington, and California in 1971 and 1972, Huerta redirected her focus to these campaigns. She went on to play a major role in the UFW for the next three decades. After Cesar Chavez's death in 1993, Dolores Huerta became the living person most identified with the farmworkers movement.

Jessica Govea is another woman whose extraordinary organizing and leadership skills found expression in the farmworkers movement and particularly in the boycott. Govea began working in the fields with her parents at the age of four and spent every summer until age fifteen picking cotton, grapes, or prunes. Her father was a lifelong activist, and by age twelve Govea was already organizing farmworker children around petition drives and rallies. She left college to join the UFW in 1966 and stayed for the next fifteen years. After two years of performing administrative tasks in the union office, Govea accepted an opportunity in July 1968 to join Marshall Ganz (with whom she was romantically involved) and Catholic priest Mark Day in Toronto to lead the Canadian boycott there. Canada was among the top five markets for California table grapes.

Govea was not deterred by her status as a single woman traveling alone in a foreign country, and she often single-handedly assembled coalitions of labor, clergy, and political activists to win support for the boycott in the small cities outside Toronto. This was Govea's first experience living outside her hometown of Bakersfield, and she became a huge hit with the Toronto media. The *Toronto Star* called her "the girl from the south," intrigued by her stories of how Mexicans were discriminated against in California. Govea won a standing ovation after speaking to the Ontario Federation of Labor, and she convinced the United Churches of Canada to support the boycott. Along with Day and Ganz, Govea succeeded in getting three major Toronto chain stores to stop selling grapes. Rising public interest in the campaign led the mayor of Toronto to proclaim November 23, 1968, as "Grape Day" in recognition of the city's official support of the boycott.[30]

Govea believed that although the boycott experience was challenging, "we learned we were capable of a lot more than we thought." She captured the message an effective boycott volunteer needed to convey:

> "What we're asking you to do is to become involved in our struggle and to help us by not buying grapes. That's what we're asking you." Actually that was the smallest thing we were asking people to do, because, when we went out, we had to lose all shame and be willing to ask for everything. And we were asking people to quit their jobs and drop out of school and

Jessica Govea inspired Canadians as she led the UFW grape boycott in Toronto and Montreal, 1968–1969. Photo by Hub Segur.

come work with us full-time. We were asking people to give us money; we were asking people to let us live in their home, and sleep on their floor. We were asking people to feed us. We were asking paper for leaflets . . . anything you could think of, we were asking for, because we didn't have it, and we needed it in order to do the boycott.[31]

In January 1969, the twenty-two-year-old Govea was put in charge of the boycott for Montreal and the entire province of Quebec. Montreal was North America's fourth largest grape-consuming city. Govea had so impressed the UFW leadership back in California that she was given complete authority over the entire boycott organizing strategy for this important region. Govea worked day and night, meeting with labor officials, religious leaders, and key community supporters to assemble a citywide campaign. She was also responsible for staff recruitment, training, and supervision and for the overall operation of the Montreal boycott office.

If Govea's "one-woman" organizing machine were not impressive enough, consider that she had been raised speaking Spanish, although she had become proficient in English by high school. In Canada, however, 75 percent of Montreal residents spoke French. In other words, Govea was taking on one of the largest challenges in the boycott operation while communicating with people who often did not speak English or Spanish. She quickly recruited a staff of bilingual organizers and implemented a door-to-door campaign in neighborhoods surrounding Dominion grocery stores. Govea supplemented the door-to-door work with a broad range of public activities, as captured in this account of an event in the summer of 1970, published in the UFW newspaper *El Malcriado:* "Jessica Govea organized a massive moving picket line that totaled over 200 at times and visited five Dominion stores, concluding the day's activity outside of the Quebec division headquarters. A street theater group traveled with the picket line on a flat-bed truck, performing a skit depicting economic links binding the growers and the supermarket."[32]

Govea had no budget in Montreal. Not only was she responsible for raising sufficient funds to keep her staff housed and fed and to cover all office costs, but she was also expected to send at least $1,000 a month back to Delano. Raising money often required her to attend labor-oriented social events, which sometimes proved awkward for a young woman dealing with an overwhelmingly male-dominated Canadian labor movement. Govea's problems with sexual harassment were greater in the provincial areas outside Montreal, where some mistook the Chicana boycott leader for a Canadian Indian. Separated from Ganz and her close-knit family, Govea never allowed her loneliness to interfere with her mission. The Montreal boycott was central to the success of the UFW's international campaign. Based on her work in both Montreal and Toronto, Govea was the person most responsible for Canadian pressure on the Delano grape growers to settle with the UFW in 1970. After the settlement, she returned to California, working in Salinas on the lettuce boycott and becoming one of the international boycott coordinators. She returned to Toronto to run the Gallo wine boycott from 1973 to 1975 and later joined Huerta as one of the two women on the UFW executive board. Both became models for women working on the boycott and in the union.[33]

As Govea demonstrated, there were few limits to the amount of responsibility women were given if they could do the job. The UFW treated organizing training like a school, and the good students, regardless of gender, were given broader responsibilities. The boycott's staffing demands were such that the union sometimes had to break down cultural barriers to get potential women leaders involved. For example, Maria Saludado Magana was from a family of farmworkers who had been dues-paying members of the UFW since holding a house meeting for Cesar Chavez in 1964. After Magana had proven herself by walking picket lines during the day, attending house meetings at night, and putting up with abuse from grower employees for two full years, Chavez asked her in July 1967 to go to Chicago with Eliseo Medina and a few others to run the boycott there. Magana did not think that her family would let her go, because "Hispanics did not let their daughters out of the house until they married." But her parents agreed to the move, and she not only succeeded in Chicago but then went on to head the Indianapolis boycott campaign. While in Indianapolis, Magana went on a spiritual fast for ten days to highlight the refusal of the Kroeger's grocery chain to stop selling grapes; the tactic succeeded in bringing Kroeger's to the table. Magana stayed with the UFW until 1980.[34]

Another cultural barrier the union had to overcome in recruiting women organizers was the media's reliance on racial and gender stereotypes. Organizer Wendy Goepel Brooks was on a picket line with Dolores Huerta in Delano in November 1965, and a photo of them together was included in a *San Francisco Chronicle* story on November 6, 1965. Huerta was second in command to Cesar Chavez, while Brooks had joined the movement in 1963 but was not part of the union's leadership. Despite their respective roles, the article did not discuss Huerta. Instead, it described Brooks as a twenty-six-year-old who looked like a "pretty Stanford coed, her silky hair, brown plaid skirt, and white blouse in sharp incongruity among the other picketers." The newspaper apparently could not believe that a Chicana could be the real leader and a white Stanford graduate a helpful assistant. By the time the right-wing John Birch Society got hold of the story, it concluded that Brooks was "the real star of the Chavez show," claiming that she "ghostwrites Cesar Chavez's speeches."[35]

During the industrywide grape boycott of 1968–70, women directed campaigns in such top UFW boycott cities as New York City, Montreal, Vancouver, Cleveland, and Philadelphia. In Philadelphia, women farmworkers Tonia Saludado and Carolina Franco joined leader Hope Lopez on an all-female boycott leadership team in 1968. Saludado, who was Magana's sister, and Franco had both walked off jobs picking grapes to join UFW strikes against Giumarra and Schenley, respectively. The three women ran an aggressive boycott campaign in both Philadelphia and the surrounding suburbs. Lopez noted that suburban women who supported the boycott "were heavy duty in the confrontation division" and "hated the sight of table grapes on their local retail store shelves." In May 1969,

Lopez fasted for eight days, until A&P agreed to stop selling grapes in the city. Saludado and Octavia Fielder, another female staffer, fasted for two weeks, and a male volunteer for three, in an effort to convince the city's largest chain, Acme, to follow suit; though the fasts did not immediately change Acme's stance, the chain announced in a full-page newspaper ad in June 1970 that it was now selling only grapes picked by the UFW. Lopez was a widow who fulfilled her duties as boycott leader while being a single parent for five children. She was among other women organizers who eventually gave up leadership positions with the UFW for jobs that allowed them more time with their children.[36]

Although the UFW provided an otherwise unavailable entry point for women organizers, this did not mean that the organization was immune to sexism and gender discrimination. For example, Dolores Huerta's formal leadership role and track record of success did not insulate her from encountering antagonism and disrespect even from longtime colleagues. Other women confirmed Huerta's experience, with one staff member noting, "Dolores is often overlooked because she's a woman. Sometimes our staff says, 'Oh, it's only Dolores. We don't take orders from her.'" Despite the persistence of male jealousy and sexism, Huerta nonetheless sent a message to other female UFW activists that they could fulfill important roles with the union.[37]

Susan Samuels Drake, who was Cesar Chavez's personal secretary from 1970 to 1973, offered this look at the leader's mixed attitudes toward women:

> When Cesar called department head meetings, sometimes he'd forget to tell the women. Or he'd leave their names off the minutes when I knew they'd attended the gathering. "How dare he overlook Dolores Huerta, Jessica Govea, and other key staff," I'd think. These were strong women whose native skills blossomed under his tutelage. He had stepped up to the union's presidency with a history of *machismo*. Whenever the habit got to him, I became determined to let him know how important our gender is.[38]

But after noting that she spent three years as Chavez's assistant while her male predecessors "changed with the seasons," Drake concluded:

> I'm only one of droves of American women, not only those who work in the fields and orchards, who believe *Sí, se puede* ("Yes, it's possible"), because Cesar believed in us, gave us meaningful work to do and appreciation when we did it. Cesar Chavez taught me when to speak, when to listen, when to negotiate—sometimes in cooperation with him, sometimes in opposition to him.[39]

The experience of Elaine Elinson confirms Drake's assessment of Chavez's ability to instill self-confidence in UFW staff and volunteers. Elinson was a senior at Cornell University in 1968 when UFW staffers Jerry and Juanita Brown came to the school to recruit for the boycott. Elinson was moved by their slide show of the deplorable working conditions faced by farmworkers, but she had already been accepted to graduate school in London for the fall. Soon after beginning school, Elinson found herself less focused on Asian studies than on world events. She called Brown (not to be confused with the future governor of California) and asked if she could return to the United States and work for the UFW. Brown stunned Elinson by saying that Cesar Chavez wanted her to stay in England and organize an international grape boycott.

California grapes were not typically sold in Europe, but growers were now dumping grapes abroad to make up for the lack of an American market. Brown told Elinson that the UFW would send her flyers, posters, and $200, which amounted to forty weeks' salary in advance. In light of Chavez's stringent attitude toward money—he personally reviewed telephone bills and in 1971 opposed raising the weekly stipend from $5 to $10—this show of confidence in a young woman with absolutely no prior organizing experience was remarkable. Yet Chavez's confidence in Elinson seemed to boost her own faith that she could handle the job, even though she knew no one in England and the UFW had no contacts to give her. She got a letter of introduction from Chavez designating her as the UFW representative and then began going through the phone book, calling and writing labor unions and student groups, asking them to support the grape boycott. Chavez's faith in Elinson paid off, as the British and Swedish labor movements effectively shut down European markets for California grapes.[40]

The UFW also drew in women activists through its emphasis on workers' families; in fact, the union built a tradition of transforming workers' struggles into family campaigns. Mothers often ran the boycott's day-to-day operations, including phone answering, record-keeping, supervising volunteers, and managing the many boycott houses. Entire families of farmworkers frequently participated in protests, rallies, and boycott activities in front of supermarkets; and the July 1, 1970, issue of the UFW newspaper, El Malcriado (literally, the "unruly child"), featured an article titled "A Woman's Place Is . . . on the Picket Line!" It was unusual for families to participate in protests at the time, but the precedent set by the UFW proved handy in organizing for the massive immigration protests in 2006. Although the "family model" of activism during the boycott often left wives in roles secondary to those of their husbands, the grape boycott never could have succeeded without the active participation of women. Cesar Chavez was credited at the time with turning the grape conflict into a "strike of families," and Dolores Huerta argued that women were "most important" to the union because "if a wife was for the union . . . then the husband would be. If she was not . . . the family usually stayed out of the union, or it broke up."[41]

The UFW's need for skilled boycott organizers created opportunities for women that were otherwise unavailable in the labor movement. No other male-dominated union of this era actively recruited female staff or trained as many women to become highly skilled professional organizers and leaders. These female staff members had the same duties as their male counterparts, despite often having the additional responsibility of raising children (Huerta had seven kids, and Lopez had five), and they received the same level of training as male staffers. In contrast, unions other than the UFW hired organizers almost exclusively from within their own ranks, which effectively excluded women from becoming organizers in male-dominated industries. Even SEIU—a union that once included many female-dominated fields and that broke with standard practice by hiring "outsider" college graduates for its research departments—had nowhere near as high a percentage of female organizers as the UFW did. When Susan Eaton, an SEIU staffer who became a labor studies professor, was hired into a staff internship program with SEIU as late as 1980, only four of the thirty-five people who had been chosen for the program since 1972 were women.[42]

The Role of Clergy and Labor

Recruits from religious institutions and labor unions were also critical to the boycott's success. In fact, Cesar Chavez's personal skill at building support for the farmworkers' cause in the religious community during the 1960s and 1970s is among his greatest achievements. The clergy's overwhelming backing of this American labor struggle remains unprecedented, and it is such an important part of the UFW's ongoing legacy that chapter 3 is devoted entirely to this issue. Here, however, it is worth noting that the involvement of the clergy in the boycott was particularly significant for four reasons.

First, one of the key aims of the boycott was to send a message to the entire liberal establishment that this was a mainstream, nonradical cause it should embrace. In a period when Chavez and others were still branded by opponents as "communists," a boycott endorsement from a local or national church organization made it "safe" for community members to stop buying grapes and express solidarity.

Second, religious approval also lent moral authority and social legitimacy to those sitting at tables in front of supermarkets asking people not to buy grapes. Such a scene was unusual in America and might have generated suspicion or confusion. But once boycott volunteers, some of them active church members themselves, publicized the endorsement of local churches, people were much more willing to talk to them and to support the UFW campaign by not purchasing grapes.

Third, because churches have a nationwide presence, grassroots religious activists were positioned to help boycott staff virtually everywhere. Boycott organizers were typically sent to unfamiliar places where they knew no one, armed only with a few names they could contact to get the local campaign going. These lists invariably included religious allies, who would then provide other names of potential supporters. Support from a major urban Catholic archdiocese, for example, granted access to the full range of church committees, greatly expanding the number of boycott volunteers. Moreover, since churches had their own internal organization, it was much easier to mobilize large numbers of people to attend a boycott rally on short notice than if the UFW had to do it alone.

Finally, a large number of boycott volunteers came to the campaign through internship programs like those run by the National Farm Worker Ministry (described in chapter 3). It was not simply Chavez and farmworkers who were strongly motivated by religious concerns; many of their boycott recruits also saw working for La Causa as a spiritual and moral imperative.

Labor also had a nationwide presence and internal organized structures that facilitated boycott support. In fact, labor's involvement in the grape boycott was international, with British, Canadian, and Swedish unions all helping to reduce grape sales in their countries. Union support was especially important because it was unionized truckers and grocery clerks who first got information about grape shipments and the unloading of grapes at stores and, in some cases, could stop such deliveries. After the New York Labor Council endorsed the boycott in 1968, the Seafarers Union stopped all shipments of grapes through the Port of New York through mid-July. The Teamsters, who did not stop grape shipments to Safeway supermarkets because of their competition with the UFW in California, nonetheless lent their support to the boycott in New York, pressuring buyers in produce markets in New York City to stop purchasing grapes. By January 1969, grape sales in New York were down 30 percent, which enabled the UFW to divert experienced boycott staff to other cities. Even when unions could not themselves shut down grape shipments, individual members could sometimes tip off boycott staff so that future deliveries would be greeted by picket lines or rallies.[43]

Support for the boycott from rank-and-file union members was also significant because the UFW was relying on tactics that America's labor unions had long abandoned. The UFW always viewed itself as a civil rights movement and a spiritual mission as well as a union, and it embraced movement-style tactics to achieve its broader goals. But since the early 1950s the AFL-CIO had pursued a "business unionism" model that focused labor's agenda on securing good contracts for members rather than pressing for the general welfare. As labor historian Sidney Lens describes it, American labor unions by the end of the 1950s were no longer a "maverick" force and had become "sluggish toward new ideas, practical rather than idealistic, legalistic rather than militant, more conformist than anti-conformist."[44]

This narrower agenda was reflected in the use of more traditional tactics. This distinction had been clear when the AFL-CIO tried to organize farmworkers in competition with Chavez and the UFW in the early 1960s. Its local leadership insisted that the battle with growers involved "a trade union dispute, not a civil rights movement or a religious crusade." The AFL-CIO approached farmworker organizing as if it were dealing with autoworkers in Detroit's General Motors plants in the 1930s, when sit-ins and stationary picket lines brought success. Chavez and the UFW understood that new tactics and strategies were needed, the most important of which was expanding the arena of labor conflict from the fields of Delano to a Philadelphia shopping center or a Chicago supermarket. Grassroots labor activists embraced the boycott's movement-style tactics even while mainstream union leaders—other than Walter Reuther and Paul Schrade of the United Auto Workers, who long backed the UFW—remained skeptical.[45]

DAILY LIFE ON THE BOYCOTT

After recruiting such a wide range of staff and volunteers, the UFW needed to train them and find places for them to live. The farmworkers movement included many who had dropped out of college to become involved (Sharon Delugach, in fact, began a lifelong organizing career at fifteen after leaving high school to work for the UFW), but the union provided a far more rigorous education than that found on most campuses. The UFW treated organizing as a serious discipline that required study, homework, and lesson plans. Nancy Carleton, a longtime political activist, describes how the UFW taught her the "methodology" of organizing in 1975:

> I use the word *methodology* quite intentionally, because there was nothing haphazard about the UFW's organizing techniques. We were trained to be incredibly disciplined about our use of time, and daily staff meetings and daily reports helped make certain that we used our time productively. Each day started with a morning meeting from 8 to 8:30 A.M., where we reviewed our progress and set our goals for the coming day and week, as well as receiving inspiring updates on breaking news. Then we made personal visits during the rest of the day and attended house meetings we had arranged through successful PVs [personal visits]. In this way, word about the union spread to increasingly larger circles of people. On evenings when we didn't have house meetings or other supporter meetings lined up, we focused on making dozens of calls to line up more PVs and to get commitments from volunteers for the upcoming weekend's actions. The UFW managed to ensure an impressively high rate of turnout from volunteers by sticking to the discipline of follow-up calls.[46]

The UFW was willing to invest time in training those who were highly motivated but needed extra attention. Larry Tramutola got off to such a slow start as a UFW organizer that he told Fred Ross Sr. that he couldn't do the job and should quit. Rather than accepting Tramutola's departure and focusing on other workers who needed help, Ross asked him to explain everything he had done to date. After Tramutola recounted his failed efforts to get people to attend a meeting, Ross told the young organizer that he had done everything wrong. Ross then told him that if he wrote down every single thing he did on the job for the next six months, Ross would make himself available by phone every night at 10:00 P.M. to review Tramutola's actions. It was akin to Harvard's most famous professor giving private tutoring each day to a first-year student who had yet to show promise. Tramutola lived up to his pledge, and Ross fulfilled his. Tramutola's meetings were soon better attended, and under Ross's tutelage he became a top organizer, spending eleven years with the UFW and the rest of his career as a political organizer. The UFW's investment in training created a boycott staff that understood how to accomplish the union's goals. Chavez, Ross, Govea, Ganz, and others also created a culture of mentoring in the union. As Ganz put it, "Organizing was taught as a discipline. There was a method, and you

Boycott reports published in *El Malcriado*.

could learn it, and be good at it, and then you could teach others." Veteran organizers were expected to become mentors, greatly enhancing the UFW's organizing prowess.[47]

While undergoing training and working on the boycott, UFW organizers had to have a place to call home. During 1968–69, the union maintained "boycott houses" in forty to fifty cities, although organizers were still encouraged to find their own lodging. The Boston boycott house was typical of many, as it was large, run-down, and located in a low-income minority neighborhood. This particular house had been abandoned by an adjacent Catholic church and donated to the union. The seven-bedroom, three-bath structure housed ten or fifteen people; some rooms had been converted to a print shop and workspace. Staff took turns cooking and cleaning, but the atmosphere was a far cry from MTV's *The Real World*.[48]

The often substandard living conditions and dangerous neighborhoods made less of an impact because boycott staff were rarely home. Mornings were spent picketing produce terminals, in the hope that a grape shipment might be refused. Organizers then went to supermarkets to picket or gave talks to interfaith committees, local unions, or any other organization that might be persuaded to lend money or time to the campaign. Some days there would be sit-ins at stores or fun tactics like creating a public scene in a store that was selling nonunion grapes. Boycotters also had to visit stores regularly to monitor those that claimed to have stopped selling grapes, with protests and picketing needed in response to violations. On Saturdays there were mass pickets, and there was also an occasional rally that had to be organized. For example, Chavez declared May 10, 1969, as International Grape Boycott Day, and rallies were held in more than a hundred cities to promote the boycott.

Planning or strategy meetings might be held in restaurants or cafés. Churches became popular stopping places because they sometimes had available office space, typewriters, or copiers. The boycott house was indispensable for one reason: making phone calls. In that pre–cell phone era, the fastest, cheapest, and easiest way to make local calls was to call from home. Phoning was an important part of the job, as potential donors had to be solicited to raise funds for the local boycott, and part-time volunteers had to be contacted to keep them involved. Given the all-consuming nature of the work, it is no surprise that many staffers formed romantic relationships with one another; there was little time available for someone not involved in the campaign and also little stability, as boycotters were moved from city to city without much advance notice.

The UFW realized that there were many committed activists who were unable to devote their entire lives to the farmworkers' cause but whose volunteer hours were nevertheless needed. The union thus became expert at recruiting and utilizing part-time volunteers. These volunteers were typically found at the omnipresent UFW boycott tables at supermarkets, on college campuses, or at community events. Staff members were trained to ask those expressing sympathy for the cause to sign up to volunteer for "a few hours" per week. Using Ross's model, the staffers would then make sure to call the potential volunteers quickly to give them an assignment. Because boycott staffers were trained never to ask volunteers to do too little, those committing to a "few hours a week" soon found themselves being regularly called to come out and help. UFW staffers were so diligent in calling part-time volunteers that it seemed as though they were following a schedule. They were. Given the disorganized aspect of most '60s-era campaigns, few could have suspected that Ross had set up a system requiring boycott staff to make a certain number of calls each night and then report the number of commitments back to their supervisors.

Ross's systematic approach to ensuring quality UFW outreach led him to devise what became one of the essential tools of the organizing trade: the ironing board "table." Marshall Ganz recalls that while UFW volunteers were staffing a table in front of a K-Mart in 1973, Ross observed that the orange folding metal tables they were using were rickety and kept falling apart. Ross went into the K-Mart to get something, "and his eyes fell upon a stack of folding ironing boards. Flash. Moment of insight. Maybe those would work better. He bought one, took it outside, set it up in place of the flaky orange table, and history was made. They were the right height, kept the petitioner from sitting down (losing energy), people could easily sign them, they were long enough that several people could sign at once, and you could carry them around in your car."[49] And thus began the ironing board brigades, launched by the UFW, which remain a staple of signature gathering drives for twenty-first-century social movements.

For Gary Guthman and other new volunteers, spending a few hours at a boycott table—or an ironing board—was the least they could do in light of the terrible conditions faced by farmworkers. And while some activists later joked about how boycott staff "guilt-tripped" them into volunteering, that was simply good organizing. Effective boycott staff developed cordial relationships with volunteers, which increased productivity and also gave them a place to visit when they got hungry at night. Guthman used to typically appear at my wife's apartment between 5:30 and 6:00 P.M. As he filled us in on the latest news from the campaign, time would pass until dinner was ready. It would have been inhospitable to ask Gary to leave at that point, and he was grateful for our offer that he stay for dinner. That's the kind of resourcefulness that living on $5 a week instills. With boycotters working for a vital cause on subsistence wages, UFW supporters were more than happy to feed them.

In many cases, people began as part-time volunteers but soon found boycott work so fulfilling that they gave up regular jobs. For example, Mark Sharwood was earning a good living working for the U.S. Geological Survey when he met Oakland boycott coordinator Bob Purcell at a local Safeway in 1972. Sharwood began volunteering for the boycott part time and ended up quitting his job in 1976 and working full time on the boycott in the Midwest. After leaving the UFW in 1982, Sharwood found his way to SEIU, where he has been an organizer for California's statewide janitors union, SEIU Local 1877, since 1987. His recruiter, Purcell, went on to work for multiple labor groups before spending more than two decades as director of the Public Employee Department of the Laborers International Union.[50]

PUBLIC SUPPORT GROWS

By the spring of 1968, public support for the grape boycott had grown dramatically. Even agricultural industry trade publications acknowledged the impact. *California Farmer* headlined its July 6 story "Boycott Jeopardizes Entire Grape Crop," while the August 1968 *Sunkist Newsletter* stated that there was "no question that the boycott of California grapes, unethical and illegal as it may be, is currently effective." After declaring "the boycott has been unsuccessful," Allan Grant, president of the California Farm Bureau, conceded that it represented "the most serious crisis that California agriculture has ever faced." Grant also accused the UFW of trying to "blackmail California." In October 1968, to increase pressure on grape growers, the UFW shifted the focus of its boycott from convincing consumers not to buy grapes to persuading them not to shop in stores that sold the boycotted product.[51]

Targeting a business that is not the primary source of a labor conflict is known as a "secondary boycott," and unions are prohibited from using this tactic under the federal National Labor Relations Act (NLRA). But when the NLRA was enacted in the 1930s, pressure from agribusiness had exempted farm labor from the act's protections. This meant, among other things, that the farmworkers' right to organize was not protected or guaranteed by law, which is why the UFW faced such steep hurdles in securing union representation. Now the union was turning its exemption from the NLRA into an asset—since farmworkers weren't covered by the NLRA, they were free to launch a secondary boycott, targeting supermarkets that sold boycotted grapes. Chain stores such as A&P and Safeway became the new "villains" of boycotters, as activists attacked the groceries' willingness to profit from exploiting farmworkers. A boycott that once financially harmed only the grape growers now threatened the bottom line of supermarkets selling nonunion grapes.

By 1969, the boycott's combined focus on individual consumers and supermarket chains was having its intended impact. Retail grape sales were estimated to be down 12 percent nationally and down more than 50 percent in major cities. Growers still refused to negotiate with Chavez and used their influence with the incoming Nixon administration to boost sales. (When Richard Nixon began his presidential campaign in San Francisco in the fall of 1967, he expressed support for the growers who had been targeted by the UFW and ate grapes to show his solidarity.) In fiscal year 1969, the Defense Department bought 2.4 million pounds of table grapes for soldiers fighting in Vietnam, a fourfold increase over the previous year. Overall, the department purchased 9.69 million pounds of grapes, nearly three million more than in 1968. (Similarly, after the UFW lettuce boycott began in 1970, the Defense Department more than tripled its purchases of nonunion lettuce in 1971 while sharply reducing purchases of lettuce picked under UFW contracts.) These purchases, however, did not make up for the lost sales, and the UFW had its own successes leveraging its political allies to help the boycott. For example, in July 1968 the administration of Mayor John Lindsay announced that it would stop New York City's annual purchase of fifteen tons of grapes for its prisons and hospitals.[52]

In July 1969, growers filed a lawsuit against the UFW, claiming that the boycott had caused losses of $25 million. In December, California's Board of Agriculture launched a grower-funded media campaign to convince consumers to buy grapes. A high-profile advertising firm came up with the idea of attacking the boycott as a violation of "consumer rights" and set up nationwide Consumer Rights Committee offices to protest supermarkets that refused to sell grapes. The campaign also featured bumper stickers boosting California grapes as "the Forbidden Fruit." The board's actions were consistent with the anti-UFW attitudes of California governor Ronald Reagan, who labeled farmworker supporters "outside agitators" and joyfully ate table grapes in front of the cameras.[53]

By 1970, both Chavez and the growers knew that the boycott was killing the table grape industry. In addition to its moral appeals, the UFW had used congressional hearings during the fall of 1969 to expose growers' use of DDT and other dangerous pesticides (see chapter 5). Boycotters tabling at supermarkets now handed out flyers charging the stores with selling "poisoned grapes" and arguing that only a UFW contract that banned hazardous pesticides could ensure healthy grapes. As those avoiding grapes out of health concerns joined consumers seeking to express solidarity with farmworkers, stories began circulating of unsold storage sheds of rotting grapes and of table grapes being sent off to wineries. The April 6, 1970, edition of *U.S. News and World Report* stated that grape sales were down an estimated 50 percent in New York City and about 46 percent in Atlanta and that "demonstrations in Boston forced most chain stores to take grapes off the fruit counters." Grape shipments were down by more than 33 percent, and wholesale prices fell below the growers' production costs. Lionel Steinberg, a grape grower who was a registered Democrat with close ties to pro-UFW politicians, tried unsuccessfully to get California growers to negotiate with Chavez. Steinberg felt that the boycott had "closed Boston, New York, Philadelphia, Chicago, Detroit, Montreal and Toronto completely from handling table grapes."[54]

Tired of waiting for his fellow growers to come to the table, Steinberg broke ranks and signed a union contract with the UFW on April 1, 1970.

UFW march on Tremont Street in Boston, 1970. Photo by Nick Jones.

His move led some other growers to follow suit, raising concern within the UFW that the union would once again be forced to boycott specific grape companies rather than the entire industry. But this risk never materialized, as stores feared that buying any nonunion grapes would provoke a picket line. Newly unionized grape growers also tipped off the UFW on where nonunion grapes were being distributed, enabling the union to quickly close down such channels. The market for union grapes grew, and soon they were bringing higher prices than nonunion grapes. As nonunion grapes continued to rot for lack of consumer demand, growers actually began calling the union and asking, "What do I have to do to get the bird on my grapes?" (referring to the black thunderbird that was the UFW insignia).[55]

On July 29, 1970, Cesar Chavez appeared before a boisterous crowd of two hundred farmworkers in the hiring hall in Delano. All around the room hung pictures of religious saints, of the late Robert Kennedy, Martin Luther King Jr., and Mohandas Gandhi. Officials of the AFL-CIO were also present, as were key Catholic and Protestant religious leaders. Chavez looked out over the crowd and used a word that those in the room had waited to hear since the strike against grape growers began in

September 1965. This word was "victory." The previous day, the Giumarra Corporation, the most powerful grape grower in the San Joaquin Valley, had agreed to sign with the UFW. This paved the way for the remaining large growers to sign as well.

After a nearly five-year strike and more than two years of an industrywide table grape boycott, the farmworkers movement had won a complete victory. John Giumarra Jr. left no doubt what had brought the large grape growers to the table. "Boycott pressures," he said, were threatening "to destroy a number of farmers." The Department of Agriculture subsequently found that 17 million Americans, or 10 percent of the population, refused to eat or buy grapes from 1966 to 1972. The union, which before the grape boycott had contracts covering only three thousand workers, soon won more than two hundred grape contracts covering seventy thousand workers.[56]

THE UFW BOYCOTT EXPANDS

If life were a movie, the story of Cesar Chavez and the UFW would end with this dramatic victory. The Delano grape strike and resulting boycott had already become the stuff of legend, achieving a cultural cachet by being chronicled not only in newspapers but also by prominent writers such as Peter Matthiessen in the *New Yorker* and John Gregory Dunne in the era's leading literary magazine, the *Saturday Evening Post*. Joan London, the daughter of famed California writer Jack London, lent further gravitas to the struggle in her 1970 book *So Shall Ye Reap: The Story of Cesar Chavez and the Farm Workers' Movement*.[57]

The UFW's grape boycott of 1968–70 deserved all this attention. It was the first of many consumer boycotts launched by the farmworkers and laid the groundwork for these future struggles. The grape boycott shifted the arena of farm labor disputes from the Central California fields to hundreds of cities across the United States and Canada, transforming a California campaign into a national movement. It ushered a generation of young activists into the labor movement and into lifelong advocacy on behalf of social and economic justice. It also created the foundation for the powerful confluence of Latino and labor power in the twenty-first century.

But because the struggle was not happening on a movie set, but in real life, the harsh reality of grower dominance of America's agriculture industry prevented the UFW from savoring its success. Within days of its historic grape victory, lettuce and vegetable growers took preemptive action against the union by signing contracts with the rival Teamsters Union (the absence of any agricultural labor law allowed growers to bind their workers to a union without the workers' approval). Employers favored the Teamsters since, unlike the UFW, the Teamsters did not push for increased wages and improved working conditions for farmworkers. The Teamsters had a different motive: they represented truckers who drove produce from the fields, so cutting a "sweetheart" deal with growers for farmworkers created leverage for improving Teamster trucking contracts. In response to the growers' action, Chavez and the UFW redirected the grape boycott staff to a campaign against nonunion lettuce and vegetables. This boycott was still ongoing in 1973, when grape growers who had signed three-year contracts with the UFW in 1970 unilaterally switched their union contracts to the Teamsters when the contracts came up for renewal.

The impact of the grape growers' action was dramatic and could have broken the will of a less committed movement. The grape growers' switch to the Teamsters left the UFW with only a dozen contracts covering about sixty-five hundred full-time workers and reduced the union's total membership to no more than twelve thousand.[58] In response to this nearly 90 percent reduction in its contracts, the UFW began a bitter grape strike in 1973, in which two union members were killed on picket lines that summer. The violence directed against UFW members by both local law enforcement and the Teamsters became so blatant and pervasive that Chavez decided to end the grape strike and to instead fight the growers from a position of strength. This involved continuing the lettuce and vegetable boycott, but also raising the stakes for California agribusiness by intensifying the UFW's year-old boycott of Gallo wine.

Of all the corporations targeted by the UFW, the wine company owned by Ernest and Julio Gallo may be the one most associated with the farmworkers boycott. To this day, one virtually never sees Gallo wine at a progressive event. While projecting a warm image of its two immigrant founders making affordable quality wine, the Gallo Corporation would neither negotiate with the UFW nor allow its workers to vote on whether they wanted UFW representation. Gallo was America's largest winemaker, and its products were sold everywhere. But its very size significantly raised the economic impact of the UFW's boycott, a fact not lost on Fred Ross Jr., son of the man who had trained Cesar Chavez in organizing. Ross Jr. conceived a strategy that used the Gallo boycott to set the stage for the UFW to win enactment of America's first labor relations law protecting farmworker rights.

THE UFW TRIUMPHS

Children often go into their parents' business, but Fred Ross Jr. followed a father who was one of the great community organizers of the twentieth century. Ross Jr. joined the UFW for the same reason many others did: the charismatic leadership of Cesar Chavez. Ross said that, after meeting Chavez, "I knew I wanted to work with him." After graduating from college in 1971, Ross Jr. began working on the lettuce boycott in Seattle. From 1972 to 1975, he was in Berkeley, organizing the lettuce boycott there and doing campus recruitment. These were challenging years for the UFW, as it was engaged in a nationwide boycott of nonunion lettuce, the continuing grape strike and conflict with the Teamsters, and a separate boycott of Gallo wine.[59]

In January 1975, the *New York Times* declared that the UFW boycotts had failed and concluded that the Teamsters union would soon control the lettuce and wine industries. Ross Jr. interpreted the article as a pronouncement that "the UFW is dead." He was outraged, believing that, for all of the union's setbacks, "the workers were on fire" and were as committed as ever to fighting for justice in the fields. Ross and other UFW organizers also knew that their close ally, California governor Jerry Brown, who had just taken office, was committed to passing a state law granting labor protections to farmworkers. The *Times* somehow missed the political significance of a pro-UFW Jerry Brown replacing the progrower, anti-UFW Ronald Reagan as governor. Believing that the UFW needed to do something to show its strength, Ross suggested a march from San Francisco to Gallo's Central Valley headquarters in Modesto. Although some staff argued that the turnout would be too low to fulfill Ross's goals, Chavez agreed with the young organizer's plan.[60]

In order to ensure a good turnout, Ross arranged for the march to begin on February 22 in San Francisco, which was a hotbed of pro-UFW sentiment. Organizers in that city had succeeded in having Gallo wines, including the Thunderbird and Night Train brands, which were popular among street alcoholics, removed from many stores in the heavily Latino Mission District. Before the Union Square rally to kick off the march began, a giant banner was unfurled from the top floor of the adjacent St. Francis Hotel. In three-foot-tall letters, the banner read GALLO'S 500 UNION FARM WORKERS BEST PAID IN U.S. . . . MARCHING WRONG WAY, CESAR? The sign referred to the Gallo workers who had been put under a Teamsters contract without having had the right to vote on representation. Although Gallo's banner was designed to intimidate the

UFW, it had the opposite effect, inspiring the marchers as they left on the 110-mile journey to the Gallo corporate headquarters in Modesto.[61]

The impact of the march exceeded Ross's expectations. By the time the marchers got to Modesto, they numbered twenty thousand, even more than had participated in the 1966 pilgrimage. As the crowd sang and chanted, "Chavez, sí! Teamsters, no!" a company-sponsored banner unexpectedly appeared in front of Gallo's headquarters bearing these words: 73 MILES TO GO. GALLO ASKS UFW TO SUPPORT NLRA-TYPE LAWS IN SACRAMENTO TO GUARANTEE FARMWORKER RIGHTS. The "73 miles" referred to the distance from Modesto to Sacramento, the state capital.

This unorthodox announcement by Gallo that it wanted to join the UFW in pressuring the new governor, Jerry Brown, to enact the farm labor bill that the UFW had long sought—but that former governor Reagan had steadfastly opposed—shocked the union. It meant that growers, supermarkets, and the California agricultural industry were tired of dealing with the UFW boycott and would accept a farm labor law in its place. In response to Gallo's overture, Chavez agreed to drop the Gallo boycott in exchange for passage of a farm labor act in 1975. With key growers such as Gallo now aligned with the UFW, the historic California Agricultural Labor Relations Act (ALRA) passed in June 1975. For the first time, farmworkers in the United States were granted the rights that industrial and service workers had received under federal law in the 1930s. No longer could employers legally fire employees for union activity; and now workers themselves, rather than growers, would decide on union representation. Ross's idea of directly confronting Gallo with the full force of the boycott was yet another example of the power of the UFW's multipronged boycott strategy.[62]

In taking stock of the farmworkers movement in the October 30, 1975, issue of the *Los Angeles Times*, longtime labor reporter Harry Bernstein concluded that the UFW grape boycott "was the most effective union boycott of any product in the history of the nation." To support this view, Bernstein cited a recent Lou Harris poll reporting that 17 million consumers had stopped buying grapes, 14 million had given up lettuce, and—explaining Gallo's push for the ALRA—11 million had stopped purchasing Gallo wine. Although the ALRA's passage in 1975 paved the way for hundreds of union elections in the fields, the UFW still saw the boycott as an important weapon against stubborn growers. In 1976, the union's boycott operation included about three hundred full-time staff members in more than thirty cities in the United States and Canada. Nearly a third of the staff had at least four years of boycott experience and could ramp up quickly as needed.[63]

In February 1979, Chavez announced that the UFW was launching an international boycott against the United Brands Corporation, owner of Sun Harvest lettuce, with whom the union was engaged in a bitter strike. The UFW's United Brands boycott extended to the company's better-known products, including Chiquita bananas, John Morrell meats, and A&W root beer. In a sign of how seriously corporate America took the threat of the boycott, it took only a day after the UFW began mobilizing this boycott on July 31 to bring United Brands to the negotiating table. On August 31, the UFW won a three-year contract with Sun Harvest covering twelve hundred workers.

But the need to prioritize resources soon led Chavez to dismantle the UFW's boycott infrastructure. The passage of the ALRA had brought the union's focus back to the fields, and the boycott fell by the wayside as the union focused on winning elections and servicing its members. Chavez subsequently tried to promote consumer boycotts through direct mail, a tactic that brought in money but had little if any economic impact on targeted companies. Chavez and the UFW continued to call for boycotts of various products and companies until his death in 1993, but, unlike the original grape and vegetable boycotts, these appeals were not accompanied by a larger grassroots movement of workers and community supporters. Chavez and the UFW had shifted in a different direction, and nearly all of the leading boycott and organizing staff had departed from the union by 1982. It would be left to UFW alumni and others to apply the lessons of the table grape, wine, lettuce, and vegetable boycotts to new struggles.[64]

2

THE UFW BOYCOTT TRANSFORMED

The UFW boycotts of 1966–79 showed that a campaign that combined worker organizing, grassroots pressure, and an appeal to consumers could triumph over corporate interests that had significantly greater resources. It was not surprising, then, that other social movements would attempt to apply the UFW's boycott model to their own campaigns. The first, and most logical, set of progressive groups to follow the UFW's lead was fellow unions.

An early example came in June 1972, when the Amalgamated Clothing Workers of America (ACWA) launched a national boycott of Farah pants. With AFL-CIO backing and a $5 million budget, the boycott reduced pants sales so greatly that Farah agreed to sign a union contract in 1974. The relatively large amount of money committed to this battle (in contrast, the total four-year income of the UFW during the grape boycott of 1966–70 was only $2 million) clearly indicated that mainstream labor was becoming a believer in the UFW's boycott strategy.[1]

In 1974, after years of organizing, workers at several North Carolina plants owned by the southern textile giant J. P. Stevens voted to be represented by the Textile Workers Union of America (a struggle captured in the film *Norma Rae*). But the notoriously anti-union company refused to negotiate a contract with the TWUA, which in 1976 merged with the ACWA to become the Amalgamated Clothing and Textile Workers Union (ACTWU). Soon after the merger, the new union and the AFL-CIO launched an international boycott against J. P. Stevens linen and bedding products. This boycott was part of a widely heralded "corporate campaign," defined by Ray Rogers, its architect, as one that "attacks an adversary from every conceivable angle . . . and that encompasses all legitimate means of pressure and might include a strike, a consumer boycott, or other traditional tactics."[2]

UFW veteran Harriet Teller was the national field director of the Stevens boycott campaign from 1975 to 1979, supervising thirty boycott staffers across the United States and Canada. Other UFW veterans included Susan Sachen and Mark Pitt, who worked full time in the Stevens boycott campaign, and Paul Milne, who set up a powerful San Francisco Bay Area J. P. Stevens Boycott Support Committee after visiting Sachen in Greenville, South Carolina. Milne built an eight-person staff that, in UFW fashion, was paid $50 a week plus rent. The Bay Area group mobilized more than two thousand union members in Alameda County alone and won broad support for the boycott from the local religious community, particularly African American churches.[3]

The J. P. Stevens campaign was strategically framed as a civil rights struggle, pitting the plant's multiracial workers against white bosses in the Old South. The AFL-CIO's involvement, the campaign's racial dynamics, and the targeting of East Coast financial institutions all contributed to drawing major national media attention. Unlike Cesar Chavez, Marshall Ganz, or other architects of the UFW boycott, Ray Rogers publicly promoted his strategies and the concept of the corporate campaign, winning well-deserved credit for the tactic of personally targeting corporate directors of J. P. Stevens and the financial institutions who lent money to the company. The workers finally prevailed in 1980, when J. P. Stevens was forced to sign contracts with the ACTWU, a victory that at the time was seen as opening the door to increased unionization of the southern textile industry. Unlike the UFW boycotts, the J. P. Stevens boycott targeted a single company and was an important part of an overall corporate campaign.

In 1980, the Farm Labor Organizing Committee (FLOC) launched a six-year boycott against Campbell's Soup to demand a guaranteed minimum wage and improved working conditions for farmworkers in the Midwest. FLOC president Baldemar Velásquez had founded the organization in 1967, crediting Cesar Chavez with "opening the world of possibility for us. He showed us that we could win in our own struggle." Chavez regularly advised the Ohio-based FLOC and was the keynote speaker at the group's first three constitutional conventions in 1979, 1982, and 1985. (Chavez missed the 1988 convention because he was engaged in a thirty-six-day spiritual fast.) Like Chavez, Velásquez ensured that FLOC was "committed to the principle of nonviolence in all of our activities," and he adopted many of the tactics that had been pioneered by Chavez and the UFW for FLOC's campaign against Campbell's.[4]

For example, in the fall of 1982, Velásquez went on a twenty-four-day spiritual fast, a tactic Chavez had first brought to America's economic justice struggles in 1968 (see chapter 3). In the summer of 1983, FLOC echoed Chavez's legendary 1966 pilgrimage from Delano to Sacramento by organizing a 560-mile march from Toledo, Ohio, to Campbell's headquarters in Camden, New Jersey. Like the UFW event, the FLOC march had powerful religious overtones and was strongly backed by many churches, mirroring clergy support for the California farmworker campaigns. The march ended with a large crowd gathered at a mass for the farmworkers, held at the Camden Catholic cathedral, in which fifteen priests washed the feet of marchers.[5]

Following the UFW model, FLOC's boycott campaign created a broad coalition of labor, religious, and student supporters; and it set up boycott offices in major cities to recruit a new generation of young organizers for social change. The UFW's Fred Ross Sr. trained many of these recruits in organizing skills. Among them was Mike Casey, who headed FLOC's Philadelphia boycott office from 1984 to 1986, learning the ins and outs of running a national boycott. Casey subsequently became president of San Francisco's UNITE HERE Local 2, where his experience with FLOC would prove critical in boycotts waged by the local and national hotel workers union, as described later in this chapter. For Casey and other young activists, FLOC was the type of organizer training center that the UFW had been for a prior generation. In February 1986, FLOC made history by signing three-year labor contracts with Campbell's Soup, Campbell's Ohio tomato growers, and its Vlasic pickle growers in Michigan. FLOC's willingness to sustain the boycott against Campbell's for eight years brought others to the bargaining table: the union signed a similar contract with the Heinz Company the following year.[6]

By the late 1970s, the UFW's boycott strategy had spread from unions to a variety of human rights campaigns, both in the United States and internationally. In 1977, the Infant Formula Action Coalition (INFACT) launched a U.S. boycott against the Swiss-based Nestlé Company to protest the corporation's unethical marketing of infant formula in the Third World. UFW alumnus Paul Milne provided training to Nestlé boycott staff and was a key strategic advisor to the campaign in the early 1980s, continuing in this role for over two decades. Milne developed the strategy of examining Nestlé's business reports and then targeting cities where the company wanted to expand; the idea was to create a hostile climate on the ground that could thwart the company's ability to open new outlets. The Nestlé boycott eventually expanded to more than twenty countries and resulted in numerous international laws to prevent the deceptive marketing practices that had sparked the protest.[7]

From 1979 through 1986, American campuses were rocked by student demands that universities divest pension funds and other investments in apartheid South Africa. The anti-apartheid divestment campaign also used the economic boycott and legal strategies to pressure banks, other financial institutions, a wide range of corporations, and local and state governments to stop conducting business with or investing in South Africa, whose white minority government enforced legal segregation and discrimination against the nation's black majority. The national divestment campaign grew in strength, and Congress finally passed the Comprehensive Anti-Apartheid Act of 1986, over President Reagan's veto, imposing sanctions against companies doing business in South Africa. Beginning in 1989, the South African government, increasingly isolated both economically and politically, moved toward reform and the dismantling of the structures of apartheid. Nelson Mandela, leader of the African National Congress and a political prisoner for twenty-seven years, was released from jail in 1990 and in 1994 was elected president in the nation's first multiracial democratic elections.

During the late 1990s, economic justice activists used consumer-based strategies to address the proliferation of sweatshops in Third World countries. These strategies fell short of calls for a boycott, and since most of these low-wage, exploitative facilities were in undemocratic nations such as Indonesia, Vietnam, Haiti, and China, worker organizing was difficult. But as anti-sweatshop campaigns began to reveal the hard facts about how goods were made, many consumers started to read labels carefully. Students across America won measures requiring that clothes with their college's name or logo be made "sweat free," and local governments prohibited the purchase of uniforms made in sweatshops. Media coverage of sweatshop workers making clothes for companies such as Nike and the Gap evoked public anger and won improvements in labor practices. During the Vietnam war, activists had attacked corporations such as Dow Chemical (maker of napalm), but the UFW boycotts had taken it a step further by giving consumers an important role in improving corporate conduct. Kevin Danaher of Global Exchange, author of numerous books and articles on corporate campaigns, noted, "I would call the UFW boycotts the predecessor of the contemporary corporate campaigns in that they innovated tactics that got picked up by later campaigns that built on and improved the earlier model."[8]

By the 1990s, the AFL-CIO, which had questioned Cesar Chavez's use of the boycott in the 1960s and 1970s, itself sponsored a long list of boycotts. Unfortunately, the key to the success of the UFW model—its combination of a grassroots boycott campaign with worker and community organizing on the ground—was ignored. Instead, unions often simply announced a boycott and added it to the official AFL-CIO list, with little grassroots action to build consumer pressure against the target. The proliferation of these "paper" boycotts (that is, campaigns that existed solely on paper) reduced the effectiveness of the boycott strategy, and it gradually fell from favor.

It took former UFW organizer Fred Ross Jr. and his fifty-thousand-member Neighbor to Neighbor organization to demonstrate the continued viability of the farmworkers' boycott model. In addition to its strategically savvy grassroots mobilizing to prevent the U.S. Congress from approving military aid to Central American dictatorships, Neighbor to Neighbor launched a boycott of Salvadoran coffee in 1990 that helped bring peace to a country plagued by right-wing death squads and a lengthy civil war.

THE COFFEE BOYCOTT

After leaving the UFW and attending law school, Fred Ross Jr. became involved with the plight of refugees who had fled war-torn Central America and were now living in San Francisco. This involvement renewed Ross's contact with Paul Milne, whose Institute for Effective Action was training organizers in Fort Worth, Texas, for the fifteen leading Central American peace and solidarity groups. Milne had contacted the UFW's former chief organizer, Fred Ross Sr., to conduct the training, which lasted five weeks. In the mornings, the trainees would learn how to run house meetings; in the evenings, over the course of the five weeks, they held more than 150 house meetings, all of which occurred in the congressional district of Democratic representative Jim Wright, who was then Speaker of the House. Soon after the training ended, Milne and Ross Jr. got together with two other UFW veterans, Nick Allen and Angie Fa, to figure out how to build a movement to stop the U.S. government from sending military supplies to right-wing forces in El Salvador and Nicaragua. Ross knew about an educational group called Neighbor to Neighbor, which was trying to get a documentary titled *Faces of War* shown on television stations across the country. As Ross began organizing showings of the film in 1986, he and his colleagues decided to transform Neighbor to Neighbor into a national grassroots campaign against the United States providing military aid to antidemocratic forces in Central America.[9]

Ross recruited the type of idealistic young organizers who in earlier years might have joined the UFW boycott staff. He also applied organizational building skills learned in the farmworkers movement and brought in former UFW general counsel Jerry Cohen as a top advisor. Ross and his team soon created a grassroots activist group that grew to fifty thousand members. In 1988, Neighbor to Neighbor, with more than one hundred organizers working in eleven states and eighteen congressional districts, helped bring about a 219–211 vote in the House of Representatives to cut off military aid to Nicaragua's contra rebels. This marked a rare setback for the Reagan administration's policy in the region.[10]

When right-wing death squads in El Salvador killed six Jesuit priests, their housekeeper, and her daughter on November 16, 1989, the shocking event galvanized Ross and others who were already concerned about ongoing politically motivated violence in that country. Seeking a way to end this violence, Ross considered the classic UFW strategy: the boycott. He visited El Salvador and asked workers in the coffee fields whether they would support a boycott of Salvadoran coffee. When the workers responded enthusiastically, Ross returned to the United States, and the boycott began in December 1989.[11]

Ross first targeted the Nestlé Foods Corporation, whose Hills Brothers coffee was headquartered in San Francisco. Neighbor to Neighbor issued a press release urging a boycott of Salvadoran coffee in response to the Salvadoran government's refusal to take action in response to the most recent killings. Nestlé responded by announcing on December 11, 1989, that it was suspending the purchase of coffee beans from the country for thirty days. Nestle's Taster's Choice and Nescafé brands were America's top-selling instant coffees, and El Salvador's ambassador to the United States immediately decried the boycott as "harming" coffee workers and "hampering" the peace process.[12]

Borrowing another tactic from the UFW boycotts, Ross arranged to bring four hundred pickets down to the San Francisco waterfront in February 1990, to protest the unloading of Salvadoran coffee. James Herman, head of the International Longshoremen's and Warehousemen's Union, had been one of the first labor leaders to go to Delano and help the UFW's struggle; and he now agreed to implement Ross's boycott strategy by having union dockworkers refuse to unload Salvadoran coffee. After the ILWU told Ross that the Salvadoran ship *Ciudad de Buenaventure* was due to dock with forty-three tons of coffee, Herman got a commitment from the ship's owner that the coffee would be sent on to Vancouver. At a dockside media event packed with boycott supporters, Herman announced that the "death squad coffee" was going to Vancouver—"but

Actor Ed Asner, International Longshoremen's and Warehousemen's Union president
James Herman, and Fred Ross Jr. at a Neighbor to Neighbor boycott rally, 1990.
Courtesy of Fred Ross Jr.

it's only going along for the ride." Herman had called his union counter-
part in that city, and the Vancouver union had also pledged not to unload
the ship. The coffee was then rejected at the Southern California port of
Long Beach before being forced to sail back to El Salvador. As a result
of Ross's relationships with Herman and other labor officials, no Salvadoran coffee was unloaded on the West Coast for nearly two years.[13]

In addition to stopping coffee imports at the docks, Neighbor to Neighbor's grassroots base quickly mobilized to build community support for
the boycott. Supporters picketed restaurants that were selling boycotted
coffee, and cafés and other businesses were encouraged to switch to other
brands. City councils passed resolutions pledging not to purchase Salvadoran coffee for city workers, and supporters placed boycott stickers
on cans of targeted coffee brands such as Philip Morris's Maxwell House
and Procter & Gamble's Folgers. After Neighbor to Neighbor produced
skull-and-crossbones stickers that read "Boycott Folgers: This coffee
helps fund death squads in El Salvador," the CEO of Procter & Gamble
sent a copy of the sticker to the White House with a letter branding the
message as defamatory.[14]

The boycott's big breakthrough came in May 1990, after Neighbor to Neighbor ran commercials on Boston's CBS affiliate WHDH-TV, claiming that Folgers coffee brought "misery, destruction, and death" in El Salvador. The ads, narrated by television star Ed Asner, were provocative, picturing an upside-down coffee cup pouring blood. Neighbor to Neighbor knew that the ad was powerful but did not expect Procter & Gamble, the nation's largest television advertiser of packaged goods, to respond by canceling $1 million worth of advertising with the station. The day after Procter & Gamble's announcement, the *New York Times* ran a front-page article on the company's decision to pull the ads and included a photo of the bloody coffee cup. Neighbor to Neighbor responded to Procter & Gamble's action by saying that the company had given "us the biggest gift they could possibly have given us. This angers people in a way that the issue itself would not have." The group had spent only $1,000 on the commercials but was now reaping national publicity for its message.[15]

Thanks to the company's overreaction, millions of coffee drinkers now knew that Folgers was the largest American buyer of Salvadoran coffee beans. Many also learned for the first time that El Salvador's wealthy coffee growers were alleged to be financing death squads and were an obstacle to a peace settlement in the country's civil war. In a story on the advertising controversy, Ross told *Time* magazine, "There's blood on that coffee." The article also quoted an independent television station manager in Worcester, Massachusetts, whose station planned to run the ads that week because "First Amendment rights" were at issue. In September, the *New York Times* revealed that Neighbor to Neighbor had an important ally in its coffee boycott: James Gamble, heir to the Procter & Gamble fortune and namesake of the company's founder. Gamble and his family placed a shareholder resolution supporting the boycott on the agenda of the company's annual meeting in October. The resolution also had the support of religious groups affiliated with the Interfaith Center on Corporate Responsibility, which meant that shareholders representing more than $1 billion in company stock were backing the boycott.[16]

The multinational corporations that owned coffee brands were beginning to feel like the Schenley and Gallo companies in their battles with the UFW boycotts: the struggle simply was not worth it. The boycott had reduced American consumption of Salvadoran coffee by 33 percent, and imports of the coffee in Europe had declined steeply.[17] (Neighbor to Neighbor relied on European labor allies to bar shipments.) Given that Salvadoran coffee amounted to only 5 percent of American coffee imports before the boycott, Procter & Gamble did not need such a public relations nightmare. In a powerful statement of a global corporation's attitude toward the nation's future, the company took out full-page advertisements in El Salvador's leading newspapers supporting the peace process. Negotiations on a peace agreement for El Salvador began in New York in September 1991. By November 1991, Procter & Gamble had accepted Neighbor to Neighbor's proposal that it recruit Nestlé and Kraft to take out full-page ads in El Salvador's four leading newspapers urging peace. These three corporations, who controlled 80 percent of that country's coffee imports to the United States, were now pressuring the Salvadoran government for a peace settlement. On January 16, 1992, a peace agreement was signed, followed by a permanent cease-fire in February. When the cease-fire agreement was signed, Neighbor to Neighbor, having achieved its goal, ended its boycott.[18]

Throughout its boycott, Neighbor to Neighbor had insisted that there was an alternative "fair trade" approach for dealing with El Salvador's coffee industry. After the boycott ended, Rob Everts, who had worked for the UFW from 1975 to 1982 and for Neighbor to Neighbor on the Folgers boycott, joined Equal Exchange, a group that promotes fair trade between the United States and Third World workers and farmers, and became its executive director. Today, cooperatives in El Salvador sell fair trade coffee throughout the United States under the Café Salvador label.

Unlike the UFW, Neighbor to Neighbor was formed for a short-term purpose: preventing U.S. military assistance to El Salvador and Nicaragua and bringing peace to the war-torn, impoverished region. By the time the successful coffee boycott ended, the political situation in Central America had changed, and the group soon disbanded. But in assessing the legacy of Cesar Chavez and the UFW, it is significant that Neighbor to Neighbor was the creation of Fred Ross Jr., with Paul Milne playing an important early role. Fred Ross Sr. trained many of its organizers. Other UFW alumni, such as Jessica Govea, who had led the UFW's Canadian boycott, and Bob Purcell, also held key positions.

In 2007, many Neighbor to Neighbor veterans were working for SEIU, including Ross Jr., Dennak Murphy, Dana Hohn, and Mary Ann Buckley. Tracy Zeluff, who in the 1990s became SEIU's California field director, got her most critical training as an organizer when she worked for Neighbor to Neighbor. John Adler, another young Neighbor to Neighbor organizer, felt that he had "learned more during two weeks of training by Fred Ross Sr. than in four years at Yale University."[19] Adler became an organizer for District 1199, a union of health care workers, in New York City in 1992 and was subsequently recruited to head up the union's equity capital division. Lauren Martens also got his organizing career started with Neighbor to Neighbor, later becoming a prominent environmental organizer and the state council director for SEIU in Denver, Colorado.

Neighbor to Neighbor demonstrated the continued viability of the UFW boycott model for achieving progressive change and winning substantive victories. The organization also replicated the UFW's role as an entry point for many who went on to build careers working for social change: an extraordinarily high percentage of Neighbor to Neighbor's recruits became key leaders in social, labor, and economic justice struggles in the twenty-first century (see chapter 11).

HOTEL WORKERS RISING: THE UFW BOYCOTT IN THE AGE OF THE INTERNET

At the start of the twenty-first century, nearly fifteen years had passed since organized labor's last successful national consumer boycott, the FLOC boycott against Campbell's. Many considered boycotts a strategy of the past, while others identified the term with the failed "paper" boycotts. But labor activists affiliated with San Francisco's hotel workers union—some of them former UFW and FLOC organizers—recognized the boycott's potential. Local 2 had waged a successful boycott of San Francisco's Parc 55 Hotel from 1990 to 1993; and a second hard-fought, three-year boycott campaign had resulted in America's first unionized Marriott Hotel. These local successes inspired UNITE HERE to apply the boycott strategy nationally, most notably with the emergence of the union's Hotel Workers Rising (HWR) campaign in 2004.

The HWR campaign became a test of the UFW boycott model's continued viability in the Internet age. It not only confirmed the value of the boycott but also took advantage of technological advances that had occurred since the UFW grape and lettuce boycotts to retool and enhance the farmworker boycott for the twenty-first century.

Background of the Boycott

After weathering the downturn in travel that followed September 11, 2001, America's hotel industry again enjoys record profits, but many of the nation's 1.3 million hotel workers still earn poverty wages. Hotel wages and benefits vary dramatically within the same occupation, and often within the same city. For example, in 2006, full-time housekeepers cleaning rooms, changing sheets, and vacuuming floors in a luxury resort in Phoenix, Arizona, earned less than half of what their unionized counterparts earned in San Francisco or New York City. In Los Angeles, Seattle, and other large cities, unionized hotel workers earned higher wages and received greater health and other benefits than those performing identical work in the same city for the same corporation's nonunion hotels. Even in highly unionized San Francisco (89 percent of hotel workers), room cleaners today earn 51 percent less in the city's nonunion hotels.[20]

In the late 1970s, Miguel Contreras, Bill Granfield, Kevin O'Conner, and Gary Guthman were among the UFW organizers who moved on to jobs with San Francisco's hotel workers union, Local 2. Although their focus changed from the fields to urban hotels, there were many similarities between farmworkers and hotel workers: both groups were primarily immigrants, who received low wages and no health benefits while performing physically demanding work. Along with their organizing skills, the UFW alumni brought to Local 2 a belief in the power of the economic boycott. The San Francisco local became further committed to the boycott strategy when Mike Casey, the former leader of the FLOC boycott office in Philadelphia, joined the union's organizing staff in 1986.

In 1990, Local 2 launched what would become a nearly three-year boycott of San Francisco's recently built Parc 55 hotel. The boycott strategy put economic pressure on the hotel without risking workers' jobs, as a strike might have done; court documents subsequently revealed that Parc 55 lost millions during the boycott. After years of picketing, protesting, and boycotting, Parc 55 agreed to a union contract. Under boycott coordinator Lisa Jaicks, Local 2 ran successful boycotts against other hotels, developing tactics that they would later use in future campaigns, such as contacting prospective attendees of special events scheduled to be held at the hotel. In 1994, Casey was elected president of Local 2. Two years later, Local 2 launched an even more aggressive boycott against the nonunion Marriott Hotel in San Francisco.[21]

The conflict began when a strong majority of Marriott workers submitted cards supporting unionization, but hotel management refused to recognize Local 2 without an election. The union believed that Marriott's aggressive opposition to unionizing and its track record of anti-union practices made a fair election impossible, so Local 2 initiated the boycott to convince the corporation to accept the workers' choice of a union based on their signed cards (a process called "card check recognition").

Located adjacent to the Moscone Convention Center, the Marriott did a huge convention business. The union began the boycott by going after this business, contacting conventions who were slated to use the Marriott two, three, and four years ahead of their upcoming events. Keynote speakers who were slated to address meetings at the hotel were also contacted, and some agreed that they would refuse to enter the hotel.

Like the UFW boycotts, Local 2's campaign involved both internal organizing of the workers and external community pressure. The union's community work resulted in large attendance at marches and rallies. Local 2 is politically popular in San Francisco, and the city's mayor, Willie Brown, boosted the union's campaign by calling for an official city boycott of the hotel. This prevented San Francisco public employees from attending meetings or conferences at the Marriott, even events that city agencies had previously agreed to sponsor. After a six-year campaign and three-year boycott, the Marriott finally accepted the union. On the day Local 2's agreement with the Marriott was reached, the company gave Casey a list of hotel groups covering twenty-three thousand nights' occupancy and asked UNITE HERE to call these guests to tell them the boycott was over—just one indication of how successful the Marriott boycott had been in deterring business. Local 2's victory over the Marriott created a confident attitude at the union: "If we can beat the Marriott, we can beat anyone."[22]

While Local 2 was using the economic boycott to chalk up victories, the hotel industry was changing. Once an industry in which local, family-owned hotels negotiated with union locals, it was becoming increasingly controlled by international corporations. The rise of these global hotel corporations meant that UNITE HERE locals had far less leverage when they negotiated on a city-by-city basis. UNITE HERE president John Wilhelm acknowledged this new reality at the union's annual convention in 2001, where he called for a campaign to organize the entire hotel industry on a national basis to raise wages and improve benefits. The campaign's goal would be to replicate for the service sector what had been accomplished in the steel, auto, and other manufacturing industries in the 1930s: the transformation of historically low-wage work into decent jobs that could bring workers into the middle class. Since international hotel chains were united at the bargaining table, labor must also take a national approach. This meant negotiating all of the major cities' hotel contracts at one time, rather than having each local face the power imbalance of dealing separately with a global hotel corporation.

It would take several years to synchronize all the major hotel contracts. San Francisco's contract expired in 2004, while those in Chicago, New

York City, Honolulu, Boston, Los Angeles, and Toronto expired in 2006. To have the contract expiration dates coincide, San Francisco insisted at the start of negotiations in 2004 that its contract end in 2006. This did not sit well with their adversaries, the thirteen hotels that had joined together as the Multi-Employer Group, including such leading global hotel corporations as the Hilton, Starwood, InterContinental, and Hyatt chains. The MEG had stated publicly that it would never agree to a two-year contract, as that would play into the union's plans for national negotiations.

The employer group could have offered Local 2 members such a "Cadillac" four-year contract that the workers would have been hard-pressed to reject it, but no such offer was forthcoming. The MEG apparently forgot that failing to reach agreement with Local 2 in 2004, or by 2005, would automatically have San Francisco's contract coincide with those expiring in 2006—as Mike Casey put it, the MEG "forgot they could not make time stand still." Negotiations began in July 2004, and the MEG's refusal to consider a two-year contract led Local 2 to launch a two-week strike against the hotels. The employers then locked out all forty-two hundred workers for seven weeks, leading Local 2 and the Hotel Workers Rising campaign to call for a national boycott of the global corporations represented by the MEG.[23]

Launching the Hotel Boycott

Having seen the success at the Parc 55 and the Marriott, and having won a boycott against another hotel in the late 1990s, Casey and his colleagues were convinced that hotel boycotts were an effective strategy. As Casey put it, "If the hotels hate boycotts so much, then let's give them a boycott." Despite Local 2's track record, Casey got a less than enthusiastic response from other UNITE HERE leaders in the summer of 2004 when he raised the idea of expanding the Local 2 boycott program into a nationwide HWR boycott. Some assumed that he was proposing the type of paper boycott that routinely failed. Union officials who had worked for UNITE before its merger with HERE were especially skeptical, having had little experience with boycotts. As HWR boycott leader Dave Glaser described it, "For many labor leaders, boycotts had a bad reputation for being ineffective."[24]

The strategy also raised a critical internal issue: a national hotel boycott targeting unionized hotels would hurt the pocketbooks of UNITE HERE members. Less business at a Hilton meant fewer tips for hotel staff, and a steep loss of business could produce shortened workweeks and even layoffs. This meant that, regardless of union leaders' faith in the power of the boycott, the hotel workers would have to decide for themselves whether to pursue this strategy. San Francisco's UNITE HERE Local 2 was the group with the greatest capacity to run a successful boycott, and when its members voted overwhelmingly in 2004 to support a boycott of the thirteen major hotels where they worked, the Hotel Worker Rising national boycott was on.

A conscious link between the UFW grape and lettuce boycotts of the 1960s and 1970s and the hotel boycott was evident from the outset. In early 2005, Sam Pullen and Paul Engler of UNITE HERE's boycott team created a PowerPoint presentation on the planned boycott. The show was designed as a tool for recruiting community groups to be part of local boycott committees and for educating and exciting union members about the strategy. Different versions were shown in Boston, Miami, Atlanta, Chicago, Seattle, San Francisco, and Los Angeles; but viewers in all cities saw two large slides of Cesar Chavez with accompanying text. The first slide, titled "Boycotts Work," pictured Chavez in a UFW march next to these words:

> Every person has an impact and you really see results. Boycotts really work. They worked for us twice in 1970 and 1975. Every time you go to the store and choose not to buy grapes you cast a vote for what you believe. You can cast this vote as many times as you want and the polls never close. These are not family farms we are talking about, these are major corporations and the only way to get through to them is by not buying grapes.
>
> *Cesar Chavez*

The other slide was titled "Boycotts = Mass Participation." Next to Chavez's photo were these words:

> To us the boycott of grapes was the most near-perfect of nonviolent struggles, because nonviolence also requires mass involvement. The boycott demonstrated to the whole country, the whole world, what people can do by nonviolent action.
>
> *Cesar Chavez*

UNITE HERE understood the power of Cesar Chavez and the UFW's historic legacy and harnessed this force to build support for its twenty-first-century Hotel Workers Rising boycott.[25]

HWR's boycott targeted four categories of hotels. First were unionized hotels currently in contract disputes with UNITE HERE, such as the MEG hotels. Second were hotels that were not currently unionized but where workers were organizing, such as the situation Local 2 confronted in its earlier boycott at San Francisco's Marriott Hotel. Third, the boycott would target nonunion hotels where no organizing was occurring, which included those owned by the InterContinental, Starwood, Hilton, and other chains represented on the MEG. Finally, the boycott would be used to win union neutrality (employer agreements pledging not to oppose union organizing drives) and card check recognition agreements at hotels not yet built. This fourth target would ensure that union membership gains followed the growth of the hotel industry, which is the model that UNITE HERE has used with great success in Las Vegas.[26]

After categorizing the targets, HWR boycott staff researched the marketing strategy used by each hotel. Some hotels primarily rely on conventions, which meant that HWR staff had to convince convention planners and board members of groups slated to hold conventions to schedule their meetings at another facility. Other hotels primarily rely on special events, which meant that boycott staff needed to focus on wedding planners, local religious schools (for example, with Jewish parents who might be planning bar and bat mitzvahs), and community organizations who might be scheduling annual dinners, conferences, or other meetings.[27]

Just as Chavez and the UFW realized in 1965 that they could not win their labor dispute solely by fighting in the local arena, UNITE HERE's national hotel bargaining meant that the union could pressure a hotel in Los Angeles by extending the boycott to the same corporation's nonunion hotels in Atlanta or Seattle. Since consumers could readily switch reservations to a hotel not being boycotted, the Los Angeles hotel owner thus faced lost business not only in that city but also in other locations across North America. For example, because the InterContinental chain had four and a half votes in the MEG, HWR ran an active boycott against its nonunion Buckhead InterContinental in Atlanta. It also ran boycotts against nonunion hotels owned by the Sheraton (Peachtree Atlanta) and Starwood (Seattle Westin) chains, both of which owned union hotels that were in a contract dispute in San Francisco and other cities. In Seattle, a UNITE HERE Local 8 flyer calling for a boycott of the Sheraton Hotel and Towers told the public that the boycott was connected "to the owner's involvement in ongoing labor disputes at hotels across the U.S. and Canada."[28]

Under national labor laws, a union cannot urge a boycott, using coercive means, of a business with which it does not have a labor dispute— for example, a business that merely buys products or services from the "primary" employer (who is the target of the labor dispute). The UFW could legally urge consumers to boycott Safeway supermarkets as part

of its grape and vegetable boycotts because farmworkers were not covered by the federal laws banning such "secondary boycotts." But hotel
workers were subject to those laws. How, then, could HWR ask the public not to patronize hotels the union was not seeking to organize? Under
a 1988 U.S. Supreme Court decision known as the *DeBartolo* case, simply handing out leaflets urging a secondary boycott is constitutionally
protected "pure speech" and is not deemed to involve the element of "co-
ercion" necessary to invoke the ban on secondary boycotts, as labor laws
stipulate. Picket lines, in contrast, while imbued with the elements of
speech, are deemed to be inherently coercive—that is, they can intimidate people. Thus, while UNITE HERE could not put up a picket line at
the nonunion Buckhead hotel, where it had no labor dispute, the right
of free speech allowed organizers to dress up as "fat cats" and use a bullhorn to urge people not to patronize the facility.[29]

HRW focused on nonunion hotels in Atlanta because the InterContinental's corporate headquarters was located in that city, and that site
could be legally picketed. This picketing also publicized the local boycott, essentially allowing the union to send two messages with each event.
In Seattle, UNITE HERE boycotted the nonunion Sheraton for three reasons: to prevent the parent, Starwood Corporation, from using revenue
from the Sheraton to fight the city's unionized Westin workers; to reduce
business at a hotel that was driving down standards in the Seattle hospitality industry; and to give Westin workers more leverage in their bargaining. HWR's boycott campaign against such nonunion hotels showed
how following the UFW model and adapting it with some creative thinking could transform a dispute with a corporation in one city to a conflict
affecting the broader industry.[30]

Boycott staff followed a standard process in encouraging conventions
or events to seek alternative lodgings. First, staff members would contact
the meeting planner who had made the reservation. If they could not convince the meeting planner to change locations, they would then call the
chief executive or the board of directors of the group holding the event.
According to boycott coordinator Dave Glaser, these calls would usually
identify at least one or two people who were sympathetic to the union
position. Sometimes HWR had to take special steps to reach key decision-
makers—for example, visiting a hospital to reach an executive of a medical group planning an event at San Diego's historic but boycotted Del
Coronado Hotel. Those who were contacted most commonly reacted by
asking, "How did you get my name?" Board members of a group holding a conference rarely expected to be involved in a labor dispute.[31]

In Seattle, UNITE HERE boycott coordinator Jessica Lawson sent a letter in 2005 to the National Association of Drug Court Professionals providing "critical information" about the "block of rooms" the group had reserved for the Seattle Sheraton Hotel and Towers for June 21–24, 2006. The letter explained that the hotel's parent, Starwood Corporation, had locked out UNITE HERE workers in San Francisco and that the union was now highlighting the "clear connection" between "workers' rights and the bottom line." Specifically, this meant that UNITE HERE and its community allies would be engaging in "ongoing communication activities, including those in front of the hotel," and that the union wanted to "alert you to the possibility" that the group's event would face such "legal communications." The letter ended by urging the group to "do the right thing" by moving its event away from the Seattle Sheraton: "The sooner you decide to move your block of rooms, the easier it will be for you to provide the experience your attendees expect."[32]

Sometimes the boycott efforts required a less friendly tone. In Boston, HWR began a boycott of two nonunion Hyatt Regency hotels in November 2004, designed to pressure the chain in its negotiations with hotel unions in San Francisco and Los Angeles. HWR followed the UFW's model of leaving no potentially winning nonviolent tactic unexplored in pursuing its goal. At the Boston Hyatt, boycott supporters handed out flyers publicizing health code violations at the hotel that city inspectors had labeled as "critical risks." The flyer, titled "Wanted: Dirty Hyatt!" made sure to tell prospective customers that these "critical risk" violations had "the potential to seriously affect public health." In case this hadn't sufficiently scared away business, HWR distributed another flyer in May 2005 whose headline screamed, "THERE ARE DEAD BODIES IN THIS HOTEL!" The leaflet announced that the Hyatt was hosting the Society for Pain Practice and Management, which was using the President's Ballroom for a "Hands-on Cadaver Course." Asking "Would you share your banquet with a cadaver?" HWR urged customers who had not been told that there would be "dead bodies being worked on at this hotel during your stay" to "demand your money back!"[33]

A major target of the Boston-area Hyatt boycott was an academic conference that had been scheduled to bring in between $300,000 and $400,000 worth of business to the Hyatt Regency Cambridge. Boston boycott coordinator Jim McNeil assembled a delegation of union members, former Hyatt workers, religious leaders, and representatives of immigrant rights groups to meet with the academic group's key decision-maker, but they were continually pushed off to underlings. McNeil then organized a phone bank that called each of the organization's twenty staff members, urging them to tell their boss to reschedule the event. When this did not work, McNeil decided that he had to personally confront the leader and explain why the group would regret not supporting the boycott.[34]

He and a colleague went to the man's office and just sat, waiting for him to leave. When McNeil confronted him about the importance of supporting workers' rights and asked him if he had contacted his members about the boycott (which HWR was clearly prepared to do), the man replied, "You think I'm going to pull out three months before the event? You are cute, kid." Unflustered, McNeil asked if he had contacted the speakers planned for the conference, who included reporters from the *New York Times* and other media figures. McNeil suggested that these speakers might not be happy to arrive at a hotel only to learn that it was under a labor boycott. The leader got angry at McNeil and told him bluntly, "Do not contact the speakers." But McNeil had finally found the winning pressure point, and a week later the group moved the event.[35]

In October 2005, HWR's Boston boycott engaged in an even more confrontational battle with a new InterContinental hotel/condo tower under construction near the city's Big Dig, an enormous highway and tunnel project. The campaign targeted InterContinental both for its failure to reach agreement with hotel unions in San Francisco and other cities and for its refusal to accept card check recognition at the new property. HWR's chief strategy was to prevent condo sales by highlighting that buyers would face increased carbon monoxide levels from auto exhaust because the condos were being built around a 287-foot vent shaft near the Big Dig's exhaust tower—a problem that was not visible from inside the building.

The *Boston Business Journal* aptly titled its September 30, 2005, story "Tactics at Condo Site Display More Aggressive Union Efforts." The campaign aggressively promoted the message "Carbon Monoxide. Tunnel Fires. Terrorism. This is Big Dig Living" on leaflets, through Google ads, and on its own website. (HRW claimed that the building was vulnerable to a terrorist attack because it was built above an underground highway, where a fire or explosion might cause the building to collapse.) McNeil and his crew put stickers on parking meters and poles in the Financial District that read "Carbon Monoxide Warning: Boycott the InterContinental Hotel." The stickers also directed people to a website that linked to information about other luxury condominiums and hotels in Boston. As the stickers proliferated and union members handed out leaflets at real estate offices and the construction site, the activities got the attention of the *Boston Globe* and other media.[36]

In addition to spreading concern about health risks at the property, HWR joined with environmental groups and WALK Boston to protest the developer's plans to change the location of the sidewalk bordering the property. HWR argued that this change could create "a frantic, if not dangerous situation for the public" and organized a letter-writing campaign to the Massachusetts Environmental Policy Act Office, the agency in charge of approving the proposed change. InterContinental produced studies refuting HWR's allegations about carbon monoxide levels, and its real estate brokers insisted that the boycott campaign was having no effect on sales. But within two months of publicly denying the boycott's impact, the hotel agreed to the union's demands. The final deal affirming that the hotel would accept card check recognition of the union was signed in April 2006, months before the hotel's opening in November.[37]

UNITE HERE Local 1, in Chicago, has also effectively used the boycott strategy against the InterContinental Chicago hotel. Organizer Reverend Teran Loeppke's flyer titled "Dead Birds!" with a picture of a dead bird told potential hotel guests that city inspectors had found "dirty unsanitary debris and dead birds" on floors 4–15 of the hotel. The flyer's effectiveness was heightened because it coincided with a breakout of avian flu.[38]

In July 2003, Local 1 began a strike and boycott at Chicago's 852-room Congress Plaza Hotel in response to management imposing steep cuts in wages and benefits. The union has drastically reduced patronage at the Congress by forging a strong worker-community support network. For example, working in concert with the Alliance for Justice (a coalition of groups including ACORN, the American Friends Service Committee, and Citizens Action Illinois) at the Congress Hotel, Local 1 convinced the Chicago International Film Festival to break its October 6, 2005, reservation at the Congress even though the hotel had given the group one hundred free rooms. The festival preferred this course to having a picket line at their opening event at the Chicago Theater, one that keynote speaker and strong progressive Susan Sarandon would have been unlikely to cross. Local 1 also stopped the Chicago Rabbinical Council from holding an Orthodox Singles Shabbaton at the Congress scheduled for December 15–17, 2006, the first nights of Channukah. The cancellation prevented circulation of Reverend Loeppke's flyer describing the Congress as a "hotel of disrepute" and as "a terrible place to meet your mate."[39]

Boycott Eagle Hospitality rally, Cincinnati, March 7, 2007. Photo by Bishaara Clark/UNITE HERE.

As this book goes to press, the strike and boycott at the Congress Plaza Hotel remain in full force. As this example makes clear, even the most effective hotel boycott does not guarantee quick success. In this case, Local 1 diverted significant business from the hotel, which soon fell into acute disrepair. But more than five years later, the hotel's wealthy offshore owners continue to accept the financial losses rather than agree to contract terms accepted by the city's other unionized hotels.

The willingness to accept ongoing losses is the exception, however. After UNITE HERE launched a boycott of Eagle Hospitality in November 2006 to protest management's refusal to accept card check recognition and union neutrality at its Glendale Hilton, just outside Los Angeles, the company's chairman, William Butler, sought to buy back control of the public company. But the shareholders—after boycott actions at nine properties, and a huge Cincinnati protest where UNITE HERE announced that it had diverted $1 million in business from Eagle's properties—had had enough. UNITE HERE lead boycott organizer Sam Pullen notes that in March 2007, only five months after the boycott began, Eagle's board moved to sell the Glendale Hilton. By May, it had been sold to the Apollo Corporation, and in April 2008 190 hotel workers won union recognition.[40]

In the Eagle dispute, UNITE HERE initiated boycotts in nonurban midwestern cities such as Dublin, Ohio, and Covington, Kentucky (outside Cincinnati), to gain leverage in a conflict involving a property outside Los Angeles. This is reminiscent of the UFW's willingness to go anywhere to wage a fight and of its ability to expand a local labor conflict into a nationwide struggle. And the Eagle boycott was not a pale imitation of the struggle in larger, more militant cities. To the contrary, UNITE HERE's Covington campaign used the union's typically aggressive strategies.

For example, boycott organizers attended wedding expos, where hotel vendors were distributing information to prospective brides and grooms who were deciding where to hold their wedding parties. Organizers typically handed out flyers explaining how labor disputes could disrupt such special events and why it was important to hold them in hotels where there would be no such risk. In Covington, boycott organizer Alicia Ortiz and her colleagues took the standard wedding action a step further: they dressed two people in formal wedding attire and had them walk through the expo with a ball and chain tied to their ankles bearing a sign that read "BOYCOTT." Several volunteers handed out flyers to the crowds in the convention center accompanying the chain's message— that weddings in boycotted hotels would encounter constraints. Ortiz noted that such actions give couples "a sense of how disastrous it could be if this 'crazed labor dispute' followed them from the expo to the very hotel where their events were taking place." It is no wonder that the union has brides signing up to be continually informed about hotel labor disputes in their area.[41]

INMEX: Steering Consumers to Pro-Union Hotels

Although Local 2's Mike Casey did not expect the hotel industry to acknowledge the economic impact of the Hotel Worker Rising boycott, this was one time that he was wrong. In January 2005, only a few months after the boycott began, both the InterContinental and Starwood chains complained to UNITE HERE that the boycott was hurting business. A major reason for their irritation was that short-term boycotts in the hotel business can cause long-term losses. A group that holds its annual meeting in the same hotel every year and then switches facilities because of a labor dispute may well continue future meetings at the new site. Boycotts similarly risk permanent loss of business among vacation travelers, wedding planners, and other important sources of steady hotel revenue.[42]

In addition, convention visitors confronted by pickets and demands for a boycott are unlikely to support plans to have their group return there in the future. Boycott staff make sure to remind meeting planners that they will be the ones blamed when convention attendees arrive at a hotel and face a noisy picket line. That the economic impact of hotel boycotts continues well after the dispute is resolved raises the stakes for global hotel owners; this was particularly true given the large number of hotels targeted by the HWR campaign.

Whereas the UFW had to convince consumers to stop eating table grapes altogether, HWR in most cities had the easier task of convincing people to switch to a non-boycotted hotel. For example, HWR leaflets promoting the boycott of the Seattle Sheraton Hotel and Towers provided a list of facilities such as the Best Western, the Edgewater, and the Hilton, noting that these establishments "treat their employees with respect and dignity and compensate them with livable wages and good benefits." Although leaflets and boycott websites were useful for steering customers to non-boycotted facilities, in the spring of 2005 HWR came up with the most innovative new boycott strategy in decades: it created a nonprofit online organization that would both help meeting planners "navigate the world of hotel labor disputes" and steer millions of dollars in business from boycotted hotels to competitors.

Known as INMEX, short for the Informed Meeting Exchange, this nonprofit acts as a hotel reservation planner for groups considering conventions or events. INMEX includes a Meeting Planning Resource Manual with negotiating tips for event planners, including how to negotiate clauses that allow a group to terminate its agreement with a hotel in the event of a labor dispute. INMEX provides not only a list of boycotted hotels but also a guide to unionized hotels, to reward hotels that treat workers well. Dave Glaser describes INMEX as "steering business on a massive scale through positive consumer power." UNITE HERE has transformed the boycott so that it includes both positive and negative consumer power, a strategy akin to the UFW being able to steer consumers to nearby supermarkets where union-picked grapes, lettuce, and vegetables were sold.[43]

Members of INMEX, which include local and state governments, nonprofit organizations, and socially responsible businesses, do more than $200 million a year in convention business. Glaser's experience with the National Association of State Insurance Commissioners during the San Francisco Marriott boycott shows why many groups would see the advantage of using INMEX. Although such an organization has little to no involvement with unions, the position of state insurance commissioner is often a stepping-stone to higher office, and few ambitious politicians seeking higher office want to be accused during a campaign of having patronized a boycotted hotel. In this case, the head of the organization's board was the Kansas insurance commissioner, Kathleen Sebelius, who played a key role in getting the group to switch hotels. When she ran for governor in 2002, her campaign reminded labor that she had stood with them in the Marriott boycott. Any politician aspiring to higher office should appreciate the political safety that arranging reservations through INMEX provides.[44]

In 2006, HWR won major contract victories in San Francisco, Chicago, New York City, Honolulu, and Monterey. Its Seattle victory occurred in 2007, but Local 8 workers won benefits retroactive to May 2006. In addition to winning improvements in wages and working conditions, UNITE HERE won a national agreement from the Hilton and Starwood chains to agree to card check recognition of union representation in hotels. Glaser believes that one reason these two powerful chains agreed to a measure that could expedite unionization of their nonunion hotels was to get the market leverage bestowed by INMEX.[45] When you consider that an increasing number of groups will be using INMEX's recommendations to seeking out hotel, the financial wisdom of the two companies' action is clear.

The Boycott as Ongoing Tool

Like the UFW of the 1960s and 1970s, UNITE HERE has made the boycott an effective ongoing tool. Hotels know that when they do not deal in good faith with the union, a boycott is not only possible but likely— and they know that the action will not be one of the paper boycotts that so rarely succeed. For example, on March 14, 2007, Local 26 members at Starwood's Boston hotels overwhelmingly voted to authorize a strike and boycott after contract negotiations stalled. A little over a month later, the union's six-month contract dispute with the four hotels ended with a successful agreement. Even its anti-union opponents acknowledge the potency of the union's strategy. As one critic noted: "The union advantage? Hotels that employ both union and non-union workforces at different hotel locations faced a tough choice—either succumb to union demands for card check and neutrality at every one of their non-union hotels, or face a national boycott and a union corporate campaign that becomes a public relations nightmare."[46]

This pattern of the boycott working in concert with worker organizing and grassroots campaigns aimed at the public is becoming the norm for UNITE HERE disputes and closely parallels the UFW's use of the boycott in its heyday. The HWR boycott includes many of the grassroots activist components of the UFW's boycotts in years past and has also implemented innovative new tactics made possible by the Internet. UNITE HERE's success underscores the relevance of the UFW's basic boycott model for progressive movements in the twenty-first century.

3

BUILDING THE CLERGY-LABOR ALLIANCE

Reviving the Fast

Just as Cesar Chavez and the UFW revived and reshaped the activist strategy of the economic boycott, they also resurrected the strategy of building a strong clergy-labor alliance. The deep partnership that the farmworkers created with the religious community represented the first time since at least the 1940s that a workers' movement had secured active support from clergy and congregants. Many in the religious community had long been troubled by the living and working conditions of farmworkers, but they had lacked a vehicle to improve the situation. Chavez's framing of the union's struggle in spiritual and religious terms gave them this vehicle and, for many, transformed farmworker organizing and support work into a religious calling. Never before in the United States had so many people of faith attached themselves to a struggle for economic justice.

Although the 1960s and early 1970s saw young, activist members of the clergy become involved in a variety of campaigns for social issues, the UFW's success at integrating the religious community into the farmworkers movement was not simply a product of its times. To the contrary, Chavez and the union took specific actions to develop and solidify clergy support, resulting in the alliance that became so pivotal to the UFW's success. This strategy, rooted in Chavez's own religious faith and in the philosophy of nonviolent struggle and enhanced by the dramatic tactic of the spiritual fast, helped to develop a model that is now often integral to the standard in America's campaigns for economic and social justice.

THE MIGRANT MINISTRY

Cesar Chavez was a profoundly religious man. While working for the Community Services Organization in the 1950s, he concluded that the church would have to be an essential and equal partner in building a farmworkers movement. During the 1950s, Chavez met Father Donald Mc-Donnell, who introduced him to Catholic Church teachings on farm labor and labor unions and to a recent encyclical from Pope Leo XIII on the church's support for workers who protested unfair labor conditions. By 1961, when Pope John XXIII issued a new encyclical promoting the organizing of rural agricultural workers, Chavez had already come to see farmworker organizing as part of a spiritual mission to end injustice.[1]

Also during the 1950s, Chavez had begun meeting with the California Migrant Ministry (CMM), a Protestant organization. When he began looking for allies in Delano in 1962, this was the first group to whom he turned. He could not have found a more receptive audience. In 1961, leadership of the CMM had passed to the Reverend Wayne "Chris" Hartmire, who had previously been actively involved in community organizing work in East Harlem. Under Hartmire, the CMM's primary mission became the empowering of farmworkers. CMM staff had spent enough time in the fields to know that social services were not the answer and that only building a movement could make a meaningful difference in farmworkers' lives. When Chavez convened the founding convention of the National Farm Workers Association, on September 30, 1962, both Hartmire and fellow CMM leader Jim Drake were present.[2]

At the time of this meeting, Chavez and Hartmire understood that mainstream churches were not supporting the farmworkers' cause. Churches were potentially powerful allies, especially if their congregations could be mobilized, but they lacked the will, or the vehicles, to become involved in farm labor struggles. Growers were the primary donors to churches in California's agricultural towns, and the overwhelmingly white local church officials were not about to antagonize these civic leaders by embracing the cause of the primarily Mexican American farmworkers. Hartmire later noted, "I used to wonder why Chavez took the time to meet with me in Delano and to attend our CMM staff retreats. It was a lonely task that he had begun, so I speculated that fellowship may have been his motivation. But looking back, I am sure he knew he would need allies when the first strikes came, and he was carefully preparing us to be among those allies."[3]

Although Chavez knew that the CMM supported his vision, he did not take the organization's loyalty for granted. Nor did he treat the CMM as subordinate. Hartmire recalls that "Cesar carefully respected the fact that the CMM was a separate entity with a board of directors of our own, a constituency of our own and financial struggles of our own. He had a very clear and down-to-earth view of what we could do."[4]

Hartmire and Drake quickly became two of Chavez's closest allies. In 1963, the CMM provided the majority of the union's staff (Chavez worked the entire year for no pay). Although Chavez remained the only full-time staffer the group could afford in 1964 (his salary was $40 a week), by that time the union had obtained around eighty thousand pledge cards and enrolled one thousand members. By the summer of 1965, on the eve of the Delano grape strike, the CMM supported three priests working full time for the UFW; they represented more than half of the union's paid staff. That year, the Migrant Ministry was providing most of the staff and budget for the farmworkers movement. Despite losing support from pro-grower donors after the strike began, Hartmire convinced his superiors to expand the CMM's commitment to La Causa. Following the model of the 1964 civil rights movement's "Freedom Summer," the Migrant Ministry sponsored a "summer of 1964" event in 1965 to recruit progressive students to help on the strike, and some stayed on as full-time volunteers. Two years later, the CMM was renamed the National Farm Worker Ministry, and its chief program supplied the union with twenty-six priests who served as full-time organizers.[5]

The CMM's staff and resources were vital in the early months of the Delano strike, but equally important was the group's intensifying role in educating Protestant congregations about the exploitation that was taking place in California's fields. CMM ministers invested the labor struggle with moral authority, and the Migrant Ministry became the chief vehicle for enlisting Protestant church support for the farmworker cause. Chavez's carefully built alliance with a small group of rural ministers eventually started a nationwide tidal wave of Protestant religious activism on behalf of the farmworkers' struggle. Chavez later declared that the CMM "stood with us, picketed with us, marched with us, *lived with us* from the first days of our strike in Delano until the battle was won. . . . Our case became the heart of their mission—despite the fact that the organized wealth and power of the rural and conservative churches [were] trying to put them out of existence."[6]

Securing Catholic Support

To Chavez's surprise, despite the recent papal encyclicals promoting farmworker organizing and support, the Catholic Church in Delano had no programs to assist the primarily Catholic rural workers toiling in the community's fields. Although the Catholic Church supported the efforts of industrial workers to unionize in the 1930s, in the 1950s "labor problems began to recede into the background of Catholic concerns." The reasons for this growing separation were likely many: Catholics had favored barring communists from unions, for example, while at other times labor had not appeared to need the church's help. As legendary "labor priest" George Higgins put it, "The UAW's Walter Reuther (who benefited from church support as much as any other labor leader) did not need Cardinal Mooney's advice on how to run a union." The Catholic Church was also estranged from the AFL-CIO during the 1960s and early 1970s over labor's official support for the Vietnam war. The increasing affluence of U.S. Catholics during these years may also have reduced church support for labor unions.[7]

In California's Central Valley, however, Chavez confronted additional obstacles. Charles A. McCarthy, associate editor of the Monterey-Fresno diocesan newspaper, the *Central California Register,* described Delano in 1962 as a place where "growers are among the leading and most respected citizens in their communities and in Catholic groups." Chavez confronted a local Catholic Church hostile to his agenda and aligned with the wealthy Catholic growers who funded Central California's rural archdioceses. Even though Chavez and the vast majority of farmworkers were devout Catholics, and the union portrayed its mission as fulfilling Catholic teachings, the church hierarchy in the Central Valley was not swayed and publicly attacked the Catholic "outsiders" who came to Delano to support the grape strike. This alignment between affluent growers and the local Catholic Church posed a challenge for Chavez and the growing union and meant that they often had to overcome strong opposition in organizing, building, and nurturing an alliance between the farmworkers movement and the Catholic Church.[8]

Chavez's breakthrough with the Catholic Church began when he cited Pope Leo XIII in a speech on September 16, 1965, as he called for the largest labor walkout in California since 1938. On October 19, ministers from the state's Northern and Southern Council of Churches responded to Chavez's entreaties by joining workers in picketing. The *Central California Register* soon ran a front-page editorial on the Delano strike titled "Our Catholic Church Is Involved." While the editorial did not endorse the strike, it forced the newspaper's Catholic readership to put the dispute in the context of papal encyclicals supporting farmworkers. When priests from Sacramento read about the strike in the *National Catholic Reporter,* they announced that they were troubled to learn that no local clergy had been involved. This highlighted what would become a major conflict between pro-worker Catholic clergy from urban communities and representatives of local Central Valley dioceses who "didn't want outside clergy making trouble in the area." Nonetheless, strike support efforts quickly spread to Catholic schools in the San Francisco Bay Area; and by December 1, a Bay Area interfaith meeting to support the strike included many Catholic priests and nuns from agricultural areas. Two weeks later, a national group of Catholic, Protestant, and Jewish leaders, who had formed a Committee of Religious Concern, visited Delano.[9]

The committee's Delano meeting on December 14 proved to be a turning point in the attitude of the Catholic Church toward the union. The committee heard from Chavez in the morning, who spoke of the conditions that had caused the strike. He then introduced the Reverend James Drake and the Reverend David Heavens from the CMM. Heavens described how he had been dragged from a car and assaulted by a local grower and how he had been arrested by local sheriffs simply for reading to workers Jack London's classic definition of a strikebreaker ("a traitor to his God, his country, his wife, his family, and his class"). After the union completed its presentation, the committee learned that the growers had canceled the lunch meeting where they were to give their side of the strike.[10]

Since some of the national religious leaders had flown three thousand miles to get to Delano, they were not pleased. The committee continued its fact-finding and then held an afternoon press conference in which it "urged the strikers to continue their strike until such time as their just demands are recognized, and we promise them our help and support." The statement infuriated growers, whose spokesperson retorted, "Anyone can find hunger and poverty if they look hard enough." When asked about the pope's statement that workers had a right to form voluntary associations, a Catholic grower said he was sure that "the Pope did not mean that all men everywhere should be organized."[11]

On March 14, 1966, Chavez testified before the U.S. Senate Subcommittee on Migratory Labor, which held three days of hearings in rural Visalia, California. Chavez stated that farmworker unrest was growing and that Kern County sheriff's deputies were harassing picketers. The following day, Catholic bishop Hugh A. Donohoe of Stockton, California, speaking on behalf of the state's eight bishops, testified in favor of federal legislation to help farmworkers. He also insisted that farmworker organizers were not "outside agitators," drawing applause. Senator Robert F. Kennedy was among those who heard the testimony. He told reporters that "he considered a bishop's first responsibility to be with the poor and oppressed." He added that he would be "surprised and considerably shocked" to hear of a bishop not allowing priests to go out and help farmworkers (a charge made against local bishops). Kennedy went so far as to argue that "bishops should encourage their priests to work with the farm laborer. They themselves should leave their homes and live among these workers."[12]

Robert Kennedy had a tremendous following among Catholics. His late brother John had been America's first Catholic president, and in 1966 the Kennedy name was akin to the gold standard in America's Catholic community. Kennedy's endorsement of the farmworkers' strike, and his chastising of less than supportive Catholic bishops, sent a powerful message to the church hierarchy about the need to more aggressively support the farmworkers' cause.

"Perigrinación, Penitencia, and Revolución"

As soon as the Senate hearing ended, Chavez announced that he would walk three hundred miles from Delano to Sacramento, the state capital. Chavez called the march a *perigrinación* (a pilgrimage), and its theme was "Perigrinación, Penitencia, and Revolución" (Pilgrimage, Penitence, and Revolution). Chavez felt that the march would rejuvenate the farmworkers and make them fit for the struggle ahead, "not only physically, but spiritually." He explained:

> In every religious-oriented culture the pilgrimage has had a place, a trip made with sacrifice and hardship as an expression of penance and of commitment—and often involving a petition to the patron of the pilgrimage for some sincerely sought benefit of body and soul. Since this is both a religious pilgrimage and a plea for social change for the farm worker, long advocated by the social teachings of the Church, we hope that the people of God will respond to our call and join us for part of the walk just as they did with our Negro brothers in Selma.[13]

Chavez and the workers began their pilgrimage accompanied by priests from four dioceses, and they sang hymns as they traveled twelve to sixteen miles each day. Marching farmworkers held portraits and a banner of the Virgin of Guadalupe, the well-loved religious and cultural symbol of Mexico. Marcher Luis Valdez, founder of El Teatro Campesino (the Farmworkers' Theater) and later director of such films as *Zoot Suit* and *La Bamba,* explained, "In their desire for freedom the Mexican people have not always had the backing of the Church or of the bishops or the priests, but the virgin is ours." Many carried large crosses representing the final journey of Christ, fitting for a march that began during the holy season

of Lent and was designed to end on Easter Sunday. No American struggle for economic justice had ever relied on such an unequivocal expression
of Catholic religious symbols.[14]

Priests from the San Francisco archdiocese celebrated the Eucharist
each day of the march, and a large number of seminarians and sisters
from the Bay Area joined the throng at the halfway point. A week into
the journey, the workers were met by more than a thousand farmworkers in West Fresno, who packed into a local theater. A representative of
Bishop Aloysius Willinger, from the Monterey-Fresno area, told the spirited crowd that the workers had the right to achieve social justice and
that the Catholic Church encouraged their efforts.

On each night of the pilgrimage, Chavez and the marchers held a meeting with local farmworkers. The gathering opened with the Mexican song
"De Colores," the theme song of the Catholic Cursillo movement, a
charismatic prayer and study association to which Chavez and many
workers belonged. A prayer would often follow. Luis Valdez would then
read "El Plan de Delano," a manifesto that combined quotes from the
pope and a tribute to the Virgin of Guadalupe with radical rhetoric describing the farmworkers as "sons of the Mexican Revolution." The Plan
of Delano ended with the words, "wherever there are Mexican people,
wherever there are farm workers, our movement is spreading like flames
across a dry plain. . . . Viva la Causa!"[15]

Bill Kircher, the AFL-CIO's national organizing director, was deeply
impressed: "The march was an organizing tool. New. Radical. Different. . . . The whole thing had a strong cultural, religious thing, yet it was
organizing people." While suffering from a "pancake of blisters on his
feet" from participating in the march, Kircher was shown a local newspaper story reporting that the AFL-CIO was boycotting the pilgrimage
because "it was not really a march, it was a civil rights thing, a demonstration, no relationship to unionism and so forth." Inspired by the farmworkers' new approach to union organizing, Kircher read the riot act to
the AFL-CIO officials responsible for the criticism. By the next evening
in Modesto, labor representatives from AFL-CIO unions were out in force
to greet the marchers, holding "Viva La Huelga" and "Viva La Causa"
signs. Kircher saw the AFL-CIO turnout as "a landmark in terms of visible solidarity."[16]

The pilgrimage was a remarkable organizing tool, as it connected farmworkers heretofore isolated in rural towns to the growing statewide
movement. A candlelight procession sometimes preceded the marchers
as they passed through these villages, and local workers held feasts. A

wave of excitement permeated the normally quiet fields as word passed that the marchers were approaching. Crowds stretched as far as two miles. Marchers spent the night in the homes of fellow workers, creating an opportunity to develop relationships and discuss the union with local families. Workers were aware of the grape strike and received reassurance from marchers that "La Huelga" would soon be coming to their field.

On Easter morning, Chavez appeared as an almost biblical figure, walking with blistered and bleeding feet to reach the state capitol building. Ten thousand workers, students, clergy, and other supporters accompanied him, in a procession headed by a farmworker carrying the large Virgin of Guadalupe banner. Dolores Huerta was the chief speaker, and she evoked the "Pilgrimage, Penitence, and Revolution" theme that had launched the march. Reading from the "Plan of Delano," which Valdez had based on Mexican revolutionary hero Emiliano Zapata's "Plan of Ayala," Huerta declared: "The workers are on the rise. There will be strikes all over the state, and throughout the nation, because Delano has shown what can be done, and the workers know now, they are no longer alone."[17]

The pilgrimage dramatically increased the sense of unity and common struggle among farmworkers, and it also cemented the unwavering alliance of the Catholic Church with the farmworkers' cause. But that alliance, and the backing of the religious community overall, did not come easily. Unable to inherit religious support for labor causes, Chavez and the union had to initiate and nurture it. No such relationship had existed in America in the previous two decades. Had Chavez not cultivated the Migrant Ministry and worked hard to overcome opposition from the Catholic Church, the religious support that proved indispensable to the union's success would not have emerged.[18]

Chavez had to fight for this alliance even within the farmworkers movement. As the following section describes, when Chavez began his 1968 fast, some secular labor activists within the UFW were wary of the influence of the Catholic Church. Chavez could have deferred to these feelings, but instead he boldly moved the UFW toward close identification with the church. Speaking at a conference that year, he publicly chastised Mexican American groups for not building ties with the Catholic Church and "ignoring this source of power." He argued that "it is not just our right to appeal to the church to use its power effectively for the poor, it is our duty to do so."[19]

No other labor struggle achieved the UFW's level of solidarity with the religious community until over two decades later, in the 1989–90 strike by Pittston coal miners in Appalachia. In the interval, labor leaders, ignoring the lessons of the UFW's battles, "seemed uninterested in coalitions with religious and civic groups that lent the movement so much of its moral credibility in its early years."[20]

Today, however, with Latino immigrants centrally involved in many unionization drives, the relationship between the religious community and labor is once again moving to the fore. Clergy-labor alliances have played an instrumental role in some of organized labor's biggest victories in the twenty-first century, including Houston's landmark union organizing drive among janitors in 2005, the successful campaign to unionize downtown security guards in Los Angeles in 2007, and Miami's Justice for Janitors campaign in 2006 (which is the focus of chapter 4). In 1996, Kim Bobo founded Interfaith Worker Justice, a national organization that coordinates local religious support for worker struggles and regularly works with SEIU's Justice for Janitors campaigns. Bobo has been among the nation's preeminent organizing strategists since her days in the 1970s with the Midwest Academy, which trained a generation of community and labor organizers. Interfaith Worker Justice committees, working collaboratively with labor unions, are using many of the same tactics and strategies pioneered by the UFW, with equally successful results. Chavez and the UFW created a model for the building and nurturing of clergy-labor alliances that is a vital part of the UFW's twenty-first-century legacy.

CHAVEZ'S SPIRITUAL FAST

As 1968 began, Cesar Chavez and the UFW faced a major challenge. After using threats of consumer boycotts to secure union contracts at such leading wineries as Almaden, Gallo, and Paul Masson in 1967, the UFW remained locked in an increasingly bitter dispute with the much larger table grape industry. The union had launched a strike against these grape growers in September 1965 and expected that its consumer boycott would force growers to the bargaining table. But after learning how Giumarra Vineyards and other growers targeted by the boycott were circumventing it by selling grapes under other labels, the UFW expanded its boycott to the entire table grape industry in January 1968.

Along with the broader boycott, the strike continued, but there was growing frustration with its lack of progress. Despite the incredible surge of empowerment and excitement that had accompanied the early days of the strike, feelings of demoralization and anger had now set in, along with the first serious internal conflicts since Chavez began organizing farmworkers in 1962. Some started to question his strategy of nonviolence. Pro-grower judges had effectively allowed strikebreakers into the fields, and violence against strikers was rising. Younger workers, influenced by recent urban riots and an emerging Chicano militancy, felt that Chavez's reliance on nonviolence left them defenseless and that his approach no longer served the movement's needs. Chavez acknowledged, "Some of our people accused us of cowardice. They told me: 'If you go out and kill a couple of growers and blow up some cold storage plants and trains, the growers will comes to terms. This is the history of labor; this is how things are done.'" Chavez disagreed. He predicted that using violence would have won the UFW contracts, "but they wouldn't be lasting, because we wouldn't have won respect." He believed that the industrywide boycott would bring victory and feared that resorting to violence would undermine the movement. "Social justice for the dignity of man cannot be won at the price of human life," he argued.[21]

With his movement's very existence at risk, Chavez made a decision that shaped the UFW's future and continues to reverberate in today's progressive movements. On February 15, 1968, he privately decided to stop eating. Four days later, he called a special noon meeting of all strikers, office staff, and their families. He spoke for an hour and a half about nonviolence, directing many of his words toward activists who were critical of the violence in Vietnam yet seemingly supportive of violence in rural California fields. Chavez reminded the group that they were a cause, not simply a union, and that if they were considering violence, it meant that they had lost their commitment to win. He closed by saying that his fast was an act of love and prayer for the movement that he led and for whose individual acts he felt responsible. He would not eat "until such time as everyone in the strike either ignored me or made up their minds they were not going to be committing violence."[22]

After reaffirming that the fast was an act of love, Chavez walked out of the hall and continued a few miles to a shed at the union's new headquarters, an old labor camp known as the Forty Acres. As strikers heatedly debated their leader's announcement, Chavez confidant LeRoy Chatfield, formerly a member of the Christian Brothers religious order, went to arrange for a bed, a fan, and water to be brought to the Forty Acres. While Chavez remained peacefully in bed over the next weeks, receiving daily communion, his fast on behalf of both his movement and the power of nonviolent activism galvanized America. The fast signified the idealism of the era and left a permanent legacy for future struggles.

The Power of Nonviolence

Cesar Chavez believed in Gandhi's adage that "if you really want to do something, be willing to die for it." For Chavez, "doing something" meant using nonviolent tactics, which he saw as having "the power to attract people and to generate power." He was a great admirer of Mohandas Gandhi, the Indian independence leader who had often fasted to publicize his message, but he also saw Mexican culture as bringing a "Catholic concept of sacrifice" and of penance to the act of fasting. Gandhi's twenty-one-day fast in 1924 was aimed at reducing violence between India's Muslims and Hindus. Chavez's 1968 fast sought to preempt the prospect of violence by recommitting the farmworkers movement to the strategy of nonviolence, which he saw as spiritually essential and as key to the movement's success. Chavez and UFW spokespersons made clear from the outset that he was on a spiritual fast, not a hunger strike. Chavez viewed a hunger strike as an action motivated by a specific demand, whereas a fast represented both an act of penitence for the talk of violence within the union and an act of rededication to nonviolence. Chavez saw his fast as "a very personal spiritual thing . . . done out of a deep conviction that we can communicate to people, either those who are against us or for us, faster and more effectively, spiritually, than we can in any other way."[23]

The initial reaction to Chavez's decision to fast was mixed. Some of the more secular and radical UFW volunteers, who included those most critical of Chavez's strategy of nonviolence, disdained the religious imagery of the fast. Saul Alinsky, whose Industrial Areas Foundation had employed Chavez as an organizer in the 1950s, told Chavez that his fast was "embarrassing" to the IAF. Labor officials were reportedly incensed about the fast. Unions were accustomed to "beating up scabs" as the best strategy for deterring strikebreakers, yet Chavez was ignoring this and instead engaging in what they perceived as a religious act.[24]

But it soon became clear that most of the overwhelmingly Catholic farmworkers saw Chavez's fast as the ultimate in self-sacrifice, a sacrifice made solely on the workers' behalf. Chavez's arrival at the Forty Acres triggered a renewed sense of purpose that could be felt throughout UFW headquarters and on picket lines. This feeling of rejuvenation also took hold on the East Coast, where the farmworkers' newly expanded table grape boycott was in full swing. In January, UFW co-founder Dolores Huerta had traveled to New York City by bus along with dozens of farmworkers to work on the boycott. When Huerta heard about Chavez's decision to fast, she and other women volunteers "broke down and started crying. I think I lost eight pounds the first week of his fast." Huerta felt that critics of the fast had an attitude of "bigotry" toward religion, and she noted that the idea of "penance, of suffering for something, of self-inflicted punishment" had a long tradition in Mexican culture. Chavez had often stated that the movement would prevail through fasting and prayer rather than violence, and La Causa had long incorporated religious imagery. But unlike a march with religious symbols or a speech with religious themes, Chavez's fast was viewed as profoundly, if not exclusively, spiritual. It created the image of a religious martyr sacrificing for the greater good. It became the best organizing tool the union had ever seen.[25]

In the early days of the fast, groups of farmworkers would arrive at the Forty Acres from great distances in order to pay their respects. Most said that they understood why he was fasting, but added that they worried about his risk of dying. On at least one occasion, a visitor took direct action to prevent the fast from killing Chavez. Although a monitor was usually outside his door to regulate visitors, no one was on duty at 2:00 A.M. Taking advantage of this, a farmworker from Merced, who had been unable to meet with Chavez during the day, entered the room and claimed that he was under instructions to make the leader eat. He told Chavez, "You don't do us any good dead," pulled out a bag of tacos, and told Chavez to start eating. When Chavez politely refused, the worker tried to stuff a tortilla into his mouth and then jumped on Chavez to force the taco into him. Cesar's brother Richard heard struggling and rushed to the room, believing that the worker was trying to kill Chavez. As the worker was being dragged away, Chavez told his colleagues to leave the man alone, and they apologized for the mistake.[26]

The UFW had strong support from the religious community before the fast, but Chavez's echoing of the biblical fasts of Jesus and Moses galvanized the union's religious base. Mark Day, a Franciscan priest assigned to work with the union, wore vestments with the UFW's red and black colors and held a daily evening mass in a converted storeroom at the Forty Acres. Day even offered union-made wine to worshippers. The number of those attending masses and the ongoing prayer sessions grew steadily, as hundreds of farmworkers drove sixty to eighty miles to attend the mass before returning home the same night. Since not all farmworkers were Catholic, Chavez also asked a Protestant minister to preach at the nightly mass. A black Protestant minister subsequently appeared, and then a group of ministers came to sing Mexican Protestant music. Chavez was conscious of how the Catholic majority in Mexico had discriminated against that country's Protestants, and the fast became a vehicle for unifying the two groups.[27]

The Fast Becomes an Organizing Tool

LeRoy Chatfield coordinated activities around Chavez's fast. Chatfield had been a Christian Brother working in Bakersfield in 1963 when he attended a National Catholic Social Action Convention in Boston. Among the speakers was famed Catholic activist Father Philip Berrigan, who talked about Cesar Chavez's efforts to organize farmworkers in Delano. Delano was only thirty miles from Bakersfield, and after returning from the conference, Chatfield went to meet Chavez. Following the meeting, he left his job to join the UFW. He subsequently became a close advisor to Chavez.

Chatfield sought to make the Forty Acres "sacred ground," barring cars from driving or parking on the property. A chapel was erected, and arrangements were made for food, water, and bathroom facilities. Although media descended on the Forty Acres, Chatfield refused to allow them to photograph Chavez in his room or to interview him there. The press corps, which included Tom Brokaw, then a Los Angeles local news reporter and later the longtime anchor for NBC national news, accepted these restrictions without protest. Chavez attended the night masses, and the press was free to photograph him then. But the goal was to emphasize the religious, sacred, and personal aspects of the fast, not to transform the act into a publicity stunt or to have it perceived in that light.[28]

Farmworkers and religious supporters also came, even from hundreds of miles away, living in tents erected outside Chavez's room. This process began when two longtime UFW volunteers, Nick and Virginia Jones, pitched a pup tent at the Forty Acres and spent the night. Others followed their example, and it eventually grew into a virtual city of three hundred to four hundred tents, each sheltering four or five people. The scene came to resemble a religious campground or pilgrimage center. Marion Moses, a nurse and UFW volunteer, described the pattern of tents as looking "like a mining settlement in the Old West." The makeshift village included children playing, the sounds of guitars strumming, and the singing of Mexican songs at night. A fireplace was built, and there was hot chocolate every night. Strikers brought Chavez religious artifacts such as crucifixes, Christ figures, and images of the Virgin of Guadalupe and St. Martin de Porres, one of the most popular saints in Latin America. One family even brought an offering of a 150-year-old handmade silver Christ of the Miners. People approached Chavez as if he were dying, and there was a very real fear among fellow UFW leaders—as well as on the part of his brother and his wife—that his death would kill the movement.[29]

As the numbers coming to pay homage to Chavez reached into the several thousands, Chatfield arranged a receiving line for farmworkers to meet with their leader on a one-to-one basis. These meetings gave Chavez a remarkable opportunity to privately connect with workers from across the state and to learn their problems firsthand. These private meetings built workers' loyalty to Chavez and the movement. It was not every day that farmworkers had a private meeting with a famous person; they no doubt left Chavez's room impressed that he had spent private time with them. Chatfield felt that people entered the room as members, "but they left as organizers." While the receiving line was created as a practical method of accommodating large numbers of visitors, it became what Chatfield describes as "the most fantastic organizing opportunity ever devised." Chavez said that he did "more organizing out of this bed than I did anywhere."[30]

On day eleven, the UFW's chief adversary made a colossal blunder. Despite the public nature of Chavez's fast, growers and their allies seemed to believe that it was a fraud. One rumor was that Chavez's nurse, Marion Moses, was shooting jackrabbits at night and then cooking them for him. John Giumarra, the leader and largest of the Delano grape growers, apparently shared this distrust of the fast. Giumarra's company asked a local judge to bring Chavez to court to face contempt charges for violating one of the many injunctions against picketing issued by Delano's pro-grower judiciary. Chavez could not avoid the court appearance, even though twelve days of fasting had left him barely able to walk on his own.

In preparation for Chavez's court visit, UFW organizing director Marshall Ganz went to the courthouse with representatives of workers' ranch committees. The purpose? To measure how many people the courthouse could hold. When a clearly weakened Chavez arrived at the court the next day, farmworkers lined every wall of the courthouse. UFW attorney Jerry Cohen estimated that there were five hundred cars full of people and three to four thousand farmworkers overall. As Chavez approached the courthouse, the path was lined with workers silently kneeling. Inside the courtroom, farmworkers sat, singing softly, and many were praying. News media were out in full force to cover Chavez's arrival, bringing national attention to events occurring on a quiet morning in a small-town courthouse in rural Delano, California.[31]

Before the court proceedings began, Cohen and the Giumarra attorneys met in the judge's chambers. The growers' attorneys expressed outrage at how the farmworkers had been allowed to take over the courtroom and urged the judge to expel them. The UFW had never won a single case in that courthouse, so it seemed to be a foregone conclusion that the court would grant the growers' request. But Judge William Quinlan told the attorneys, "If I kick these workers out of this courthouse, that will be just another example of goddamn gringo justice. I can't do it." The judge continued the case because of Chavez's condition. About a year later, Giumarra dismissed the contempt request. The farmworkers' presence had changed the balance of power at the courthouse, and growers did not want to give them an excuse to return.[32]

Organizing for the court appearance had forced all nine ranch committees—one for each of the wineries where the UFW had already won contracts—to work together for a common goal. As Cohen recalls, this helped transform what had previously been isolated groups into a true union. In diverse and mutually reinforcing ways, the fast brought forth the best impulses of the farmworkers movement and reminded everyone of the importance of keeping their eyes on the prize.[33]

By day twenty-one, pressure on Chavez to stop the fast had increased. His doctor forced him to take medication and to sip some bouillon and unsweetened grapefruit juice. He informed Chavez that he could be doing permanent harm to his health if he continued fasting. Many felt that Chavez had already achieved his goal, with the UFW clearly more unified than ever, particularly around its commitment to nonviolence. Chavez's family, constant delegations of workers, and his closest allies all urged him to end the fast. Senator Robert Kennedy, who had established a close relationship with Chavez while holding hearings on the farmworkers in Delano in 1966, sent a telegram asking him to consider the implications for the movement if his health failed. But Chavez rejected these pleas, feeling that the process of penance required him to put his health at risk, and told people that he "wasn't hungry."[34]

When Chavez finally decided to end his fast after twenty-five days (one day more than Gandhi's longest fast), he asked Kennedy to join him. Kennedy was on the verge of announcing his candidacy for the presi-

Cesar Chavez ends his twenty-five-day fast, Delano, 1968. *Seated:* Helen Chavez, Robert F. Kennedy, Cesar Chavez, and Juana Chavez, Cesar's mother. *Standing, with the banner:* Pete Cardenas, Larry Itliong, Andy Imutan, and Julio Hernandez. Photo by Jon Kouns.

dency, and he and his aides feared that a trip to visit Chavez would lead to charges of political posturing. But he could not turn down Chavez's request. He chartered a plane from Los Angeles, arriving at the Delano county park where Chavez planned to break the fast just before the mass of Thanksgiving started. A crowd estimated at eight thousand, including priests, nuns, farmworkers, and their supporters, attended the mass, which was held before an altar that had been assembled on the flatbed of a truck. In keeping with the ecumenical tone set by Chavez and the UFW, the mass began with a prayer in Hebrew, the sermon was delivered by a Protestant minister, and Catholic ritual preceded the breaking of the bread. Chavez had lost a great deal of weight, going from 175 to 140 pounds during the fast, and could barely keep his head up. The most publicized picture was of Kennedy handing the completely worn-out movement leader a piece of bread. As Kennedy took his own piece of the homemade Mexican bread, he described Chavez "as one of the heroic figures of our time." Kennedy endorsed all of the UFW's legislative goals and praised those "locked with Cesar in the struggle for justice for the farm workers and for justice for Spanish-speaking Americans."[35]

Chavez was too weak to speak. Migrant minister Jim Drake read a few words written by Chavez, which captured the mission of the movement and are among his best remembered:

> Our struggle is not easy. Those who oppose our cause are rich and powerful, and they have many allies in high places. We are poor. Our allies are few. But we have something the rich do not own. We have our bodies and spirits and the justice of our cause as our weapons. When we are really honest with ourselves, we must admit that our lives are all that really belong to us. So it is how we use our lives that determines what kind of men we are. It is my deepest belief that only by giving our lives do we find life. I am convinced that the truest act of courage, the strongest act of manliness is to sacrifice for others in a totally non-violent struggle for justice. To be a man is to suffer for others. God help us to be men.[36]

The photo of Chavez and Kennedy remains a lasting image of the 1960s. It became more poignant with subsequent events. Six days after leaving Chavez's side, Kennedy announced that he was running for president. Less than three months later, the UFW's voter mobilization in Latino precincts was widely credited with bringing Kennedy victory in the critical June 6 California presidential primary. It was on the night of this great victory, with the UFW's Dolores Huerta standing beside him on the podium, that Robert Kennedy's drive for the presidency ended with his assassination.

In the wake of his fast, Chavez was hospitalized for three weeks with back pains caused by a lack of calcium. He spent much of the next eight months directing the UFW while in bed at home. But Chavez was convinced that all the pain of his ordeal was well worth it. This historic fast, like the 1963 March on Washington or other large civil right marches, was a cathartic and unifying event that deepened participants' investment in the movement's success and promoted the value of shared sacrifice. Chavez's willingness to put his life on the line for the movement sent a powerful message to both his allies and his adversaries. His fast rejuvenated farmworkers picketing in the hot Delano sun, solidified the clergy-farmworker alliance, and inspired students and others to redirect their lives toward working on the grape boycott. For the growers, Chavez's fast meant that they faced an adversary who would either win or die trying.

Chavez's fast typified his strategic creativity. His efforts to build the UFW were not limited to a certain range of "acceptable" tactics, and his example inspired UFW activists to think and act "outside the box," even when other leaders of the era criticized such unorthodox approaches. Saul Alinsky, for instance, told Dolores Huerta and Fred Ross Sr. after the fast began that "we've had a terrible time trying to explain it." Ross responded that Alinsky did not understand "what a good organizing technique it was," because the fast had been able to "unify the farm workers all over the state." Ross argued that Chavez had "brought everybody together and really established himself as the leader of the farm workers," which might not have happened if he had allowed outsiders to restrict his plans.[37]

Cesar Chavez's 1968 fast would not be his last. He began a fast of "thanksgiving and hope" in 1970 in preparation for planned mass civil disobedience by farmworkers in opposition to a court injunction against picketing a lettuce grower. In 1972, he undertook a highly publicized fast in Arizona following that state's passage of legislation barring farmworker boycotts and strikes during the harvest season. The UFW had launched a signature-gathering drive to recall the governor, who had signed the measure.

Around the fifth day of the fast, Chavez was resting in a Phoenix hotel room when some of his Arizona labor and political supporters told him that he should end his commitment because the campaign to get the law overturned could not succeed. They told him in Spanish, *"No se puede, no se puede"* (it cannot be done). Dolores Huerta responded, *"Sí! Sí se puede!"* (yes! yes it can be done!), and Chavez immediately announced that *"sí se puede!"* would become "the battle cry" of the Arizona campaign. *"Sí se puede!"* became the inspirational slogan not only of the UFW but also of other labor struggles, immigrant rights marches, and—in the English version "Yes we can"—Barack Obama's 2008 presidential campaign. Under doctor's orders, Chavez ended his fast before a crowd of four thousand farmworkers. Although the Arizona law was not repealed, the UFW's voter registration efforts led to the election of Raul Castro, the state's first Mexican American governor, in 1974.[38]

In July 1988, the sixty-one-year-old Chavez undertook his last fast, which aimed to highlight the problem of pesticides in the fields. He had been concerned for decades about farmworkers' exposure to pesticides and hoped that his "Fast for Life" would cause growers to rethink their stance and at least sit down and talk about reducing pesticides in the fields. Chavez fasted for a record thirty-six days, losing thirty pounds and putting his life at risk. UFW alumni, including Marshall Ganz, Jerry Cohen, and Fred Ross Jr., drove out to Delano to plead with him to end the fast, but the UFW leader remained frustrated by the growers' lack of response to his spiritual act. Finally, before a crowd of eight thousand at the Forty Acres, Chavez broke his personal fast on August 21. But he initiated a new twist that increased the power and utility of the strategy: he announced that union supporters would continue the fast in three-day increments. The Reverend Jesse Jackson took up the first three-day period of fasting, and the fast was then passed to a variety of celebrities and civil rights activists, including actors Martin Sheen, Edward Olmos, Emilio Estevez, Whoopi Goldberg, and Danny Glover; singer Carly Simon; the Reverend Joseph Lowery, president of the Southern Christian Leadership Conference; and Kerry Kennedy, daughter of Robert F. Kennedy.[39]

Because it avoided the problem of fasters risking their lives for the cause, this "rolling fast" became a far more commonly used tactic than the one-person fast. Unfortunately, Chavez's thirty-six-day fast took a permanent physical toll. Some even believe that it contributed to his death five years later. But the 1988 fast did force the media to increase publicity about pesticides in the fields, demonstrating the power of a fast as a tool to focus public attention on issues.

PROGRESSIVE MOVEMENTS ADOPT THE FAST

After Cesar Chavez and the UFW demonstrated the powerful moral force of the spiritual fast, other progressive campaigns increasingly adopted the tactic. Student activists have regularly turned to the spiritual fast to highlight concerns about sweatshops and other campus labor issues, and the incidence of fasting for social justice appears to be on the rise. In 2000, more than fifteen hundred religious leaders and janitors across New York State fasted to protest low wages and inadequate working conditions. This was the fifth year that the labor-clergy coalition had held a fast to encourage the state legislature to enact laws helping low-wage workers. Kim Bobo of Interfaith Worker Justice, interviewed by the *New York Times* about the New York effort, observed, "There's been a definite increase in fasting. . . . As people of faith seek increasingly to struggle for justice in this time of abundance, it's a natural outgrowth that fasting would be something they do."[40]

Maria Elena Durazo's USC Fast

In 1999, Maria Elena Durazo, then president of the Hotel Employees and Restaurant Employees (HERE) Local 11, initiated a rolling fast in Los Angeles that was likely the most highly publicized such event since Chavez's 1988 effort. Durazo had grown up as one of ten children in a migrant farmworker family, joining her parents as a field worker throughout California and southern Oregon. After graduating from college, she organized immigrant garment workers from 1978 to 1981 for the International Ladies Garment Workers Union in Los Angeles. She then joined HERE Local 11 as an arbitration specialist and organizer from 1983 to 1987, a time when the union's white male leadership was so resistant to empowering its own immigrant members that it would not even translate union meetings and contracts into Spanish.

Durazo was stunned by the racism of the union's leadership, its lack of respect for members, and its disconnection from the city's broader labor movement. Encouraged by UFW veterans Marshall Ganz, Scott Washburn, and Larry Frank, as well as union activist and future Los Angeles mayor Antonio Villaraigosa and others, Durazo sought to transform Local 11 by running for president in 1987. After the votes were cast but before they were counted, the incumbent union president sought to avoid possible defeat by turning control of the local over to the international union, under a trusteeship. The international sent in two organizers to run Local 11 until the questions about the election could be resolved. One was Bill Granfield, a former UFW organizer who had left the farmworkers to work for HERE and who later became the head of UNITE HERE's New York restaurant operation. The other was Miguel Contreras, an ex-UFW organizer who had been active in building strong HERE locals.

Although some of Durazo's backers thought she should lead a war against the international for voiding the election, she took a wait-and-see attitude. Before long, she was offered a job on the staff. Contreras was running the daily operations of the union, helped by John Wilhelm, who eventually became UNITE HERE's international president. Contreras and Wilhelm showed Durazo how to build a progressive "movement" union, and when the trusteeship ended in 1989, Durazo was elected president.[41]

In 1995, Durazo's union began a fight against the University of Southern California (USC), a school best known for its football team. The conflict began when the school refused to guarantee that the jobs of HERE's 350 workers would not be subcontracted out. The union found this lack of job security unacceptable, believing that it signaled USC's likely intent to eliminate these jobs once the union agreed to a contract that permitted subcontracting. After a year of negotiations with no progress, Durazo broadened and escalated the conflict. USC students began openly supporting the workers' struggle, forming a group in 1996–97 known as SCALE (Student Coalition against Labor Exploitation). Worker protests accompanied the school's May 1998 graduation, and students and workers held an "alternative" graduation ceremony offering "diplomas of justice." The following September featured a large march by students, workers, and clergy to support the union's cause. In addition, 135 national religious leaders signed a statement criticizing USC for "valuing the bottom line over and above human dignity."[42]

By May 1999, USC's intransigence had continued for over four years. Seeking to return the spotlight to the workers' struggle, Durazo chose Cesar Chavez's tactic of the spiritual fast. She began her fast on May 10, 1999, and was joined by forty others. On the eleventh day, she passed the fast on to California state assemblyperson Gilbert Cedillo, who then passed it to Durazo's former mentor Miguel Contreras, who was now her husband and head of the Los Angeles County Federation of Labor. The rolling fast continued for 150 days, with more than two hundred participants, including Martin Sheen. Students would pass the fast to each other in a ceremony at the statue of Tommy Trojan, the USC symbol. Finally, in early October 1999, the school agreed to provide the necessary guarantees against subcontracting. Like Chavez's effort, Durazo's spiritual fast had changed the momentum of the struggle and proved decisive in changing her adversary's position.[43]

Fasting for the Homeless

Chavez's legacy of transforming the spiritual fast into an organizing tool for economic justice campaigns came full circle when LeRoy Chatfield, who had coordinated Chavez's 1968 fast, joined with Rev. Chris Hartmire, one of the UFW's earliest allies from the religious community, in leading a public fast in Sacramento in 2002. Chatfield had become executive director of Loaves & Fishes, a full-service center for homeless persons located in Sacramento, which combined advocacy with its food and shelter programs. Hartmire worked with the group from 1989 to 2003. In 2001, Loaves & Fishes began pressing county officials to open a year-round shelter for homeless women and children. These officials appeared sympathetic to the problem, but they suddenly reversed course and told the county board of supervisors that the existing shelter beds were sufficient to meet current needs. Chatfield then called for a public fast to pressure the county to change its position. County officials told Chatfield that he was wasting his group's time, since the supervisors had already resolved the issue. But, in typical UFW style, Chatfield followed his strategic sense, not that of outsiders or his adversaries.[44]

Starting during Holy Week of 2002, Loaves & Fishes held a public fast in the waiting room of the Sacramento County board of supervisors. All participants pledged to fast for a twenty-four-hour period (or longer); at the end of the commitment period, each participant would hand the pledge to the next person. This use of the rolling fast meant that the protest could continue indefinitely, and Chatfield prepared for a campaign that would last at least one year. The group commandeered one of the room's large tables, arranged their chairs in a circle, brought fresh flowers and potted plants for decoration, and displayed two freestanding poster-size photographs of homeless women and children. Loaves & Fishes provided a guest register for visitors to sign and a journal for participants to write about their experiences and reflections. In addition to Chatfield, twelve of the organization's thirteen board members attended the fast twice during each month. There were usually five people at the table at a time. As word of the fast spread, more than a hundred individuals joined, including clergy, supporters of Loaves & Fishes, and county employees.

The genius of Chatfield's fast was that it assumed control over a public space that every member of the public who wanted to meet with a supervisor had to encounter. These visitors, as well as county staff, were visibly reminded that people were fasting in order to bear witness to the lack of shelters for women and children. Since the waiting room was public, the fasters could not be arrested or otherwise removed from the premises. Unlike protests in which activists seek to highlight their cause and pressure politicians by such confrontational actions as loud disruptions or illegal sit-ins in public buildings, Loaves & Fishes disturbed the status quo by its persistence and quiet presence. Chatfield described the public fast as a "scriptural knock on the door in the middle of the night at the home of a judge. Once the judge finally opened the door to confront the supplicant, his resistance turned to acceptance of the legitimacy of their request." Although Chatfield had anticipated that the fast could take a year or more to have its impact, five months after it began the supervisors voted to open a year-round shelter for homeless women and children. This victory would not have been won without the fast—further evidence that this tactic, inherited from Cesar Chavez and the UFW, continues to play an important role in the struggle for justice in the twenty-first century.[45]

4

YES WE CANE

Miami's Janitors Struggle for Justice

We viewed janitors as farmworkers in highrises.
Stephen Lerner, founder of Justice for Janitors

During the 1980s, America's janitorial industry changed dramatically. As commercial real estate values declined, building owners began outsourcing janitorial duties to an increasingly small and concentrated group of independent contractors. These outsourced jobs were nonunion and poorly paid and were primarily filled by Latino immigrants.

Until the late 1970s, janitors in Chicago, San Francisco, New York City, and Los Angeles had been heavily unionized. SEIU in fact began as the Building Service Employees International Union (BSEIU) in 1921 and had organized janitors with great success. BSEIU had a history of racial and ethnic inclusiveness, with many African American and Mexican American members. But when the trend toward eliminating union jobs in America's major industries hit the janitorial industry in the late 1970s, the renamed SEIU saw its janitorial ranks plummet. Local union leadership was unfamiliar with and often hostile to the Latino immigrants who were coming to dominate the janitorial business and did not understand how to organize them. By the middle of the 1980s, SEIU was losing janitor members by the thousands. The union still had powerful locals in San Francisco, New York City, and Chicago, but it considered getting out of the business of organizing and representing janitors in other cities.[1]

JUSTICE FOR JANITORS EMERGES

In 1986, Stephen Lerner became the organizing director of SEIU's Building Services Division. He had volunteered on the UFW's Manhattan boycott during high school, graduated in 1973, and skipped college to become a full-time boycott volunteer. After years of working on the boycott in the New York City metropolitan area, Lerner left the UFW in 1976 to work as a janitor at a local hospital that had been organized by District 1199, an independent health care workers union that is now affiliated with SEIU. Lerner began organizing health care workers for District 1199 in 1977, and in 1978 he moved to North Carolina to organize for the International Ladies Garment Workers Union. In the early 1980s, he became an organizer for the Communication Workers of America, where he crossed paths with former UFW executive board member Eliseo Medina, who was then with CWA in Texas. Lerner brought this full range of union organizing experience with him when he moved to Washington, D.C., in 1986 to head SEIU's janitorial division.[2]

Lerner inherited a division in which "old guard" locals closely defended their own prerogatives and were often hostile to new ideas from the international union. He decided to launch his first janitors' organizing drive in Denver primarily because the Denver SEIU janitor local was one of the few that would allow the involvement of someone from the international. Lerner had worked with former UFW organizer Susan Sachen in North Carolina, and he now asked Sachen to go to Denver and head the organizing drive. The Denver campaign was the first time that SEIU became identified as a union that welcomed Latino immigrants. Many of the janitors were undocumented immigrants; during the campaign, the workers' entire leadership team was deported. (Border crossings were easier in those days, and the workers soon returned.) Denver was also the first time that an SEIU janitors' campaign used UFW-style nonviolent civil disobedience and the first time that the union hired a full-time community organizer to build citywide support for the janitors. The UFW had aggressively sought broad public support for its struggles from its earliest days, but Lerner recognized that "it was still relatively rare for a union to say, 'We are going to make this a citywide cause.'"[3] The organizing efforts in Denver showed that the UFW's organizing framework and "movement" mentality could be replicated among janitors, who, like farmworkers, could be organized on an industrywide basis even though their workplaces were scattered.

Additionally, the Denver campaign borrowed from the UFW an emphasis on conveying vivid imagery that illustrated the workers' situation. As Lerner explained, "Whereas boycott volunteers would tell the story of farmworkers living in poverty and being brutalized by [being forced to use] the short-handle hoe, in Denver we told the story of janitors having to clean the equivalent of thirty houses a night. The details were different, but the image of exploitation of workers was the same." John Sweeney, who was president of SEIU at the time, visited Denver to see for himself what Lerner and Sachen were doing. He was "incredibly moved" by his conversations with the Latino janitors, and the Denver

Justice for Janitors founder Stephen Lerner *(at right with beard)* attacked by police in Century City, June 15, 1990, as janitors blocked the intersection. Courtesy of Stephen Lerner.

campaign changed his entire perspective—and that of the union—on the issue of organizing Latino immigrants. Lerner joked, "Everyone said you can't win in building services because people work part time, many are undocumented, and Latino immigrants don't want to unionize. After [we prevailed in] Denver, everyone said we won because undocumented, Latino, part-time workers were ripe for unionization."[4]

When the first Justice for Janitors campaign began, Denver janitors working in downtown office buildings were earning less than $4 an hour with no benefits. By early 1987, more than eight hundred Denver janitors had joined the union. Following this initial success, JFJ soon undertook major organizing drives in Washington, D.C., Los Angeles, and other urban centers. Like the UFW, JFJ relied on such tactics as demonstrations, street theater, vigils, and hunger strikes. JFJ continued to successfully transfer the UFW's nonviolent civil disobedience and confrontational style to an urban context—janitors blocked commuter bridges in Washington, D.C., and closed down an entire office complex in Century

City, in Los Angeles—and to follow the farmworkers' example of building broad-based coalitions of religious groups, students, and community organizations to support the workers.

Lerner acknowledges that, from its conception, JFJ "was enormously influenced by the campaign tactics and strategies of the farmworkers movement." He is one of many UFW veterans who have played key roles in building JFJ. The rallying cry for JFJ campaigns is *"sí se puede,"* the famous slogan identified with the farmworkers movement. Janitors now march through downtown business centers chanting, *"Sí se puede!"* just as farmworkers first sang out those words in the fields more than thirty years ago.[5]

In 2006, JFJ launched an organizing drive at the University of Miami (UM), in Florida, among the university's primarily Cuban American janitors. This campaign utilized many of the strategies and tactics pioneered by the UFW nearly forty years earlier and provides a case study of how the legacy of Cesar Chavez and the UFW still influences progressive movements. Even the campaign's theme echoed the UFW: its slogan, "Yes we cane," was a clever twist on the English translation of the familiar *"sí se puede."* The motto fit a region known for its sugarcane fields and the sports excellence of the University of Miami Hurricanes.

THE BATTLE AT THE UNIVERSITY OF MIAMI

During the union's June 2004 convention, SEIU president Andy Stern had announced a major new commitment to helping workers in the South and the Southwest form unions—with a focus on workers in health care, public service, and building services. Part of this commitment involved SEIU opening a major beachhead for organizing in South Florida, primarily focusing on the crews of workers who cleaned condominiums. Miami had the third biggest condo market in America, but, unlike workers in New York City and Chicago, Miami's condo workers were not unionized. While preparing its condo organizing campaign, SEIU was contacted by janitors at the University of Miami who wanted to organize a union. As SEIU assessed the potential of this organizing drive, three factors emerged.

First, the workers were eager to join a union. UM janitors, who were employed through the Massachusetts-based cleaning contractor UNICCO, earned an average wage of $7.53 an hour, with many earning as little as $6.33. Most lacked health insurance, including those who cleaned the university's teaching hospital. In an August 3, 2001, study, the *Chronicle of Higher Education* revealed that of 195 universities, only one paid its janitors less than UM did. Following this revelation, the UM faculty senate recommended that the university require a living wage for employees in its contracts with UNICCO, but the school's only response to the study was to offer janitors a health referral service, along with English and computer classes. When UM's workers learned that UNICCO's janitors at Harvard, who were now part of SEIU, earned $13 or $14 an hour, it was easy to see why most supported unionization.[6]

Second, SEIU wanted to expand its contracts with UNICCO. After defeating UNICCO at Harvard, SEIU reasoned, a win at UM could convince the giant campus janitorial company to stop battling unionization at its other campuses.

Third, Donna Shalala, who had been U.S. secretary of health and human services in the Clinton cabinet, was president of the University of Miami, and she was expected to back—or at least not to oppose—the union drive. The university's stance would be critical, given the peculiar nature of organizing janitors. Since building owners (in this case, universities) typically contract out janitorial services to companies like UNICCO, the owners avoid direct responsibility for janitors' wages and working conditions. Instead, they focus mainly on selecting contractors who submit the lowest bids. Building owners frequently change contractors to obtain the lowest price and can often terminate contracts on only thirty days' notice. Thus, a contractor has great incentive to keep wages low, in order to ensure the continuation of contracts, whereas unionization—and the resulting higher wages—could cause owners to shift to a cheaper company. However, as long as Shalala assured UNICCO that unionization would not affect its UM contract, UNICCO would have little incentive to battle SEIU.

These positive factors were countered by the challenge of organizing in a city and state where unions had found little success. In 2005, only 5.4 percent of Florida employees were unionized, compared to more than 12 percent nationally. Florida had little history of significant labor struggles, and neither did UM, which was known during the 1960s as "Suntan U." A nonactivist campus, located in a twenty-four-hour party city and in a region not hospitable to unions, meant that JFJ's organizing drive at UM might not be easy.[7]

Building a Clergy-Labor-Student Alliance

Like Cesar Chavez and the UFW, JFJ made it a practice to build a strong clergy-labor alliance during its organizing drives. In Miami, JFJ began with a faith-based community that, according to Jeanette Smith of the Quaker Peace Center on the UM campus, "had suffered from apathy for a long time." Anthony Vinciguerra of the Center for Justice and Peace at St. Thomas University noted that religious groups had lobbied for various issues such as expanded health care and a living wage, but he felt that no single issue had brought South Florida clergy together in a "a broad response." To change this dynamic, SEIU teamed with Kim Bobo, founder of Interfaith Worker Justice. Bobo believes that one of Cesar Chavez's greatest legacies was his recognition that "the religious community has to be brought into worker campaigns at the outset, not simply trotted out later to speak at press conferences." When Stern announced SEIU's plan to target Miami, JFJ coordinated with Bobo to enlist the South Florida Interfaith Committee for Worker Justice in the struggle to raise wages for the area's working poor. SFICWJ included representatives of the Catholic, Protestant, and Jewish faiths, and among its participants was Miami's influential Catholic archdiocese.[8]

SFICWJ had launched a Workers' Rights Initiative in 2002 and a campaign in 2003 to improve job opportunities for Miami residents. In early 2005, the group joined SEIU's organizing drive among Miami's condominium workers. Clergy subsequently "adopted" a condominium by writing letters to each building's governing board urging support for higher wages for janitors. To bolster SFICWJ's work, SEIU asked the Reverend C. J. Hawking, a United Methodist pastor consulting with Bobo's group, to come to Florida for a month or two to help organize the interfaith campaign. Hawking was experienced at developing relationships both among clergy and with workers. She also had a keen understanding of the tensions that can emerge when clergy and workers who "had a liturgical rhythm to their lives" interacted with union organizers, who often did not (recall, for example, that Cesar Chavez's 1968 fast was criticized by secular UFW staff). The mother of two young girls, Hawking was so committed to the janitors' cause that she agreed to travel to Florida each week from her Bloomington, Indiana, home. Two weeks after her arrival in Miami, the UM janitors asked SEIU to help them organize. Hawking was unwilling to walk away from their struggle and flew back and forth from Miami to Bloomington for nearly a year.[9]

Enlisting students in the janitors' cause was more difficult. UM did not have much history of student activism, though students had been involved in investigating the low wages and lack of health benefits of school janitors. After the 2001 *Chronicle of Higher Education* study showed that UM's janitors earned poverty wages, student Shelly Stromoski interviewed janitors and found that some had worked there for fifteen years without the right to a single paid sick day. On Valentine's Day 2002, Stromoski and her friends tried to highlight the problem by putting up handmade paper hearts and writing on them, "Having a heart for a living wage." Seventy of these hearts were displayed around Shalala's office. But because the hearts had not been produced by an official student organization, they were not approved for posting, and the janitors the hearts had been designed to help were forced to remove them.[10]

Stromoski's efforts did not raise janitors' salaries, but did establish a history of concern that a skilled organizer could capitalize on. The right catalyst appeared in the form of Eric Brakken, the organizing director for SEIU Local 11, which represents the Miami area. Brakken had formerly been the lead organizer of United Students against Sweatshops, a nationwide coalition of campus activists who won "anti-sweat" purchasing policies—which prevented schools from buying or selling clothes with collegiate logos if the apparel had been made in sweatshops—in colleges and universities across America. Brakken knew how to mobilize students, and he began the fall 2005 semester by working with Miami students who had formed STAND, Students toward a New Democracy, to support the janitors' cause.

Recognizing that students typically respond best to training from fellow students, Brakken brought in a delegation from Georgetown University to help train STAND in organizational tactics. He also connected STAND to students at Harvard, whose Student Labor Action Project (SLAP) had played a major role in SEIU's hard-fought victory in 2002 over UNICCO. As the fall semester got under way, STAND built an e-mail list of student supporters, created a website, handed out flyers at Miami Hurricane football games, and gathered signatures in support of better pay for workers. Most important, STAND helped students recognize that they had the power to raise campus workers' salaries, a critical prerequisite for expanding student involvement.[11]

With its religious and student allies in place, JFJ publicly launched its organizing drive on September 14, 2005, with a speakout at a campus location known as the Rock. The event, which included about forty workers and twenty to thirty students, gave workers the chance to testify about their low wages, lack of health insurance, and the impact on themselves and their families. SEIU then planned a second speakout for October 6, 2005, but the UM administration told Brakken that a nonstudent group could not hold events on campus and that it was too late for STAND to apply for permission.

Brakken then contacted the university chaplain, Father Frank Corbishley of the Episcopal Student Center, who agreed to hold the speakout at his facility. Although the center was located on campus, UM had sold it and other school sites to religious groups in the 1950s, which meant that it was like an embassy within the UM campus, able to make its own decisions. Corbishley saw his job "not simply as the chaplain for the students, but for the entire university, including the workers and President Shalala." He had become involved in the SFICWJ in June 2005 to show support for his associate bishop, James Ottley, who was on the group's board of directors. Corbishley had been looking for a way to make a difference in the world, and when Rev. Hawking told him that the janitors on his own campus were organizing, he felt that "the Holy Spirit was hitting him on the head." Corbishley would play a critical role in the janitors' struggle.[12]

Following the workers' testimonies at the October 6 event, Brakken and the janitors headed to President Shalala's office to ask her to support unionization and to give her written copies of the testimonies. Although Shalala was not available to meet with the workers, a UM spokesperson stated that the school would "remain neutral" in SEIU's dispute with UNICCO. Meanwhile, UNICCO's spokesperson told the *Miami Herald* that it "was open to negotiating wages and benefits," but that this would require a renegotiation of its contract with the university. In a statement that must have made Shalala cringe, the UNICCO official further stated, "We were probably the most cost effective for them, and that resulted in the wages we pay." In other words, on the same day that UM disclaimed responsibility for the janitors' low wages and lack of health benefits, its contractor publicly disagreed. This mutual fingerpointing was a pretty good result from a small event early in the campaign.[13]

Targeting Donna Shalala

Shalala soon became the campaign's chief target. UNICCO could raise salaries if she agreed to have UM pick up the increased costs. SEIU organizer Brakken had encountered a similar contractor issue when campaigning against sweatshops: companies such as Nike disclaimed responsibility for the low wages of those making their sneakers, even as they routinely switched labor contractors in search of a lower price. But whereas apparel companies prevented union organizing by shifting production facilities to repressive regimes abroad, UM's janitorial contractor worked on an American campus. Further, unlike heads of apparel companies, Shalala had a political reputation to uphold.

Shalala's political history as an outspoken advocate for health care for the poor made her a perfect target for Yes We Cane. This became clear when the *Miami New Times,* part of a national chain of weeklies whose owners are no friends of unions, wrote a strong piece on November 24, 2005, titled "Donna vs. Donna," with the subhead "The UM President Talks out of Both Sides of Her Yapper." The article juxtaposed her past statements in favor of universal health care, ethical business practices, and the need to eradicate poverty ("Shalala Says") with her refusal to support UM's low-paid janitors ("Shalala Does"). The article previewed how Shalala's history as an advocate of the poor now opened her to charges of hypocrisy, a theme that attracted critics of the university president from both the right and the left.[14]

Later in the fall, STAND organized a march in the center of campus, where students and workers carried "Support Janitors at UM" signs. This led to a December 20, 2005, *Miami Herald* story on UM's student activists that legitimized and highlighted their role in the struggle. The story quoted Julio Ramos, a janitor employed by UNICCO, who asserted, "Without students we cannot succeed. They are the ones who can get to Shalala." STAND leader Jacob Coker-Dukowitz, whose mother was associate dean of the UM law school, noted that STAND was working on bringing new groups into the campaign. He said that student support was forthcoming because of "the issue. It's just so duh! You make $6.30 an hour. You can't feed a family of four." This story, which ran only a few days before Christmas, foresaw that the new semester was likely to attract even more students to the janitors' cause. On December 30, as the Miami Hurricanes football team played the Louisiana State University Tigers in the Peach Bowl in Atlanta, SEIU and UM janitors wearing full UM regalia attended the game and passed out thousands of notes in the shape of footballs that read, "Kick the Tigers, Not UM Janitors."[15]

On January 8, 2006, the *Miami Herald* published a letter from Coker-Dukowitz and members of STAND that disputed Shalala's claim of neutrality. A month later, the group reiterated this point in the *Miami Hurricane,* the UM student newspaper. Coker-Dukowitz charged Shalala with ignoring recommendations from the student government and the faculty senate that UM require its contractors to pay a living wage. He also accused her of refusing to meet with student organizations to discuss the janitors' demands and of unduly restricting SEIU's campus access.[16]

On January 16, Martin Luther King Jr. Day, SFICWJ took out full-page ads in support of the janitors in the *Miami Herald,* the *Miami Hurricane,* and the *Coral Gables Gazette.* In a signal of labor-clergy unity, Andy Stern attended a King Day prayer rally, where Catholic bishop Felipe Estévez and the Reverend Dr. Joaquin Willis were keynote speakers. More than four hundred people participated in the event, and religious leaders were impressed that Stern had spent the day in their community.[17]

As Shalala was being targeted by the campaign, the usually savvy school president agreed to be interviewed for what she no doubt believed would be a harmless two-page puff piece in the February 12 *New York Times Magazine.* Normally such an article would have been quickly forgotten, but for a school president under fire because campus janitors were being paid poverty wages, a story disclosing that Shalala lives in a 9,000-square-foot mansion and had recently purchased a 29-foot motorboat came at the wrong time.[18]

Critics had a field day with this depiction of Shalala's lavish lifestyle. As the title of the February 22 "Reliable Source" column in the *Washington Post* put it, "For Donna Shalala, Nice Digs, Lousy Timing." The column starts with this caution: "Note to the Haves: When involved in labor disputes, skip the luxury home profile." It went on to observe that SEIU organizers were "just tickled" to see Shalala's palatial residence profiled in the *Times.* The February 17 edition of the online blog Wonkette was titled "Let Them Eat Mangoes" and included quotes from an unidentified source who reported that "the students at the famously apathetic school are side-by-side with the janitors in protesting Shalala's stance." As the blogger stated, "The Miami janitors are about to go on strike—making this NYT mag 'profile' truly poor form."[19]

After the janitors announced that they had scheduled a strike vote for February 26, UM sought to influence the vote by announcing on February 23 that it would begin a review of compensation and benefits for all contract employees working on its campuses. Shalala said that the university could no longer remain "quiet or idle while our integrity is called into question by the people we hold dearest." A working group was assigned to collect data and report back to Shalala in thirty days. But SEIU replied that the formation of this group would not delay a strike vote. Janitor Nelson Hernandez recalled that twenty-five years ago "the university formed a committee to talk about our wages. I was making barely over minimum wage then, and I still am now."[20]

On February 26, the janitors voted to strike. Because they were striking prior to joining a union, they based their action on UNICCO's unfair labor practices, which included the alleged firing of one worker for union organizing activity and the alleged suspension of six others. SEIU did not reveal any specifics about its strike plans, but some speculated that a strike at UM could lead to picketing by 258 UNICCO workers at Miami International Airport. Mike Scott, president of Teamsters Local 769, told the *Miami Herald* that if UNICCO janitors did set up a picket line at the airport, "my advice would be that nobody works as long as that picket line is up."[21]

The UM janitors began their strike on March 1, which was also Ash Wednesday. Father Richard Mullen, parochial vicar of St. Augustine parish, presided over a noontime Spanish-language Ash Wednesday mass, which many janitors attended before beginning to picket. Mullen was a member of SFICWJ and served as the archdiocese's chief representative during the strike. He had come to Miami after spending the previous two decades in Peru, where he had become a strong advocate for economic justice.[22]

SEIU's Lerner used the beginning of the strike as an occasion to return the focus to Shalala. He told the Associated Press, "I think that it is shocking that Donna Shalala hasn't used this as an opportunity to help make people's lives better." Shalala was also targeted by *Miami Herald* columnist Ana Menendez, who provided consistently persuasive coverage of the campaign. Menendez's March 1 column, "While Shalala Lives in Luxury, Janitors Struggle," personalized the dispute by describing a day in the life of Zoila Garcia, a fifty-one-year-old Cuban immigrant who "has the toughest job at the University of Miami. From 10 P.M. to 6 A.M., five nights a week, she washes windows, cleans desks and picks up the potato chip bags and used condoms that students leave behind in the library. 'Ay mamita! And when they decide to draw on those tables, it's scrub scrub scrub,' Garcia said." Garcia lived in a 24-by-57-foot trailer, had high blood pressure, and took pills for pain in her arms. She also had a blood clot on her calf and needed an operation but could not afford the $4,000 cost. She earned $6.70 an hour with no health insurance.[23]

To contrast Garcia's life with Shalala's, Menendez asked Garcia some of the same questions that had been posed to Shalala in her *New York Times Magazine* profile. Garcia's responses to questions about "her perfect day," "what she drives," and "her favorite vacation spot" brought home the stark differences between a janitor's life and that of a university president. This comparison made Shalala's labor stance look particularly heartless, and many likely agreed with Menendez that Shalala should "get these people health insurance and a dignified wage. The bare minimum, that's all they're asking."[24]

The Campaign Intensifies

On March 3, the janitors held a march, accompanied by more than five hundred students, community members, faculty members, and religious leaders under the auspices of the SFICWJ. It was the largest protest march in the school's recent history. Media reports found that the vast majority of the faculty backed the strikers, and SFICWJ arranged for more than two hundred classes to be held off campus in churches and synagogues so that faculty members could express their solidarity without interfering with students' education.[25]

Two days later, on March 5, the Most Reverend Felipe Estévez, the auxiliary bishop of the archdiocese of Miami, presided over a special "Janitors' Mass" at St. Augustine Catholic Church. Months earlier, in October 2005, SFICWJ had brought three workers to meet with the bishop and apprise him of their situation. He was so moved by their stories that he committed to hold a mass in their honor on the next available date. Fortuitously, that date was March 5, the first Sunday of Lent, so the mass ended up coinciding with the start of the strike. With striking janitors and their families in attendance, the bishop called on Shalala, or her representative, to sit down with SEIU and a board member from the SFICWJ to resolve their differences.[26]

By the following week, the janitors' strike had spread to UM's Medical Center. SEIU then planned to expand picket lines to the airport but agreed to delay this while Joe Martinez, chair of the Miami-Dade Board of County Commissioners, sought to mediate the dispute. Martinez acknowledged the potential harm to Miami's tourist business if janitorial service at the airport ceased: "people are going to say Miami's a dirty city." Despite this risk, Shalala refused Martinez's mediation offer. In response, SEIU began picketing at the Miami airport on March 14.[27]

Recognizing that UM was losing the battle of public opinion, Shalala announced on March 16 that the school would be giving 25 percent raises to all its contract employees, including the striking janitors. This raised the starting base pay from the state minimum of $6.40 to $8 an hour, with landscapers making at least $9.30 an hour. UM also promised to offer health care benefits in the near future. Shalala stated that the higher wages would go into effect immediately, as part of the school's effort to "lead the market." She said that the raise had been prompted by public concern over the existing low wages and claimed that the pay hikes were necessary because the school's wage survey had found that the labor market "had changed dramatically in the past year." Shalala was not asked to reconcile that statement with the 2001 *Chronicle of Higher Education* survey showing that UM's wages were nearly the lowest in America.[28]

Miami's local television news shows framed Shalala's offer as a "bombshell." Reporters announced that UM was generously picking up the tab to resolve a dispute between UNICCO and its workers. Channel 7, Miami's Fox News affiliate, said that Shalala's action meant "workers will actually get what they want"; another station reported that while UM's agreement to fund the higher wages and benefits would cost the school "hundreds of thousands of dollars," the university "does not expect it will result in tuition increases." Earlier in the day, before Shalala's announcement, more than a hundred janitors and their supporters had traveled to exclusive Star Island, where several UM trustees, including singing star Gloria Estefan, lived in multimillion-dollar homes. Estefan's spokesperson said that she had already expressed to UM her support for "fair pay." News coverage of the protest, which included marchers chanting *"sí se puede"* and banging on Estefan's gate, implied that the workers would not have been protesting if they had known about the pay raise. The television news coverage transformed Shalala and UM into pro-worker heroes who were rescuing janitors from their exploitative employer, while SEIU was described in one report as "not being happy" that Shalala had raised janitors' salaries and granted them access to health care.[29]

But the proposed raises failed to defuse the janitors' growing campaign. The same day that Shalala announced the raises, janitors in Westchester County, New York; Hartford and Stamford, Connecticut; and Piscataway, New Jersey, walked off the job in support of Miami's striking workers. Mike Fishman, president of SEIU Local 32BJ, noted, "In New Jersey, UNICCO respected the will of the workers and recognized the union through card check. In Miami, UNICCO fired and threatened workers in response to their efforts to organize. Cleaners here are willing to stand up to end this unfair treatment." With more than eighty-five thousand members covering six states and the nation's capital, Local 32BJ had the capacity to pressure a broad range of businesses over a labor dispute two thousand miles away. JFJ's Stephen Lerner had long argued that unions must gain sufficient density in an industry to achieve maximum leverage, and SEIU was now calling on its unionized janitors to take the UM battle against UNICCO nationwide.[30]

The most immediate impact of Shalala's wage hikes in response to the unionization threat was that janitors across South Florida began calling SEIU Local 11 to express interest in organizing a union at their workplaces. Two hundred and sixty workers at nearby Nova Southeastern University, also employed by UNICCO, felt that they too deserved a raise and had been meeting at Plantation United Methodist Church with the Reverend Tim Smiley to discuss their plans. UNICCO was now looking at a JFJ drive at a second South Florida school.[31]

While UM's janitors and their supporters remained committed to forming a union, the *Miami Herald*'s March 21 editorial, "New Deal for Janitors," appeared to argue that the UM workers should stop striking now that they had received a pay hike. But Father Corbishley responded in a March 23 letter to the editor that Shalala's announcement had failed to address either UNICCO's alleged unfair labor practices or the workers' "documented desire to unionize." The chaplain argued, "As individuals, the janitors are powerless. Without a union to protect them, they remain vulnerable." Corbishley's letter was courageous, as his position as chaplain was up for renewal in July 2006. Shalala even called Associate Bishop James Ottley to complain about Corbishley's advocacy on behalf of the workers, but by this time Ottley was president of the SFICWJ board, and his superior, Bishop Leo Frade, stated, "I decide who is the chaplain here, not Donna Shalala."[32]

Shalala clearly recognized, as growers opposed to the UFW had done, that the religious community had the moral authority to promote economic justice in spiritual terms. Framing the janitors' struggle as a moral issue, rather than as a question of dollars and cents, was persuasive. Had SEIU been the lone critic of the wage hike, the union would have been accused of caring only about its own self-interest. Shalala's effort to halt the union organizing drive by raising wages was a critical turning point for the janitors' campaign; the *Miami Herald* and most of the local media were reporting that the dispute had been resolved. But SFICWJ's involvement with the janitors' cause from the outset enabled Corbishley and others to quickly understand the inadequacy of Shalala's offer, and they effectively reaffirmed the legitimacy of the janitors' ongoing struggle—an action that proved pivotal in maintaining public support for the strike.

Jacob Coker-Dukowitz argued that Shalala "had pulled a fast one," and he and other UM students felt compelled to send a public message to the university president and the Miami community that the wage increase would not end the workers' battle. On March 28, more than three hundred janitors, faculty, students, and clergy blocked traffic on the six-lane South Dixie Highway outside the campus, shutting down traffic for miles, in an act of nonviolent civil disobedience. Seventeen people entered the intersection, led by eight union members, six members of the clergy, two community leaders, and SEIU Local 11 president Rob Schuler. The three hundred protesters chanted, "Yes, we can!" as police arrested the seventeen, and Bishop Ottley led a prayer. Following the arrests, STAND student Alana Lopez told the crowd that students had just taken over the Admissions Office in the Ashe administration building. The crowd rushed to the building, and about fifty protesters and a few members of the media made it into the lobby before the police could stop them. Once inside, the protesters announced that they would not leave until Shalala called a meeting with SEIU and UNICCO and publicly stated that UM would not tolerate further intimidation of workers who were attempting to form a union. After more than twelve hours, at 1:40 A.M., sixteen students and Chaplain Corbishley left the building after UM agreed to hold the requested meeting within forty-eight hours.[33]

Miami Herald columnist Ana Menendez used her March 29 column to situate the labor dispute in the broader context of Miami-Dade County's large population of working poor. She wrote that many saw the janitors' fight as "a referendum on business as usual in this county." Striking janitor Reinaldo Hernandez told Menendez that the workers did not trust that Shalala's promises would be kept unless they had a union. He added that, while "the money is needed, what we want is dignity and respect."[34]

The Fast

Two weeks after Shalala's March 15 pay raise, the janitors' struggle escalated. On April 5, ten janitors and six students began a hunger strike in protest of UNICCO's alleged firing, threatening, and otherwise intimidating pro-union workers and UM's refusal to agree to recognize the union through card check rather than a lengthy NLRB election process. The group set up an encampment under the Metro Rail outside UM's main gate, which was dubbed "Freedom Village." Freedom Village soon featured a medical tent with a round-the-clock nurse, a meeting tent, sleeping tents, artwork, musicians, portable toilets, and a steady stream of high-profile visitors such as actor Ed Asner and author Barbara Ehrenreich, whose best-selling *Nickel and Dimed: On (Not) Getting By in America* profiled the problems of the working poor.[35]

While some of the media questioned the point of a hunger strike, given the pay hike, the workers saw their struggle as involving more than wages. One of the janitors who was fasting, Feliciano Hernandez, who had been suspended for refusing to carry heavy equipment up a flight of stairs, explained, "They are treating us like dogs. We can't allow that to continue." Many in Miami's Cuban American community viewed fasting as a winning campaign tactic. UM's Cuban American janitors were influenced by the successful fasts of Miami activist Ramon Saul Sanchez, leader of the anti-Castro Democracy Movement. Sanchez's hunger strikes in 1999 and 2005 had made the Clinton and Bush administrations back down.[36]

While SEIU did not initiate the hunger strikes, the tactic was consistent with Stephen Lerner's belief that successful union organizing requires "militant action" that "forces people to take sides." The hunger strike brought new urgency to the labor dispute, which intensified as workers fell ill. On April 8, janitor Isabel Montalvo collapsed and was rushed to the hospital after an on-site nurse concluded that Montalvo was at risk of a stroke. On April 9, janitor Odalys Rodriguez also collapsed and required emergency medical assistance. On April 10, janitors at Nova Southeastern University—whose organizing had been triggered by Shalala's pay hike—began their own strike against UNICCO. Seeking to expand what was already a multilevel campaign, SEIU asked the Student Labor Action Movement at Harvard to join Boston's downtown office workers in a one-day hunger strike on April 12 to support the Miami campaign. There was no way to know how many Bostonians complied with the request, but the union's call for downtown workers to "give up their lunches" caused Boston media to cover the Miami struggle.[37]

That same day, seven UM students joined the eight Miami janitors in their hunger strike. More than 175 supporters, including a hundred striking janitors from Nova and a delegation from the Association of Community Organizations for Reform Now (ACORN), joined the fasters in marching to Shalala's office, only to find the doors to the Ashe administration building locked. Many stayed at the building for over two hours, chanting their demand that the school intervene in the dispute. Janitor Clara Vargas gave a speech, saying, "We know that with just one phone call, this can change." The "one phone call" she referred to would have been from Shalala to UNICCO—an argument that had been pushed by SEIU's Lerner. Jacob Coker-Dukowitz of STAND charged, "They haven't eaten in eight days and Shalala won't even meet with them." As she addressed the crowd, student hunger striker Tanya Aquino captured just how quickly the UM labor dispute had become identified as part of a larger movement: "This is not just about the over 400 families on strike, this is for all of working America. It's bigger than the hunger strikers, it's bigger than me, it's bigger than UM, and it's not going to stop."[38]

Confirming Lerner's belief in militant action, the hunger strike shook UM's public relations operation. A UM spokesperson said that the university did not want to see a hunger strike but added, "They're not on university property, so it's hard for me to say." UM then filed an unfair labor practice charge against SEIU because it had bused in supporters for the protest. Shalala explained that it was "off limits, unacceptable and potentially dangerous" to bring in third-party protesters to "disrupt the educational mission of the University and to encourage them to trespass on private property." While she may have felt that filing the charges would put SEIU on the defensive, the chief impact of this action was to boost solidarity between the Nova janitors who had been bused in and their Miami counterparts.[39]

The hunger strike returned the janitors' struggle to the national spotlight. SEIU president Andy Stern told the media on April 13 that "it appears to only have a tragic end in sight," raising the specter that janitors could lose their lives in pursuit of a living wage and fair treatment in their workplace. While the union had hired medical staff to monitor the workers' health, Stern said that it was difficult to know "when to intervene and urge janitors to end the perilous strategy." Continuing SEIU's focus on Shalala, Stern charged that she "held the health and safety of these workers in the palm of [her] hands. At any time she chooses, it can be over." Although UNICCO had become a secondary campaign target, its spokesperson, Douglas Bailey, ruffled feathers by suggesting on his blog that hunger strikers were "cheating" by eating fruit and vegetables. "That's what we used to call a diet," joked Bailey, who later said that his comments were "misunderstood."[40]

By week three, most of those who were fasting were getting sicker by the day. Many were suffering from high blood pressure and were in deteriorating health. Mewelau Hall, one of the fasting students, had grown up in Miami and chosen UM because she viewed Shalala as a role model. Now Hall accused Shalala and the other administrators of "forcing me to go on this hunger strike," asserting that the labor dispute could "end in an instant" if Shalala intervened. On April 18, STAND leader Tanya Aquino became the first student casualty when she was rushed to the hospital on the thirteenth day of her fast. Although clearly in distress, Aquino refused to get medical treatment until a UM vice president agreed to ask Shalala to call UNICCO and ask them to return to the bargaining table. Shalala met with civil rights leaders about the conflict the next day, which also featured a mass of students blockading the entrance to the Ashe building. But Shalala remained firm. She issued a press statement on April

19 insisting that while UM "was caught between a rock and a hard place," the workers were not UM employees and the university was not a party to the union campaign.[41]

In response to this intransigence, Andy Stern and Eliseo Medina, who was now the first vice president of SEIU, arrived in Miami on April 21. The two immediately attended Father Richard Mullen's evening prayer service for campaign supporters at St. Augustine Catholic Church. The appearance of the two union leaders came at a critical time. Workers were suffering health problems from the hunger strike and the stresses of the campaign; and despite their dedicated efforts, the struggle's outcome remained very much in doubt. The arrival of Stern and Medina was welcomed, leading hunger striker Clara Vargas to say that she "never imagined janitors in Miami would have so much support, but now we know the world is watching and our voices are being heard."[42]

During his days with the UFW, Medina had been widely viewed as Cesar Chavez's likely successor before he left the union in 1978. In more recent years, he had led SEIU's organizing campaigns in the South and the Southwest, and he was fresh off a November victory in Houston that had won union representation for more than five thousand janitors. Medina had been in post-Katrina New Orleans when he learned that some of the hunger strikers were jeopardizing their lives by continuing their fast. In an action that recalled Chavez's unwillingness to relinquish his 1988 fast without assurances that others would continue it, Medina decided that he and Stern would continue the fast on the janitors' behalf. The fast would then be passed to others, enabling janitors to resume eating without feeling that they had given up the fight. At the prayer service at St. Augustine, Medina announced that they would be taking up the janitors' fast and moving into Freedom Village. The workers and students then ended their seventeen-day fast with bread and soup. Eric Brakken described the scene as "a deeply spiritual moment for the workers, who showed great emotion over Medina and Stern taking over the fast."[43]

Before Medina's arrival, everyone involved with the janitors' struggle had referred to the fast as a "hunger strike." But both Medina and UFW stalwart Dolores Huerta, who now had also arrived in Miami, shared Cesar Chavez's view that there was a distinction between a hunger strike and a spiritual fast. Whereas the former sought to extract a concession from an opponent, the latter was seen as part of a spiritual appeal to the opponent's conscience to do what is morally right. The janitors had not been aware of this distinction, but from that point forward, the event

Eliseo Medina joins fasting janitors on strike at the University of Miami, April 2006.

was transformed into a spiritual fast. The UM campaign had clearly become a test of the union's capacity in South Florida, and the arrival of
its top leaders showed that SEIU was prepared to use all means necessary to prevail.[44]

In preparation for the planned rolling fast, Medina had asked the Reverend Wayne "Chris" Hartmire to come down to Miami and explain to
others what a spiritual fast could mean. In 1962, Hartmire had been director of the California Migrant Ministry, and he and his staff worked
side by side with Cesar Chavez on his mission to organize farmworkers.
Hartmire had worked for the farmworkers movement for more than two
decades, and, as chapter 3 described, he had been involved in Chavez's
1968 fast as well as the thirty-one-day 1988 fast that had been continued by the Reverend Jesse Jackson and others. Hartmire explained to
SEIU and SFICWJ how the nightly religious ceremonies surrounding
Chavez's 1968 fast had had a powerful spiritual and unifying impact,
and he suggested that similar nightly events occur in connection with the
rolling fast in Miami, to symbolize the passing of the fast by some, and
the taking up of the fast in the janitors' name by others.[45]

The first ceremony was held on April 22, and on this and every subsequent night, Chaplain Corbishley conducted a prayer service. As in

Chavez's 1968 fast, people testified about what the fast had meant to them, and, as Hartmire described it, "it was powerful stuff." The nightly ceremonies also recognized that not all of those participating in the rolling fast were religious. Those leaving the fasts could receive a handmade cross, a Star of David, or a handmade design in the shape of a little broom. The ceremonies always included announcements. One night, Dolores Huerta reported on a meeting she had with Shalala. The UM president had refused private meetings with virtually everyone identified with the janitors' cause, but she did agree to meet with the prominent labor rights activist. In the meeting, Shalala speculated that Huerta did not understand that Miami's workers were Cuban American, not Mexican American, and that the Cubans "don't like unions." According to Father Corbishley, "this angered the janitors more than anything else. It said to them that Shalala was unfairly stereotyping them and did not believe in their commitment to the union cause."[46]

The arrival of Stern and Medina prompted other key leaders to show their support for the janitors. More than 150 political, religious, and community leaders agreed to take up the janitors' fast in their name. David Bonior, formerly Democratic majority whip in the U.S. House of Representatives, and John Edwards, former senator and 2004 Democratic vice presidential candidate, publicly asked Shalala to accept the union's use of card check rather than an election to end the conflict. On April 25, Edwards joined Teamsters president James Hoffa Jr., civil rights leaders, and two hundred other supporters in a campus march. Edwards's appearance brought national media coverage, including a story in the *Washington Post*.[47]

The combination of Edwards, Hoffa, Huerta, and Medina created a media field day, as Freedom Village became ground zero for a national social justice campaign. It also fulfilled one of the hopes of the Change to Win labor federation, which included SEIU, UNITE HERE, the UFW, the Laborers, the United Food and Commercial Workers, the Carpenters, and the Teamsters, unions that had broken away from the AFL-CIO in August 2005 in order to "revitalize" the labor movement. Change to Win was backed by the unions most associated with UFW alumni. In fact, the SEIU UM campaign director, Stephen Lerner, had authored the defining critique of the AFL-CIO in December 2002 that eventually led to the new federation. Hoffa's appearance reflected the type of cross-union support for the UM janitors that Change to Win sought to achieve nationally. The next day, SEIU brought a group of international labor leaders to visit with the strikers. Leandro Avila, from the Panamanian

Federation of Public Employees, issued a press statement, saying, "It's time for University President Donna Shalala to do what's right and just." A website based in the United Kingdom resulted in trade unionists from around the world sending more than four thousand e-mail messages to Shalala, urging her to tell UNICCO to stop breaking the law.[48]

SFICWJ played a vital role as the strike intensified. According to board member Anthony Vinciguerra, "The Catholic community got involved because the issue of low-income workers gets at one of the core challenges in Catholic social teaching, which is 'How do we treat the most poor and vulnerable in our society?'" Fellow board member Bishop Felipe Estévez used his mass on the first Sunday of Lent to offer to personally arbitrate the dispute, but Shalala refused. Father Richard Mullen ministered to the fifteen strikers who lived in Freedom City from April 5 to April 21; on Holy Thursday, in remembrance of the Last Supper, he washed the fasters' feet. As Mullen said, "This whole strike was conducted in a prayerful environment. These workers are very humble, spiritual people." Janitor Reinaldo Hernandez, who had lost thirty pounds by day fifteen of his fast, was among the devout workers who spent considerable time praying with Mullen. In addition to working forty hours a week for UNICCO at $6.40 an hour, Hernandez also supported his wife and infant son by working another thirty hours a week washing cars at Alamo and dishes at Denny's. Hernandez said that he passed the time during his fast "dreaming about his hilltop church" in his native Cuba and "thinking about God—my belief in God and my belief that he is here with us in this fight for human rights."[49]

While other commitments forced Stern to leave Miami after fasting for seventy-two hours, Medina's fast in Freedom Village continued. This ensured daily media coverage and brought one of America's most skilled organizers directly into the conflict. Medina was SEIU's highest-ranking Latino officer and had recently become the nation's leading spokesperson for immigration reform. He remained centrally involved with the congressional battle over immigration legislation while showing support for UM janitors by fasting and living in a tent. Rev. Hawking observed, "Eliseo had a presence and aura that was almost priestly. He was fasting for spiritual reasons and conveyed the impression that this is what life was about and that he would stay with the workers until the end." Medina's personal commitment to the janitors' cause sent a powerful message to Donna Shalala that SEIU viewed this campaign as a top priority. While SEIU sought to publicly pressure Shalala through high-profile visits from Edwards, Hoffa, Huerta, and other nationally known figures, it was also relying on backchannel communications involving former Clinton administration officials and other prominent figures privately urging Shalala to resolve the dispute.[50]

On May 1, 2006, the historic day when millions of Latino immigrant families took to the streets shouting *"sí se puede!"* for immigration reform, the UM janitors finally had occasion to chant *"sí se puede!"* as they declared victory in their own struggle. The janitors and UNICCO agreed to recognize the union if 60 percent of the workers submitted cards saying they wanted to join the union. Lerner stated, "We're elated that these workers, who have sacrificed so much and have been so dedicated to winning a voice and winning a union, will go back to work with their heads held high, winning a breakthrough for immigrant workers throughout the country."[51]

The agreement enabled Eliseo Medina to break his eleven-day fast, and he felt "ecstatic" over the victory: "I think it's a wonderful beginning for Miami, and it sets an example for the rest of the country." Having been involved in many lengthy battles for social justice over the past four decades, Medina also noted, "It's a great day for Miami's workers because it shows that if you persevere, you can win." He praised Shalala, saying that her work behind the scenes had made a "big difference." UM's public reaction was muted, with a spokesperson simply stating, "The university has always maintained a neutral stance on this issue and encouraged UNICCO and SEIU to negotiate a swift resolution. It is now up to the UNICCO employees to decide." While UM refused to give the Yes We Cane campaign the satisfaction of acknowledging that its pressure campaign against Shalala had worked, labor expert Richard Hurd told the *Miami Herald*: "I don't think the company caved; I think the university decided it no longer wanted to be subject to such public pressure." Nevertheless, Medina knew that UM would always have the last word over the wages and working conditions of its contract janitors and was savvy enough to give Shalala credit for working on the janitors' behalf. He also signaled to Miami's condominium industry and to Nova and other area universities that the janitors' victory at UM was only the beginning of a broader South Florida unionization drive, not the end.[52]

On May 3, UM janitors returned to their jobs for the first time since February 28. This gave the media the opportunity to assess the impact of the campaign and to speculate about what the next steps might be. The May 7 *Miami Herald* reported that while the union's Freedom Village under the Metro Rail tracks was gone, for "the SEIU and its supporters, the fight to organize cleaners in South Florida is just beginning." Securing card check recognition "is the first major Florida win for [SEIU's] local Justice for Janitors campaign," the *Herald* noted, a campaign that had added "significant strength to the labor movement here, because it has spawned a whole new set of union organizers—the workers themselves, who are already active on other campuses." Lerner said that Miami reminded him of the environment in Los Angeles during JFJ's famous organizing effort in that city, which was profiled in the film *Bread and Roses*. Although both battles began with workers feeling beaten down, with low wages and no health insurance, Lerner observed, "UM showed that people can win. What about the hundreds of thousands of workers in Miami who are watching?"[53]

Others were less sanguine about SEIU's future prospects in South Florida. A spokesperson for Nova indicated that the school president remained insistent that union recognition would require a secret ballot election rather than card check, and the Continental Group, whose Miami's condominium workers SEIU sought to organize, also announced that its position against card check recognition would not change. *Miami Herald* columnist Ana Menendez, whose March 1 column on janitor Zoila Garcia had helped to personalize the struggle, offered some post-campaign advice for these employers: "If there's a lesson for Miami's union-shy bosses in all of this, it's to pay attention to your workers before someone else does."[54]

As Andy Stern observed, the janitors' victory would not have been possible without "the incredible support of the faith-based community, the students, and the faculty of UM." It was Cesar Chavez and the farmworkers movement who first developed the strategy of building clergy-labor-student alliances for unionizing workers, and this model had again proved its effectiveness in Miami. SEIU hosted a post-victory awards luncheon for the clergy, with both Lerner and Local 11 president Rob Schuler emphasizing how the religious community's moral voice had profoundly influenced the struggle. The Miami archdiocese had played a critical role in resolving the strike, with clergy, archdiocesan social justice groups, and Bishop Estévez all urging UM to ensure that UNICCO met the janitors' demands. No member of the clergy took greater personal risks than UM chaplain Father Corbishley, who could have lost his job for publicly siding with the janitors against his employer. Student leader Mewelau Hall later recalled that students built "a great relationship" with Corbishley, who facilitated campus support for the janitors by turning the Episcopal Center into a "second home" for student activists. The crowd of workers and clergy at the luncheon gave him a standing ovation for his efforts.[55]

As for the students, never again would UM be known solely for its partying and football team. STAND leader Jacob Coker-Dukowitz felt that "students have gotten a better education out of this than they could have gotten in any classroom." Students affiliated with the national Student Labor Action Project sent more than fifteen hundred e-mails and faxes to UM and UNICCO, and students at several other schools staged events to show solidarity with STAND and the workers at UM.[56]

On June 15, the janitors' victory was complete, as well over 60 percent of workers submitted cards expressing a desire to be represented by SEIU. While the janitors cheered at the press conference announcing the result, they mixed their happiness with vows to help raise janitors' wages at Nova and in local shopping malls. After the campus media event, the janitors delivered a letter to the local Sunset Place mall management company, which employed UNICCO as its cleaning service. The letter requested that Sunset hire a contractor who would provide higher wages and health insurance to its workers. As Henry Ruiz, deputy director of SEIU Local 11, put it, "We're hoping that the inspiration from the janitors' victory at UM is going to encourage not just workers at Nova but throughout the local area of Miami-Dade and Broward to realize that they too can lift themselves out of poverty." South Florida janitors no longer have to rely on stories about high wages and good benefits at faraway Harvard—they can now look to nearby UM for the economic and social benefits of unionization.[57]

5

THE UFW BATTLES PESTICIDES

Jessica Govea began working in California's fields at the age of four, picking cotton and prunes with her parents. The fields where they worked often had no bathrooms or clean drinking water. Govea and others had no choice but to drink water that she later concluded had been contaminated by pesticides. In 1967, Govea, now nineteen years old, was working at the Farm Worker Service Center, a project of the UFW, when three female farmworkers came in complaining about dizziness, nausea, severe rashes, and double vision. The grower and the foreman claimed that the women were suffering from mild heat exhaustion, but Govea felt otherwise. Recalling her own experience in the fields, she believed that the women were suffering from pesticide exposure.

Soon after this incident, Govea went to work for the UFW legal department, headed by general counsel Jerry Cohen. She asked Cohen what the union was doing about pesticides and urged him to press the UFW to address the issue. As Govea later proved while leading the union's Canadian grape boycott (described in chapter 1), she could be quite persuasive. Cohen soon began looking into the pesticide issue and was troubled by the increasing number of farmworkers suffering health problems that had likely resulted from pesticides. During his investigation, Cohen was denied access to public records showing which chemicals were being sprayed in proximity to workers. This stonewalling confirmed the UFW's suspicions about the dangers of the pesticides sprayed in the fields. To protect its workers, the union had no choice but to combine its David versus Goliath battle against America's most powerful growers with an equally uphill fight against the nation's rapidly growing chemical and pesticide industry.[1]

AMERICA'S UNREGULATED PESTICIDE INDUSTRY

In 1962, Rachel Carson published *Silent Spring*, a landmark work that blamed "chemical insecticides indiscriminately sprayed on the land" for the "direct killing of birds, mammals, fishes, and indeed practically every form of wildlife." Carson's work, which helped launch America's modern environmental movement, was published three days before Cesar Chavez began the nation's first successful campaign to organize farmworkers. Carson and Chavez shared more than the launching of two major grassroots movements in the same week. Although *Silent Spring* focused on the impact of the pesticide DDT on wildlife, Carson wrote her book while suffering from breast cancer, which she believed had been caused by "agents in our environment." The UFW, for its part, would become the first organization to take up the challenge of eliminating the environmental causes of cancer. One can only imagine what a critical ally Carson might have been had she not died of cancer in 1964.[2]

Silent Spring did not focus on DDT's impact on the farmworkers who picked America's fruits and vegetables. The plight of farmworkers was little publicized in those years, and no attention was paid to the indiscriminate spraying of insecticides by airplane or field cart into the fields. Growers were certainly aware that insecticides posed hazards to their workers; they were careful to tell those spraying pesticides by hand that they should be sure to wear masks. But this did not eliminate the unreasonable dangers caused by the use of highly toxic chemicals. For example, Elijah Boone of Pahokee, Florida, told the U.S. Senate Committee on Labor and Public Welfare in 1969 about a case "where a man was spraying in an orange grove, and he took the mask off for a second and inhaled, and died." The grower blamed the worker, saying he "should have kept his mask on." The victim's family received no compensation.[3]

The women who told Jessica Govea about their health problems were not the first farmworkers to feel the impact of DDT; nausea, itching, and vision problems were common. But when workers have no health insurance, no overtime pay, no unemployment compensation, no social security, no minimum wage guarantee, and none of the protection offered by labor laws, addressing these fundamental survival issues usually takes precedence. Once Jerry Cohen began investigating the pesticide problem, however, he learned that the health risks to farmworkers were far worse than previously realized. New studies were linking insecticide exposure to disorders of the central nervous system, and many of the pesticides that were supposed to be a boon to the nation's agriculture were beginning to look more like poisons in terms of their health effects.

From 1950 to 1969, spending on pesticides in the United States grew by 15 percent a year: whereas growers spent only twenty-five cents an acre on pesticides in 1950, they were spending $3.65 an acre by 1968. The agriculture industry's increasing reliance on dangerous pesticides posed a major challenge for the UFW. As the union analyzed the best way to proceed, two events in the summer of 1968 made action imperative. In June 1968, a crew of farmworkers became seriously ill after exposure to sprayed pesticides. Then, a month later, sixteen workers who had been exposed to the deadly pesticide parathion in a grape field had to be hospitalized. For Chavez and the UFW, protecting farmworkers from pesticides was now a top concern.[4]

The pesticide industry in the 1960s was almost entirely unregulated. Federal and state governments, which allowed growers to flout labor laws and did not even ensure that toilets and safe running water were available for farmworkers, were unlikely be concerned about pesticide exposure. Federal regulations regarding pesticides did exist, however: there were, in fact, quite stringent guidelines to protect growers who were using pesticides from being wrongly accused of causing harm. This meant that if a union, a physician, or a consumer publicly claimed that pesticides hurt workers' health, the grower could actually sue for damages, which was a great strategy for deterring bad publicity and complaints. Before 1970, the U.S. Department of Agriculture was the federal agency primarily responsible for monitoring pesticides. But the USDA was primarily a lobbying arm for agribusiness; of the $132 million it spent on research and development in 1969, only $160,000 went toward ensuring that pesticides met federal standards.[5]

Congress's attitude toward pesticide hazards was reflected in the comments of Mississippi representative Jamie Whitten, longtime chair of the House Appropriations Subcommittee on Agriculture. Disputing claims that the pesticide residue remaining on leaves after spraying was a health hazard, Whitten declared in 1969, "The worst residue problem we have to face today is the residue of public opinion left by Rachel Carson's book, *Silent Spring.*" State regulation was no better. California was among the few states that gave the appearance of regulating pesticides, but enforcement was in the hands of local agriculture commissioners, who were firmly controlled by growers. An incident in 1963 demonstrated the attitudes of the regulators. When California health officials warned that it was dangerous to permit farmworkers to go into peach orchards sprayed with the pesticide parathion because residue on the leaves would cause poisoning, state agriculture officials called such precautions "unwarranted." The reason? At that point, 60 percent of the crop had not yet been harvested, and ensuring that the crop was picked took precedence over farmworkers' health.[6]

THE CAMPAIGN BEGINS

In response to the increasingly obvious health threats posed by pesticide use, the UFW developed a strategy that linked unionization to strict pesticide regulation and outright bans on dangerous chemicals. Including landmark pesticide restrictions in UFW contracts provided a way to circumvent lax federal, state, and local enforcement. This new emphasis meant that the UFW grape boycott would now highlight the link between a union contract and the safety of both the workers who picked the food and the consumers who bought it.

The UFW addressed this new challenge by following the same strategy that had inspired the grape boycott: it sought to transform what could have remained a local struggle involving pesticides in California's Central Valley into a national campaign for social justice. The UFW pursued this strategy in two key ways. First, the pesticide issue became part of its boycott message. UFW boycott staff informed consumers that nonunion grapes not only were picked under terrible labor conditions but also posed a health danger because of pesticide residue. Whereas the standard UFW pitch appealed to the conscience of consumers, the pesticide threat appealed directly to their own self-interest. Since Chavez had publicly committed to include pesticide regulation in all UFW contracts, supporting the boycott would both improve conditions for workers and ensure that consumers had access to grapes that were safe to eat.

Second, Chavez and the UFW sought to nationalize the pesticide issue by setting in motion a series of events that would eventually lead to two U.S. Senate hearings in 1969. The March 1966 Central Valley hearings of the Senate Subcommittee on Migratory Labor had represented a huge national breakthrough for the union, leading Senator Robert Kennedy to announce his support for the grape strike and to urge religious leaders and others to do likewise. The UFW hoped that Senate hearings on pesticides could similarly bring national attention to the issue and rally opinion to the union's side.

To build momentum for a future Senate hearing, the UFW began turning up the heat around pesticides in August 1968. In what should have been a very nonthreatening act, UFW general counsel Jerry Cohen visited the office of the agriculture commissioner of Bakersfield, California, with a simple request—he wanted to review various public records of

Pesticide poisoning brings poor health and short lives to farm workers. Jerry Cohen, UFWOC attorney, wages constant court battles to end such conditions in the fields.

January 1971

Sunday	Monday	Tuesday	Wednesday	Thursday	Friday	Saturday
					1 New Year's Day	2
3	4	5	6	7	8	9

UFW calendar (designed by Andy Zermeno), January 1971: Jerry Cohen wages a battle against pesticides.

pesticide spraying. The union had heard from workers that they were being sent into fields too soon after spraying had been done (there was a legal minimum time before work could resume after spraying); some workers had even been sprayed while picking crops.

Although the spraying records were public, this meant little to the Central Valley's grower-controlled justice system. The agriculture commissioner denied Cohen's request, saying that the public records had been given to him "in confidence."

Cohen left the commissioner's office at approximately 11:30 A.M. By 1:34 P.M., the Agricultural Chemicals Association had obtained a temporary restraining order from the Kern County Superior Court preventing Cohen and the UFW from inspecting the only records that could determine whether the spraying had violated the law. Attorneys for the crop-dusting corporations seeking the restraining order acknowledged that there was no legal authority for their request, but this proved to be no impediment for the court. Even worse, although such temporary restraining orders are typically terminated as soon as a fully briefed court hearing can occur, in this case the Kern County court continued the ban for six months. The order might have stayed in effect indefinitely had the UFW not filed a lawsuit against the agriculture commissioner in January 1969, demanding to examine the records.[7]

At the court hearing on the UFW's request, Cohen and fellow UFW attorney David Averbuck elicited testimony from leading experts, including the chief of California's Department of Public Health and a University of California professor of economic entomology, on the importance of worker access to pesticide information. Attorneys for the crop dusters and the local agriculture commissioner argued that the spraying information was a "confidential trade secret" and brought in their own UC professor of entomology—also a consultant to the state Department of Agriculture—to rebut his colleague's claims. A representative of the state agricultural director's office told the court that the state did "not make tests of our own. We take the word of the chemical companies."[8]

Cohen argued that it was the UFW, not the state, who was acting as "public defender" and told the judge, "We don't trust government agencies. We rely on ourselves, and would rather rely on public law." To nobody's surprise, the court upheld the order keeping the public spraying records secret. To rule otherwise, the judge found, "would seriously hamper the essential cooperation existing between all segments of the pesticide industry and the farmers on the one hand with the commissioner on the other." In California's fertile San Joaquin Valley in 1969, the health of farmworkers was not even part of the court's calculation. But Cohen's request to inspect the records and the UFW's subsequent lawsuit had exposed the state's failure to enforce pesticide regulations and forced regulators to take a stance that they must have known would never be upheld by higher courts.[9]

In late 1968, Cohen filed a landmark lawsuit on behalf of a seventeen-year-old farmworker who had been unable to work after exposure to an organophosphate pesticide, a type of pesticide that had originally been developed by German engineers during World War II as a form of nerve gas and that was increasingly replacing DDT. Until the mid-1960s, growers had relied on the notorious pesticide DDT, a chlorinated hydrocarbon whose threat to wildlife had been highlighted in Rachel Carson's *Silent Spring*. But insects were becoming immune to DDT, so the new organophosphate pesticides came into use, a type that was even more toxic in the short run but had a shorter duration of toxicity. This shorter duration reduced risks to wildlife, which could suffer harm from exposure to DDT residue well after spraying. But it increased risks to farmworkers who were directly exposed to the more lethal chemical. Growers often sued their neighbors for damages caused by the neighbors' wrongful use of land, but no farmworker had ever recovered damages for nuisance activities on the land of a grower. In January 1969, Cohen prevailed with his novel claim, and the young worker received $447 for five months of lost salary as a result of his incapacitation. According to Cohen, it was the "first time a farmworker had ever been so compensated." But it would not be the last, as the UFW and other legal groups increasingly used traditional nuisance and tort theories to recover damages for farmworkers injured by pesticides.[10]

As word of the pesticide problem spread, the UFW got an unexpected boost in January 1969, when the California Department of Public Health released a survey showing that 71 percent of the 548 farmworkers tested had symptoms of pesticide poisoning. The public health director concluded that only 1 percent of poisonings from pesticides were being reported, which meant that nearly a hundred thousand farmworkers were likely suffering health problems as a result of pesticide spraying. The state report helped legitimize farmworkers' concern over pesticides and became an important element in negotiations between the UFW and twelve leading table grape growers in the first half of 1969. In fact, the pesticide issue became such a major issue of dispute that the growers terminated the negotiations over the UFW's refusal to accept the standard contract provision stating that the union "will not embark on any program which will in any way harm the industry to which the employer belongs."[11]

Chavez acknowledged that many UFW supporters felt he was making a major mistake in allowing the pesticide issue to get in the way of a labor settlement with the table grape industry. He was advised to "settle for what you can" and to "get your foot in the door—that's the important thing." But Chavez knew the importance of the pesticide issue to farmworkers, and he was adamant that the UFW not accept any contract clause that would prevent the union from pushing for pesticide restrictions: "If they think that once we sign a contract, we are going to become docile little lap-dogs, they're crazy." The growers were equally adamant in refusing to accept any limitations on the use of DDT on table grapes, even though Michigan, Arizona, and Sweden had already banned the pesticide.[12]

PESTICIDES IN THE NATIONAL SPOTLIGHT

The growers would soon regret their hard-line pro-pesticide stance. The first hearing of the Senate Subcommittee on Migratory Labor on the pesticide issue convened in Washington, D.C., on August 1, 1969. Jerry Cohen led off the union's presentation and told subcommittee chair Walter Mondale and the other senators the full details of the complicity between the state and the growers in concealing pesticide risks. Cohen described the record speed at which his attempt to view the spraying records had produced a restraining order and revealed the Kern County agriculture commissioner's own report, which showed extensive spraying of poisonous pesticides on more than a thousand acres of grapes in that county alone. From the committee's reaction, it was clear that Kern County's approach to pesticide regulation did not play well on the national stage.

Cohen then asserted that "to eat a Kern County grape is to play Russian roulette with one's health." He supported this statement by announcing that the UFW had tested grapes purchased in supermarkets in the state of Washington and had found DDT residue on each batch—despite the claim by California's agricultural director that the state's grapes had no residues and similar assertions by Washington's department of agriculture. Cohen also revealed that UFW tests had found DDT-tainted grapes from Delano and other Central California fields in stores in Sacramento, Seattle, and Buffalo. Using humor to pound home his point, Cohen displayed a newspaper article on a "scientific" finding that cannibals in certain primitive Pacific islands ate British missionaries and soldiers but not North Americans. The scientists concluded that "cannibals are naturally selecting out those people who don't have as much DDT in their bodies," meaning that the spraying of fruits and vegetables with the pesticide had left the American people "unfit for human consumption."[13]

The subcommittee hearing provided Cohen with a national stage on which to highlight the risks posed by DDT for consumers and farmworkers, and it clearly raised public relations problems for the agricultural and chemical industries. But the hearing might have been quickly forgotten had Republican senator George Murphy of California not raised a huge ruckus by publicly attacking Cohen and the UFW and accusing them of "deceit."

The controversy ignited when, at the conclusion of his testimony, Cohen asked one of his colleagues to bring in the results of a test performed by an independent laboratory on grapes that the UFW had purchased from a nearby Safeway supermarket in Washington, D.C. The test found that the grapes were contaminated with the toxic pesticide known as aldrin and that the levels of aldrin on the grapes were 180 times above human tolerance levels. The notion that grapes were being sold containing such dangerous doses of pesticide represented the hearing's most controversial and explosive revelation. California growers claimed they had not used aldrin for three years, so the presence of aldrin residue on grapes raised doubts as to whether the testing procedures designed to protect consumers from pesticides could be trusted. And, as Cohen later put it, once consumers learned that grape growers could not tell whether their grapes were tainted by aldrin or sulphur (and UFW boycott staff across the nation would soon make sure that consumers got the message), "nobody in their right mind would take the health risk of purchasing a California table grape."[14]

California agribusiness understood the dire implications of the UFW's lab test and used the period after the subcommittee's adjournment to figure out how to respond. The growers decided to have Senator Murphy insert a statement in the *Congressional Record* on August 12, 1969, attacking the UFW for engaging in a "vicious type of deceit." Murphy also charged that the union's claims were "part of an attempt to mislead the subcommittee by presenting false testimony" in the form of fraudulent lab results. Accompanying Murphy's attack on the UFW's integrity was an affidavit signed by grower Anthony Bianco, whose grapes had been tested, swearing that he had not used aldrin in six years. But when the Mondale subcommittee reconvened on September 30, the growers and Murphy paid dearly for this line of attack. Since Safeway Stores did not want to knowingly sell aldrin-tainted grapes, it had engaged labs to conduct tests similar to those performed by the UFW's independent lab. Cohen revealed at the September 30 hearing that these tests had also found aldrin on the grapes, confirming the UFW's tests. He also told the committee that Safeway had canceled its contract with the grower who had signed the affidavit denying that he had used aldrin.[15]

Senator Murphy, like California governor Ronald Reagan, was a former actor and a harsh critic of the UFW. Not known for his intellect or political savvy, he now looked foolish for his public attack on the UFW's test results. At the hearing, Mondale accused Murphy of "kicking a dead horse," arguing that "it is abundantly clear the union took an honest sample, took it to an honest laboratory and came up with an honest report." Murphy responded by charging that "playing games with California table grapes has done enormous harm to the industry and to the workers," but he conceded that, while he "was not in the habit of accusing without facts and knowledge," he had been mistaken in his August 12 criticism of the UFW.[16]

Had the hearing ended then, the storyline still would have been, as the front-page headline in the October 1, 1969, *Los Angeles Times* read, "Murphy Retracts Accusations against Union on Pesticides." But officials of the pro-agribusiness Food and Drug Administration and the grape growers were furious about the lab results and decided to dig themselves a deeper hole. FDA officials, concerned that the lab finding undermined their assurances that the grapes sold in America's supermarkets were safe, questioned the accuracy of the tests. But under harsh questioning from Mondale, FDA commissioner Dr. H. L. Ley acknowledged that the agency had not even bothered to check the reports from two of the independent labs used by Safeway. Other FDA officials stated that "it was not worthwhile" to check the lab reports because they conflicted with the agency's own findings. This led Mondale to suggest that the FDA did not want to confirm that independent labs had found aldrin when its own tests had not. John Giumarra Jr., of the powerful Giumarra Vineyards, then further undermined his industry's credibility when he told the subcommittee that the UFW's charge of aldrin use was "an irresponsible and deceitful act." Citing expert witnesses who argued that lab results on pesticide use were hard to interpret, Giumarra suggested that what the lab had determined was aldrin could instead be sulphur. He concluded by asserting that either the grapes the UFW had tested were "doctored" or the lab analyses were wrong.[17]

The statements of Murphy, FDA officials, and Giumarra at the hearing greatly boosted the UFW's entire table grape campaign. The credibility of Senator Murphy, the grape industry's leading backer in the U.S. Senate, was irrevocably compromised on this issue. On September 30, 1969, the *Sacramento Bee* reported on the hearing, with this headline: "Witnesses Disprove Murphy: Murphy's 'Doctored Grape' Tale Fizzles." While Murphy's credibility plunged, California's other senator, Democrat Alan Cranston, also on the subcommittee, introduced Cesar Chavez as "an outstanding citizen not only of my state but of the entire country, in the tradition of Mahatma Gandhi and Martin Luther King." Murphy sat quietly throughout the second hearing, leaving growers without a strong advocate on the subcommittee. In addition, the FDA showed that it had little interest in monitoring health problems with grapes and that the public could not trust the agency's claims of safety. Another powerful ally of the grape industry was thus compromised.[18] .

The growers' own explanation for the lab results made consumers even less likely to buy table grapes. A leading grower had told consumers that the grapes sold in stores were probably tainted with sulphur rather than aldrin, a claim that likely made the situation worse. Few consumers had heard of aldrin, but everyone knew about sulphur—which was not typically seen as a chemical that makes food more attractive to eat. Further, Giumarra's insistence that growers were not using aldrin contradicted Safeway's own lab report. This sent a powerful message that growers refused to be bound by scientific findings on pesticides, even when the lab tests had been conducted by a supermarket chain that was one of their strongest retail allies. Finally, Giumarra's statements raised a basic question for consumers: If the lab tests could not be trusted, then what alternative exists for protecting consumer safety other than to bar pesticides altogether? Recall that in July Giumarra and other growers had broken off negotiations to end the grape strike and boycott because the UFW refused to sign a contract pledge that the union would "not embark on any program which will in any way harm the industry to which the employer belongs." At the September 30 hearing, however, the growers' representative did more to harm the industry's credibility on pesticides than anything that had been said by Cesar Chavez, Jerry Cohen, or the UFW.[19]

This public relations disaster soon forced growers to return to the bargaining table and to eventually sign contracts with the union. Following the Senate hearing, the UFW signed a contract with A. Perelli-Minetti & Sons prohibiting the use of "hard" pesticides (those that persist in the environment long after application) on wine grapes. This landmark agreement was the first time any union had won this restriction, and it demonstrated that the UFW's best strategy for combating pesticides was through contract language, given the lack of enforcement by state and federal authorities. The agreement required the company to inform workers of which pesticides were being sprayed, and it banned DDT, aldrin, and other common pesticides. The company was not prohibited from using the newer organophosphate pesticides, but the union's Health and Safety Committee would recommend how long fields had to be closed after the spraying. Because organophosphates were more toxic but dissolved more quickly than DDT, the UFW's regulation of the spraying was crucial. The contract also required the company to pay for testing workers to determine the impact of pesticide exposure and used the same testing standards for farmworkers that state law already required for crop dusters and workers in the pesticide industry.[20]

In a further demonstration of the significance of the Mondale hearings, the same state agricultural director who had imposed the secrecy policy denying Cohen and the UFW the right to inspect spraying records quietly announced at the end of 1969 that he was barring 91 pesticides from use on crops and would impose new restrictions on 120 others. He declared that the state was now taking "a much broader view of pesticide usage."[21]

The pesticide issue gave boycott staff a powerful new message to offer wary consumers, increasing the campaign's effectiveness. Boycotters tabling at supermarkets handed out flyers that read, "This market sells poisoned grapes," while other flyers listed the pesticides used on grapes and their negative effects on health. One handout showed a bushel of grapes in the shape of a skull with the caption "A Peligro de Muerte! Danger! Deadly!" It also charged, "California grape workers are killed and maimed every year by the pesticides you are eating," and described the death of a scientist who accidentally swallowed the common pesticide parathion. A consistent theme of these handouts was "Warning: Eating Grapes May Be Hazardous to Your Health," often with a picture of a plane dropping pesticides on crops. One flyer cautioned: "All California grapes are sprayed with poisonous pesticides. Neither washing nor cooking can completely destroy pesticide residues. Only a union contract can protect farm workers and consumers from the dangers of poisonous pesticides." This latter point was crucial. Organic produce was not widely available in the late 1960s and 1970s, and many consumers shared the UFW's skepticism about government regulation of pesticides. Consumers could logically view a UFW contract as the chief guarantee of safe grapes.[22]

To further increase pressure on growers, the UFW filed a class action lawsuit in February 1970 in federal court in Los Angeles on behalf of "all consumers and farm workers" to outlaw the use of DDT and thirty other pesticides deemed "even more dangerous." Although California's agricultural director had announced widespread restrictions on pesticide use at the end of 1969, the new restrictions contained multiple loopholes, and the union moved to file suit. UFW attorney Charles Farnsworth described the state's action "as a deceptive move to protect the chemical companies and the growers, and we will not let them get away with it."

Negotiations soon resumed between the UFW and three growers who had been involved in the previous year's discussions. With the National Conference of Catholic Bishops playing an important role in bringing the parties together, an agreement was reached on March 31 with the first grower, and the two others soon followed.[23]

On July 29, 1970, John Giumarra Jr., who had denounced the UFW's pesticide concerns at the last Mondale hearing, joined twenty-eight other growers in signing contracts with the UFW. By the fall of 1970, the UFW had signed contracts with 150 table grape growers involving about twenty thousand workers. The agreements brought grape workers an immediate raise, from $1.65 an hour to $1.80, and increased piece-rate bonuses; employers also agreed to pay a dime an hour per worker into the union's Robert F. Kennedy Health and Welfare fund. Joint employer-worker committees were set up to regulate pesticide use. Realizing that they had lost all public credibility on pesticides following the Mondale hearings, the growers agreed to provisions banning DDT, parathion, aldrin, and other pesticides in union fields. These were the same provisions that had led them to break off negotiations the preceding year. The UFW accomplished through its organizing drive and contract provisions what had not been won through the political process—and government was clearly lagging in this area. When the landmark Occupational Safety and Health Act (OSHA) was enacted in 1970 to safeguard employees in the workplace, farmworkers were excluded from its protections. The federal Environmental Protection Agency did not ban DDT from agricultural use until 1972, and aldrin was not prohibited until 1974. And the EPA imposed no restrictions on the spraying of parathion, a nerve gas type of insecticide that has been described as responsible for more deaths worldwide than any other pesticide.[24]

The events of 1969 and 1970 showed that pesticide regulation in the fields depended on the UFW's organizing strength. When the UFW used its organizing clout to secure a contract, workers covered by the contract had the highest level of protection from pesticides. Without a UFW contract, workers were at the mercy of unsympathetic local, state, and federal regulators. The link between UFW contracts and the battle against pesticides made it imperative for worker safety that the union continue to grow. This link also helps explain farmworkers' incredible anger when the initial UFW contracts expired in 1973 and grape growers switched to sign agreements with the Teamsters. Unlike the UFW pacts, the Teamsters' "sweetheart" contracts merely required that growers "strictly comply with all federal and state laws, rules and regulations" for the health and safety of employees regarding "dangerous chemicals and sprays." Given the regulatory agencies' history of nonenforcement and growers' longtime control of these departments, shifting the contracts to the Teamsters meant that farmworkers, without a representation election, had lost the critical protections against pesticides that they had won in 1970.

A preview of the harm grape workers could suffer under the lax Teamster contracts occurred in December 1972, when farmworkers in the lettuce fields—the UFW was boycotting lettuce as part of its organizing drive—were exposed to a new pesticide known as Monitor-4 (M-4). Workers noticed that the outer leaves of the lettuce were burned, and they themselves soon experienced nausea, dizziness, burned skin, and other symptoms of toxic poisoning. The California Department of Food and Agriculture (CDFA) investigated complaints regarding M-4, but its tests found no pesticide residue on the lettuce. (Ronald Reagan was governor at the time and was notoriously anti-UFW.) When the U.S. Food and Drug Administration investigated further, however, it became clear that the CDFA had found no residue because it had removed the outer leaves; when heads of lettuce that still had their outer leaves were tested, residue levels were six times the legal limit. In response, the EPA temporarily banned M-4 but then quietly lifted the ban in March 1973.[25]

FORGING ALLIANCES WITH ENVIRONMENTALISTS

The UFW's campaign against pesticides began in 1968, two years before the first Earth Day and before the full-fledged emergence of America's environmental movement. The growth of environmental groups in the early 1970s created potentially strong allies for the UFW's anti-pesticide campaign, but mainstream organizations were reluctant to make the issue a top priority. Believing that environmental groups concerned about pesticides would be motivated by the growers' actions to help the UFW's cause, Cesar Chavez sought to build an alliance with the growing environmental movement in 1972 and 1973, arguing that "the unity which the union movement can have with the environmentalists is crucial to our survival." Many of the smaller environmental groups responded favorably to Chavez's request and began urging the EPA to restrict pesticides in the fields. These groups also lent formal support to the UFW grape and lettuce boycotts.[26]

But the larger, more influential organizations, including the Audubon Society, the National Wildlife Federation, and the Sierra Club, did not want to get involved in what they perceived as fundamentally a labor dispute. These organizations were involved with pesticide issues but did not want to endorse the UFW boycott or formally align with the farm-workers movement. In some ways, this rebuff to the UFW was surprising. Contrary to the popular notion that labor and environmentalists were continually at odds during the 1960s and 1970s, the two constituencies often effectively collaborated during these years. This labor-environmental alliance led to the passage of such critical measures as the Coal Mine Safety and Health Act in 1969 and OSHA and the National Environmental Policy Act in 1970. The Sierra Club played a role in the passage of all the labor-backed environmental legislation of the era and formally endorsed the strike against Shell Oil Company called by the Oil, Chemical, and Atomic Workers (OCAW) in 1973, the same year it refused to endorse the UFW boycott.[27]

OCAW's January 1973 strike was sparked by concerns over the numerous toxic chemicals and other dangerous substances to which production and refinery workers were exposed. When Shell refused to include health and safety provisions in the upcoming union contract, including monitoring requirements and a joint labor-management health and safety committee, five thousand workers walked off the job. Environmental groups quickly supported the workers' demand for a safe workplace, and while the Sierra Club engaged in vigorous internal debate over the issue, its board endorsed OCAW's strike in March. According to Robert Gordon's analysis of the campaign, "for six months, striking workers and environmental activists battled the world's second largest oil corporation to a virtual standstill. Workers and environmentalists returned Shell credit cards by the thousands, endured threats and harassment, walked picket lines side-by-side, and argued that toxic wastes not only fouled the environment, but also threatened the lives of workers, their families, and their communities." Although OCAW fell short of a clear victory, the campaign strengthened bonds between environmentalists and labor unions through the 1970s. This collaboration helped lead to the passage of the Toxic Substance Control Act (1976), the revised Clean Water Act (1977), the Humphrey-Hawkins Full Employment Act (1978), and the Superfund Act (1980).[28]

Why did OCAW secure the active support of the Sierra Club and other mainstream environmental groups around workplace safety issues while the UFW did not? One factor was the identity of the wrongdoer. Les Leopold, biographer of OCAW health and safety pioneer Tony Mazzocchi, notes that the union's dispute with Shell Oil resonated among environmentalists angry about oil spills that had killed wildlife and despoiled beaches. OCAW's strike also coincided with skyrocketing oil company profits and long lines at gas stations that infuriated consumers. But another reason was the cultural distinction between the UFW, with its "movement" style and its 90 percent Latino membership, and OCAW, whose struggle was more of a traditional labor strike involving a primarily Caucasian workforce. The Sierra Club and other longtime environmental groups in the early 1970s were disproportionately made up of white male professionals who did not view environmental problems as a function of deep-seated racial or social injustices. This narrow vision of environmental problems was demonstrated in a 1972 internal survey of 800 Sierra Club members, which found that "only 15 percent wanted the club to become more involved in nonwilderness issues." Most flatly opposed the group's involvement in such issues.[29]

It was the Sierra Club leadership, acting against the views of the majority of its membership, that pushed for the endorsement of OCAW's strike. Sierra Club president Mike McCloskey even spoke at the union's August 1973 convention to express the club's strong solidarity. Gordon convincingly suggests that the club was under pressure to endorse OCAW's struggle in order to rebut charges that it was anti-labor; having done so, the group believed that it did not have to also back the UFW. Almost two decades later, the Sierra Club would adopt many of the grassroots electoral and organizing strategies made popular by the UFW. But at the time Chavez requested help, the Sierra Club's approach to environmental activism was not broad enough to see the UFW's battle against pesticides as a priority, leaving smaller and less influential environmental groups to heed the UFW leader's call.[30]

In later years, it became clear that the conflicting responses of mainstream environmental groups to the OCAW and UFW labor struggles in 1973 were part of a larger pattern, a failure to recognize that low-income people and communities of color were disproportionately subjected to environmental hazards. As the environmental justice movement emerged, it began to address these issues and, in the process, highlighted this blind spot in the work of many established environmental groups. Environmental justice campaigns often relied on grassroots tactics and strategies evocative of the UFW and eventually helped lead the Sierra Club and other mainstream organizations to adopt more broadly progressive agendas and a more activist approach.

If a group such as the Sierra Club had been more cognizant of racial and class issues in its environmental campaigns in the early 1970s, would it have made a difference in the UFW's pesticide campaign? It is tempting to think so, particularly given the incredible growth of the environmental movement in the past decades. Since most Sierra Club members lived in the UFW's home state of California, perhaps the organization could have played a particularly potent role in broadening support for the boycott and increasing pressure on retailers and politicians. But neither the Sierra Club nor the environmental movement enjoyed such political clout in the early 1970s. Even if these groups had universally endorsed the boycott and worked hard on the UFW's behalf, it is doubtful that such support would have pressured growers to the bargaining table before the passage of the ALRA in 1975.

As Jerry Cohen puts it, "The UFW's success on pesticides was not dependent on endorsements by other groups, but on our ability to organize workers on the ground."[31] Chavez was seeking whatever backing he could get in 1973, as the years from 1973 to 1975 represented the most challenging of the UFW's history. The union was battling both grape and lettuce growers, and table grape workers had lost their hard-won protections against pesticides as the growers signed contracts with the Teamsters. But after Governor Jerry Brown took office and the ALRA became law, the UFW's success at winning union elections again ensured that hazardous pesticides would be banned or strictly regulated in the fields. The UFW's historic victory in the 1979 Salinas lettuce strike and the Teamsters' decision to stop competing with the UFW rendered the lack of mainstream environmentalist support irrelevant and gave the UFW enough contracts to exert its strongest control ever over pesticide spraying.

As the 1980s began, the UFW appeared to have both California agribusiness and the state's pesticide industry on the run. It seemed only a matter of time before the UFW's organizing prowess secured enough labor contracts to protect most California farmworkers from toxic chemicals. The union's success would effectively free workers from having to rely on state and local pesticide regulators, who were largely progrower. And Chavez and the union leaders saw the UFW's success in California as the launching pad for what would become a national union of farmworkers. The UFW had had contracts with Minute Maid in Florida and had worked with farmworker groups in Texas, Arizona, Oregon, and Washington. The UFW also had close ties with the Midwest-based Farm Labor Organizing Committee (see chapter 2), whose founder and president, Baldemar Velásquez, had been mentored by Cesar Chavez from the start. The battle to unionize farmworkers throughout the United States would not be easy, but the UFW represented a model that could be replicated in the fields across the nation. Relying on the spirit of "sí *se puede,"* it appeared possible, and perhaps even likely, in 1979 that the country's farmworkers would soon be unionized and would be protected from harmful pesticides by union contracts.

PROGRESS ON PESTICIDES IS REVERSED

But, for the reasons discussed in chapter 10, the UFW's 1979 success was soon followed by a steady decline. Nowhere was this decline more evident, and the consequences so extreme, as in the union's battle against pesticides. By the 1980s, American farmers were using 2.6 million tons of chemical pesticides each year, and three hundred thousand people were suffering health problems as a result. Cancer clusters had emerged among farmworker children. But the UFW was increasingly frustrated by its inability to transform election victories in the fields into actual labor contracts. With the boycott staff dissolved, and lacking the grassroots organizing capacity of the 1960s and 1970s, Chavez took the UFW on a new course.[32]

Encouraged by Richie Ross, a former UFW volunteer turned political consultant, Chavez and the UFW sought to pressure growers through a nationwide direct-mail campaign targeting pesticides. Whereas boycott staff had earlier asked consumers at supermarkets not to buy grapes because they were unsafe, this appeal now came by mail. Not surprisingly, the campaign prompted people to write checks to the UFW but did not reduce consumer grape purchases. Although some religious groups actively worked on behalf of the new grape boycott, the UFW's direct-mail appeal was precisely the type of paper boycott that the AFL-CIO used so frequently—and that typically failed. In this case, growers responded with their own media campaign, accusing Chavez of using the pesticide issue for political purposes. Volunteers on the ground could have directly rebutted such claims, but in a battle waged through the mail and the media, it was more difficult for consumers to figure out the truth. Despite these problems, the UFW's political clout in the Democratic-controlled California legislature remained strong. The legislature passed a union-sponsored bill in 1985 requiring growers to post signs warning that spraying had occurred (which was then vetoed by Governor George Deukmejian). The UFW also played an important role in Monterey County's enactment of tough new pesticide regulations, which contributed to improvements in the state guidelines.[33]

As the 1980s proceeded, news continued to spread about farmworker families who were experiencing health problems as a result of pesticide exposure. When a cancer cluster was detected in the San Joaquin Valley, which included Delano, in 1987, Chavez got some Hollywood allies to produce a powerful fifteen-minute video, *The Wrath of Grapes*. Featuring the voices of parents castigating regulators' unwillingness to enforce pesticide regulations, the pictures showed disfigured and fatally ill children who were the victims of pesticide spraying. The UFW distributed more than fifty thousand copies of the video, which they hoped would raise money and spur public concern about pesticides. But growers attacked the video's fundraising component and succeeded in getting some of the mothers shown in the film to complain that money from the video should go to help their children, not the UFW. These mothers sued the union, claiming misrepresentation, and a court suspended distribution of the film.[34]

With the new grape boycott faltering, and increasing evidence of pesticide-caused illnesses, Cesar Chavez announced in 1988 that he would undertake a fast to refocus attention on the pesticide problem. The sixty-one-year-old Chavez engaged in his longest fast ever, ending it after thirty-six days only when others promised to keep it going on his behalf. Chavez's fast brought the media, celebrities, Ethel Kennedy, and the Reverend Jesse Jackson out to the Forty Acres compound, where the UFW leader had engaged in his first spiritual fast twenty-one years earlier.[35]

But while the location of Chavez's 1988 fast was the same as it had been in 1968, the meaning and the surrounding actions were quite different. In 1968, Chavez's fast became a vehicle for farmworker unity. Workers drove for hundreds of miles to see him, and hundreds packed tents and lived alongside the leader who was risking his life for the farmworker cause. This earlier fast was a defining moment for the UFW, and a transformative event for many of those involved. In contrast, Chavez's 1988 fast was more personal than communal. Some farmworkers did come to pay their respects, but this fast lacked the religious and ceremonial aspects that had made the earlier one so inspiring and emotionally moving. Chavez's 1967 fast was one part of a broader grassroots campaign, whereas in 1988 the UFW had no real campaign on the ground against pesticides. In fact, the fast, along with the UFW's direct-mail appeals, essentially constituted the campaign. Unlike 1968, the end of Chavez's 1988 fast left the union no stronger than before and its leader suffering from grave health problems.

Despite the fast's failure to galvanize the public, Cesar Chavez spent the remainder of his life battling pesticide spraying. After spending months recovering from the fast and a subsequent fall, Chavez hit the speaking trail urging consumers not to buy grapes until they were pesticide-free.

In 1990, the UFW joined with California environmental groups in a far-reaching "Big Green" ballot initiative that included a provision reducing the use of farm pesticides. Chavez had lost faith in the initiative process after Prop 14's defeat in 1976, but enjoyed leading anti-pesticide rallies across the state in support of the measure (which eventually lost). Chavez told an environmental conference convened by Ralph Nader in 1991 that "Americans who are truly interested in working for social change can look less and less to the political process for redress." This statement harkened back to the UFW strategies and tactics of the 1960s and 1970s and was a clear departure from Chavez's heavy reliance on campaign donations to Sacramento politicians throughout the 1980s. By the time of his death in 1993, the UFW, environmental groups, and the Pesticide Action Network were still battling pesticides, with the most effective fights being waged in the courts by attorneys from California Rural Legal Assistance (CRLA); the Center on Race, Poverty and the Environment; and the Farmworker Justice Center in Washington, D.C.[36]

In assessing the ongoing legacy of the UFW's anti-pesticide campaign, two pioneering strategies stand out: the union's use of contract provisions to ensure worker safety, and the framing of environmental hazards in a broader social justice context. Whereas the effectiveness of the contract provision strategy was limited by the union's decline after 1981, the UFW's historic role in educating the public about the concept of environmental justice has been largely overlooked. When the UFW sought to bar DDT and other dangerous pesticides from the fields in 1969, environmental problems were not being discussed in the context of deeper social injustice. In fact, many environmentalists were uncomfortable addressing such issues, which helps to explain the lack of mainstream organizational support for the UFW's struggle. Both OCAW and the UFW broke from other labor unions in the 1970s in seeking alliances with environmentalists, but it was the farmworkers movement that embodied the cause of environmental justice. The UFW did as much as any group during the 1970s and 1980s to help the public understand environmental risks in social justice terms, and the widespread emergence in the 1990s of environmental justice campaigns in low-income areas and communities of color is an important part of its legacy.[37]

In 1993, former UFW boycott leader and executive board member Jessica Govea was diagnosed with breast cancer. Govea had inspired the UFW's campaign against pesticides, and while she could not prove that she contracted cancer from working in the fields, she believed that pesticide exposure was the cause. Described by Jerry Cohen as "the heart and soul of the union when it was at its best," Govea left the UFW in 1981 and spread her commitment to social justice beyond the fields. During the 1980s, she worked with Marshall Ganz and other UFW alumni on increasing Latino voter turnout for Democratic candidates in California; and, in 1990, she developed a pilot project in New York City to train city council candidates and campaign managers from underrepresented communities.

Govea learned of her cancer after she returned from training the national leadership of the coffee-processing workers union in El Salvador, in connection with Neighbor to Neighbor. She was providing strategic and administrative guidance to the workers as they developed a plan to rebuild the union after the country's long civil war. Govea was never bitter over the circumstances that led to her cancer and did not allow the diagnosis to interfere with her work. After having a bone marrow transplant, she was even heard singing "We Shall Overcome" from her hospital bed.[38]

In 1992, Govea had joined the faculty of the Labor Studies and Employment Relations Department at Rutgers University. She later became part of Cornell's School of Industrial Relations, where she applied her broad UFW experience to training organizers, shop stewards, and union administrators affiliated with the nation's largest health care local, SEIU's Local 1199. After years spent increasing union activism among non–English-speaking immigrant farmworkers, Govea was now developing leadership among the union's Chinese immigrant home care workers. After one extensive training conducted by Govea, her associate Ken Margolies, and Local 1199 organizer David Ho, which was designed to prepare ten Chinese workers to become facilitators for other Chinese-speaking staff, one of the trainees stood up before the group and told Govea, "For the first time, I really feel like I am part of my union and part of my country." Jessica Govea was dedicated to the empowerment of immigrant workers, and this tribute was a fitting coda to a life cut short when she died of cancer at age fifty-eight in 2005.[39]

6

THE UFW GRASSROOTS
POLITICAL MODEL

Legislative Advocacy and Voter Outreach

The way I see it, everything is like a big machine with
a lot of buttons. You never know which is the one that
starts things, so you just have to go out there and push
all kinds of buttons. Pretty soon, if you go and start a
campaign, and it's not going anywhere, you know that
it's not the right approach. So you try something else.
Eliseo Medina, 1974

During the UFW's critical decade of growth, from 1966 to 1976, farmworker activists became experts in holding politicians accountable, conducting voter registration drives among low-income and minority voters,
and operating get out the vote (GOTV) drives to boost turnout in traditionally low-voting, working-class neighborhoods. The UFW responded
to political attacks from growers by adopting innovative approaches for
almost every type of electoral and legislative campaign. These strategies
brought the union victories in statewide initiative campaigns, state legislative fights, races for public office, and a major battle against the Nixon
administration.

In 1966, the farmworkers movement had no more experience with
politicians and elections than it had with boycotts. Cesar Chavez's previous job as an organizer for the Community Services Organization had
included voter registration drives, but the CSO did not make political
endorsements or engage in partisan electoral work. The UFW did have
one experienced hand, however: Fred Ross Sr., who had become a legendary electoral organizer after running Edward Roybal's winning campaign for a seat on the Los Angeles City Council in 1949. Roybal, who
was president of CSO, was the first Mexican American to win a Los Angeles city council election in more than seventy years, a victory described
as marking "the birth of Latino politics in California."[1]

Ross used the same painstaking approach to voter registration and
GOTV in the Roybal campaign that he later brought to the UFW's first

representation election at the DiGiorgio ranch in 1967, and his methods would soon become central to the union's grassroots electoral approach. Using Ross's lessons as a starting point, UFW activists were not deterred by their lack of financial resources or political experience; in fact, these circumstances forced them to pursue innovative electoral and legislative strategies. Not all of these efforts succeeded, but by "pushing all kinds of buttons" and being willing to "try something else," the UFW developed a model for grassroots voter outreach to Latino and other low-income and minority voters that has spearheaded winning progressive campaigns in subsequent years.

DEVELOPING THE UFW
ELECTORAL MODEL: 1966–1972

When Chavez began organizing farmworkers in 1962, growers retained the solid backing of local, state, and national politicians. Farmworkers could never match the growers' ability to make campaign contributions, and they lacked the numbers to outvote the opposition in local council or congressional contests. So Chavez and the union approached political battles much as they had approached the boycott: whereas boycotts could turn Central Valley–based fights into national struggles, the union sought to gain political superiority over its adversaries by becoming a statewide electoral force.

This strategy for dealing with politicians and elections became clear as early as 1966. One goal of Chavez's 1966 pilgrimage to Sacramento (described in chapter 3) was to win a show of support from Governor Edmund G. "Pat" Brown, who faced a tough reelection fight that November against Republican Ronald Reagan, the former movie actor. The UFW had asked Brown to meet with its representatives when the marchers reached Sacramento, but he refused. Chavez described Brown as "deathly afraid of the growers," noting that the governor was so "frightened" that, instead of meeting with the marchers, he spent Easter Sunday with Frank Sinatra in Southern California. When Brown later changed his mind and asked to meet with Chavez and his allies, the UFW refused the offer. Chavez said, "When he changed his mind afterward, it was too late. We didn't want him to come. We knew ultimately he couldn't do anything for us."[2]

Rather than trying to protect Brown from liberal criticism over his pro-grower stance, the UFW targeted him at the Easter Sunday rally that ended the pilgrimage. Dolores Huerta told the crowd of ten thousand:

"On behalf of all the farmworkers of this state, we unconditionally demand that the governor of this state, Edmund Brown, call a special session of the legislature to enact a collective bargaining law for the state of California. We will be satisfied with nothing less. . . . You cannot close your eyes and ears to us any longer."[3]

The UFW played hardball with Brown despite having little to offer him politically. The farmworkers had no track record of success in electoral politics; and organized labor, other than the anti-UFW Teamsters, already backed Brown. Meanwhile, the Central Valley was full of Democrats who would have shifted their votes to Reagan if they had seen Brown as an ally of Cesar Chavez. But these pragmatic political considerations did not change Chavez's insistence that Brown fully back the UFW cause. He believed that politicians who helped the farmworkers deserved overwhelming support, while those who opposed them or who equivocated in offering support invited political attack. This would be a principle that Chavez and the UFW would repeatedly apply in future years. (It turned out that even an all-out UFW effort for Brown would not have prevented his defeat by the staunchly pro-grower Ronald Reagan.)

California's 1968 Democratic presidential primary put Chavez and the UFW on the state and national political map. New York senator Robert F. Kennedy was a staunch ally, whose public support for Chavez and the farmworkers during Senate hearings in the fields in 1966 had greatly boosted national sympathy for the union, especially among Catholics. Chavez developed a close personal bond with Kennedy and considered it "heroic" that the powerful senator had publicly embraced the UFW without asking anything in return.[4]

Kennedy announced his 1968 presidential candidacy just days after joining Chavez at the end of his fast. Although the UFW was busy organizing workers and running the grape boycott, it could not pass up the prospect of electing a strong ally to the presidency. Chavez was asked to be a Kennedy delegate at the Democratic Convention, and UFW members unanimously endorsed Kennedy and committed to campaign all-out for him in California's June 6 primary. It was yet another sign that the UFW was willing to pursue a political strategy different from that of mainstream organized labor: the AFL-CIO was supporting Vice President Hubert Humphrey in the primary.

In April and May of 1968, UFW organizers spread throughout the state's Mexican American neighborhoods to build support for Kennedy. Chavez himself made as many as six public appearances a day on the senator's behalf. Rallies were held across the Central Valley. In the long-ignored and politically disenfranchised Mexican American neighbor-hoods of East Los Angeles, the UFW set up an electoral operation that included personal visits to all registered voters, phone banks, and walking committees. To build election excitement, the campaign even hired kids to hand out thousands of leaflets. A key strategy the UFW developed during the Kennedy effort was the recruitment of volunteer organizers who could be counted on to turn out their neighbors to vote on election day. These volunteers were recruited at their doors by UFW campaign workers, who were simultaneously contacting voters, training them to conduct voter outreach on the spot, and enlisting them for GOTV efforts on Kennedy's behalf. This emphasis on developing volunteer leadership was as central to the UFW's electoral work as it was for the boycott, and it would become a major component of Latino voter outreach efforts in Los Angeles three decades later.

Marshall Ganz was the chief organizer of the UFW's Kennedy campaign, and he later recalled the effort as "the model" for grassroots campaigns that the UFW and its alumni would run at the local and state levels over the next three decades. Journalist Sam Kushner observed that the UFW volunteers "worked as no other political activists. Hours meant nothing to them and they accepted hardships such as sleeping on floors in churches and meeting halls as a necessary part of the struggle." Chavez later compared the experience to organizing a strike; the fact that the UFW assembled its campaign operation without much prior electoral experience likely contributed to its functioning more as a community organizing effort than a traditional political campaign.[5]

The UFW was not the only organization helping to mobilize the Mexican American vote for Kennedy—Latino activists such as Bert Corona, head of the national "Viva Kennedy" campaign, also played key roles—but to Kennedy delegate Paul Schrade of the United Auto Workers union, "the farm workers had made the difference." Schrade's conclusion was echoed by three journalists from the *London Sunday Times*, who wrote: "In the end, the votes of Chavez's Mexican-Americans contributed most of the slender margin by which Kennedy beat McCarthy in California."[6]

The UFW's Dolores Huerta stood near Kennedy on the podium when he gave his historic victory speech at the Los Angeles Ambassador Hotel on the night of June 6, 1968, after winning the California primary. After pledging to win the presidential nomination at the next month's Democratic National Convention in Chicago, Kennedy left the stage, only to be assassinated. Kennedy's death eliminated any joy that would have resulted from the UFW's successful voter outreach and denied the union the opportunity to have its leading political ally in the White House. But, through the Kennedy campaign, the UFW proved that it could exercise statewide electoral clout, and the farmworkers movement gained experience in grassroots electoral politics that would prove vital in the years to come.

Growers Launch Political Attacks

In 1971 and 1972, the UFW increased its involvement in legislative and electoral politics in response to political attacks from growers in several states. Concerned about the increasing success of the boycott and the farmworkers movement, the American Farm Bureau Federation—the political arm of the large growers—asked legislators in several states to pass anti-farmworker laws. These measures typically outlawed boycotts and strikes at harvest time and changed election procedures to effectively deny farmworkers the right to choose a union. Opposing these measures required UFW staff to drop everything and travel to the state in question, where they had to quickly assemble political opposition. No movement would willingly divert its proactive agenda to wage such uphill defensive struggles—but having been forced to do so, the UFW gained enormous political and organizing expertise.

FORCING A VETO IN OREGON

The Oregon legislature passed an anti-farmworker law in August 1971 that the UFW did not learn about until the bill was on Governor Tom McCall's desk. The governor had a week in which to sign or veto the bill. Chavez immediately sent Fred Ross Jr. and UFW chief legal counsel Jerry Cohen up to Oregon and told them to mount an all-out "war" during that week. Cohen quickly got into the spirit of things when he told the governor, in a meeting that McCall had insisted be open to the press, "If you sign this bill, Oregon will become the Mississippi of the Northwest. We're going to put a picket line up around your state and stop people from coming in." While Cohen later acknowledged that such a threat could not have been carried out, the media loved the audacity of the assertion, and it made headlines.[7]

As Chavez called for a nationwide boycott of Oregon products, Ross arranged for farmworkers, members of the clergy, and Portland boycott supporters to set up a round-the-clock religious vigil on the steps of the capitol building in Salem. A women's vigil prayed for four days that the

governor would support justice for farmworkers, and five thousand workers came to hear Chavez denounce the bill at a rally before the state capitol. With thousands of telegrams and calls flooding McCall's office and
the UFW's threat to mount a nationwide boycott of Oregon lumber loom-
ing, McCall vetoed the bill. Describing what the UFW learned from the
victory, Ross later noted, "We generated real, measurable pressure, which
put us in a position to negotiate from a position of strength and save our
movement. We learned not to negotiate hat in hand and not to agree to
unacceptable laws."[8]

DEFEATING LEGISLATION IN FLORIDA

The UFW next confronted anti-farmworker legislation in Florida. In early
1972, the union signed contracts to represent Coca-Cola's Minute Maid
citrus workers in Florida and workers at H. P. Hood and Sons, a major
dairy firm in the northeast part of the state. Most of these workers were
African Americans who migrated up and down the Atlantic Coast, joined
during peak periods by workers brought in from the Caribbean. The
UFW's success at organizing these workers led Florida farm interests to
propose legislation that would restrain further organizing and restrict the
power of unions. Some of the legislators sponsoring the bill freely admitted
that its target was the UFW. One key provision was a ban on farmworker
hiring halls. Hiring halls run by the union prevented growers from choos-
ing which farmworkers would get work; without the halls, growers had
a surefire way to retaliate against employee complaints and union organizing. Although a similar bill had been defeated in 1971, the UFW's recent success led the Farm Bureau to make the legislation a top priority
for 1972. Eliseo Medina, who had headed the Midwest boycott and was
now a seasoned six-year UFW veteran at age twenty-five, was charged
with organizing opposition to the bill. He began his battle against Florida's
wealthy corporate farmers with fewer than twenty-five staffers from the
boycott and union field offices, some Coca-Cola workers, and no money.[9]

Since the bill included provisions that affected other unions, Medina
initially tried to join with mainstream Florida labor groups to kill the
measure. But labor officials told Medina, "Look, you're fooling your-
self. This bill is going to pass. Instead of wasting your efforts trying to
kill it, . . . compromise and get out." But compromise was not the UFW
way. Medina argued with the other unions: "Once your beginning point
is a compromise, then you're going to have to compromise on your compromise." He later recalled, "Everybody told us it couldn't be done. Well,
I guess we just didn't know any better."[10]

Eliseo Medina talks to Florida legislators, 1973.
Photo by Mark Pitt.

Medina and his allies explored many strategies for defeating the bill. An idea to use a farmworker relay system that would carry mass petitions five hundred miles from the fields to the state capital in Tallahassee appeared promising, but it was rejected because of fears that Ku Klux Klan members in rural areas might attack the farmworkers. The group then decided on a letter-writing campaign and launched an aggressive outreach effort to churches and schools in cities such as Miami and Jacksonville, forming local committees to solicit letters. People were asked to contribute the dime for postage, as the UFW did not even have money for stamps. Medina used the opposition campaign as an organizing opportunity. He traveled to labor camps to meet workers in their homes, got them to write letters expressing their opposition to the bill, and informed them about the UFW. In two months, the UFW had amassed twenty thousand personal letters opposing the measure. Medina then brought committees of workers to meet every member of the state legislature, so they could explain why the hiring hall was important and why the bill should be defeated. Many legislators had never previously spoken directly to farmworkers and were impressed with their ability to articulate their concerns. Establishing a personal connection between workers and key decision-makers was a UFW hallmark, later adopted by SEIU's Justice for Janitors campaigns and other struggles for economic justice.[11]

In the weeks prior to the legislative hearing, Medina seized on two events to build opposition to the bill. The first was a report of a typhoid epidemic in Florida's most highly regarded labor camp. Medina learned that the local health department had known for two years that the camp's running water was contaminated but had taken no action. Now county officials were trying to hush up the typhoid outbreak, in order to protect Florida's tourist industry. To prevent a cover-up, the UFW convinced congressional investigators to inspect the state's labor camps, and they found so many health violations that it appeared Florida officials had recklessly endangered farmworkers' lives. As Medina framed it, a state that was jeopardizing farmworkers' health was now trying to pass a bill that would deny them basic labor rights. He got a second opportunity to link the mistreatment of farmworkers to the pending bill when the UFW uncovered a case of a labor contractor who had kept twenty-nine farmworkers as slaves. Again utilizing the tactic of having the victims of injustice tell their stories to decision-makers, Medina brought one of the men to the state capital to talk to the media and to give powerful testimony at the legislative hearing. By the time the anti-farmworker bill was slated to be heard, in March 1973, the public mood had shifted. As Medina recalled, "All of a sudden people were saying, 'What are they trying to do to farm workers?'"[12]

Trained by Chavez and Fred Ross Sr. never to take victory for granted, Medina used the days leading up to the hearing to organize a phone bank that resulted in about a thousand telegrams being sent to key legislators. Farmworkers then flooded legislators' offices on the eve of the hearing. By the time the vote occurred, Florida legislators wanted nothing more than to get far away from the anti-farmworker measure. The bill was killed in committee by a fifteen to seven vote.[13]

The UFW proved in Florida that it could do more than rely on the "outsider" tactics of boycotts and marches; it also understood how to win on the political battleground. Rather than relying on the insider lobbying used by other Florida unions, the UFW showed how community organizing tactics could bring success in the legislative arena.

THE ARIZONA RECALL

In Arizona in 1972, Governor Jack Williams signed a Farm Bureau–sponsored bill directed against farmworkers forty-five minutes after it passed the legislature, perhaps seeking to avoid the pressure the UFW had placed on Oregon's Governor McCall. Williams's action led Chavez to initiate a spiritual fast (discussed in chapter 3) and also to launch a campaign "to make the governor who signed the bill pay for it." Chavez asked Marshall Ganz, LeRoy Chatfield, and Jim Drake to consider the best strategy, and they came up with the idea of trying to recall the governor. The UFW assumed that the recall election would have a low voter turnout, so it embarked on a massive voter registration drive among farmworkers and their allies that enabled them to sign the recall petitions and later vote.[14]

This was the campaign that led Cesar Chavez to adopt the battle cry *"sí se puede!"* (it can be done!) in response to some Arizona supporters who claimed *"no se puede"* (it cannot be done). In only four and a half months, the UFW registered almost 100,000 new voters, most of whom were Navajos, Mexican Americans, and poor people who had not previously voted. The group also got 168,000 signatures on recall petitions, which was 40 percent of the total number of voters in Arizona's previous gubernatorial election.[15] Collecting such a staggering number of signatures in such a short time was a remarkable accomplishment, considering that the UFW had no labor contracts in Arizona, had to import many of its volunteers from California and other states, and had no funds to hire paid signature gatherers. The union popularized the tactic of mass petitions, as the ironing boards and tables once used for distributing boycott materials became the tools of the trade for gathering signatures on recall petitions. The UFW proved in Arizona that it could go virtually anywhere and quickly assemble sufficient staff to implement mass petition drives, which helped deter the future passage of anti-farmworker legislation.

The Arizona attorney general eventually blocked the recall election, handing a short-term victory to the UFW's adversaries. But the entry of the UFW into Arizona politics changed the state. That same year, the union's massive voter registration drive and its voter outreach to long-disenfranchised Mexican Americans and Navajos helped to send four Mexican Americans and two Navajos to the state legislature, and Mexican Americans were elected to local councils, judgeships, and school boards across the state. In 1974, Arizona elected its first Mexican American governor, Raul Castro, whose 4,100-vote margin of victory was attributed to his 7,000-vote margin among newly registered Navajos. Mexican Americans were elected as majority leader of the state senate and minority leader in the lower house of the legislature. Cesar Chavez had vowed to send a message by taking on Arizona's governor over the anti-farmworker bill, and the UFW clearly did just that.[16]

CALIFORNIA'S PROP 22

While battles against anti-farmworker measures in Oregon, Florida, and Arizona were important, these campaigns were relatively short-lived and hastily organized; none gave the UFW the opportunity to develop an ongoing, statewide, grassroots electoral model. The union had mobilized Mexican American and low-income voters during Robert Kennedy's 1968 California presidential campaign, but it had not built on this experience in subsequent years.

But the UFW was forced back into the California electoral arena in 1972 to face a political challenge that threatened the union's very existence. Growers had tried to pass an anti-UFW measure in the legislature in 1971, but the union mobilized forty-five hundred people in a rally in front of the state capitol building to successfully defeat it. Farm interests then put an initiative on the ballot, known as Proposition 22, that included the standard provisions forbidding boycotts and strikes and added such extreme provisions as barring farmworker unions from bargaining on work rules.

Chavez assigned LeRoy Chatfield to head the No on Prop 22 effort, which became one of the largest grassroots initiative campaigns in California history. The lettuce boycott came to a virtual halt as boycott volunteers joined hundreds of farmworkers who traveled across the state registering voters, handing out leaflets, and waiting in parking lots to ask drivers to place bumper stickers saying "Justice for Farmworkers, No on 22" on their cars. After growers paid for billboards all over Los Angeles using the misleading slogan "For Farm Workers Rights, Yes on 22!" the UFW responded with "human billboards"—volunteers standing on freeway off-ramps and major streets holding "No on 22" signs. After the *Los Angeles Times* did a story on the novel tactic, which further publicized the No on 22 message, volunteers encouraged motorists to honk to show support. This may have been the first activist campaign to use human billboards on such a widespread scale and as part of an organized strategy.[17]

The No on 22 campaign initiated a new approach to electoral politics that would become a prototype for the successful grassroots labor campaigns that began reshaping Los Angeles and California politics in the late 1990s. In many respects, the UFW's model replicated on a larger scale the detailed approach that Fred Ross Sr. had developed for winning the union's first representation election at DiGiorgio farms. Ellen Eggers, who extended her summer stint with the UFW in Los Angeles to help fight Prop 22 and ended up staying on with the farmworkers for fifteen years, describes the incredibly tight organization of the campaign:

> We always kept totals of what we did and reported in to our coordinator. Whether it was bumpers "stickered," leaflets passed out, voters registered, or declarations signed, we always kept accurate tallies. The numbers were turned in, added up, and reported on, probably to Cesar and LeRoy, but

always, also, to those of us who were "out there." The union leadership was excellent about this. Always keeping us going and lifting our spirits by showing us that our little piece of the puzzle was important. Each of us was doing our job, and as grinding and boring as it could be at times, we knew we were part of something much larger.[18]

At the end of each day's billboarding, the Reverend Chris Hartmire announced how many cars had seen the signs, a number based on UFW research on traffic patterns at the various intersections. This recordkeeping reinforced the importance of the volunteers' efforts, a critical encouragement for an activity that required people to wake up at 4:00 A.M., be out on freeways by 6:00 A.M., and then continue working into the evening. Boycott volunteers normally worked six days a week, but the Prop 22 campaign required an all-week, morning-to-night commitment.[19]

It is possible to get a sense of just how persistent UFW volunteers were by looking at the union's effort to have Prop 22 removed from the ballot. In a two-week period in September 1972, volunteers collected six thousand declarations from people who had originally signed the petition to put Prop 22 on the ballot, swearing that they had been misled about the purpose of the initiative. The volunteers had to obtain the phone numbers and addresses of signers, knock on their doors, inquire about whether they had been deceived as to the measure's real intent, and then ask them to sign a preprinted declaration attesting to the misrepresentation. As Eggers noted, "This was not altogether an easy task, as you might imagine. We were telling them they had been swindled by a stranger into signing a legal document. Now we wanted them to sign another legal document based upon what we (another stranger) were telling them." When you consider how many doors had to be knocked to get these six thousand declarations in just two weeks, it gives some sense of the unprecedented grassroots force assembled by the UFW. Although Secretary of State Jerry Brown's lawsuit based on the declarations failed to knock Prop 22 off the ballot, the process of gathering the declarations facilitated the UFW's door-to-door campaign against the measure.[20]

Knowing that Latino voters would strongly oppose Prop 22, the UFW targeted this constituency by establishing precinct operations in East Los Angeles and other Latino communities across the state. In East L.A.'s Lincoln Park, the union set up a tent city to house the hundreds of farmworkers coming from the fields to help the campaign in the month before the election. Boycott staff across the nation had also been redirected to the campaign. Although Chavez was still recovering from his Arizona fast, he toured the state attacking Prop 22 as a "fraud which would destroy the farm workers union in California." The UFW had strong backing from the Democratic Party, the AFL-CIO, California's Catholic bishops, and Secretary of State Brown. Growers spent nearly $500,000 (a large sum by 1972 standards) on television ads supporting Prop 22, but they were outmatched by the UFW's massive grassroots effort. The initiative was defeated by over one million votes, 58 percent to 42 percent, despite California voters' strong support for pro-grower Republican Richard Nixon over pro-UFW Democrat George McGovern on the same ballot. As Dick Meister and Ann Loftis conclude in their book on the farmworkers' struggle, after Prop 22, "no one could doubt the union's ability to wage an extremely effective political campaign, and no other state would make a serious attempt to enact such legislation."[21]

In addition to battling growers at the state level, the UFW was also fending off attacks from the National Labor Relations Board. President Nixon opposed the UFW boycott and publicly criticized Chavez. "Nixon Eats Grapes" buttons, showing a jowly Nixon stuffing himself with non-union grapes, were a popular sales item at boycott tables. In March 1972, the chief counsel of the NLRB, a Nixon appointee, sued the UFW to stop its use of the secondary boycott. The suit claimed that the union's secondary boycotts against sellers of non-union grapes, lettuce, and wine were illegal because the boycotts also included nine small wineries with nonagricultural workers.

In response, the UFW began a massive letter-writing campaign, picketed Republican Party headquarters in 150 cities, and threatened protests at the 1972 Republican National Convention scheduled for San Diego. Over one million letters were sent to Republican Party chair Robert Dole. Two months later, the NLRB dropped the suit in exchange for the UFW agreeing to end secondary boycotts involving the small wineries. While the UFW missed out on holding massive protests at the Republican Convention, its lettuce boycott got a boost at the Democratic Convention when it was formally endorsed and included in the party's platform. A leading lettuce grower targeted by the boycott said that the convention publicity reduced lettuce shipments from Salinas by 20 percent, a loss of $200,000 a day.[22]

In less than two years, grower attacks had transformed the UFW into a sophisticated political and electoral operation. UFW organizers had learned the voting patterns of every nook and cranny in California, which would prove handy in future years. A union whose Prop 22 campaign leader LeRoy Chatfield had no prior experience running election campaigns, and which once operated according to Eliseo Medina's philosophy of "you just go out there and push all kinds of buttons," quickly became the era's leading training ground for Latino and labor political organizers. In addition to boosting the skills of UFW organizers, the campaigns in Oregon, Florida, Arizona, and California during 1971 and 1972 increased Latino voter registration and gave many activists their first experience in mobilizing Latinos for political action. It also led the UFW to create an intense, precinct-based model of outreach to low-income and minority voters at a time when most political campaigns were increasingly relying on television advertising.[23]

HOLDING POLITICIANS ACCOUNTABLE

Following its statewide electoral success in 1972, the UFW went on to play a leading role in Jerry Brown's 1974 campaign for California governor. After eight years of hostility from Ronald Reagan, Chavez and the UFW felt it was imperative to elect an ally to the governor's office. Brown's Catholic background made him particularly sympathetic to La Causa; as secretary of state, for example, he had unsuccessfully sued to remove Prop 22 from the ballot. The former Jesuit seminarian had also developed a close personal relationship with Chavez. Brown saw the UFW as an important political ally, and he hired LeRoy Chatfield as a top campaign aide.

Despite Brown's sympathy for Chavez and the farmworkers' cause, he was a politician, and, as a former aide put it, "You had to rattle his cage a bit if you wanted to get his attention." Nobody was happier to rattle a politician's cage than Chavez, as became clear during Brown's campaign. In 1974, attempting to assess support for a farm labor law, the UFW had its allies introduce legislation similar to what the union hoped to enact after Brown's election. But when the UFW sought Brown's endorsement of the measure, the candidate was evasive. Resorting to the UFW's longstanding tactic of demanding political accountability, Ross Jr. and Sandy Nathan (an attorney and Jerry Cohen's top assistant) held an unannounced sit-in in September, with farmworkers and college students carrying the union's red and black Aztec eagle flag into the Brown for Governor San Francisco headquarters. Chatfield, who had helped to organize Chavez's initial fast and had headed the union's No on Prop 22 campaign, was running this office and now found himself the target of his own tactics. Jerry Cohen had instructed Nathan that the UFW delegation was not to leave the building until Jerry Brown got on the phone and agreed to publicly support the pending legislation.[24]

The event threw Brown's campaign "into a tizzy," as the candidate's race with his Republican opponent was tightening. Brown's staffers raised concerns that "if Cesar had undertaken an extended, well-publicized sit-in or picket line, he could have cost Jerry 25,000 votes in the Mexican-American community, enough perhaps to swing the election the other way." Brown immediately began making calls around the state, talking to leading Democrats, including the heads of the assembly and the state senate, as he put together his position. At the end of the day, Brown called Nathan and agreed to support the bill. Nathan, Ross, and the UFW delegation then left the office. The next day, before the media learned about the UFW sit-in, Brown publicly announced his full support for the proposed bill, which included a particularly controversial provision invalidating contracts the growers had signed with the Teamsters. As Brown biographer J. D. Lorenz put it, Chavez "had delivered his rabbit punch at just the instant in the campaign when Jerry was most vulnerable." Although Brown did not appreciate Chavez's tactics, he spent the balance of the campaign emphasizing that one of his top priorities would be signing a farm labor bill.[25]

The UFW's hard-nosed approach to politicians was also demonstrated when its 1974 bill ran into problems from liberal West Los Angeles assembly member Howard Berman, who introduced a competing farm labor bill that tilted more toward growers. When Berman refused to drop his sponsorship, the UFW's hundred-strong Los Angeles boycott team spent a Sunday leafleting his district. The leaflets attacked Berman's position and urged his constituents to write or call him to express their opposition. The UFW also convinced top Democratic officials to call Berman. On Monday, he asked the UFW to call off the campaign. Although he did not follow through on his commitment to drop the bill, it ceased to move in the assembly. The UFW's willingness to play hardball with Berman had the additional benefit of turning the future congressional representative into a strong ally. In 1980, the UFW initiated a major intraparty fight in Sacramento when it backed Majority Leader Berman's attempt to replace fellow Democrat Leo McCarthy as assembly Speaker. McCarthy had never been a UFW ally, and his battle with Berman created bitter rifts among Democrats. When the dust cleared, a third candidate, Willie Brown, was elected Speaker. Although Chavez was unable to get Berman elected, the UFW achieved its goal of replacing McCarthy with a Speaker who would defend its interests: Brown assured the UFW that he would not allow pro-grower legislation to pass the assembly.

After Jerry Brown took office in January 1975, he avoided meeting with Chavez to discuss plans for enacting a farm labor law. Chavez's response to this snub was predictable. When Fred Ross Jr. organized the March 1975 march against Gallo to pressure the company to support farm labor legislation (described in chapter 1), Chavez announced at the rally of twenty thousand that if Brown broke his promises to the UFW, "we may have to march on Sacramento as we did when his daddy was in office." This threat did more than simply "rattle the cage" of Brown and his administration. Among Brown's staff, Chavez's threat conjured up images of "ten thousand" farmworkers: "dressed in their straw hats and carrying the red and black flags and marching [to Sacramento] behind the sign of the Virgin of Guadalupe, they would make a nice 'visual' on the evening news." Brown staffers feared that the farmworkers would "stay on the television screens as long as it took," would pray and hold vigils; they envisioned that "women would be kneeling on the capitol steps" while "Chavez fasts."[26]

In other words, Chavez's public threat to Brown had conjured up a virtual catalog of the UFW's previously successful tactics—now, even the threat of their use became part of the movement's power. While Brown was motivated by the threat of UFW actions against him, he also recognized that maintaining a strong alliance with Chavez and the farmworkers had many positive sides. Given Brown's interest in seeking the presidency in 1976, he surely felt that "the boycott network would be very useful in building a grassroots campaign" for his presidential bid.[27]

Chavez's pressure and the value of the UFW and its charismatic leader in boosting the governor's political standing finally led Brown to institute the pro-farmworker policies he had long claimed to support. The nation's first Agricultural Labor Relations Act was signed into law in June 1975 and took effect in August. The UFW reciprocated, as was its practice, by lending Marshall Ganz and other key staff to coordinate Brown's 1976 and 1980 presidential campaigns. Cesar Chavez even gave the nominating speech for Brown at the 1976 Democratic Convention.

PROP 14: THE UFW TAKES THE OFFENSIVE

The UFW's defeat of Prop 22 in 1972, its key role in the election of Jerry Brown in 1974, and the enactment of the Agricultural Labor Relations Act in 1975 enhanced Cesar Chavez's confidence in the union's ability to win California elections. This led him to promote a farm labor initiative on the November 1976 ballot primarily aimed at preventing legislative interference with the funding of the Agricultural Labor Relations Board. Although some of the issues the initiative addressed were quite technical, Chavez was so confident that the voters who had backed the UFW in 1972 would do so again that he vowed, "We're going to teach the growers a lesson they'll never forget once and for all." The union collected 720,000 signatures on initiative petitions in just twenty-nine days, a remarkable show of strength for an all-volunteer effort. Most California initiatives reach the ballot by partially or entirely relying on paid signature gatherers. Growers were so impressed by the UFW's display of grassroots mobilizing that they soon agreed to most of the provisions included in the ballot measure. Nevertheless, Chavez was tired of having to fight over implementation of the 1975 Agricultural Labor Relations Act, and Proposition 14 proceeded to the ballot.[28]

In many ways, the campaign was a remarkable tribute to the grassroots political machine Chavez and the UFW had built. Prop 14 volunteers were seemingly everywhere, and the campaign exceeded the successful Prop 22 effort in money raised and volunteer hours spent. Prop 14 volunteer Larry Tramutola, who had worked for the UFW for years and later became a leading California campaign consultant, described the effort as "probably the best statewide grassroots campaign you can imagine." Marshall Ganz, by now recognized as one of the nation's leading political strategists, managed the campaign. Prop 14 brought virtually the entire nationwide staff together for the first time, and the national UFW boycott structure was transformed into a statewide political operation. The campaign also built working relationships among boycott staff that would later benefit the labor movement. For example, Susan Sachen, who had spent years working on the Boston boycott, met Mark Sharwood, a Midwest boycotter, while working for Prop 14 in East Los Angeles. After leaving the UFW in 1982, Sharwood worked with Ganz to elect San Diego's first woman mayor in 1985. Sachen was working on SEIU's first Justice for Janitors campaign in Denver in 1987 when she recruited Sharwood as an SEIU organizer, and he then spent the next two decades working with other UFW alumni to organize immigrant janitors.[29]

Although the Prop 14 campaign enhanced activists' electoral skills and established long-term working relationships among UFW veterans, the measure suffered a landslide defeat. Some voters were simply unwilling to make changes only a year after the ALRA's passage. But Prop 14 was hurt most by a provision granting labor organizers a constitutional right to enter fields to meet workers. State regulations upheld by the California Supreme Court already granted organizers a right of access, but Chavez was tired of growers denying this right and local sheriffs arresting organizers for trespassing. Prop 14 sought to enshrine the right of access in the state constitution. This provision, however, allowed growers to frame Prop 14 as an attack on homeowner and privacy rights by "big government." Opponents ran television commercials in which a farmer and homeowner expressed fear for his daughter's privacy and safety if union organizers—assumed to be nonwhite—had unrestricted access to their property. Even more effective were statewide newspaper ads offering the passionate testimony of a Japanese American farmer who had been sent to an internment camp during World War II. The farmer, whose photo appeared in the ad, linked his wartime deprivations to the battle against Prop 14: "I was 20 years old and I gave up my personal rights without a fight," he said. "Never again."[30]

Prop 14 was the last time Chavez and the UFW put a ballot measure before the California electorate. The UFW remained as politically involved as ever, but instead sought to win the support of California legislators through lobbying, campaign donations, and distributing workers for get out the vote operations.

Despite Prop 14's defeat, Chavez and the UFW in the decade from 1966 to 1976 developed a model for labor and Latino political involvement that laid the framework for today's grassroots campaigns. The farmworkers movement brought community organizing tactics and strategies—voter registration drives, mass petition drives, intensive door-to-door and street outreach, public visibility events to catch the attention of voters and the media, and election day voter outreach efforts—into the electoral and legislative arena. In contrast, mainstream labor unions did little to mobilize their rank-and-file members. As one union member described it, while the UFW was running grassroots electoral campaigns, other unions' political programs focused on "writing checks to political candidates and party organizations, lobbying entrenched members of Congress, and— shortly before Election Day—sending mailings to union members informing them of our endorsements."[31] The UFW also sought to increase Latino voting at a time when most campaigns ignored infrequent Latino voters. UFW activists developed particular expertise in the strategy and tactics necessary to boost voter turnout among Latinos, immigrants, and low-income workers. This expertise paid particular dividends in California, where many of the activists continued to work and where the number of infrequent Latino voters and those eligible to vote but not registered was highest.

THE 1980s: EXPANDING
THE UFW ELECTORAL MODEL

Because of their experience in operating statewide grassroots election campaigns, many UFW alumni were hired to run mainstream election campaigns in the 1980s. These veterans used these campaigns to enhance and expand the UFW electoral outreach model, laying the foundation for organized labor's successful voter mobilization strategies in the twenty-first century. The electoral approach developed by former UFW activists in the 1980s included aggressive vote-by-mail campaigns, computer-assisted targeting of infrequent (occasional) voters for GOTV operations, door-to-door voter registration, the use of house meetings to build the campaign volunteer base, more-intensive voter outreach, and the creation of city and statewide precinct operations.

The first such campaign was the attempted recall of San Francisco mayor Dianne Feinstein in April 1983, initiated by an obscure group called the White Panthers. Angry over Feinstein's support for gun control legislation, the White Panthers collected thirty-five thousand signatures in favor of the recall. Many of those who signed were from the gay and lesbian community, as well as progressives, who were angry about Feinstein's veto of domestic partners legislation the preceding December. Although the recall's prospects for success seemed remote, the mayor did not take victory for granted; she also saw defeating the recall as a way to discourage challengers in her bid for reelection that November.[32]

Faced with getting people to the polls during an unusual April 26 election, Feinstein used her virtually unlimited budget to retain the top campaign strategists available. Prominent political consultant Clint Reilly managed the overall campaign, and UFW veterans Fred Ross Sr., Fred Ross Jr., Larry Tramutola, and Scott Washburn ran the field effort. Accustomed to operating on shoestring budgets, these four field organizers showed what they could accomplish when given greater resources. One of their key innovations was a massive drive to get opponents of the recall to vote by mail. This labor-intensive effort required volunteers to make contact with the voters by phone or door knocking and give them a form to officially request an absentee ballot, which would then be mailed to the registrar. Campaign volunteers then had to recontact the voters to make sure that they had mailed the completed ballot back to the registrar. This effort, which resembled the UFW's door-to-door efforts to collect legal declarations during the Prop 22 campaign, was designed to secure the participation of infrequent voters as well as those who might forget to show up at the polls (since April 26 was an unusual election day). The UFW veterans assembled what may have been the largest grassroots campaign in San Francisco's history; and after all the door knocking, phone calling, and large campaign rallies every weekend, the recall was defeated with an astonishing 80 percent of the voters supporting the mayor.[33]

Also in 1983, Marshall Ganz joined with Reilly to run Maureen O'Connor's campaign to become San Diego's mayor. Although she lost narrowly (but won a special election in 1985 after the incumbent mayor resigned, becoming the city's first woman mayor), Ganz and Reilly used the campaign to advance the occasional-voter methodology conceived during the Feinstein recall. Candidates are always interested in reaching potentially supportive constituencies who otherwise might not vote. In this election, technological advances in collecting and utilizing voter data enabled Ganz and Reilly to more systematically identify which specific voters to target. The key was access to individual voting histories. According to Ganz, the traditional GOTV approach could identify precincts containing a high number of infrequent voters but could not distinguish individual voters within the precinct. Outreach staff were thus forced to contact all three or four hundred registered voters in the precinct rather than the eighty or ninety infrequent voters who needed to be contacted to ensure their vote. With more specific identification, the campaign could focus its GOTV resources on those voters. Since a huge bloc of occasional voters consisted of low-income and minority voters, who were more likely to support progressive causes, getting them to the polls could easily spell the difference between victory and defeat. While a far more sophisticated occasional-voter methodology is now common in political campaigns, the fundamental assumption of the methodology—that GOTV resources should be carefully targeted rather than spread throughout the electorate—would prove critical to expanding Latino voter outreach.[34]

In 1986, California senator Alan Cranston sought to apply this enhanced UFW electoral model in his reelection campaign. Cranston found himself in a tight race two months before the election, as he sought a fourth term in the U.S. Senate against a wealthy Republican opponent. He asked Ganz to put together a statewide field campaign to increase minority voter turnout. Ganz set up operations in San Diego, East and South Central Los Angeles, and Oakland. Jessica Govea ran the Los Angeles operation, with a team that included the future mayor of Los Angeles, Antonio Villaraigosa, and the future head of the hotel workers union in Los Angeles, Maria Elena Durazo. Cranston's decision to put his electoral future in the hands of Ganz's grassroots GOTV effort was a significant step for a senator who had won three previous Senate races without a field operation.[35]

Cranston had been elected California's controller in 1958 through grassroots electoral mobilizing. But, like other politicians, particularly in the large state of California, he had subsequently relied primarily on television campaign ads for statewide races. This time, however, Cranston felt that television ads would not produce the huge turnout of low-income and minority voters he needed to win. He was familiar with the UFW's success in building statewide grassroots campaigns, and he gave Ganz an unlimited budget to work the farmworkers' magic in the campaign's last stages. Cranston's decision to turn to a field campaign only six weeks before the election proved prescient—a solid turnout in the state's Latino and African American neighborhoods brought Cranston victory by a 1 percent margin among the millions of votes cast.[36] Senator Cranston recognized in the mid-1980s what other mainstream politicians did not: the UFW's grassroots field mobilization model represented the best strategy for reversing the steady decline in working-class and low-income voting that was tilting the electorate toward the middle and upper classes.

After his narrow victory, Cranston provided funding for Ganz to set up an ongoing statewide field operation, named the Campaign for Participation and Democracy (CPD), which was intended to help secure California's electoral votes for the Democratic presidential candidate in 1988. Ganz recruited longtime UFW colleagues Govea and Washburn to help run the operation, and Washburn recruited a young African American named Martin Ludlow. While the CPD registered thousands of new voters and ran a strong precinct operation for Democrat Michael Dukakis's presidential campaign against George H. W. Bush in 1988, the Republicans carried California, as they had in every presidential election since 1968. Even worse, Cranston had funded the CPD through donations from Charles Keating, a central figure in the multibillion-dollar savings and loan scandal of 1987. Cranston was among five senators eventually reprimanded for the scandal. As Harold Meyerson observed, "Cranston surely knew this was very bad money that he was putting to a very good cause." The CPD did not survive Cranston's fall.[37]

In 1987, Ganz teamed with Fred Ross Jr. and UFW veteran Paul Milne to run the field campaign for a longtime Democratic Party fundraiser and former California Democratic Party chair who was trying to win election to Congress in San Francisco. The candidate's name was Nancy Pelosi. The congressional seat had once been held by Phil Burton, a leg-

Congresswoman Nancy Pelosi with Fred Ross Jr. at a Neighbor to Neighbor meeting.
Photo by Mark Pitt.

end in California politics; after his death in 1983, his wife, Sala Burton,
had assumed the office. But it was now vacant because of her death in
early 1987, and a special election had been called. Earlier, in 1982, when
Phil Burton's brother John gave up his adjacent San Francisco congressional seat, the powerful Burton had offered to back Pelosi for the position. At that time, she demurred, feeling that her kids were too young
for her to go off to Congress. Now Sala Burton had summoned Pelosi to
her deathbed to urge her to run for the seat, and Pelosi agreed. Although
she was the chair of the state Democratic Party, she was relatively unknown in San Francisco and faced a tough primary opponent in progressive supervisor Harry Britt. Britt's supporters saw his candidacy as
a historic opportunity to elect the first openly gay member of Congress.[38]

Pelosi's backers emphasized the importance of electing a woman who
would know how to get things done in Washington, D.C. In order to
overcome the perception that Pelosi was a wealthy socialite who could
not relate to average San Franciscans, the UFW alums followed the strat-

egy initiated by Fred Ross Sr. in the 1950s and used by Cesar Chavez in 1962 to launch the UFW: the house meeting. Ross Jr. and Milne were experts in organizing house meetings, both from their work with the UFW and from their ongoing effort to build Neighbor to Neighbor into a mass organization that could stop American military aid to Central America (described in chapter 2). In an election campaign of only sixty days, Ross and Milne arranged for Pelosi to attend 120 house meetings.[39]

Few San Franciscans knew that Pelosi's father was Tommy D'Alesandro, who had served in Congress and had been mayor of Baltimore during a political career in which he won twenty-two straight elections. Her brother had also served as Baltimore's mayor, so politics ran in her blood. From the outset, Pelosi worked a room like a veteran campaigner. Ross observed that she had "an organizer's instinct. An organizer has to have imagination, has to have a very strategic mind about how to think about a campaign, how to organize a campaign and how to win it. What are the vulnerabilities of the other side? What are the resources you can amass? She understands all of that."[40] Pelosi won the race by four thousand votes, launching a political career at age forty-seven that would make her the first female House Speaker in 2007.

The value of the farmworkers' grassroots mobilization approach was further confirmed by the work of two UFW veterans in the 1987 San Francisco mayor's race. Larry Tramutola and Richie Ross both began careers as political consultants after leaving the UFW. Tramutola focused on building field campaigns, while Ross specialized in direct mail and had become the chief political consultant for the California Democratic Party. In 1987, Tramutola and Ross were working to elect Art Agnos, then a member of the state assembly, whose chief competitor in the mayor's race was John Molinari, president of the San Francisco Board of Supervisors.[41]

San Francisco residents had seen the UFW campaign model in action during the Feinstein recall and Pelosi's special congressional election, but both of those campaigns were unusually short, only two months' duration. In contrast, the San Francisco mayor's race allowed Tramutola and Ross to spend nearly a year recruiting volunteers, holding house meetings, and finding a coordinator for nearly every precinct in the city. As in the UFW's No on Prop 22 campaign, they kept detailed daily counts of virtually any campaign action that could be tabulated: voters contacted, signs put up, calls made, new volunteers recruited, and literature distributed. Progress reports were updated daily on large butcher-paper displays in the campaign headquarters, and mass campaign meetings were held weekly for the vast army of volunteers. At the start of the campaign, Agnos trailed by more than 20 percent—and even four months before election day, many political insiders felt that he could not win. But the daily phone calls and door knocking from Tramutola's massive field campaign steadily chipped away at Molinari's lead, and polls showed Agnos pulling ahead as the election approached. The combination of the field effort and a state-of-the-art GOTV campaign that brought occasional voters to the polls in droves resulted in Agnos winning the primary election with 48 percent of the vote. He then won a whopping 70 percent in the runoff.[42]

By the late 1980s, it was clear to those familiar with the Feinstein, O'Connor, Cranston, Pelosi, and Agnos campaigns that grassroots mobilizing could overcome television advertising as a strategy for bringing low-income, infrequent, and minority voters to the polls. But as much as this enhanced UFW model had succeeded in winning these elections, it would take UFW veteran Miguel Contreras to institutionalize this successful model, first in Los Angeles and then throughout California.

7

THE LABOR-LATINO ALLIANCE

MIGUEL CONTRERAS, THE "ARCHITECT"

The story of how Miguel Contreras used the UFW electoral model to transform Los Angeles politics, as well as boost Latino voter turnout in California, begins with his birth in 1952 in the small Central Valley farm town
of Dinuba. Contreras and his five brothers worked with their parents in
the fields, picking grapes and tree fruit. When Contreras was a teenager,
his family became active with the UFW. He and his father were later elected
union leaders at their ranch, and Miguel was a picket captain during the
strike that began in 1973 after grape growers across California refused
to renew their UFW contracts. He was arrested eighteen times for violating anti-picketing injunctions. Those were the days when the UFW was
running multiple boycotts in addition to organizing in the fields, and Cesar
Chavez was always on the lookout for potential leaders. He asked Contreras to join the union staff, and the young man spent more than two
years in Toronto, organizing support for the grape boycott.[1]

In Canada, Contreras was supervised by two of the UFW's most talented strategists, Marshall Ganz and Jessica Govea. Ganz acquired some
insight into Contreras's ability to build relationships with people who
could help, as it quickly became clear that, of all the UFW staff in Toronto,
Miguel had found (a) the most places to stay, (b) the most places to eat,
and (c) the most overcoats. How had he done this? Ganz recalled, "For
single male farmworkers who were working on the boycott, Father
Robert Madden, rector of St. Basil's Seminary, had offered housing, meals
(including an open kitchen), and use of the facilities, including television, pool tables, et cetera, for the duration of the boycott. So the first
people Miguel organized in Toronto were Basilians. He learned that they
took a special interest in you if they thought you could be recruited [to
their order]. So it turns out the rooms, meals, and overcoats came from
Jesuits, Dominicans, Paulists, Franciscans, and ordinary parish priests.

Miguel Contreras in his office at the Los Angeles County Federation of Labor, with pictures of Cesar Chavez and the UFW logo in the background, 2002. Photo by Stephanie Diani.

Somehow, it seems, they had all gotten the idea that Miguel was a 'hot prospect.'"[2]

Ganz believed that Contreras found his calling in Toronto. When California's Agricultural Labor Relations Act passed in 1975, Contreras joined other boycott staff in returning to the fields to organize farmworkers for union elections. He then became a UFW contracts negotiator, a departure from his organizing experience, which was a factor in his leaving the UFW in 1977. Along with other former UFW staff, he began organizing for the San Francisco Hotel Employees and Restaurant Employees union, Local 2 (HERE, the precursor to UNITE HERE). UFW veteran Larry Tramutola, who worked with Contreras during this period, observed, "Miguel really came into his own when he began working with Local 2. He had an engaging personality, was a fun guy to be around, and, because he recognized the power of organizing, he attracted good people." Contreras became staff director for Local 2 and helped coordinate a citywide twenty seven-day hotel strike in 1980. The strike produced the greatest increase in wages and benefits in Local 2's history, and Contreras was soon appointed as a HERE international representative.[3]

In 1978, Marshall Ganz assembled field campaigns in cities across

A young Miguel Contreras.
Photo courtesy of LACFL.

California for Governor Jerry Brown's reelection campaign. Contreras was the area coordinator for a portion of East Los Angeles, working with his Toronto boycott colleague Jessica Govea. Joining them were Victor Griego, who later became a career political organizer in Los Angeles, and Richard Polanco, who went on to serve in the state legislature from 1986 to 2002. Polanco chaired the Latino Legislative Caucus from 1990 to 2002 and authored the legislation creating a California state holiday honoring Cesar Chavez. Ganz described his East L.A. group as an organizer's "dream team." The group followed the UFW's door-to-door precinct work model that had worked so successfully in East Los Angeles during the 1968 Robert Kennedy for President campaign. Through his work in Brown's reelection campaign, Contreras gained experience with the most effective Latino electoral outreach model of its time—a model he would later improve upon when he became head of the Los Angeles County Federation of Labor nearly two decades later.[4]

In 1980, Contreras joined Ganz in organizing for Brown's ill-conceived presidential bid. He had the unenviable task of getting Democratic primary voters in North Milwaukee to abandon incumbent president Jimmy Carter for California's young governor. The Wisconsin primary campaign culminated with movie director Francis Ford Coppola engineering a high-tech television broadcast from the state capital that showed, among other oddities, candidate Brown with holes in his head. Contreras was not happy with the campaign but stuck it out. After the summer 1980 Democratic Convention, Contreras, representing the HERE international, returned to the task of rebuilding troubled HERE locals in San Francisco, San Diego, and Los Angeles. He also spent considerable time organizing undocumented workers in Las Vegas, which soon became a HERE stronghold under the leadership of Vincent Sirabella and John Wilhelm. Contreras noted that when he traveled throughout the nation organizing members and staffing picket lines for HERE, "it was an extension of Cesar. Everywhere I went I ran into farm worker organizers."[5]

In 1986, Contreras was working for Sirabella and the HERE International when Ganz invited him to his home on the California coast to meet with a young union firebrand named Maria Elena Durazo. Ganz and fellow UFW alum Scott Washburn had previously interviewed Durazo for a study on the next generation of labor leaders. She now was running an insurgent campaign for president of HERE Local 11 in Los Angeles. At the time, Local 11 represented the worst stereotype of "business unionism." The union was not affiliated with the county federation of labor, members were excluded from negotiations, and the leadership refused to translate meetings into Spanish. Durazo's candidacy threatened to overturn this status quo, and the international did not know what to make of her. Contreras came to Ganz's house to determine whether Durazo was someone the international could work with; she was there to ascertain the international's view of her candidacy and to assess whether Contreras was someone she could trust.[6]

The meeting went well. The Local 11 election was held in March 1987. After ballots were cast and Durazo seemed headed to victory, the international halted the process and put the local into trusteeship. Bill Granfield, a UFW veteran who had worked at San Francisco's Local 2 before becoming head of New York City's UNITE HERE Local 100, a restaurant local, became the trustee. But the person put in charge of running Local 11 day to day was Miguel Contreras, who quickly confirmed Durazo's impression from the Ganz meeting that he could be trusted. Durazo accepted an offer to join the union's staff, and after the trusteeship ended in May 1989, she was elected president of Local 11. She and Contreras eventually married, becoming the "dynamic duo" of the Los Angeles labor movement. (For more information on Durazo, see chapter 5.)[7]

Contreras's first major involvement in a Los Angeles election campaign occurred in 1993, when he was a key strategist in Mike Woo's insurgent campaign for mayor. Although the city's political climate in the wake of the Rodney King riots was not hospitable to Woo's progressive agenda, and he eventually lost to wealthy investor Richard Riordan, Woo did better than expected. The Woo campaign showed Contreras which constituencies had to be brought together in order to have progressives win a citywide campaign. He soon got the chance to assemble this coalition after he was named political director of the Los Angeles County Federation of Labor in 1995. When LACFL's leader died in 1996, Contreras became the first Latino elected to head the organization (and one of the few Latinos in America to head a county labor federation).[8]

Although LACFL had long engaged in electoral work, Los Angeles was not viewed as a political stronghold for labor. Longtime mayor Tom Bradley had increasingly tilted toward the downtown business community, and had been elected on a platform claiming that he was "Tough Enough to Lead L.A." Veteran *LA Weekly* columnist Harold Meyerson noted that when Contreras became head of LACFL in 1996, "the city was just beginning to climb back from the worst recession since the Thirties." Unions participated in electoral politics "largely by writing checks to candidates" or by making deals with "behind-the scenes power brokers"; LACFL rarely if ever asked union members to walk precincts and directly engage in election campaigns. In Riordan's election, labor had been reduced to "a marginal player at best." Of great significance, as Meyerson observed, "a whole new population, an entire new working class, had descended on L.A. from Mexico and Central America, but they did not figure in L.A.'s civic life, in its politics, at all."[9]

To be sure, some movement toward Contreras's vision for the city's labor movement had preceded his election to the leadership of LACFL. SEIU's Justice for Janitors campaign won a widely publicized victory for two thousand workers in the Century City area of Los Angeles in 1990, and UCLA's Center for Labor Research and Education had become an intellectual hotbed for organizing. (Kent Wong, the center's director, got his start as an activist working on the UFW boycott when he was a high school student.) In 1994, a teachers union official named Antonio Villaraigosa won a state assembly primary in northeast Los Angeles, overcoming opposition from the Latino establishment and sending a strong reform message to the city's power structure. That same year also saw Republican governor Pete Wilson's effort to boost his reelection chances by putting an anti-immigrant initiative, Prop 187, on the November ballot. LACFL supported a No on 187 rally at city hall in downtown Los

Angeles, despite concern from many Democratic politicians that the Latino event would trigger a political backlash. Labor, immigrant rights groups, and the ethnic media turned out more than a hundred thousand people, the city's largest rally in over fifty years. Prop 187 galvanized the political consciousness of California's Latino community as never before and gave Contreras a motivated constituency from which to draw new progressive, pro-labor votes.[10]

Contreras thus began his tenure as LACFL's leader in 1996 with a large, untapped, but potentially mobilizable Latino constituency base. He brought to this challenge vast experience in the labor movement, cutting-edge electoral skills, personal relationships with other UFW veterans working in the Los Angeles area, and a history of Latino immigrant organizing—all factors that enabled him to quickly capitalize on the community anger spawned by Prop 187. His most immediate political priority was to help Democrats regain control of the state assembly, which they had lost in 1994 for the first time in decades. LACFL targeted six seats in the 1996 election and, through its field operations and independent mail programs in longtime Republican districts just outside Los Angeles County, helped Democrats take back five of the seats. This victory returned control of the state legislature to the Democrats, greatly boosting LACFL's political credibility in Los Angeles and across California.[11]

In 1997, Contreras took LACFL in a new direction. The group broke with the traditional Democratic Party Latino establishment and supported local SEIU official Gilbert Cedillo in a special election for an assembly seat representing the overwhelmingly Latino neighborhoods of downtown Los Angeles. Contreras's campaign for Cedillo included a voter registration and outreach drive targeted at union members and new immigrant voters, an independent precinct walking program, and mailers targeted to occasional voters and newly registered Latinos. When Cedillo won by nearly two to one over the old guard's better-known candidate, it became clear that Contreras and LACFL had found the strategy for building Latino voting power that could bring success in future races.[12]

Contreras also demonstrated in 1997 that, unlike his predecessors, he understood the strategic and political value of establishing strong labor-community alliances. He committed LACFL to helping build the Los Angeles Alliance for a New Economy (LAANE), a research and policy center that has used grassroots organizing tactics to win living wage laws, an anti-sweatshop ordinance, and "community benefits" criteria for business development. In the past, LACFL had rarely extended itself to organizing around community issues. But Contreras had seen the benefits of community participation from his days running a UFW boycott, and he steered LACFL in a new direction. In virtually every major economic justice struggle in Los Angeles County during his leadership—from union organizing drives at hospitals to living wage and worker retention laws, from legislation regulating "big box" stores in Los Angeles to the successful campaign to stop the construction of a Wal-Mart in Inglewood— LACFL built strong alliances with community groups.[13]

Contreras's focus on labor-community alliances was particularly evident in his approach to electoral work. To boost voter turnout among low-income residents, he helped launch a nonpartisan, nonprofit corporation called the Voter Improvement Program. VIP was a community-based coalition whose nonpartisan status enabled 501(c)(3) nonprofit groups, who could not legally work on behalf of candidates, to carry out voter registration, education, and outreach efforts in underrepresented communities. VIP allowed hundreds of charitable groups in Los Angeles to walk precincts, make phone calls, and mail election materials to the immigrants, Latinos, African Americans, and women whose increased voting rates would likely help pro-labor candidates. By 2004, VIP was raising up to $1 million annually from labor, key corporate allies, and community groups throughout Los Angeles.[14]

While he helped to promote nonpartisan voter registration through VIP, Contreras was well aware of the limitations of this approach. During the 1980s, Los Angeles unions and the Democratic Party had found that their investment in nonpartisan registration work in Latino neighborhoods produced a group of new voters that was less than 50 percent Democratic and more than 30 percent Republican. Labor's more targeted registration drives among Latinos greatly increased the number of Democratic registrants: for example, voters who became naturalized citizens during Governor Wilson's attacks on immigrants in the mid-1990s voted overwhelmingly Democratic. Labor's direct involvement in voter registration signed up not only more Democrats but also voters who were strongly pro-labor.[15]

In 1998, Contreras, LACFL, and California's entire labor movement faced a June ballot measure that would have banned unions from using any portion of members' dues for political campaigns without annual written authorizations—a difficult standard that would have greatly reduced labor's electoral clout. Proposition 226, the so-called Paycheck Protection initiative, prompted an all-out opposition campaign from organized labor. LACFL coordinated the hundreds of Los Angeles–area union staff members loaned to the No on 226 effort, and labor's massive statewide field campaign managed to defeat the measure. (Unions defeated a similar California initiative in 2005.) In a testament to labor's voter education and outreach efforts in 1998, 75 percent of Latino voters rejected Prop 226, compared to only 53 percent of voters overall. That fall, labor activism spearheaded the election of Gray Davis as California's first Democratic governor since 1982, and the election also brought commanding majorities for Democrats in the state legislature. New Latino Democratic assembly members were also voted into office, which in turn led to the election of California's first Latino Speaker of the assembly, Cruz Bustamante.[16]

Contreras's strategy in the 1998 election was to hire immigrants with campaign experience to work in Latino communities and to focus LACFL's voter outreach effort in these primarily immigrant communities, most of which had historically low voter turnout. Working with SEIU, HERE, and the UFW, LACFL brought thousands of union members to the streets, distributing literature and talking to voters. About 95 percent of the members of SEIU's statewide janitors union, Local 1877, are Latino immigrants. According to Local 1877 president Mike Garcia, "in the election of November '98, we turned out for 1,500 shifts [a shift is either walking a precinct or staffing a phone bank]—more than any other union." Janitors, who primarily work after offices close at night, were coming home from their jobs at 4:00 A.M. and beginning precinct walks at 7:00 A.M. When Latino immigrants show this kind of dedication to electoral work, it is easy to understand their effectiveness at persuading fellow immigrants to support the labor agenda and to get out and vote. As a result of the intense political mobilizing strategy that Contreras had learned from the UFW and honed while working with Marshall Ganz, LACFL and its allies increased Latino immigrant voter turnout 26 percent in areas where they campaigned.[17]

Labor's political success was matched by its increasing success in organizing Latino immigrants in the workplace. In 1999, Local 434B, SEIU's Los Angeles health care local, won union representation for seventy-four thousand home health care workers, the largest union organizing victory since the 1930s. Antonio Villaraigosa, now Speaker of the assembly, sponsored the bill that allowed such workers to join unions and used his powerful position to win passage of the legislation. The bill was then signed into law by the new Democratic governor, Gray Davis, who had been elected with strong labor support.[18]

In 2000, SEIU's Justice for Janitors won wage hikes of 22 to 26 percent over three years, following a nearly three-week strike that saw virtually every elected official in Los Angeles—including the city's Republican mayor—speak out on the workers' behalf. Los Angeles cardinal Roger Mahony, who had embraced the cause of Cesar Chavez and the UFW in the 1960s, when he was a Central Valley auxiliary bishop, conducted a public mass for thousands of striking janitors; Mahony even got arrested to show support for the janitors. Several elected officials were also arrested, fulfilling Contreras's demand that the politicians LACFL supported be "warriors for working people." Contreras's leadership of LACFL led the group to "lift the bar for our endorsements." No longer would labor be content with politicians who simply voted their way. Rather, Contreras expected the candidates his group helped to elect to "really push legislation" and to undertake civil disobedience on workers' behalf if necessary.[19]

In 2000, Contreras demonstrated just how serious he was about holding labor's political allies to higher standards. That year, LACFL waged an all-out primary campaign to unseat an incumbent Democratic congressional representative, Marty Martinez, who had an 80 percent prolabor voting record. Contreras felt that Martinez had betrayed his "very blue-collar" district by voting for the North American Free Trade Agreement (NAFTA) and failing to introduce pro-labor bills or champion labor's cause. Establishment Democrats questioned Contreras's decision to wage an intraparty fight while Republicans controlled the House of Representatives. But Contreras was making the same point about political accountability that Cesar Chavez and the UFW had made when they ran Democrat Art Torres against incumbent pro-business Democrat Alex Garcia in 1982; both wanted a labor champion, not a bystander, representing core Latino districts. To challenge Martinez, Contreras recruited California state senator Hilda Solis, who had helped lead the fight to defeat Prop 226 and the successful campaign to increase the state minimum wage. Contreras explained that Solis "would not be 80 but 100 percent" for unions and that backing her "was sending the message to Democrats that we expect more and we're going to hold them accountable." Backed by LACFL's tenacious voter outreach program, Solis defeated Martinez and became one of labor's strongest allies in Congress.[20]

Contreras continually sought new ways to increase LACFL's power. After labor and immigrant rights groups drew twenty thousand supporters to a downtown rally in 2000, Contreras, Maria Elena Durazo of HERE, SEIU international vice president and UFW veteran Eliseo Medina, and Ben Monterroso, who was Medina's assistant and SEIU regional coordinator, created a new structure for linking labor and immigrant power. They named it the Organization of Los Angeles Workers (OLAW), which sounded like the Spanish word for hello *(hola)* but actually meant "big wave"—a reference to the cascade of voting the project hoped to produce. OLAW's goals were twofold. First, it would use Spanish-language media and public events to build a sense of Latino-labor solidarity. Second, it would pay trained union members to take a leave from their regular jobs to participate in political campaigns. In addition to members of HERE Local 11 and SEIU Local 1877, full-time campaign walkers would also come from immigrant rights groups in Los Angeles.[21]

OLAW and LACFL also worked with Spanish-language Univision (Channel 34) to conduct citizenship fairs. At one such event, every consulate in Los Angeles set up a booth, and more than three thousand people attended to inquire about the process of attaining U.S. citizenship. Channel 34 set up call-in shows with a toll-free number connected to an SEIU Local 99 phone bank. Univision started airing other call-in shows with labor, marketing them as *Treinta Cuatro en Su Lado* (Channel 34 on Your Side). The station promoted and televised a question-and-answer session with fifty immigration attorneys who had been recruited to staff SEIU Local 99's call center; more than two hundred thousand phone requests were received. For a question-and-answer session on Los Angeles schools, "the union recruited school district and union representatives to field another barrage of questions, and a session on community-police relations filled the phone bank with LAPD community affairs representatives." Describing the importance of such events, Eliseo Medina observed: "With the phone bank at Local 99, the TV has the SEIU logo behind all of the experts and people start to understand that labor has a role in all these key issues."[22]

OLAW followed the UFW model in prioritizing leadership development and organizer training for its worker/participants. Tracy Zeluff, SEIU's California state council field director, saw the importance of such training when she honed her own organizing skills in the 1980s at Neighbor to Neighbor, the group founded by Fred Ross Jr. (described in chapter 2). According to Zeluff: "They start with the task of delivering a message, working as a team, being accountable, being more assertive. They develop politically, organizationally, personally, and they take these skills back into the workplace for their union. And the next campaign they are there again, but this time as a team leader or possibly running several teams."[23]

OLAW's test run occurred in 2000 when it assigned sixty full-time precinct walkers to two Republican-controlled congressional districts just outside Los Angeles. In a parallel effort, the UFW took on a third congressional race in L.A. Unlike LACFL's usual effort, which focused on voter outreach in Latino neighborhoods, the two congressional districts included predominantly white voters, though when the districts were combined, they had forty thousand potential Latino votes. The strategy was clear: dramatically increase Latino voting numbers in order to tilt the districts to the Democrats.

The union members working on the campaigns went door to door to get Latino registered voters to sign a *compromiso,* or commitment sheet. As Eliseo Medina explained, "The commitment was focused on making voting a social act. The commitment forms said, *'Por la amnistia, por derechos, mi familia vota 100 percento.'* [For amnesty, for rights, my family is voting 100 percent.] . . . We tried to make everything a family act to magnify the work and make it resonate." The strategy worked: Latinos voted in higher numbers, and two of the three Republican seats were won by Democrats. Increased Latino voting has switched these onetime Republican districts to Democratic control.[24]

In 2001, Contreras and LACFL launched a campaign to elect longtime labor ally Antonio Villaraigosa as mayor of Los Angeles. After his election to the state assembly in 1994, Villaraigosa had risen to the position of assembly Speaker. He had performed impressively in the assembly, but few gave him much of a chance in the mayor's race. Contreras's labor-community electoral machine had proved successful in district-based races, but not in a citywide contest.

To support Villaraigosa, OLAW provided 150 full-time precinct walkers for six weeks before the election and 450 walkers in the four days prior to both the primary election and the runoff. In addition, LACFL operated a labor-to-labor campaign and a separate independent expenditure campaign. Contreras reported that on the Saturday before the runoff, 2,700 people walked precincts for Villaraigosa. Villaraigosa finished first in the primary and faced a runoff against a fellow Democrat, former city attorney James Hahn. Hahn's father was a political hero in the city's African American community, and the combination of blacks and conservative whites defeated labor's candidate by seven points. But Villaraigosa's campaign exceeded all expectations, demonstrating the power of the city's labor-Latino-progressive alliance.[25]

The large numbers of Latinos in the ranks of janitors, health care workers, and hotel workers meant that building union power was also enhancing Latinos' political clout. In the face of this growing influence, the African American community's overwhelming support for Hahn over Villaraigosa in the 2001 mayor's race raised concerns that many black voters felt threatened by the Latino-labor alliance. However, demonstrating that its support for pro-labor candidates was multiracial, LACFL backed African American Martin Ludlow in a crucial city council race in 2003. Ludlow had been recruited by Scott Washburn in 1988 to work with Marshall Ganz's Campaign for Participation and Democracy (see chapter 6), and he went on to organize for SEIU before becoming LACFL's political director. Ludlow trailed his establishment opponent, also an African American, by thirteen points in the primary, but labor's vaunted voter outreach program brought him to victory in the runoff.[26]

Harold Meyerson described a meeting during the campaign in which Contreras, writing with a black marker on a whiteboard, explained how Ludlow would win the race:

> In the Latino northeast quadrant, Contreras said, the Latino activists from the Hotel Workers were walking. Over here, in the more Jewish neighborhoods, Ludlow was spending all his time going door-to-door; the guy was a great advertisement for himself. Over in this corner, there was an operation funded by unions that didn't care much about Ludlow but that wanted to ingratiate themselves to newly elected councilman Villaraigosa, who'd ask them to deliver for Ludlow. And so it went, neighborhood by neighborhood, until Contreras wound up predicting how many votes the leading candidates would receive. On election day, he was accurate within a couple of hundred votes for each of them.[27]

In the next local race in 2004, LACFL backed Karen Bass, an African American community activist and close labor ally, in her successful assembly race. When Bass took office in 2005, she became the first African American woman in the state legislature in a decade. Three years later, she was elected Speaker of the state assembly, the first Democratic woman to hold that post in California's history. She is also the first African American woman to serve as assembly Speaker not only in California but in the entire United States. The twin victories of Ludlow and Bass showed an emerging alliance among labor, Latinos, and African Americans, which could help avoid the rifts that had surfaced in the 2001 mayoral runoff; the wins also showed that labor's power would boost Los Angeles's progressive black leadership. This growing alliance was further solidified in 2006, when LACFL helped win an agreement unionizing the city's predominately African American security guards. These estimated five thousand security guards, who work in the downtown office buildings cleaned by SEIU janitors, represent a new pool from which LACFL can draw to provide training and leadership development for electoral work in the black community.[28]

In 2003, Antonio Villaraigosa beat an incumbent city council member and returned to public life. It was the first primary loss by an incumbent in the history of Los Angeles's nonpartisan council elections and showed Villaraigosa's continued popularity. His return to city politics was accompanied by the ascension of his close ally Fabian Nuñez, LACFL's former political director, to the position of assembly Speaker in 2004 (because of a six-year limit on assembly terms, the Speakership now rotates with regularity). Latino political clout both in Los Angeles and in state government was growing rapidly, and the big question was whether Villaraigosa, who had pledged in his council race that he would finish his term, would instead challenge Mayor Hahn in 2005. Hahn's first three years as mayor had been lackluster, and he had alienated his African American base by firing black police chief Bernard Parks. Hahn's political weakness was inviting strong challengers for 2005, and Villaraigosa eventually joined them.

Miguel Contreras had great personal affection for Villaraigosa, whose 2001 mayoral campaign had been fueled by LACFL's voter registration and grassroots political work. But Contreras operated by a political calculus dictating that labor must remain loyal to politicians who proved willing to champion labor's causes. Hahn had done virtually everything LACFL asked of him, including risking the loss of his conservative base by leading the successful fight against a ballot measure in 2002 that would have allowed the predominately white San Fernando Valley to secede from Los Angeles. This plan would have caused massive layoffs of unionized city workers due to the loss of the tax base in the valley. LACFL and Hahn had forged a close alliance to defeat the initiative, and after the election the mayor had appointed Contreras to the city's powerful Airport Commission. With Hahn happy to do labor's bidding, and with Los Angeles's long history of reelecting first-term mayors, some in labor argued that Villaraigosa should wait until 2009 to seek to become Los Angeles's first Latino mayor in more than a hundred years. But Villaraigosa thought he could beat Hahn in 2005. In August 2004, he announced his candidacy. One person who was not by his side was Miguel Contreras, whose LACFL stood by its ally, Hahn, in the race.

There were two great ironies associated with Antonio Villaraigosa's historic May 17, 2005, election as mayor of Los Angeles. The first is that the Latino leader won without LACFL's official support. The second cruel irony is that Miguel Contreras, the architect of the transformation of Los Angeles into a labor-Latino stronghold, and the person who for nine years had laid the groundwork for Villaraigosa's election, did not live to see Los Angeles elect a Latino mayor. Contreras died of a heart attack on May 6, 2005, at the young age of fifty-two. He was accustomed to conflict and tension as election days approached, so it is hard to attribute his heart attack to the pressures of the campaign. Some unions were complaining in the weeks preceding the runoff that LACFL was not doing enough for Hahn, but Contreras was undaunted by such criticism. He understood that the powerful electoral apparatus he had designed, based on "shoe power," was less effective when labor activists did not want to walk precincts for LACFL's endorsed candidate.[29]

Miguel Contreras used skills gained from the UFW, and from election campaigns led by UFW alumni, to build America's most successful Latino voter outreach operation. Not only was he the architect of the transformation of Los Angeles and nearby cities into progressive, pro-labor bastions; his outreach model also transformed California politics. Increased Latino voting has created strong, pro-labor Democratic majorities in the state legislature and helped to place California in the Democratic column in presidential elections. It has also built Latino political power in the state. In 1990, there were seven Latino state legislators in California; in 2006, this number had increased to twenty-seven, the most in history. The only California Republican who won a major statewide office from 1996 to 2008 was Arnold Schwarzenegger, whose victory in the 2002 recall of Gray Davis downplayed his party affiliation and who won reelection in 2006 after pledging peace with labor and by adopting much of the Democratic Party's agenda.

In addition, Miguel Contreras used the UFW grassroots voter outreach model to set the direction for future statewide labor campaigns. Labor's proficiency at electoral outreach steadily advanced during his tenure, as training and leadership development of union members built the skills of precinct walkers and other volunteers, allowing many to go on to run voter registration and get out the vote drives. Contreras had helped create OLAW as a vehicle for worker participation in electoral work, and this innovative approach to Latino voter outreach has greatly expanded in recent years. During the November 2004 national elections, several OLAW full-timers ran significant pieces of field operations in key battleground states. After the election, OLAW leaders concluded that a nonpartisan voter registration and outreach program was less effective than partisan outreach efforts at securing pro-labor Latino votes in California. This led SEIU and UNITE HERE to replace OLAW in 2006 with a similar but partisan organization known as Strengthening Our Lives, or SOL.

SOL: CONTRERAS'S ELECTORAL LEGACY LIVES ON

Although it is primarily known for its electoral work, SOL is a coalition of labor, community, and faith-based groups that focuses on the ongoing organizing of immigrant worker families. It was conceived as a vehicle for increasing labor's political clout, and its leadership includes many prominent union figures: in 2008, for example, such key union officials as Mike Garcia of SEIU Local 1877, Jack Gribbon of UNITE HERE, and Maria Elena Durazo, head of LACFL, served on SOL's board of directors.

Contreras's death in May 2005 had raised concerns about the future of the voter outreach juggernaut he had helped to build. But Contreras had always stressed leadership development, and he had been an important mentor to Javier Gonzalez, who would lead SOL's effort in the November 2006 elections. Gonzalez headed SOL while also serving as political director of SEIU 1877, the statewide janitors union. Based in Los Angeles, he had been trained in electoral organizing and political strategizing by both Contreras and Tracy Zeluff.

Gonzalez recalls some key aspects of Contreras's approach that became central to the implementation of SOL: "Miguel always made sure his precinct walkers were happy. They had to get enough food, be introduced to politicians, and if they had an idea on how to change the rap or do things differently, he would listen." Contreras also impressed on Gonzalez the notion of "trophy" campaigns, the contests in which labor can make a "statement" by winning a race that "everyone was watching." Gonzalez cites as an example Contreras's backing of Hilda Solis against incumbent Marty Martinez in the 2000 Democratic primary; her victory put all Latino and Democratic politicians on notice that merely voting for labor most of the time would no longer be sufficient.[30]

Contreras always emphasized that no politician or political party controlled LACFL's electoral machine. Gonzalez shares this analysis, viewing SOL's independence as critical to its success. He notes, "We are interested in building a movement, not in being a vehicle for a candidate or political party. People are more willing to volunteer for SOL because we are independent." SOL's "movement mentality" attracts people who ask "what else can I do?"—not "what time do we get to go home?" Contreras had come from a UFW culture in which everyone worked long hours six days a week in normal times and seven days a week during the peak of election campaigns. Nobody outworked the UFW, and Gonzalez has brought this farmworker ethos to SOL. When I asked him why other groups across the nation were not replicating the voter outreach model he learned from Contreras, he replied, "They say it is too expensive and too hard. Our walkers are working twelve to fourteen hours a day for six and even seven days a week in the six weeks leading up to election day."[31]

In addition to running partisan campaigns, SOL differs from OLAW in emphasizing ongoing political education and training over large, one-day events. Gonzalez felt that as a young organizer he would have benefited from ongoing working groups on Latino voting and other issues. SOL has developed as a year-round program for voter registration, organizer training, community education, strategic planning, leadership development, and increased civic participation in the Latino community. Just as Cesar Chavez and the UFW turned hundreds of farmworkers into skilled organizers, Gonzalez hopes that SOL can help accomplish this aim for the janitors, hotel workers, and others who get involved in the group's electoral work.[32]

One of his most promising recruits was Blanca Perez, a young Latina immigrant janitor who had come to America in 1991. She got involved with OLAW in 2000, when her employer threatened her with deportation. An OLAW organizer told her that by getting involved she could help people like herself "get what they needed, and from that point I was involved." Perez's first organizing experience occurred in 2002, when the school district announced that it would be closing the bilingual program at her child's school. Accompanying SEIU 1877's Committee on Political Action (COPA) on a Sacramento lobbying visit, Perez asked Gonzalez during lunch if he would translate something for her. She then pulled out a notebook with more than three hundred signatures from parents at the school, which so impressed Gonzalez that he agreed to accompany her to a few legislators' offices. It took Perez only one meeting with an aide to figure out the process, and "by the second and third offices, she was handling everything by herself." Perez won her battle with the district, and the bilingual program continued.[33]

Gonzalez knew he had a future organizer on his hands. He began giving Perez assignments and trained her to run phone banks, structure committees, run meetings, and hold volunteers accountable. Still working as a SOL volunteer, she was put in charge of SOL's San Fernando Valley office and was heavily involved in recruiting undocumented immigrants for the massive street protests in Los Angeles in 2006. Perez discovered that "people became less afraid, because they were so exhausted of being afraid. I believe that if everyone ignored their fear and fought and worked, there is much we can accomplish." Perez was herself undocumented at the time of the mass rallies, so her urgings to others resonated. In 2007, Gonzalez hired Perez as a full-time organizer for SOL, in the same way that countless young Latino farmworkers made the transition from full-time worker to full-time organizer during the 1960s and 1970s. Gonzalez believes that Perez is just one of the many "diamonds" within the immigrant worker community whose organizing prowess is "just waiting to be found."[34]

In the November 2006 elections, SOL targeted 300,000 infrequent Latino voters and knocked on 140,000 doors. The group spoke to 112,000 voters, a remarkable 86 percent of whom (96,000) went to the polls. The impact of SOL's campaign to contact Latino voters was significant. Voter turnout among new Latino registrants contacted by SOL was 22 percent higher across the state than among those not contacted by the organization. In every city where Sol worked, Latino voter turnout among occasional voters (defined as those who had voted in one or two of the last five elections) increased by 9 to 14 percent, and increased among those defined as somewhat likely to vote (individuals who had voted in three of the last five elections) by 3 to 12 percent.[35]

The November 2006 election was a test of whether SOL's voter outreach model was transferable to diverse communities and states. Prior to the election, the group became involved for the first time in the Central Valley city of Fresno. Although the organization was dealing with entirely new territory, turnout among Fresno's new Latino voters who were contacted by SOL was 14 percent greater than among similar voters who were not contacted; SOL's outreach increased the turnout rate among occasional Latino voters by 12 percent. The organization's voter outreach efforts in Fresno resulted in victory for an entire slate of school board candidates whose opposition was hostile to labor. The Fresno effort showed SOL's ability to quickly expand geographically, as well as its capacity to link up with new allies such as SEIU's United Health Care Workers (UHW) and Oaxacan farmworker groups organized through diaspora clubs. SOL also played a critical role in Democrats narrowly winning an open state senate seat in Orange County, ensuring that the party maintained its huge majorities in the legislature. SOL's three hundred full-time staff members for the November 2006 election were spread from Los Angeles County to San Jose, and the group had a thousand staffers getting out the vote on election day.[36]

SOL's door-to-door work also revealed an important fact about Latino voting that is typically overlooked by election analysts: the dispropor-

tionately large number of Latino registered voters who move their residence skews voter turnout rates downward. Gonzalez described SOL's
experience in one California assembly district that was supposed to have
7,000 Latino registered voters. After SOL walked the district, they found
that a full 41 percent of these voters (2,902) no longer lived at the address where they were registered. Even if every registered Latino who lived
in the district had voted, the record would have reflected only a 59 percent Latino turnout, creating a negative image at odds with the facts. The
widespread presence of these phantom voters in Latino neighborhoods
explains why SOL devotes considerable resources to registering voters and
creating new voter files when it expands to new areas and why voter
turnout in these new areas is likely to increase in future elections.[37]

Salvador "Chava" Bustamante, the elected first vice president of SEIU's
Local 1877, led SOL's Northern California operation in 2006. He had
joined the UFW as a farmworker in 1968, and he and his brother Mario
were rank-and-file leaders in the union's successful Salinas lettuce strike
in 1979. Chava and Mario were also among the worker leaders who
attempted to win executive board representation at the UFW's September 1981 convention, during a period of internal conflict. When Cesar
Chavez canceled the election and fired Mario Bustamante from his job
as a paid union representative, Chava left the UFW. He then began working with Central Valley migrant workers and on immigration reform
efforts. Having gained his "basic schooling in activism" from the UFW,
Bustamante was recruited by former UFW colleague Susan Sachen to
begin organizing janitors for SEIU in 1988. His successful campaign to
organize janitors in San Jose played a critical role in building the state's
Justice for Janitors campaign. He views such campaigns as "carrying out
many of the same tactics and strategies as the farmworkers." Despite the
circumstances in which he left the UFW, Bustamante still believes it "is
a symbol of what the labor movement can be."[38]

Bustamante gave the keynote address at SOL's Northern California
campaign kickoff on September 30, 2006. The event brought together a
wide spectrum of Latino community groups, Associated Community Organizations for Reform Now (ACORN), and several unions, including
the Laborers and Carpenters, whose members had not previously been
involved in SOL. For the November 2006 elections, SOL's Northern California operation worked in both Fresno and San Jose. The group had
thirty-five staff members for six weeks before the election, and more than
a hundred on the streets as election day neared. Mark Gomez, SOL's communication director, noted that half of the group's Northern California

participants were not from labor, creating "a rare vehicle for labor and Latino community members to work in a single organization for the advancement of their common interests." Gomez sees SOL as "offering a strategic vision for increasing Latinos' share of the state's prosperity," a concept Bustamante described in his convention speech as "reviving the American Dream, voter by voter." SOL's success in 2006 outside its home territory of Southern California represented the further expansion of the UFW-Contreras voter outreach model into a statewide electoral force.[39]

WHY CALIFORNIA'S LATINO VOTING INCREASED: LABOR OUTREACH OR HOSTILE POLITICAL ENVIRONMENT?

Inspired by the efforts of Miguel Contreras and the LACFL, California labor unions have come to rely on a grassroots mobilization model that was pioneered by the UFW and then enhanced by UFW veterans in the 1980s. This model has dramatically increased Latino voter turnout in the state. This trend began in the mid-1990s, overwhelmingly benefiting Democrats, organized labor, and pro-labor Latino politicians. But it has become part of the legend of recent California politics that a Latino voter backlash in reaction to the anti-immigrant initiative Prop 187 on the November 1994 ballot—and not labor's mobilization strategies— has been responsible for increasing Democratic and Latino voter turnout ever since. As Adrian Pantoja, Ricardo Ramírez, and Gary Segura note, not only did Prop 187 drive California's Latino voters to the polls, but a "hostile" political environment persisted, with a 1996 initiative opposing affirmative action (Prop 209) and a 1998 measure opposing bilingual education (Prop 227). As the following pages explain, however, an examination of Latino voting in California and other states since 2000 reveals that the chief variable increasing turnout was the presence of a labor movement that implemented the UFW voter outreach model.[40]

Post–Prop 187 Latino Voting

California's Prop 187 sought to deny undocumented immigrants a wide range of public services, including medical care. Governor Pete Wilson launched the initiative as a strategy to secure his reelection, and it accomplished his goal. But Prop 187 galvanized Latino immigrants as never before. More than a hundred thousand people attended a No on 187 rally at Los Angeles city hall, and in future elections Latino voting in California rose dramatically. To wit:

- The Latino share of the electorate doubled during the 1990s, rising from 7 percent in 1992 to 14 percent in 2000. This represented an increase of one million Latino voters.

- More than 90 percent of all new voters who registered in California from 1990 to 2000 were Latinos.

- Among Latino voters eligible to vote in 2000, 46 percent had registered since 1994.

- In Los Angeles between 1992 and 1998, 62.8 percent of newly registered Latino voters were Democrats, and only 10.3 percent were Republicans, a pro-Democratic slant far more striking than the 60 percent to 22 percent margin among Latinos statewide.

- In California's February 2008 Democratic presidential primary, exit polls showed that Latinos made up 30 percent of the electorate, nearly double the figures from 2004.[41]

Although a federal court quickly struck down Prop 187 as unconstitutional, the measure unleashed deep anger in the Latino community against the primarily Republican politicians who had promoted it. But it took a strategy to harness the fury of the No on 187 campaign into greater Latino voting. Specifically, Latinos had to register to vote and then be mobilized to cast ballots. Sergio Bendixen, a pollster and longtime student of Latino voting, has observed that "there isn't much of a grass-roots infrastructure in the Hispanic community to register people to vote. It is not a matter of just motivation and explaining to them the importance of voting. They get that. It's more a matter of somebody holding their hand and taking them through the process."[42]

Henry Flores, a professor at St. Mary's University in Texas and a researcher with the William C. Velasquez Institute, a respected center for studies of Latino voting, shares Bendixen's assessment. Flores believes that Latinos' lower economic status and lack of education translate into reduced voting. In Texas, he notes, as of 2006 there was "no coordinated effort to get Latino voters to the polls. The Democrats half try, the Republicans don't try." Significantly, Flores reports that a hostile, Prop 187–type initiative in Arizona in 2004 did not generate greater Latino turnout in that state. He also argues that the destruction of the labor movement in Texas from the 1920s to the 1940s eliminated the key institutional power base for strengthening Latino voter outreach. Flores sees the voter registration and outreach efforts of labor unions as key to California's increased post–Prop 187 Latino voting.[43]

If the rise in Latino voting in California were primarily caused by an anti-immigrant political context, the numbers should have declined after 1998, when California elected a Democratic governor, a Latino Democrat as lieutenant governor, and large, pro-immigrant Democratic majorities in the legislature. These statewide election results reflected the end of the state's overtly hostile political environment, prompting some Republicans to reassure Latino voters that they shared their values and wanted their votes. To that end, in January 2000 the Republican National Committee announced that likely presidential nominee George W. Bush would wage an "unprecedented Latino-aimed television and print advertising campaign" prior to California's March primary. At the 2000 Republican National Convention, California assembly member Abel Maldonado gave the first-ever convention speech in Spanish, further shifting the national party away from Pete Wilson's harsh anti-immigrant attacks. Bush spent little time in California during the general election campaign, but his campaign invested millions of dollars in the state's Latino media in the weeks before the election.[44]

Without a threatening political environment in 2000, Latino voting power in California nonetheless registered huge gains. Latino voters played key roles in winning swing districts for Democrats. In one congressional district, Latino voting enabled a white Democratic incumbent to defeat a Republican Latino challenger. In a district just south of Los Angeles County, a four-term Republican incumbent won his House seat by only eighteen hundred votes, with eleven thousand more Latinos voting in 2000 than had voted in 1998. Democrats took three Republican congressional seats in 2000, and in each case Latino votes proved pivotal. In a Los Angeles County district covered by Contreras's various electoral outreach programs, the Latino share of the electorate rose from 9.2 percent in 1994 to 13.7 percent in 2000. In the coastal areas south of Los Angeles, a Democratic challenger won by only 1.7 percent of the vote in a district that historically had a Republican registration advantage until Latino registration grew by almost a third from 1996 to 2000. In San Diego County, a Democratic challenger won by 3 percent in a Republican district that had seen Latino voter registration rise by 25 percent since the 1996 elections.[45]

The impact on state legislative races in 2000 was even greater. In the 1994 elections, Republicans had won a one-vote majority in the California assembly and were close to a senate majority. Democrats then picked up additional seats in both chambers in 1996, 1998, and 2000, with the number of Latino Democrats rising from seven in 1990 to twenty-three after the 2000 elections. After 2000, Latino Democrats represented 32 percent of the party's votes in the assembly, which helped former LACFL political director Fabian Nuñez to be elected assembly Speaker during his first term in office. As Luis Ricardo Fraga, Ricardo Ramírez, and Gary Segura conclude in "Unquestioned Influence," their study of Latino voting in California's 2000 elections, "Latino influence in the state legislature is clear, growing and demonstrating a level of political sophistication that was unimaginable just ten years ago."[46]

California's Latino voting power continued to build in the 2002 midterm election, the 2004 presidential election, the 2005 statewide special election, and the 2006 elections. None of the first three involved a political environment hostile to immigrants. Although the actual number of Latinos voting in California declined in 2002, two new Latino congressional representatives were elected, and Latino-supported candidates did well in local and state legislative races. OLAW's voter outreach drive contacted sixty-five thousand voters and got about 70 percent of them to the polls. In 2002, which featured a lackluster governor's race, total voter turnout and turnout among whites decreased by 6 percent from the prior comparable election in 1998; the Latino vote declined by only 4 percent. Rather than demonstrating that Latinos do not vote in large numbers in the absence of a hostile environment, the 2002 election actually shows that the UFW grassroots mobilization strategy gets Latinos out to vote even in low turnout elections, and at greater rates than other voters.[47]

Further evidence for the centrality of labor union mobilization efforts comes from a field experiment that analyzed various voter outreach methods among infrequent Latino voters for the 2002 election. The Voces del Pueblo (Voices of the People) project, sponsored by the National Association of Latino Elected and Appointed Officials, used three types of communication—live phone calls, automated "robo" calls, and direct mail—to mobilize more than four hundred thousand Latino voters in Los Angeles and Orange counties in California, Harris County in Texas, metropolitan Denver, New York City, and the state of New Mexico. The not-surprising conclusion: robo calls had little effect on voter turnout, and direct mail had a modest effect, while live phone calls increased voter turnout by a statistically significant 4.6 percent. As Ricardo Ramírez concludes in his analysis of the experiment, the impact of live phone calls "underscores the importance of the *quality* of communications with voters." Labor's preferred method of reaching Latino voters—knocking on doors and engaging in personal contact—is of an even higher quality than live phone calls and would almost certainly increase turnout by an even higher percentage.[48]

California versus Texas and Florida

Comparing Latino voting patterns in California, Texas, and Florida also supports the argument that labor's voter outreach is key. In 1994, California's election climate was far more anti-immigrant than that of any other state. But this situation changed in 1996, after President Bill Clinton joined with Congress in enacting a federal "welfare reform" measure that denied important financial benefits to legal immigrants. This new law affected Latino immigrants in California and Texas equally, and the level of media coverage of immigration issues in the two states in the month before the November election was also similar. But California's recently naturalized Latino immigrants registered and voted in high numbers, while the same group in Texas had low registration and voter turnout rates. Florida's newly naturalized Latino immigrants in 1996 followed the Texas pattern. The political environments in all three states were equally hostile during that year's election, but only California had a labor movement with the sophisticated registration and voter mobilization programs necessary to draw Latino immigrants to the polls.[49]

California and Texas both elected Republican governors in 1994, but then went in dramatically different political directions. Whereas the 1994 elections in California preceded a decade of Latino-influenced Democratic Party growth, that same year in Texas saw Republican George W. Bush defeat incumbent Democratic governor Ann Richards, ushering in a decade of unprecedented Republican political power in the state. A major factor distinguishing the two states was California's labor-led voter outreach, which changed the state's political calculus by increasing Latino turnout. S. Karthick Ramakrishnan has found that electoral mobilization among Latinos in Texas was consistently lower than in California. The limited mobilization that did occur in Texas focused less on registering new voters—a central focus of Contreras's agenda and a key to Latinos influencing particular races—and more on getting those already registered out to vote. Regardless of how hostile the political environment was—from the 1996 federal elimination of public benefits to legal immigrants to Congress's proposed criminalization of those assisting immigrants in 2006—Latino voting in Texas barely increased.[50]

These patterns were repeated in the 2006 midterm elections, which followed nationwide marches for immigrant rights in response to the House of Representatives passing the Sensenbrenner bill. Named after its sponsor, Wisconsin Republican James Sensenbrenner, the bill would have turned all undocumented immigrants—and those lawyers, social workers, and medical workers who assisted them—into felons. Congress's subsequent failure to enact immigration reform was viewed as a slap in the face of Latino immigrants in particular, and the question heading into the November 2006 election was whether a Prop 187–type anti-Republican backlash would occur. California, where SOL was conducting its $3.5 million grassroots field campaign, saw Latino voter turnout rise 18.2 percent over the comparable 2002 election despite a noncompetitive governor's race and little on the state ballot to stimulate turnout.[51]

The percentage of Latinos in California's electorate also rose from 2002 to 2006, from 12.6 percent to 16 percent. But Latino voting in Florida and Texas, which lacked significant labor-backed grassroots mobilization programs, declined from 2002 by 16.3 percent and 32.9 percent, respectively. Florida's decline occurred despite a 25 percent increase in Latino registrants, further confirming the importance of UFW-style GOTV campaigns in getting Latinos to the polls. Texas's steep decline in 2006 is a little misleading: there had been a record high Latino turnout in 2002 to support Democrat Tony Sanchez's campaign for governor, but there was no comparable motivating race in 2006. The hostile environment created by Sensenbrenner's legislation did not result in Latino turnout exceeding 1994 levels in Texas, despite a 15 percent increase in Latino registration since 2002. In fact, the 2006 election saw huge reductions in turnout in the heavily Latino communities in South Texas, despite the Sensenbrenner bill and rising Latino turnout nationally.[52]

The steep decline in Latino voting in Texas's traditional barrios in 2006 does not mean that people were not contacted. To the contrary, "block-walkers were falling all over each other. . . . Many of the low performing neighborhoods had 4 or 5 visits to each door." But unlike the issue-based voter outreach strategy developed by the UFW and now used by SOL and organized labor in California, the Texas mobilizing efforts assumed that Latino voters would simply come out to vote for Democrats. Democratic state representative Aaron Peña attributed the state's low Latino turnout to a history of using patronage to secure Democratic votes and blamed "the sad legacy of South Texas boss or strongman politics which relied heavily on patrón-managed turnout rather than the advocacy of ideas."[53]

Support for Peña's thesis came in the surprising 54 to 45 percent victory of Democratic challenger Ciro Rodriguez over well-funded incumbent Republican Henry Bonilla in a December 12, 2006, runoff election for a House seat. Bonilla had alienated Latino voters by supporting the construction of a seven-hundred-mile border fence with Mexico (the congressional district borders the Rio Grande) and by voting for the Sensenbrenner bill. The backlash resulted in a massive defection of Latinos to the Democratic Party. For the first time in his political career, Bonilla lost Bexar County, which includes San Antonio. In 2004, Bonilla had carried Maverick County, which lies along the Mexican border and is 95 percent Latino, with 59 percent of the vote. In the December 2006 runoff, he received only 14 percent of the vote, to Rodriguez's 86 percent. According to the *National Journal*'s Charles Mahtesian, who is also editor of the *Almanac of American Politics*, "Maverick is a border county and home to Eagle Pass, where the border fence issue was huge. Bonilla's vote in favor of the fence made an enormous difference here." Once the runoff became a litmus test on immigrant rights, Latino voters altered their traditional voting patterns and overwhelmingly supported the candidate whose ideas they came closest to sharing. With Texas Republicans promoting an anti-immigrant agenda and SEIU expanding its operations in the state, Rodriguez's upset victory could be a sign that Latino voters will finally move that state's politics in a more progressive direction.[54]

Arizona: Voter Outreach Is Key

Arizona's electoral history also shows that in the absence of a labor-led grassroots voter outreach drive, a hostile political environment is insufficient to significantly increase Latino voting. In 2004, Arizona voters easily approved Prop 200, which required individuals to show proof of citizenship in order to vote or to receive public benefits from state or local sources. This measure was directly aimed at Latino immigrants and, while not as harsh as California's Prop 187, was certainly more "hostile" than any subsequent California ballot initiative.

Although many predicted that Prop 200 would galvanize Arizona's Latino electorate, this did not occur. In fact, without a grassroots mobilizing vehicle, Arizona's Latino voter registration actually fell from 33.4 percent in 2000 to 30.5 percent in 2004, and Latino voter turnout declined in 2004 from the 2000 presidential election (27.1 percent to 25.5 percent). This decrease sharply contrasts with the spike in California Latino voter registration and turnout after Prop 187. Moreover, 47 per-

cent of Arizona's Latino voters favored Prop 200. The hostile environment was only part of the reason for the failure to generate increased
registration or turnout; the lack of an effective voter outreach campaign
by labor left Arizona's Latino electorate far less likely to identify with
the cause of immigrants.[55]

In response to Arizona's disappointing results in 2004, Eliseo Medina
of SEIU brought Mi Familia Vota (MFV) into the state for the November 2006 election. MFV was a coalition of SEIU, ACORN, People for
the American Way, and other local and national groups that engaged in
nonpartisan Latino voter outreach modeled on the successful approach
Medina had created with OLAW. MFV had begun registering voters in
Florida in 2004, and Medina expanded the group to both Arizona and
Colorado for 2006, with the goal of mobilizing infrequent Latino voters. In both states, MFV linked its outreach program to a statewide minimum wage initiative.

According to Scott Washburn, a longtime Medina ally who had become SEIU's state council director in 2003, it was actually easier to boost
Latino voting by campaigning for a positive initiative than by mobilizing people to vote against something, as had been done in 2004. In fact,
if MFV had believed that a hostile environment was a better motivator
for Latino voting than a positive message, the campaign could have focused on a state ballot measure making English the official language of
Arizona. But veteran electoral campaigners Medina, Washburn, and
SEIU's Martin Manteca, who headed Arizona's MFV campaign in 2006,
saw the positive message of raising the state's minimum wage as more
likely to get infrequent voters to cast ballots.[56]

Implementing a strategy developed with Washburn and Medina, Manteca's voter outreach campaign made it a priority to increase the number of infrequent Latino voters who cast ballots by mail. Research had
found that infrequent voters who requested mail ballots were twice as
likely to vote as those who did not. To accomplish this goal, Manteca
supervised a staff of twenty full-time paid canvassers, ten part-time canvassers, and twenty-five to thirty volunteers a week during the two
months preceding the election. The effort targeted 85,000 infrequent
Latino voters and got 27,000 to request vote-by-mail ballots—an extraordinarily high percentage for a nonpresidential election. Of the 27,000,
23,000 told outreach staff that they would be voting for the minimum
wage initiative. MFV called or visited each of these voters to ensure that
they had mailed their ballots back to the elections department in time to
be counted. Overall, 62 percent of the infrequent Latino voters targeted

by MFV cast ballots, compared to 55 percent of Latino frequent voters who were not contacted by the campaign. This result shows the enormous impact of MFV's UFW-style voter outreach campaign. MFV helped boost Arizona's Latino turnout by 11 percent over 2002, and, in the wake of this initial effort, both Washburn and Manteca expressed great optimism for building a much larger voter outreach effort in future Arizona elections.[57]

Colorado

Colorado also had a Mi Familia Vota campaign conceived by Eliseo Medina, which was linked in the November 2006 election to a state initiative raising the minimum wage. SEIU's state council director in Colorado was Lauren Martens, who had grown up in Fresno, California, without ever learning about the UFW. Martens received his formative organizer training from Fred Ross Sr. while working for Fred Ross Jr.'s Neighbor to Neighbor organization in 1988. Like other disciples of the two Rosses, Martens soon learned the discipline of organizing, along with "tangible skills, political savvy, and strategic thinking." He had worked for SEIU's Justice for Janitors campaign in Colorado in 1993, had become involved in a number of successful environmental campaigns, and then had returned to SEIU in 2005. SEIU was "a significant part" of MFV's effort in Colorado in 2006, a campaign that was housed at the Denver Labor Federation offices.[58]

The 2006 Latino voter turnout in Colorado is extensively analyzed in chapter 9. Much of the state became a litmus test for the impact of the notorious Sensenbrenner bill on Latino voting patterns. While Colorado's 38 percent increase in Latino voting over 2002 could be viewed as a response to the hostile environment created by the threat of the bill, this dramatic rise in voting was primarily produced by intensive voter registration and outreach efforts by MFV and other groups affiliated with the national immigrant rights movement. No initiative on the November 2006 Colorado ballot attacked or even addressed Latino immigrants; rather, the chief push behind Latino voting was to back up the claims by marchers across America that "today we march, tomorrow we vote." Colorado Latinos voted in record numbers in 2006 out of hope for the future, not out of fear.

After the 2004 national election, many argued that Republicans had prevailed by more systematically mobilizing their political base. But Peter Wielhouwer's study of that election foreshadowed the possibility

that the Latino voter outreach strategies pioneered by the UFW and enhanced by Miguel Contreras could soon give a turnout edge to Democrats. Wielhouwer found that those with lower educational levels and
low incomes—the profile of the typical infrequent Latino voter—were
the most likely to respond to mobilization contacts by voting at higher
rates. Despite their greater susceptibility to voter outreach, this group
had been the least likely to be targeted in 2004. In 2006, Democrats in
key races prioritized outreach to those with low levels of education and
income, boosting Latino turnout and decreasing the historical disparity
in voting along class and educational lines. The Democrats' success in
the 2006 election began to alter the perception of the party's mobilization efforts, though organized labor's successful grassroots electoral efforts in California throughout the preceding decade were still overlooked.
Contreras's lack of interest in nationally promoting his organizing model
is one reason for this, but a greater reason was likely the mistaken belief
that it was the Latino backlash to Prop 187, not labor voter mobilization, that transformed California politics. The comparison of Latino voting in states such as Colorado, however, shows otherwise. A hostile political environment has been a factor, but more important in driving
Latino turnout has been labor's investment in Latino voter registration
and getting infrequent Latino voters to the polls.[59]

Cesar Chavez and the UFW laid the groundwork for California's increase in Latino voting, and Marshall Ganz and other UFW veterans then
refined and expanded the UFW model in a series of 1980s campaigns.
After Miguel Contreras and the Los Angeles County Federation of Labor
found success using this approach during the 1990s, this grassroots mobilization and voter outreach model spread throughout California through
labor-backed organizations such as SOL, fueling the transformation of
California politics. These efforts continue to expand nationally as SEIU
and other unions build their presence in Colorado, Florida, Arizona,
Texas, and other states where greater Latino voter turnout could boost
progressive candidates and issues. To the extent that much of America's
Latino electorate is described as a "sleeping giant," its awakening de-
pends not on reacting to a hostile political environment but rather on
the spread of a UFW organizing model that has proven successful for
over forty years and is advancing the struggle for economic justice across
the nation.

8

BUILDING THE IMMIGRANT
RIGHTS MOVEMENT

Sí Se Puede!

In 2006, millions of Latino immigrants and their allies marched through America's streets to demand legalization for the nation's undocumented immigrants. Protests occurred in more than two hundred cities, with huge turnouts not only in cities such as Los Angeles and Chicago but also in small cities and rural towns across the country. This unprecedented public outpouring stunned many Americans, who had been largely unaware of the nation's growing immigrant rights movement.

Beginning with community-based immigrant advocacy groups in the mid-1990s, the movement had expanded to include labor and church groups in central roles. Its ranks quickly swelled after the passage of the Sensenbrenner bill, HR 4437, in December 2005, a bill strongly backed by President Bush and House Republicans. The measure would have made undocumented immigrants, and those who provided services to them, guilty of felonies. Opposition to the bill sparked a series of mass protests from March to May of 2006, and activists vowed to boost citizenship applications, Latino voter registration, and Latino voter turnout in the November 2006 midterm elections.

The marchers' rallying cry in cities large and small was the same: the farmworkers' chant *"sí se puede!"* That millions would identify the cause of immigrant rights with Cesar Chavez and the UFW is fitting, as the union helped to lay the groundwork for today's immigrant rights movement. Such UFW veterans as Eliseo Medina, Fred Ross Jr., Miguel Contreras, and others played an important role in building the labor-clergy-community alliance that had once been key to the UFW's success and now was the vehicle for bringing millions to march, apply for citizenship, register to vote, cast ballots, and otherwise work on behalf of America's increasingly powerful immigrant rights movement more than thirty years later.

CHAVEZ, THE UFW, AND IMMIGRANTS:
SETTING THE RECORD STRAIGHT

Although the UFW strongly backed the 2006 marches, some still hold misconceptions about the union's stance on the issue of immigration over the years. Many who recall Chavez's support for crackdowns on immigration in the 1960s and early 1970s are not aware of his battles with the Immigration and Naturalization Service in the 1950s. Nor do his critics appreciate the historical context of the UFW's pro-enforcement position, adopted at a time when growers routinely brought in undocumented immigrants to break farmworker strikes. In fact, by the mid-1970s, Chavez had become a strong supporter of immigrant rights.

When Chavez worked for the Community Services Organization in the 1950s, organizing in the small town of Madera, near Fresno, one of his duties was to help immigrants become citizens. He quickly confronted a problem. The Immigration and Naturalization Service citizenship examiner for the area would not give the tests in Spanish, even though federal law authorized him to do so. When Chavez confronted the INS official, the man told him, "If they can't speak English, they shouldn't become citizens." He then implied that Chavez was a communist. This charge from a government official was taken seriously by the CSO's Madera board, which held a sort of "trial" of Chavez to determine whether he was in fact a communist. When Chavez learned that the board was holding a public meeting about his background, he rushed to the event and denounced the INS as "Gestapos." He then succeeded in electing new officers to the board, all of whom were farmworkers who supported his tough approach to INS abuses of immigrant rights.[1]

In 1958 and 1959, Chavez's organizing took him to Oxnard, California, which had the biggest bracero camp in the country. The bracero program had begun during World War II; because of labor shortages, growers won federal legislation allowing them to bring workers from Mexico to pick crops. But the program continued after the war, enabling growers to employ braceros rather than paying higher wages to local workers. Braceros were also used as strikebreakers. Given the impact of these Mexican workers on the local labor market, experts believed that killing the program was a prerequisite for improving the wages and living conditions of farmworkers. Chavez described the bracero program as "a vicious racket of the grossest order." As he saw it, "The jobs belonged to local workers. The braceros were brought only for exploitation. Braceros didn't make any money, and they were forced to work under conditions the local people wouldn't tolerate. If the braceros spoke up, if they made the minimal complaints, they'd be shipped back to Mexico."[2]

During his time in Oxnard, Chavez was struck by the community's overwhelming demand "to get those jobs from the braceros," and he believed that this desire represented the potential organizational base for a union. He spent much of the next year waging a grassroots campaign to get growers in Oxnard and the surrounding county to hire local farmworkers rather than braceros. Through marches, demonstrations, and sit-ins, he won a major but temporary victory, when the growers began to hire local workers directly from the CSO offices. But when Chavez proposed that it form a union and essentially operate a hiring hall, the CSO did not want to invest the necessary resources. Chavez later recalled, "If I had had the support of CSO, I would have built a union there." He moved on to organize in Los Angeles, and the progress he had made in Oxnard soon fell apart in his absence. After two years of trying to persuade the CSO to take up the cause of organizing farmworkers, Chavez left the group and, at age thirty-five, moved to Delano to take up the challenge.[3]

The beginning of the farmworkers movement coincided with the demise of the bracero program, so the union did not have to address the issue. But two lessons from Chavez's CSO days would come to shape his views of undocumented immigrants. First, he could not support workers being brought from Mexico, or anywhere else, for use as strikebreakers. The issue was not their illegal status—the UFW had undocumented immigrants within its ranks for years—rather, it was their key role in helping growers deny labor rights to local workers. Second, he saw the importation of these Mexican workers as a "vicious racket," in which the undocumented workers themselves were left in abject poverty while jobs were eliminated for local workers, who were Mexican nationals legally living in the United States.

Both principles came into play in October 1966, a year after the start of the grape boycott, when the farmworkers union was involved in supporting melon workers along the Rio Grande border in Texas who were striking for better conditions. The strike had failed to produce a union contract because growers were importing strikebreakers from Mexico. In response, the melon workers and their UFW supporters began stopping vehicles that were carrying workers across the border. A struggle with a local sheriff ensued, and in protest the UFW blocked traffic on the international bridge at the border for over an hour. The resulting public controversy led Mexican unions to set up their own picket line on their side of the border, aimed at dissuading workers from crossing to break the strike. With the UFW and its Mexican counterparts demonstrating cross-border solidarity, and growers demanding legal and political action to halt the strike, it was clearer than ever that the UFW was not anti-immigrant, only anti-strikebreaker.[4]

During the grape strike and boycott, the UFW held ongoing demonstrations against the INS for its failure to stop growers from bringing in Mexican immigrants to break the strike. Chavez continually demanded that the INS enforce the federal law prohibiting employers from recruiting green card holders (who had legal status) as strikebreakers. The INS refused, and the Justice Department eventually ruled that it lacked sufficient evidence to prosecute. Convinced that the UFW could not raise wages and improve working conditions for farmworkers so long as immigrant strikebreakers were freely available, Chavez testified before a U.S. Senate committee in support of sanctions for those employing illegal immigrants and fines for green card holders who acted as strikebreakers. He made it clear to the committee that all the UFW was asking for was "some way to keep the illegal and green carders from breaking our strikes."[5]

In 1973, the UFW adopted a new constitution that provided a bill of rights for all members and committed the union to uniting "all individuals employed as agricultural laborers, regardless of race, creed, sex or nationality." The constitution made no distinction based on a worker's legal status. The UFW had never sought to exclude or penalize farmworkers who were undocumented. But pushing for the enforcement of laws to prevent undocumented immigrants from working as strikebreakers was another matter. This became clear in Yuma, Arizona, in 1973, when growers brought workers across the border to undermine a UFW strike over a contract dispute. The union began monitoring the border to prevent strikebreakers from coming in and asked the INS to stop the entries. When the INS took no action, some UFW members took the law into their own hands and physically attacked those trying to cross the border. Several strikers were arrested for assaulting undocumented immigrants, prompting civil rights groups to denounce the UFW and embarrassing a movement that was publicly committed to nonviolence. Activists affiliated with Latino civil rights groups also expressed anger that year when the UFW endorsed tough new immigration restrictions proposed in Congress.[6]

In 1974, with the UFW still battling grape growers after ending a bitter and violent strike, Chavez publicly stated that there were "more than

2,200 illegal aliens working on ranches in the Fresno area." Just as he felt that the INS had intentionally failed to stop strikebreakers from crossing the border in Yuma, he saw the pro-grower agenda of the Nixon administration behind the government's effort "to make sure this flood of desperately poor workers continued unchecked."[7]

While the UFW held protests against the INS throughout 1974, a national coalition of Latino groups criticized Chavez for his support of strict border controls. But when the Justice Department announced late that year that it would begin a massive deportation drive, Chavez wrote a letter to the *San Francisco Examiner* denying charges that the UFW supported any plans to deport millions of immigrants. The letter reiterated his long-held position that the INS was siding with growers by failing to prevent the use of undocumented immigrants as strikebreakers. Significantly, the letter expressed support for an amnesty that would lead to the legalization of undocumented workers. The public commitment of Chavez and the UFW to legalization and the union's longtime willingness to include undocumented immigrants as members refute the often repeated but erroneous views about where Chavez and the union stood on immigrant rights.[8]

As Richard Griswold del Castillo and Richard Garcia observe, "The hard realities of farm labor organizing compelled Chavez and the UFW to support immigration restrictions that were not popular with Chicano activists." These activists were focused on building a movement based on ethnic and nationalist unity, and they saw this unity being undermined by immigration restrictions. But, unlike many of the union's critics, Chavez had to live in a world where people's livelihoods depended on preventing an unrestricted flow of immigrant labor. Whereas today's immigration opponents care little about Latino workers, Chavez and the UFW made empowering Latino workers their top priority; the farmworkers movement saw undocumented immigrants as jeopardizing the jobs, wages, and working conditions of Latinos already in the United States. In other words, seeking border restrictions as part of a strategy to build the power of Latino workers represents a much different agenda than attacking undocumented immigrants on the basis of racism and xenophobia, as some do today.[9]

In 1986, the UFW joined with other labor unions in supporting the Immigration Reform and Control Act (IRCA). Opposed by both immigrant rights advocates and Latino civil rights groups because it increased employer sanctions and strengthened border enforcement, the bill also had a far-reaching (and largely unanticipated) impact on the process of building Latino political power, because it created a path to citizenship for millions of undocumented immigrants. Chavez believed that the measure would encourage these immigrants to unionize, as their path to legalization created rising expectations for improved wages and working conditions. Referring to these soon-to-be-legalized farmworkers, he observed, "I think they'll always support, if not our union, the idea of a union. . . . When a work force is not afraid, it bargains for itself." When Chavez made these comments, few saw undocumented immigrants as a future source for new union members. Those were the days when such immigrants were still considered "unorganizable," a perception that UFW alumni such as Steven Lerner of Justice for Janitors would begin to change by decade's end.[10]

Throughout the 1980s, the percentage of the UFW's Mexican-born membership increased. Chavez became more involved in Mexican politics, and in 1990 his lobbying won legislation that encouraged Mexican immigrants to join the UFW by allowing UFW members living in the United States to receive Mexican social security benefits. He continued to form relationships with Mexican unions and government officials, and by the 1990s the UFW was seen as one of America's few "binational" unions. Some attribute Chavez's adoption of a more international perspective to his increasing alignment with civil rights groups on immigration issues, but a more significant factor may have been that the UFW had largely abandoned the strike strategy by the 1980s. Since the UFW's problems around immigration arose entirely from the use of undocumented workers as strikebreakers, the lack of strikes reduced the importance of the issue.[11]

LAYING THE GROUNDWORK:
THE ACTIVE CITIZENSHIP CAMPAIGN

In the two decades that preceded the public emergence of a broad-based immigrant rights movement in 2006, UFW veterans forged some key alliances. Through Neighbor to Neighbor (described in chapter 2), Fred Ross Jr. and other former UFW activists helped strengthen links between labor unions, religious groups, nonprofits, and Central American solidarity organizations. In 1986, the passage of the Immigration Reform and Control Act, which offered a route to citizenship for nearly 2.7 million undocumented immigrants who entered the United States before January 1, 1982, provided another opportunity to build support for immigrant rights. To seize this chance, immigrants would have to navigate the notorious complexities of the Immigration and Naturalization Service. It soon became clear that immigrants would need assistance in becoming citizens, and Ross and other UFW veterans were again there to help facilitate Latino citizenship and support the broader political movement for immigrant rights.

IRCA imposed a five-year waiting period on applications for citizenship, and immigrants also had to take courses in English and U.S. civics before they could get permanent visas. So the law's impact in boosting citizenship was delayed. At first, there was no sense of urgency in applying for citizenship, and only forty-seven thousand applications were filed in Los Angeles County when the first wave of IRCA-eligible immigrants could apply for citizenship in 1992. Nor was there a steep rise in applications in 1993.[12]

In 1994, however, California governor Pete Wilson qualified the anti-immigrant Prop 187 for the November ballot, an initiative that punished undocumented immigrants by denying them access to medical care and public schools. Its harsh provisions and its passage by a resounding 59 percent to 41 percent spurred Latino immigrants to seek citizenship. The governor's aggressively anti-immigrant stance had particular significance: more than two million of those affected by IRCA were from Mexico, and California became their main state of residence. As it turned out, 53.5 percent of all IRCA applications came from California; Los Angeles alone included eight hundred thousand applicants.[13]

Understanding that California and the Los Angeles region would be the focus of any citizenship drive, four faith-based groups in Los Angeles that were affiliated with the Saul Alinsky–created Industrial Areas Foundation launched the Active Citizenship Campaign in 1995. The ACC's goals were threefold: to help immigrants apply for citizenship, to end the two-and-a-half-year backlog in processing applications at the INS, and to register voters and reach out to the newly naturalized Latino immigrants. The third component was critical, as there was a widespread feeling in the community that only increased voting by Latino immigrants could defeat future anti-Latino measures. As ACC director Father Miguel Vega put it, "The campaign is not about making citizens. It's about making active citizens."[14]

To spearhead what became a critical drive for immigrant rights throughout Los Angeles County, one of the four IAF groups—the Valley Organized in Community Efforts (VOICE), based in the San Fernando Valley—hired Fred Ross Jr. as its executive director. The Ross family had a long history with the IAF, as Fred Ross Sr. had been an organizer with the IAF's CSO when he became a mentor to Cesar Chavez. Ross Jr. became the ACC's chief organizer and political strategist, using skills he had developed with the UFW to boost the ACC's political clout. When he began working with VOICE in 1994, the San Fernando Valley was primarily a conservative white enclave. According to Ron Kaye, who was then managing editor of the San Fernando Valley–based *Los Angeles Daily News,* "Ross got the wealthy white portions of the community to support VOICE's agenda, which gave the group broader credibility. He translated the group's message in such a way that even the valley's insulated white leadership supported 'citizenship' as a worthy goal."[15]

Ross and the ACC faced two immediate challenges: the immigrants' need for assistance in applying for citizenship, and the huge backlog of completed applications at the INS. To address the first problem, VOICE requested on June 29, 1995, that its site at Mary Immaculate Catholic Church, in the suburb of Pacoima, be officially designated an INS outreach location. The other three ACC groups, located in such heavily Latino areas as East Los Angeles, South Central, and the Pomona and San Gabriel Valleys, sought similar designation, which would make it far more convenient for Latinos to apply for citizenship. They predicted that opening these sites would also speed up the citizenship process from its current twelve to fourteen months to four months.

Citizenship as Political Empowerment

Ross approached the campaign with the same focus on grassroots organizing that he had employed during the UFW boycott days. Cecilia Barragan, a VOICE leader, recalled that she and Ross walked block by block through San Fernando Valley neighborhoods, talking to people about the campaign and encouraging residents to get involved. Much of Ross's time was devoted to training and developing the leadership skills of VOICE volunteers. Barragan described herself as a "little Mexican girl from a small mining town in Arizona" who was convinced by Ross that "she could have a say in what was going on." Ross taught Barragan and other volunteers "how to speak to the powers that be," and he inspired VOICE members to believe that the campaign would achieve its goals.[16]

Richard K. Rogers, the INS district director, was the person who had to approve the four satellite outreach sites. Rogers initially claimed that the INS "liked to see CBOs [community-based organizations] get real heavily involved," because these groups could "educate applicants and bring the fear out of the process." But efforts by VOICE to set up a meeting with Rogers continually faltered. He finally agreed to meet with seven members of the group at his downtown office, refusing requests that he come out to Mary Immaculate Church. Ross figured that "since Mr. Rogers would not come to our neighborhood, we thought we would go to his." Translation: VOICE brought three hundred members to INS headquarters for the meeting. Consuelo Valdez, who was associate director of the ACC, recalls that INS staff members were not suspicious about the large crowd of Latinos, assuming that they were there to apply for citizenship. The group proceeded to Rogers's fifth-floor office and occupied the hallways, holding American flags. Rogers was not pleased by the turnout and told Barragan, "All you want to do is cause trouble." It became clear that VOICE would have to seek out higher authorities to get its needs met.[17]

As Ross and the ACC pressed the INS to reduce the backlog, the troubled agency was undergoing a "reengineering" to expedite the citizenship process. In August 1995, this led INS chief Doris Meissner to launch a new INS initiative, Citizenship USA, targeting INS districts in Chicago, Los Angeles, New York City, San Francisco, and Miami—areas that accounted for 75 percent of the pending application caseload. The program's goal was to ensure a maximum six-month turnaround on naturalization applications by the summer of 1996. Its implementation was accompanied by a 20 percent increase in funding.[18]

Unfortunately, Meissner's initiative did not account for the zeal with which Ross and the ACC were getting immigrants to file citizenship applications. The sheer volume of applicants recruited by the ACC quickly overwhelmed the bolstered INS staff, and by late January 1996, the backlog was worse than before. This led Father Vega to publicly announce that "INS incompetence will stop 300,000 California new citizens from voting in the 1996 presidential election."[19]

On January 30, 1996, Ross, Barragan, other Los Angeles ACC leaders, and representatives of the IAF's Active Citizenship Campaigns in New York, San Francisco, and Chicago joined Representative Xavier Becerra from Los Angeles at a Washington, D.C., meeting with INS commissioner Meissner. The Los Angeles ACC submitted a memo to Meissner setting forth in detail what the group could accomplish to fulfill the expectations of immigrants applying for citizenship pursuant to IRCA. The tasks included producing thousands of volunteers to process applications and help the INS screen applicants, with a specific pledge to submit at least

1,200 applications per month. The ACC was also committed to registering 26,000 new citizens to vote, turning out 52,000 occasional voters by focusing on 960 underrepresented precincts, conducting 5,000 house meetings, and creating voter interest around issues of affirmative action and the minimum wage. The memo echoed Father Vega's cautionary words, warning that "INS inaction will deny 300,000 Latinos the right to vote in the 1996 presidential election in California." The document pledged that the IAF's ACC was willing to "fight along side the Clinton Administration in efforts to maximize INS efficiency and effectiveness and to decrease massive backlogs while increasing the number of New Americans."[20]

This detailed and number-filled work plan, along with the focus on house meetings, was right out of the UFW playbook. The memo also made an explicit connection between citizenship and Latino political empowerment; these new citizens were going to be *active* participants in the elections that shape city, state, and national policies. Ross and others had effectively transformed a 1986 legalization bill into a potentially powerful long-term vehicle for greatly boosting Latino political power and immigrant rights. But the 1996 presidential election was rapidly approaching, and this would be California Latinos' first opportunity to respond to 1994's Prop 187 campaign. Time was of the essence, and the ACC believed that it was imperative that its applicants become eligible to vote.

Vice President Gore Enters the Fight

When ACC's meeting with Meissner, who had spent five years as a top INS official in the Reagan administration, did not resolve its concerns, Ross and his allies went over Meissner's head and contacted Henry Cisneros, secretary of the Department of Housing and Urban Development (HUD), and Leon Panetta, White House chief of staff. Both men forwarded ACC's concerns to Vice President Al Gore, who also received a letter from Cardinal Roger Mahony of Los Angeles expressing a "sense of urgency" over the INS backlog. Ross's longtime relationship with Mahony, who had been an associate bishop in Fresno and a close ally of Cesar Chavez, came in handy, as it would on many occasions in future years.[21]

In addition to turning to political allies, Ross organized a protest by VOICE and the Southern California Organizing Committee (SCOC) outside Rogers's office in the Federal Building in downtown Los Angeles on

February 28, 1996. Members waved American flags, chanted "We want to vote," and demanded to meet with Rogers. Father Pat Murphy of Our Lady of the Holy Rosary Church accused Rogers of "not completing his promise" and said that the group was still praying to "get four more outreach teams." According to VOICE and SCOC, Rogers had promised a three-month turnaround for citizenship interviews when he approved the satellite outreach locations, but the process was instead taking eleven months. Rogers told the media that he had never made such a promise— and never would have, given the overwhelming number of applications. In case the Clinton administration was not sufficiently troubled by Cardinal Mahony's letter, Rogers was now essentially accusing some of Mahony's parishioners of lying about the INS's commitment.[22]

On March 8, 1996, Vice President Al Gore extended his California schedule so that he could meet with Ross, Barragan, Vega, and other Los Angeles ACC representatives. At the meeting, Gore pledged the Clinton administration's full cooperation with their efforts to expedite citizenship applications and reduce the backlog. He promised that the INS would hire more temporary workers, increase office space, and address the unexpectedly large volume of applications. When Gore's commitment was not promptly followed by action, Elaine Kamarck of the vice president's staff sent a memo on March 21 to Doug Farbrother of the National Performance Review (the agency working to use its "reinventing government" principles to address the INS backlog). The memo said, "The President is sick of this and wants action. If nothing moves today we'll have to take some pretty drastic measures." Results soon followed. By early April, Gore's intervention, along with pressure from Panetta, swayed Rogers, who had been avoiding a meeting with the ACC all year. On May 1, Rogers announced at an ACC meeting at Our Lady of Lourdes Church in East Los Angeles that the INS would process 220,000 applications by the end of September. He even claimed that the agency, which until recently had been hostile to the ACC, had a "duty to apply every resource to process every application."[23]

To avoid any doubt about this commitment, Rogers signed his name to a pledge on a giant card while the crowd of eight thousand immigrant rights activists cheered. The pledge included the ninety-day turnaround that Rogers had previously claimed could not be achieved. ACC leader Orinio Opinado of the SCOC in South Central again highlighted the chief purpose of the citizenship campaign, telling the crowd, "We don't count unless we vote. We don't count unless we're active citizens. We

Vice President Al Gore meets with ACC representatives Father Miguel
Vega, Father Pat Murphy, and Fred Ross Jr., Los Angeles, March 8, 1996.
Courtesy of Fred Ross Jr.

don't count unless we are organized." The Reverend George Schultze was
even more specific, saying that only through political involvement could
the nation's anti-immigrant sentiment be reversed.[24]

From Citizens to Activists

The ACC's successful pressuring of the Clinton administration to end
the INS backlog did not slow Ross's efforts to build grassroots support
for the citizenship drive. On July 14, 1996, the IAF held its first West
Coast convention at the Grand Olympic Auditorium, which was attended
by more than 5,000 low-income and working-class people. The keynote
speaker was HUD secretary Cisneros, who had helped get Gore's attention on ACC's concerns about the INS. Richard Rogers, the INS district
director, was among the speakers, showing the agency's willingness to
turn onetime adversaries into allies. VOICE turned out more than 1,500
people for the event, which included the introduction of 750 soon-to-be
citizens who had been helped by the ACC. ACC leader Rosalinda Lugo
of the East Los Angeles–based United Neighborhoods Organization de-

scribed the meeting as a "Get Out to Vote" campaign. Lugo asserted that people were coming "because they want to take back the election process" and that they realized that if they did not get involved, "then our communities are in danger of being neglected." Lugo's comments demonstrated the ACC's clear linkage between achieving citizenship and getting Latino immigrants to exercise their civil right to vote.[25]

ACC's grassroots campaign to increase Latino voting in Los Angeles County coincided with Miguel Contreras's efforts to implement the UFW's successful Latino voter outreach model at the Los Angeles County Federation of Labor (LACFL) (described in chapter 7). While the media largely ignored the ACC's connection to organized labor, the ACC's voter outreach efforts benefited greatly from the support of both Contreras and Eliseo Medina. Medina had headed SEIU's San Diego local since 1986 and won election as a national officer with SEIU in 1996. Ross recognized the value of Medina's national connections, and since Medina was also spending time working to strengthen SEIU's Los Angeles locals, Ross contacted him and reunited with his longtime UFW ally.

Medina was attracted to the ACC for two reasons. First, he was eager to promote civic engagement among immigrant workers. Second, he saw the ACC's work as "empowering immigrant workers to have political power and create a much more progressive electorate in the state." As is often the case with Medina's contributions, there is little public record of his role with the ACC. But VOICE leader Cecilia Barragan recalled that Medina "was very involved" in the ACC; "Eliseo," she commented, "was someone who cared about our community and was always there for us." Medina was a frequent speaker at VOICE events and helped secure critical financial assistance for the campaign from SEIU's state and national offices. With Contreras's labor federation providing local financial support for ACC's voter registration and outreach efforts and Medina bringing in state and national resources, organized labor played an important role in the citizenship campaign.[26]

While Contreras was assembling a grassroots Latino voter outreach team of unionized workers through LACFL, Ross was building a similar Latino voter mobilization operation through VOICE. Many of Ross's precinct walkers were recent citizens, who were fulfilling Father Vega's pledge to become "active" in the community. Among them was Augustina Garcia, a single parent of two, who became a citizen in April 1996. On October 5, she was among 3,000 volunteers out knocking on doors, registering people to vote, and encouraging noncitizens to apply for naturalization. Garcia told the *Los Angeles Daily News* that she was "deter-

mined to fight for my rights. I don't want to be anonymous anymore."
Garcia was among many who would meet at weekly workshops at Mary
Immaculate Catholic Church to receive training from Barragan and other
leaders before going out to hit the streets. ACC's Latino voter outreach
campaign included members from eighty churches and synagogues, who
had committed to cover 960 precincts and reach 96,000 voters for the
November 1996 election.[27]

As a result of securing INS approval to use churches, school cafete-
rias, and community centers for conducting citizenship interviews, rather
than requiring immigrants to go to the INS's downtown offices, the ACC
generated historic increases in the number of new citizens. VOICE alone
processed more than 3,000 citizenship applications through election day.
In August 1996, 60,800 applicants were granted citizenship in Los Angeles, the district's highest one-month total ever. By September 30, the
INS had processed 1.3 million naturalization applications and approved
1.1 million, more than double the prior year. The ACC's efforts had
forced the INS to clear the backlog of 225,000 citizenship applications,
and 25,000 immigrants had become citizens by 1998. The impact of the
combined efforts of LACFL and the ACC became clear on election day,
when Latino turnout in Los Angeles reached record levels and Tony Cardenas became the first Latino elected to the state assembly from the San
Fernando Valley. According to an election night survey by Professor
Chuck Hotchkiss of California Polytechnic State University in Pomona,
the ACC's get out the vote efforts in 140 targeted precincts turned out
an estimated 16,500 voters.[28]

How did the ACC do it? The organization employed the same approach that Fred Ross Jr. had used with the UFW in the 1970s and that
Miguel Contreras brought to the LACFL in 1995. Father Pat Murphy of
Our Lady of the Holy Rosary Church, one of the churches affiliated with
VOICE, described it as a "door-to-door, neighbor-to-neighbor" recruitment effort that involved citizenship classes, voter registration drives, and
phone banks, all aimed at Latinos and other ethnic groups in the 140
precincts. Murphy claimed that watching Latino voters go to the polls
on election day was a "joyous exercise."[29]

As the media hailed VOICE's successful citizenship drives and Latino
voter turnout, Fred Ross Jr. remained out of the limelight. But Cecilia
Barragan, Consuelo Valdez, and Ron Kaye all noted that Ross had been
the chief strategist and organizer of the ACC campaign. Valdez noted
that it was Ross who understood "the big picture" and who had inspired

and trained a single working mother like Barragan and hundreds of other VOICE members to become committed and skilled organizers for social change. Cesar Chavez and Fred Ross Sr. had created a model for this process of leadership development, and what worked among farmworkers in the 1960s and 1970s was proving successful among the urban immigrants in the San Fernando Valley and elsewhere in the 1990s.[30]

The Anti-ACC Backlash

While the ACC's citizenship drive won broad support by appealing to the American spirit of civic engagement, the Republican Party was not happy about the group's success in expediting citizenship applications. A week prior to election day, Republican congressional representative William Zeliff of New Hampshire called for the appointment of an independent counsel to investigate how the Clinton administration had allegedly used the Citizenship USA program to benefit its reelection campaign. Zeliff charged Clinton and Gore with putting "enormous pressure on the INS to naturalize as many new citizens as possible, regardless of the consequence."[31]

Particularly targeted were "private contractors" such as VOICE, who Zeliff claimed were responsible for an "alarming" pattern of fraud in the citizenship application process. Zeliff had held hearings in September 1996 on the many "violent criminals" who had allegedly been rushed into citizenship with insufficient INS review. California governor Pete Wilson expressed his own alarm that "perhaps thousands of criminal aliens" had wrongfully been granted citizenship as a result of the Clinton administration's "rush to naturalize new voters before Election Day." Wilson's concerns, however, were never substantiated.[32]

Foreshadowing the party's shift to a strong anti-immigrant stance in 2005, Republicans continued challenging the Clinton administration's processing of citizenship applications long after the November 1996 election. In fact, three years after the election, Vice President Gore responded to a detailed list of questions from the special counsel to the inspector general at the Justice Department about his role in the Citizenship USA program and his meetings with the ACC. The inspector general sought specific information about Gore's meeting with Father Vega and the ACC's widely publicized claim—included in a February 14, 1996, letter to Gore—that the backlog would "deny 300,000 Latinos the right to vote in the 1996 presidential election." This letter had also hinted that the backlog could lead to a perception of the Clinton administration as "anti-Latino," which Republicans claimed was evidence that the Clinton administration had illegally expedited the citizenship process for political reasons.[33]

Although nothing ever came of the Justice Department investigation, the notion that "Gore pressured the INS" to win the 1996 election and that Citizenship USA "turned criminals into citizens just in time to vote" remained articles of faith among Republican anti-immigrant activists. This helps to explain the Bush administration's inadequate response to a later citizenship backlog in 2007 and 2008: expediting applications from Latino immigrants was likely seen as bringing more Democratic voters to the polls in November 2008 (see chapter 9).[34]

WELFARE REFORM AND THE ATTACK ON LEGAL IMMIGRANTS

After Fred Ross Jr. and Eliseo Medina reconnected during the ACC citizenship drive, Medina urged Ross to join him at SEIU in Los Angeles. But Ross's mother in Marin County was in poor health, and he was committed to moving back to the San Francisco Bay Area after the 1996 election. Once there, Ross became the top district aide to his good friend Representative Nancy Pelosi. Almost immediately, he became involved in fending off a major attack on immigrants' rights.[35]

In order to fulfill his 1992 campaign pledge to "end welfare as we know it," President Clinton had signed into law a "welfare reform" bill on August 22, 1996, at the height of the ACC citizenship and voter registration drive. Most of the discussion concerning the measure focused on how to address poverty among low-income families. But the bill also included little-noticed provisions denying legal immigrants such critical federal benefits as Supplemental Security Income (SSI) and food stamps. Nancy Pelosi's San Francisco congressional district included thousands of elderly Chinese and Filipino immigrants who had entered the country legally decades earlier but had never bothered to become citizens. For many, their entire income, even their food budget, was now at stake. Ross joined with San Francisco's immigrant rights groups to change the provisions affecting legal immigrants before the law was implemented.

From his work with the Clinton administration during the ACC effort, Ross knew who to contact about this new struggle. Initiated by a broad coalition of San Francisco–based Asian American and immigrant civil rights groups, a national campaign quickly emerged to protect vulnerable elderly immigrants. This campaign, like the ACC, created another bridge between immigrant rights groups nationwide that would later help to build a broader movement.[36]

As activists generated sympathetic news stories about the plight of elderly immigrants facing the loss of all their benefits, the congressional Republicans who had insisted on inserting the anti-immigrant provisions in the bill found themselves on the defensive. The political demands for a resolution required action with record speed in order to beat the deadline for the law's implementation. The coalition that Ross helped organize eventually won a new law that prevented existing legal immigrants from losing benefits but maintained the ban on food stamps and SSI for future legal immigrants. The short-term battle was won, but Congress's backroom elimination of benefits for legal immigrants as part of the welfare bill showed that building immigrant political power to avoid such bills in the future was imperative.

THE AFL-CIO JOINS THE
IMMIGRANT RIGHTS MOVEMENT

Although the AFL-CIO was among the key groups pushing to reinstate public benefits to legal immigrants in 1996, this stance ran counter to its history. Since the early 1900s, the AFL-CIO had consistently supported restricting immigration, claiming that the entry of foreign workers suppressed wages and slowed the growth of union membership. While labor's reasons for opposing immigration may have differed from the often race-based anti-immigrant attitudes of political conservatives, the AFL-CIO's alignment with such forces created a powerful political base against progressive immigration reform. For example, in 1985, the AFL-CIO endorsed employer sanctions for hiring undocumented workers, a provision of the 1986 Immigration Control Reform Act that was strongly opposed by immigrant rights groups. The AFL-CIO was so proud of its support for IRCA that it passed a resolution in 1987 calling the bill "the most important and far-reaching immigration legislation in 30 years." The UFW's primarily Latino immigrant workforce, and its refusal to distinguish between undocumented and legal immigrants in its membership, may have moderated the AFL-CIO's anti-immigrant rhetoric, but even Cesar Chavez could not alter the federation's official policy at that time.[37]

Starting with organizing drives among immigrant workers by HERE and SEIU in the 1980s, however, union attitudes began to change. Unions that were organizing undocumented immigrant workers no longer blamed immigrants for lowering wages or taking union jobs. As a result, with UFW veterans playing important roles, the AFL-CIO's historical anti-immigration stance began to shift. The federation's 1993 convention adopted a resolution praising immigrants for helping build America and criticizing efforts to make immigrants "scapegoats for economic and social problems." The resolution also urged affiliated unions "to develop programs to address the special needs of immigrant members and potential members" and to work with "immigrant advocacy groups and service organizations" to protect the interests of new immigrants.[38]

In 1994, organized labor aggressively opposed California's anti-immigrant Prop 187, and the Los Angeles County Federation of Labor, which had rarely backed community struggles in the past, helped mobilize a massive rally of seventy thousand people at Los Angeles city hall to protest the measure. When the U.S. Commission on Immigration Reform (CIR) recommended greater immigration restrictions in a 1995 report, the AFL-CIO spoke out against all the proposed changes. At its 1995 convention, the labor federation passed a resolution that declared: "The notion that immigrants are to blame for the deteriorating living standards of America's low-wage workers must be clearly rejected." According to Vernon M. Briggs Jr., "rather than immigration reform," the resolution "proposed increasing the minimum wage, adopting universal health care and enacting labor law reform as the remedies for the widening income disparity in the nation." When Congress sought to enact many of CIR's punitive recommendations in 1996, the AFL-CIO joined immigrant rights groups in killing the key proposals.[39]

Although organized labor's stance toward immigration had changed by the mid-1990s, Eliseo Medina and others recognized that simply stopping bad proposals was not enough. Medina believed that labor should help lead the fight for immigrant rights, and he saw immigrant workers as the future of organized labor. Medina himself was an immigrant, whose family had come to Delano from Mexico in 1956. He began picking grapes at the age of ten and began organizing with the UFW in 1965. Medina learned from Chavez and the union that people working in the fields could challenge the growers and be treated with respect. Describing years later what the UFW meant to him and others, Medina observed, "For the first time, people actually felt we have some rights, we can stand up for ourselves, we can fight, and we can win." He believed from his early UFW days that the surest route for Latino immigrants to win respect, fair wages, and decent working conditions was by joining a union.[40]

After leaving the UFW in 1978, Medina worked briefly for the American Federation of State, County, and Municipal Employees (AFSCME) and then moved on to organize public employees in Texas for the Communication Workers of America from 1981 to 1985. Despite the state's restrictions on collective bargaining, Medina boosted the membership of CWA's Texas State Employees Union from about six hundred to more than four thousand. Medina then joined fellow UFW alumni Stephen Lerner in leaving CWA for SEIU. Marshall Ganz had been working on some projects for SEIU, and, after seeing Medina in Houston, Ganz suggested to SEIU organizing director Andy Stern that the union should consider hiring Medina to run its troubled San Diego local. In 1986, Medina went to SEIU's Washington, D.C., headquarters to be interviewed by President John Sweeney and Stern. But the UFW veteran was asking his own questions: Medina wanted to know about Sweeney's commitment to fund organizing efforts, and he wanted assurances that he would get the resources he needed to succeed. Having spent the previous years organizing in Texas, Medina told the SEIU president, "I [am] not interested in going to San Diego to get a suntan, because I already have one."[41]

Sweeney and Stern agreed to provide the necessary organizing resources, and Medina took up the challenge. When he arrived in San Diego, his former UFW colleagues Marshall Ganz and Scott Washburn were both there, trying to clean up the mess left by Medina's predecessor. Medina quickly turned the situation around. He helped the union's primarily Latino janitors to win pay raises of 40 percent and successfully organized paramedics, health care workers, and other county staff. In just five years with Medina's leadership, the membership of the San Diego local increased from seventeen hundred to ten thousand.[42]

Medina was eager to change the AFL-CIO's anti-immigration policy, but he did not believe that it was possible until longtime AFL-CIO leader Lane Kirkland was replaced. In October 1995, John Sweeney was elected to succeed Kirkland as president of the AFL-CIO. His election gave Medina and others the opportunity to align the federation with the immigrants' cause and to unite the power of the labor and immigrant rights movements. Medina saw Sweeney as a strong supporter of immigrant rights but knew that the new president liked to operate by consensus: Sweeney would not change AFL-CIO immigration policy until a broad consensus was organized from below. Medina took up the task of creating this popular groundswell. As the newly elected executive vice president of SEIU and the highest-ranking Latino in the labor movement, he used his new base in Los Angeles to make it happen.[43]

When Medina arrived in Los Angeles in 1996, the city had a pro-business Republican mayor and a weakened though recovering labor movement. SEIU's Justice for Janitors had begun to revitalize labor in 1990 with its historic Century City campaign (later profiled in the film *Bread and Roses*), and Miguel Contreras, Medina's former UFW ally, had become political director of the county federation of labor in 1994. But there was much work left to be done. Medina told his assistant, Ben Monterroso, who had been the Los Angeles regional director of SEIU, that they had to launch the "L.A. project." Monterroso had no idea what Medina was talking about and asked what "the project" involved. Medina replied that he "wanted Los Angeles to be as labor-friendly as San Francisco" and that Monterroso would be responsible for making sure this happened. Having frequently been asked by Cesar Chavez to run campaigns without being given detailed directions, Medina clearly thought he was giving Monterroso a great opportunity to display his talents. While Monterroso met with Los Angeles union heads to discuss how to fulfill this goal, Medina set out to ensure that Contreras would be elected to head the county federation. SEIU was the largest affiliate of the LACFL, and Medina secured enough additional support to allow Contreras to take over the reins.[44]

Medina had a vision of unifying labor with community, religious, and immigrant rights groups; he spent 1997 and much of 1998 discussing this vision and how to implement it in Los Angeles with Contreras, UNITE HERE president Maria Elena Durazo, the UFW, and the United Food and Commercial Workers. By late 1998, when Sweeney had been in power for three years, the group decided that it was time to offer a resolution to the 1999 AFL-CIO convention to shift the labor federation's immigration policy. Medina "had his doubts whether they could change it" that year, but two factors worked in the group's favor.[45]

First, the October 1999 convention was held in Los Angeles, and there was not a more dramatic illustration of the importance of labor supporting immigrant rights. Union officials from across the country could see first-hand how a city's growing union-immigrant alliance was expanding labor's political clout. Immigrant janitors, drywallers, home health care workers, and hotel workers had become the face of the city's labor movement. Second, HERE president John Wilhelm was achieving great success boosting his union's membership in the Las Vegas hotel industry. He was close enough to Los Angeles to have attended some of the reform group's strategy meetings. With Wilhelm and Andy Stern, now president of SEIU, increasing their influence and both backing a new pro-immigrant policy, a shift in the AFL-CIO's longstanding position was at hand.

Medina took the lead in debating the resolution on the convention floor. He told the assembled leaders that his recent experience working with Los Angeles's unionized janitors showed the importance of aligning labor with the cause of immigrant rights. "While we do everything to bring justice and dignity to janitors in the workplace, the minute they leave the worksite, they revert to their undocumented status." Medina knew that Sweeney was in full support of the resolution and accepted his strategy of forming a special committee on immigration that would study and recommend changes to the AFL-CIO's policy. Since Wilhelm chaired the committee and Medina was a member, the outcome of its deliberations was not in doubt. But the committee's formation gave union leaders from every sector the opportunity to assess the proposed new policy and provide input, moving toward the broad consensus that Sweeney sought.[46]

In February 2000, on the committee's recommendation, the AFL-CIO executive board met in New Orleans and reversed its 1985 policy favoring employer sanctions for hiring undocumented immigrants. Since the AFL-CIO had extolled its support for this policy as recently as 1987, this reversal was dramatic. The labor leaders justified the shift on the grounds that some employers were circumventing the sanctions and the federal government's lack of enforcement made the current system unfair and unworkable. The federation also called for a new system that ensured a level playing field for all employers and urged amnesty for the nation's estimated 6 million undocumented workers. Wilhelm was among those who argued that standing up for the rights of immigrants was good for workers, unions, and communities. "We weren't trying to do anything special—we just wanted to do what was right," he said. Reflecting the increasing number of union members who were undocumented, the AFL-CIO urged strong penalties against employers who abused workers' immigration status to deny them job rights and labor protections.[47]

The AFL-CIO's new policy immediately changed the longstanding political calculus around legalization for undocumented workers The federation's action also showed how the Los Angeles labor movement, with Medina and Contreras playing key roles, was helping to transform organized labor nationally. While some labor supporters argued that unions would regret their support for increased immigration, immigrant workers had been in the forefront of America's labor movement from the fight for the eight-hour day in the 1880s to the passage of the National Labor Relations Act in the 1930s. Backers of the new, pro-immigrant policy pointed out that much of labor's historical opposition to immigration from Mexico and Asia had been based on racism and a fear of foreigners, which helped split the labor movement, to the benefit of employers. The AFL-CIO highlighted the example of Cesar Chavez as someone who had helped the union movement understand that it must accept the responsibility to represent all workers regardless of their immigration status. But neither his example nor the UFW's successes had been able to change the AFL-CIO's immigration policy; instead, it had taken years of effort by individuals such as Medina, Contreras, Ross, Stephen Lerner, and Chava Bustamante, along with other farmworker veterans and labor activists, to move immigrant rights to the forefront of the American labor movement.[48]

BUILDING A POWERFUL ALLIANCE
FOR IMMIGRANT RIGHTS

The AFL-CIO accompanied its February 2000 policy shift with a request that unions hold forums across the country where immigrant workers could explain their struggle to find a better life through union membership. Most unions expected these events to involve around three hundred people. But Medina, Contreras, and the Los Angeles labor movement had a broader vision. Medina saw the Los Angeles forum as an opportunity for organized labor to solidify its partnerships with church, community, and immigrant rights groups. He had sensed the potential power of the immigration issue when, after returning to Los Angeles after the AFL-CIO's policy shift, he scheduled a news conference with church, community, and immigrant rights groups to discuss the decision. He was shocked to see at least ten television stations and a huge number of newspaper and radio staff at the event. Even in comparison to the UFW's high-profile press events, Medina "had never seen so much media coverage." The media turnout told him that labor and immigrant rights activists were not the only ones who saw the AFL-CIO's policy shift as a "huge deal"—the "outside world" did as well.[49]

After getting the SEIU international to cover most of the cost of a larger event, Medina went to the participating groups and asked them to contribute according to their ability to pay. He wanted to convey the message that labor was looking for a "true partnership" in fighting for immigration reform and wanted the broader community to "feel ownership" of the event. The response to Medina's overtures exceeded his highest expectations. The "community forum" on June 10 became a massive rally in the Los Angeles Sports Arena, with seventeen thousand people in the arena and three thousand more outside. Contreras described the crowd as representing "the birth of a powerful new alliance." Medina was "blown away by the number of people who had shown up" and credited labor's organizational partners and the Latino media with generating the huge turnout. Medina believed that the crowd demonstrated the huge untapped potential of the immigrant rights movement, and he also felt that the event signaled a willingness on the part of the religious community to wage a major fight for immigration reform.[50]

The speakers at the Sports Arena rally included Antonio Villaraigosa and other prominent Latino politicians and labor officials. Longtime activist Bert Corona gave the keynote address. Corona had begun organizing with the International Longshoremen's and Warehousemen's Union in 1937; in 1960, he was among those who formed the Mexican American Political Association. Corona and MAPA had provided support to workers during the UFW's Delano grape strike in 1965 against DiGiorgio farms. As Corona later stated, "MAPA unconditionally endorsed the farmworkers' cause. It inspired and energized us." Corona was also inspired by Chavez's leadership and particularly appreciated the UFW leader's success in fusing the symbols of Mexican nationalism with a broader, class-based approach.[51]

But in the late 1960s, Corona ran into conflict with Chavez and the UFW over the union's policies toward undocumented immigrants. Corona had been organizing these immigrants in Los Angeles on behalf of the Hermandad Mexicana Nacional (a group formed by union members in 1951 to support the rights of Mexican residents working in Southern California), and he opposed the UFW's support for deporting undocumented immigrants who were working as strikebreakers. Chavez and the UFW had no sympathy for such "scabs," but Corona and the Hermandad believed that they should be organized rather than deported. Corona understood and sympathized with the UFW position, and his disagreement with Chavez's stance did not diminish his support for the UFW cause. He later pointed out that by the 1970s, Chavez and the union supported positive immigration reforms and that "in the main, we have agreed on ninety percent of what the farmworkers have done or advocated."[52]

Since the 1970s, Corona had focused on battling anti-immigrant legislation at the state and federal level. His selection as keynote speaker for labor's high-profile event symbolized the AFL-CIO's new strategy and sent a powerful message that the labor movement was now on the side of immigrants. Although eighty years old and physically frail, Corona had lost none of his fire, as he delivered an inspiring speech at the June

10 event: "There is no mine, no bridge, not a row in the fields or a construction site in all the United States that hasn't been watered with the tears, the sweat and blood of immigrants. We demand an amnesty for the workers who have made the wealth of this country possible. Amnesty is not a gift, but a right, for those who have contributed so much."[53] Corona's lifelong dream of labor-immigrant unity had been fulfilled in Los Angeles, and this alliance would soon spread across the nation. Those whose organizing experience had begun with Cesar Chavez and the UFW were the driving force in transforming Corona's vision into reality.

After the event, Medina scheduled a concert and fundraiser for immigrant rights, which was also held at the Sports Arena. News of the remarkable June 10 rally in Los Angeles had spread nationally, and Medina made a special effort to invite labor officials from across the country to be part of the second event so that they could view the power of the emerging labor-clergy-community alliance firsthand. The successful concert and fundraiser further confirmed that a model for the American labor movement was being created in Los Angeles and that momentum for immigrant rights legislation was growing.[54]

During 2000, many AFL-CIO unions, especially those in the food, service, and building trades, began restructuring their organizing efforts to include immigrant workers. In April 2000, the benefits of immigrant organizing became even clearer, as Medina worked with SEIU 1877's Los Angeles janitors to win the largest wage increases in the history of the union's Justice for Janitors campaign. This victory was another step in the process of transforming Los Angeles into a pro-union town, and it sent a powerful message nationally about the power of the labor-immigrant alliance.

In April 2001, Medina followed up this success by securing a historic agreement between SEIU and Catholic Healthcare West to facilitate union representation in the largest nonprofit health care system in the western United States. SEIU had been engaged in high-profile conflicts with CHW over its attempts to unionize hospitals since 1997, and CHW had fought back with full-page newspaper ads attacking SEIU's "corporate campaign" and "disruptive activities." This conflict between labor and a Catholic institution disturbed Medina, a deeply spiritual man whose UFW experience had taught him the importance of labor-church unity. In 1999, Medina reached out to a former UFW supporter, Los Angeles cardinal Roger Mahony, to help resolve the dispute.

Although Mahony had been a close ally of Cesar Chavez and the UFW, he had backed away from involvement in labor causes since 1989–

90, when his diocese successfully defeated efforts by the Amalgamated Clothing and Textile Workers Union to organize the church's cemetery workers. Some union activists accused Mahony of hypocrisy, but Medina understood how to approach Mahony, assuring him that the labor movement needed, and would appreciate, his support. Mahony worked behind the scenes to pressure CHW, which reached a settlement with SEIU in 2001. By 2002, SEIU had won contracts covering nine thousand workers at more than twenty CHW hospitals. This "peace accord" between SEIU and the hospital operator would have dramatic implications for the immigrant rights movement, as it repaired a rift and re-unified two powerful forces supporting the immigrant community. In addition, Cardinal Mahony would prove to be a critical ally of the labor and immigrant rights movements in the years ahead.[55]

As support for immigration reform grew throughout 2000, among both the public and policy makers, Eliseo Medina joined Randall Johnson of the U.S. Chamber of Commerce and other business, labor, and political leaders from both the United States and Mexico on an immigration reform panel convened by the Carnegie Endowment for International Peace. Mexico's involvement on the panel became key in 2001, as its newly elected conservative president, Vicente Fox, seemed to have a good relationship with President George W. Bush. Fox supported increased migration to the United States—money flowing back to Mexico from undocumented immigrants in America, in the form of remittances, was Mexico's biggest source of income—and many assumed that the Bush administration would want to boost a conservative ally by supporting his immigration reforms. With the AFL-CIO and the Fox government supporting legalization for undocumented immigrants, and key business groups such as the U.S. Chamber of Commerce believing that "we were on a roll," as Randall Johnson put it, there was a growing sense in 2001 that a progressive immigration measure was on the horizon. This sense of momentum continued through the day that Johnson presented the panel's recommendations to a U.S. Senate committee—the Friday before September 11, 2001.[56]

The September 11 tragedy stopped this momentum in its tracks. Although the attacks on the World Trade Center and the Pentagon had no connection to undocumented Latino immigrants, new fears were raised about foreigners who might be in the country illegally. Unions and immigrant rights groups tried their best to counter rising anti-immigrant feelings. They highlighted the large number of immigrant workers in New York City's UNITE HERE Local 100—headed by UFW alumni Bill

Granfield—who had died in the collapse of the World Trade Center and the essential role played by unionized firefighters and police officers in rescue efforts. Eliseo Medina argued that "the terrible events of September 11 should serve to unite Americans, not to divide us between immigrants and native-born." Citing the many SEIU and UNITE HERE members who had rushed to help people get out of the fallen buildings, Medina noted, "Nobody asked the people who were helping them what their immigration status was." He correctly pointed out that 9/11 actually demonstrated the human tragedy of America's immigration policy: undocumented families of 9/11 victims were left "totally unprotected because of their legal status" and had to continue "to live in the shadows, fearful that, if they go and ask for public help, they could be deported."[57] Nonetheless, it was clear that efforts to implement progressive immigration reform had ground to a halt. An issue that had seemed ripe for resolution suddenly shifted off the political radar screen, and there was no choice but to wait out the aftereffects of the attacks.

In 2002, however, reform efforts were revived with the launch of the "Reward Work" campaign, a brainchild of Eliseo Medina. This was an effort by the AFL-CIO and more than four hundred religious, community, political, student, and immigrant organizations to collect signatures on one million postcards urging legalization for undocumented immigrants who work and pay taxes. The campaign, also known as "One Million Voices," brought an important new element into the burgeoning immigrant rights movement: the notion of civic participation.[58]

Medina's faith in the power of civic engagement came from his UFW days, when he saw how the union negotiated contracts that included a provision for grower-funded "Citizen Participation Days." Workers received a paid holiday for participating in voter registration, campaign work, or other acts of civic engagement. A worker who chose not to participate could sign over the amount of the paid day to the UFW's citizen participation fund, which then used the money to advance the union's political agenda. According to Bill Carder, who negotiated some of the UFW's first grape contracts in 1970 and spent over three decades negotiating contracts for a wide range of unions, such provisions "are extremely uncommon. I cannot think of another union contract that included a civic participation clause."[59]

A 1972 study of the impact of the UFW's civic participation drive found that UFW members had a much greater sense that voting was a civic duty and had much more faith in democratic institutions than farmworkers who supported the union but were not members or those who opposed the union. Interviews with 244 farmworkers in and around the Central Valley city of Fresno supported the assertion that "the UFW has served as a mobilizing agent for its members, inducing them to new and expanded citizenship roles." Based on his experience while working for the UFW, Medina strongly believed that Latino immigrants must advocate for themselves in the political arena. He also argued that this was the lesson of immigrant empowerment throughout U.S. history. Noting the examples of the Irish, the Jews, and the Italians, Medina described how "they organized and made their issues an important part of the American agenda. We're trying to do the same."[60]

Cesar Chavez used to tell workers that they had two contracts—a collective bargaining contract that covered them at work, and a "social contract" that covered them outside the workplace. This latter protection, reflected in the UFW's civic participation days, required union members to be involved with community organizations and churches and to work to ensure fair treatment of farmworker children at school. UFW members also used civic participation days to organize voter registration drives in the many small, rural California towns where the farmworker population dominated numerically but had no political power. As Latino voting in these communities increased, local governments became more accountable to farmworkers. Medina was deeply troubled that even though unions could achieve equality and fairness for undocumented immigrants in the workplace, many of these workers felt they had to avoid public engagement because of their legal status. He conceived his civic participation plan as a way to send a message to undocumented immigrants that they had the right to circulate petitions, attend rallies, and otherwise engage in American civic life. Such participation would bring them out of the shadows and allow them to positively shape policies that affected their lives.[61]

Medina, Ben Monterroso, Maria Elena Durazo, and Miguel Contreras had created a model for civic participation for immigrant workers in Los Angeles when they founded the Organization of Los Angeles Workers (OLAW) in 2000. But that group's activities primarily involved elections. Now Medina was using the One Million Voices campaign to expand immigrants' participation from elections and union meetings to local and national advocacy campaigns, particularly those involving immigrant rights. And his plan was to expand this project nationally as a strategy for engaging hundreds of thousands, if not millions, of undocumented immigrants in the fight for legalization.

The New York Civic Participation Project (NYCPP) was an early example of how Medina's strategy could be successfully implemented. The NYCPP was created in 2003 as a collaboration between SEIU 32BJ, the nation's largest janitors' local; HERE Local 100; District Council 37, New York City's public employees union; Make the Road by Walking, a community organization based in Bushwick (Brooklyn); and the National Employment Law Project, an immigrant advocacy group. Confirming its strong identification with the legacy of Cesar Chavez and the UFW, a quotation from Chavez appeared in both English and Spanish in the center of the original home page of NYCPP's website (http://nycpp.org): "We don't need perfect political systems; we need perfect participation." The page was headed with multiple photos of immigrants carrying banners with the UFW rallying cry, *"sí se puede!"*

According to Gouri Sadhwani, NYCPP's executive director until 2007, the group was created "because there was a big vacuum among New York City community organizations in having a way for immigrant workers to be engaged in civic participation." Unlike OLAW, NYCPP does not focus on electoral politics. Rather, the group seeks to "change the framework about how immigrant workers could contribute to civic life." NYCPP accomplishes this by involving immigrants in local campaigns around such issues as ensuring language access in city services and protecting libraries in immigrant neighborhoods from proposed budget cuts. The group also focuses on national immigration reform, with its participants collecting tens of thousands of signatures for the national Reward Work campaign. In its first three years, NYCPP created an active base of more than one thousand active new immigrants, both union and community members. As the project expands to several other states, the potential activist base for local, state, and national immigrants rights advocacy will grow exponentially.[62]

In addition to working with NYCPP, SEIU 32BJ makes a separate effort to get union members involved in civic participation through its American Dream Fund. The fund uses voluntary donations from union members to back legislation and candidates and brings union members into these campaigns. Under the leadership of Secretary-Treasurer Hector Figueroa, the union has used its campaign to "Stand Up for the American Dream" to double the wages of state-contracted workers in New Jersey and to expand the workplace rights of building service staff. In the 2006 election, the American Dream Fund helped SEIU 32BJ put more than three thousand members on the streets during the campaign season and more than one thousand on election day.[63] Many of the union's members are immigrants, and their growing electoral participation creates the opportunity for an East Coast version of California's powerful Strengthening our Lives voter mobilization organization (described in chapter 7).

Having rebounded from 9/11 with a series of campaigns to reenergize the drive for legalization, the AFL-CIO sought to renew efforts for progressive federal immigration reform by linking immigrant rights to the 1960s civil rights movement through the Immigrant Workers Freedom Ride. The IWFR became a critical vehicle for refocusing the debate around immigration away from domestic terrorism and toward enacting legislation that would meet the needs of America's millions of hardworking undocumented immigrants.

IMMIGRANT WORKERS FREEDOM RIDE

The Immigrant Workers Freedom Ride was a nationwide event chiefly organized and sponsored by UNITE HERE, SEIU, and the AFL-CIO. UNITE HERE and SEIU played a leading role in building a broad coalition of religious groups, students, immigrant rights organizations, and community groups in support of the event. The IWFR largely escaped national consciousness at the time, and many labor allies questioned the allocation of union resources for the event. I was at a meeting of national organizers in December 2002 when the proposed IWFR was discussed. The group of veteran labor allies was incredulous that, after major Republican gains in the November 2002 elections, so much union staff time and money would be devoted to an event that involved neither a labor election nor a political election. I shared this skepticism and was encouraged when I learned that the IWFR had been delayed and might never happen. But all of us were wrong. We failed to foresee how the IWFR would reenergize and broaden America's immigrant rights movement as well as building and deepening labor-clergy-community alliances.

The IWFR was named after the 1961 Freedom Rides of the U.S. civil rights movement, in which student activists rode buses in the Deep South to challenge segregation on interstate transportation and in bus and train terminals. The chief organizer of the IWFR was Dave Glaser of UNITE HERE, who later went on to head the national Hotel Workers Rising boycotts (see chapter 2). The national chair of the IWFR was Maria Elena Durazo, who then headed UNITE HERE's Los Angeles local. Durazo believed that the IWFR would "take the fight for immigrant rights to a new level of unity and strength" and would show that "immigrants are also fighting for good jobs, access to health care and rights on the job—the same issues all workers are seeking." The LACFL showed its commitment by donating $100,000 to offset the cost of the Freedom Ride.[64]

A critical aim of the IWFR was to strengthen working relationships between labor unions and the many community, civil rights, religious, and student groups that collectively made up the nation's immigrant rights movement. The Freedom Riders included immigrants themselves, both documented and undocumented, as well as union and community allies, who planned to promote the need for immigration reform when stopping in dozens of communities across the country. The IWFR also hoped to return immigration issues to the national political agenda a year before the 2004 elections and to encourage greater civic participation by immigrants. IWFR organizers planned to emphasize that immigrants were also workers, and part of the U.S. working class. "Immigrants built this country and the union movement," said HERE president John Wilhelm, chair of the AFL-CIO executive council's committee on immigration. "Today, millions of immigrants are working hard at jobs many of us don't want to do, paying taxes and playing by the rules. They deserve the same freedom and equality we all strive for in America." Laborers president Terence O'Sullivan echoed this, noting, "Exploiting any group of workers is an attack on the living standards of all workers."[65]

As the start of the IWFR approached, key relationships were being forged that would expand and strengthen the immigrant rights movement. In Chicago, a crowd of fifteen hundred rallied in support of immigration reform on August 9 before marching to the Congress Hotel, whose primarily immigrant workers had been on strike for eight weeks (see chapter 2). Seattle unions used the IWFR to reach out to diverse community groups, with Steve Williamson, executive secretary-treasurer of the King County Labor Council, noting, "Labor is saying that immigrant issues are union issues, and other groups are talking about unions as never before. The energy is growing exponentially." Houston's Central Labor Council also sought new alliances in support of immigrant rights. "We are building ties with groups that have never had a relationship with the union movement before," said Richard Shaw, secretary-treasurer of the Harris County (Texas) Central Labor Council.[66]

The religious community was also gearing up. In Maryland and Washington, D.C., Labor in the Pulpits programs emphasizing immigrant rights were held at 125 religious services over Labor Day. "Just as the Freedom Rides in the 1960s set the stage for a national movement to secure the rights of African Americans in this country, the Immigrant Workers Freedom Ride can create the platform for a real national dialogue about immigration reform," noted Fred Mason, president of the Maryland State and D.C. AFL-CIO. More than 160 religious groups, including affiliates of Interfaith Worker Justice, endorsed the IWFR. Throughout the rides, meetings and rallies were often held in churches, just as they were during the UFW grape boycott.[67]

Buses carrying more than nine hundred activists began departing on September 23, 2003, from ten major cities—Boston, Chicago, Houston, Las Vegas, Los Angeles, Miami, Minneapolis, Portland, San Francisco, and Seattle—with plans to converge in Washington, D.C., and New York City in early October. Glaser described the buses as "traveling freedom schools," which would "enable workers to share personal experiences and discuss the need for immigrants to gain legal status, have a clear road to citizenship, reunite their families, be free to form unions without regard to legal status and enjoy full civil rights protection."[68]

The IWFR got off to a rousing start. In Los Angeles, an estimated ten thousand people gathered on September 23 to send the riders off. Cardinal Roger Mahony held a service in the city's cathedral and offered his blessing to the riders and the event. This inspirational start came in handy when, on September 26, the Los Angeles Freedom Ride delegation was detained for over three hours while immigration officials interrogated some of the riders at a border checkpoint eighty-eight miles east of El Paso, Texas. The riders braved the threat of deportation by refusing to disclose their immigration status and singing "We Shall Overcome." Protests over the INS action poured in to the Bush administration from union presidents, members of Congress, and bishops from around the country. At the bus's next scheduled stop, in San Antonio, hundreds of people outside city hall chanted "sí se puede!" while awaiting the arrival of the buses from Los Angeles that had been "routinely detained." Faced with resistance by the riders and the national outcry, immigration officials finally gave up and released them.[69]

Although no one expected the riders to be brutally beaten, as had occurred in the 1961 bus trips, the INS did not ignore the IWFR. In another incident, two buses that left from Las Vegas encountered about two hundred anti-immigrant protesters when they arrived in Little Rock, Arkansas. The protesters surrounded the buses, and although police had been notified about the buses' arrival, no officers were present at the scene. Legal observers accompanying the ride contacted a hotline staffed by the Los Angeles chapter of the National Lawyers Guild, who in turn contacted the police. The officers soon arrived to defuse the situation.[70]

The journey east gave Freedom Riders a great opportunity to meet local supporters and build alliances along the route. When Houston's delegation of about ninety-five riders reached Atlanta, they joined with five thousand supporters in what was the state's largest immigrant rights demonstration ever. The Houston delegation visited churches, community centers, and union halls in fifteen southern cities. In Selma, Alabama, the group marched across the Edmund Pettis Bridge, where local and state police had viciously attacked civil rights activists in 1965 as marchers sought to reach Montgomery. Overall, the riders visited 103 cities. Various delegations attended a rally in Sacramento, a march in downtown Palm Springs, a welcome event in Phoenix, a mass in Tucson, and rallies at the Bureau of Citizenship and Immigration Services in Reno, Nevada. They heard rousing speeches at St. Joseph's Catholic Church in Yakima, Washington, and a boisterous crowd welcomed them to Denver. Immigrant rights supporters in St. Louis welcomed riders at a city hall rally with gospel music and held a memorial in honor of a rider's son, a legal immigrant who died while in INS custody. In Toledo, bus riders and a group of farmworkers met at the headquarters of the Farm Labor Organizing Committee.[71]

The IWFR highlighted the diversity of cities in which a burgeoning immigrant rights movement was taking root. Neither Tulsa, Oklahoma; Knoxville, Tennessee; Birmingham, Alabama; Grove Springs, Florida; Charleston, South Carolina; nor Des Moines, Iowa, had been well known for immigrant rights activism, yet riders were warmly received by local supporters in each of these cities. At one level, the stops in more than a hundred cities were simply a function of logistics: riders needed places to eat and sleep. And it was only logical that they would meet local supporters from labor, the religious community, and student and community groups while staying in or passing through town. But beyond the practical necessity, the plan represented a brilliant strategy for laying the groundwork for a national immigrant rights movement. This proved particularly true in the smaller cities in the Midwest and the South, where little infrastructure for such a movement existed.

The riders converged in Washington, D.C., to lobby Congress on October 1. The delegations urged representatives to support three legislative goals: creating a path to legalization and citizenship for all immigrants, making it easier to reunite the families of undocumented immigrants, and protecting immigrants' workplace rights. But the IWFR was less about pushing specific legislation and more about announcing the emergence of a larger movement. Eliseo Medina captured the broader vision of the IWFR, saying, "We need to organize and use the power of our vote. That's the next step in the struggle. It's not just about immigrant workers' rights, but about living wages, about decent education. This is the beginning of us taking back America." IWFR national director Dave Glaser echoed Medina's assessment of the broader implications of the Freedom Ride. He felt that the experience of organizing the Freedom Ride had changed the labor movement and the immigrant communities; and he predicted that "employer resistance to organizing is going to have to reckon with the deep passion for justice we saw as we traveled across the country," as immigrant workers were increasingly seeing unions as a vehicle for achieving that justice.[72]

After leaving Washington, D.C., eighteen buses carrying the Freedom Riders headed for New York City, where they were met by hundreds of additional buses sent by churches, unions, and student organizations on October 4. The ride concluded with a rally of more than a hundred thousand people. Speakers included numerous representatives of the religious community. Cardinal Edward M. Egan, the archbishop of the Catholic archdiocese of New York, was warmly received by the crowd and spoke of how "shameful advantage is being taken of men and women in the work force who do not have proper papers." Bishop Nicholas DiMarzio of Brooklyn echoed Egan, condemning the way that immigrants are "often ridiculed, exploited, and abused. This must stop, and this immoral system must be changed." Congressman John Lewis, Democrat from Georgia, a Freedom Rider in the 1960s, declared, "Martin Luther King would be very proud. We are white, Black, Hispanic, Native American— we are one family, in one house, and we are not going to let anybody turn us around."[73]

Maria Elena Durazo, IWFR national chair, summed up the essence of the organizers' strategy when she told the crowd that the Immigrant Workers Freedom Ride was not an event, "but the creation of a new movement. Immigrants now understand we are not alone, we have allies. . . . Whether you are second generation, or fourteenth," she said, "we have to build a new movement in the United States of America." By setting a movement in motion and building a framework for future action, the Freedom Ride helped pave the way for the mass immigrant rights marches of 2006.[74]

9

THE IMMIGRANT RIGHTS
MOVEMENT EXPLODES

Despite the success of the Immigrant Workers Freedom Ride, its immediate impact was not visible nationally. As much as its organizers hoped that the event would put immigrant rights on the 2004 national political agenda, the issue was overshadowed during the presidential campaign by the Iraq war, growing economic and social inequality, and so-called moral issues such as gay marriage. President Bush seemingly opened the door to reform efforts when he declared in January 2004 that America's immigration system was "not working" and called for a guest worker program that would provide temporary workers with a path to citizenship. But the speech created a huge backlash among Bush's conservative base, who interpreted his remarks as a call for amnesty. The president subsequently stayed away from the issue, although it continued to be a hot topic on conservative talk radio.[1]

At the start of 2005, Representative F. James Sensenbrenner, a Republican from Wisconsin, sought to seize upon the anti-immigrant attitudes of conservatives by introducing legislation that required states to verify legal immigration status for anyone who applied for a driver's license. The bill was attached to a measure that funded U.S. troops in Iraq and Afghanistan, so that a vote against the bill could be portrayed during campaign season as a vote against the troops. Some conservatives argued that passage of this "Real ID" bill was a prerequisite for their support of comprehensive immigration reform.

But after Senators Edward Kennedy of Massachusetts and John McCain of Arizona agreed on a comprehensive reform proposal, Sensenbrenner raised the stakes by introducing HR 4437, which made it a federal crime to live in the United States illegally. Not content to criminalize 10 to 12 million hardworking immigrants, Sensenbrenner's bill also made it a felony to assist or offer services to undocumented immigrants; health care workers, teachers, and priests would be risking five-year prison terms and seizure of their assets.

The House of Representatives passed HR 4437 on December 16, 2005, only ten days after it was introduced. While the bill long remained identified with conservative Republican House members, Sensenbrenner stated during the floor debate on the measure that he was making "unlawful presence" in the country a felony "at the administration's request." Accordingly, Bush issued a statement that day to "applaud" what he described as a "strong immigration reform bill." He also urged the Senate to take action on immigration reform so that he could sign a "good bill" into law.[2]

Heavily influenced by vocal anti-immigrant sentiments on right-wing media outlets, House Republicans appeared unaware of how the immigrant rights movement had grown since the passage of California's Prop 187 in 1994. When immigrant advocacy groups learned that HR 4437 had passed, the response was fast and furious. The U.S. Conference of Catholic Bishops sent a letter to Congress and the president urging them to publicly oppose the measure, and the bishops' spokesperson noted that it "would place parish, diocesan and social service program staff at risk of criminal prosecution simply for performing their jobs." An immigrant rights movement that now included labor unions and churches on its front lines, and that had solidified its infrastructure through the Immigrant Workers Freedom Ride, was ready for battle. As Eliseo Medina later observed, "Sensenbrenner could not have imagined the historic mobilization he would help spark when he introduced his bill to criminalize hardworking, taxpaying immigrants and the teachers, healthcare professionals, clergy members and others who assist them."[3]

The House passage of HR 4437 set in motion not only a series of mass mobilizations but also a plan by immigrant rights advocates to win Senate approval of a pro-legalization bill, with Medina as lead negotiator on the Senate legislation. On February 11, 2006, immigrant rights activists from across the country met in Riverside, California, to discuss their strategy for responding to the Sensenbrenner bill and to develop a schedule for protest activities. The group decided to hold the first mass protests on or around March 25, the date on which many cities in the Southwest celebrate Cesar Chavez's birthday. The second would be held on Monday, April 10, a workday; and the third was slated for May 1, International Workers Day.

But before any immigrants took to the streets, Los Angeles cardinal Roger Mahony, who had begun advocating for Latino immigrants as a strong ally of Cesar Chavez and the UFW in the 1960s and '70s, sent a powerful message that foreshadowed the massive protests to come. Mahony's Catholic archdiocese of Los Angeles was the nation's largest, and the cardinal had become the de facto American Catholic Church leader on immigration policy. This status made Mahony's statement on Ash Wednesday, March 1, 2006, particularly significant. He directed parishioners to spend the forty days of Lent in prayer and reflection on the need for humane immigration laws. He then announced that if the Sensenbrenner bill was enacted and if providing assistance to undocumented immigrants became a felony, he would instruct both priests and lay Catholics to break the law.

As the *New York Times* put it, "it has been a long time since this country heard a call to organized lawbreaking on this big a scale." Cardinal Mahony's pledge to ask even lay Catholics to violate a federal law considerably raised the stakes over HR 4437. His declaration made it clear to millions of Catholics that all the services the church was providing to undocumented Catholic immigrants—job training, child care, counseling, emergency shelter, and much more—were now at risk. Mahony's solidarity with undocumented immigrants not only inspired action among the nation's Catholic clergy and lay Catholics, but it sent a pointed message to Latino immigrants of that faith that the church supported their taking to the streets to assert their rights. Sensenbrenner also heard Mahony's message and tried to deny that Catholic nuns would "have to demand a green card before dishing out soup to a hungry immigrant"; he insisted that "Sister Mary Margaret and Brother Rafael have nothing to worry about." But American Catholics trusted Mahony and fellow cardinals and bishops, not the man whose name had become a "Spanish curse."[4]

MARCH 2006: MASS PROTESTS BEGIN

Although the opening protests were not set to begin until later that month, the Illinois Coalition for Immigrant and Refugee Rights helped organize a March 10 demonstration in Chicago that brought out a previously inconceivable 500,000 persons. On March 23 in Milwaukee, a city that had not seen mass protests in years, a crowd of 30,000 rallied for immigrant rights under the theme "A Day without Latinos." Crowd estimates ranged from 10,000 to 30,000 in Phoenix on March 24, perhaps the city's largest protest event ever. An estimated 80,000 Latinos skipped work in Atlanta to protest passage of Prop 187 type legislation by the Georgia House. In Detroit on March 27, a crowd of more than 50,000 protesters chanting *"sí se puede!"* wended its way from Holy Redeemer

Catholic Church to the McNamara Federal Building, in yet another event many described as the city's largest political rally in years. Los Angeles saw more than 2,000 students walk out of schools in protest on March 24, and at Sacramento's March 25 rally, an estimated 5,000 protesters gathered, carrying Cesar Chavez posters.

In Denver, SEIU Local 105 overcame objections from political consultants and some Latino community leaders, who feared a public backlash, to help lead a March 25 rally of between 50,000 and 75,000 protesters at the state capitol. Among the speakers was Monica Martinez, a sixty-one-year-old Mexican immigrant who had participated in the nation's first successful Justice for Janitors campaign in 1986 and had later become a member of Local 105's executive board. Once so shy that she hid behind a sign during union picketing of an office building, Martinez now told the crowd that "all immigrants have dreams and deserve to be treated with dignity." Also on March 25, there were between 5,000 and 10,000 protesters, primarily students, in Houston; in Charlotte, North Carolina, there were about 7,000; and there were large rallies in areas as diverse as Boise, Idaho, and Knoxville, Tennessee.[5]

On Saturday, March 25, in Los Angeles, the city whose labor-Latino alliance had sparked the AFL-CIO's shift to a pro-immigrant stance, between 200,000 and 500,000 people marched in one of the largest demonstrations in the city's history. Organized labor and the Catholic Church played important roles in generating this turnout, but when an event that was predicted to draw 20,000 protesters mushrooms to 500,000, a new element is likely in play. This element was the Spanish-language media, specifically popular radio hosts whose Spanish-language talk shows were among the city's highest rated in any language. Eliseo Medina had cultivated an alliance with Los Angeles's Spanish-language media when forming OLAW in 2000 and had subsequently harnessed this power to boost attendance at the Sports Arena events following the AFL-CIO's adoption of a new immigration policy (described in chapters 7 and 8).

After being contacted by SEIU and other protest organizers about the impact of HR 4437, Los Angeles's leading Spanish-language radio personalities went all out to mobilize their listeners. Eddie Sotelo, known to listeners of his highly rated morning talk show as "El Piolín," or Tweety Bird, said he felt personally obligated to fight on this issue because he had entered this country illegally in 1986 and had gained legal status as a result of the 1986 Immigration Control and Reform Act. Sotelo arranged for a March 20 summit on the steps of city hall that included such rival deejays as Ricardo Sánchez ("El Mandril," the Baboon) and

Renán Almendárez Coello ("El Cucuy," the Bogeyman), often described as the Latino version of Howard Stern. After these leading Spanish radio personalities joined forces to promote the March 25 protest, momentum "just blew up." According to Mike Garcia, president of California's statewide janitors union, Local 1877, Sotelo, Coello, and their radio colleagues "were the key to getting so many people out. If you listened to Spanish-language media, they were just pumping, pumping, pumping this up."[6]

While the mass protests in March involved different players, they included some common threads that would also be manifested in future events. First, the spirit of Cesar Chavez dominated the marchers' call for amnesty for undocumented immigrants. Although some civil rights activists of the 1960s and '70s had criticized Chavez and the UFW on the immigration issue, immigrant rights marchers in 2006 repeatedly told the media that they saw their actions as carrying out Cesar Chavez's legacy. Many of the protests were consciously timed to coincide with the week of Chavez's March 31 birthday, and his picture was pervasive. Latino marchers clearly identified the UFW's struggle with their own, which is why in virtually every march the major chant and the most common phrase on banners was the UFW's rallying cry, "sí se puede!"

Second, the peaceful nature of the marches—with few arrests and virtually no acts of violence—echoed the nonviolent UFW protests of the past, sending a clear message that America's immigrants were law-abiding. In this respect, the tone projected by these marches differed from that of the "Battle in Seattle" protests against the World Trade Organization in 1999, the huge nationwide marches opposing the Iraq war in 2003, and the demonstrations at the Republican National Convention in New York City in 2004. Although those marches were primarily peaceful, media footage typically portrayed some protesters battling police or engaging in conduct that detracted from their message. Activists often criticize the media for promoting such images, arguing that random acts are inevitable in mass events and cannot be controlled by event organizers. But such acts were absent from the immigrant rights marches of 2006. This was attributable, in large part, to the leadership of the labor movement and the clergy, the alliance that had helped organize so many of the UFW's mass events. Medina and the Catholic clergy sought to ensure that the marches would not link immigrants with disorder in the public eye. In city after city, SEIU and other unions took responsibility for security. For example, at the massive March 25 protest in Los Angeles, SEIU Local 1877 trained nearly 500 people to deal with potential problems; and two dozen SEIU members posted on each block, wearing orange vests, kept marchers on the prescribed route. The following month, SEIU was in charge of security at a march in Phoenix, where organizers predicted 50,000 participants but between 100,000 and 200,000 showed up; according to SEIU state director Martin Manteca, "the event did not result in even one arrest."[7]

Third, the immigrant rights marches differed from other protests by conveying an overtly patriotic message. Backers of the massive Los Angeles protest urged immigrants to wave American flags, and these flags became a potent and highly visible symbol in events across the country. Deejay Eddie Sotelo, who played a major role in boosting turnout at all the Los Angeles marches, explained, "We wanted them to show that we love this country. Bringing the U.S. flag, that was important. There are so many people who say 'I'm glad my parents came here and sacrificed like they did for us.'" Susan Meehan, a veteran antiwar protester who attended the April 10 national rally in Washington, D.C., noted, "I've been to 10 zillion marches and this is the first one with people shouting 'USA! USA!' and with so many American flags." Reflecting this conscious attempt to send a patriotic message, Jaime Contreras, formerly secretary-treasurer of SEIU Local 82 and now president of the National Capital Immigration Coalition, a lead organizer of the national events, ended his speech by leading the crowd in chanting "U.S.A.! U.S.A.! U.S.A.!"[8]

The UFW understood the symbolic potency of American flags, which were regularly seen at UFW marches and rallies in the 1960s and '70s. During the 1970 Salinas lettuce strike, the union's red flags with a black Aztec eagle were hung along a hundred-mile stretch from Watsonville to King City. The Teamsters and other UFW opponents attacked these "red" flags, implying a connection to communism, and had their members waving American flags throughout the area. In response, Cesar Chavez told his staff to buy up every American flag they could get their hands on. Soon the UFW strikers were also seen waving these flags, and Chavez himself was captured waving a huge American flag. The many U.S. flags at the immigrant rights events of 2006 were designed to show immigrants' allegiance to their newfound home. UFW veteran organizer Fred Ross Jr. had used this same symbolism when he brought immigrants and their supporters to the INS Los Angeles headquarters as part of VOICE's Active Citizenship Campaign; as chapter 8 described, the hundreds present that day stood in the INS halls waving American flags.[9]

Despite the positive message of the American flag, conservative opponents of legalization highlighted the presence of Mexican flags in the crowds to claim that those marching put allegiance to Mexico first. While Mexican flags never outnumbered American flags, activists became conscious of the messaging and, after the initial group of rallies, encouraged protesters to leave their Mexican flags at home. Rafael Tabares, a senior at Los Angeles's Marshall High who helped plan that school's March 24 walkout, "ordered classmates to put away Mexican flags they had brought to the demonstration—predicting, correctly, that the flags would be shown on the news and that the demonstrators would be criticized as nationalists for other countries, not residents seeking rights at home." Although Mexican flags were not often seen in future marches, groups like the anti-immigrant Minuteman Civil Defense Corps, based in Phoenix, continued to insist that the sight of "people marching on the streets and waving Mexican flags" was resulting in "a quiet rage building."[10]

Patriotic spirit was also reflected in the rallies' support for veterans and current members of the military. Latinos accounted for 16.5 percent of marine recruits at the time of the marches, a steady increase since 1997. Uniformed soldiers were sometimes singled out for applause, and military personnel were a "popular presence" at the immigrant rights rallies. Medina noted that at the April 10 rally in Houston, which was attended by more than 50,000, "speakers repeatedly pointed to people in uniform at a nearby bridge, and they received roaring applause." He added, "When [demonstrators] see people in uniform, it gives them tremendous pride and validates that we are contributing to this country." At San Diego's huge April 9 rally, Latino veterans carried signs that read WE FOUGHT IN YOUR WARS. Jorge Mariscal, a Vietnam veteran who went on to become director of Chicano studies at the University of California, San Diego, observed that "after serving our country, to see our relatives now criminalized through this legislation [HR 4437] is provoking a lot of people."[11]

In addition to marchers' identification with Cesar Chavez and the UFW's *"sí se puede"* spirit, their peaceful conduct, and their patriotism, the 2006 marches resembled past UFW events both in their demographics—not since the heyday of the farmworkers movement had so many Latinos participated in public protests—and in their ability to convey a powerful moral message about the function of immigrant workers in the U.S. economy. What had made the farmworker marches so compelling, in addition to the music, singing, and colorful religious imagery, was that workers were coming out of the Central Valley fields to remind Americans that the fruit and vegetables on their dinner tables had been picked by human beings, who should be fairly treated. California's Central Valley was far from major population centers, and the media rarely exposed Americans to the realities of the nation's agriculture system.

But from the start of the UFW's grape boycott, Americans became exposed to the truth. Farmworkers told shoppers and the nation about the harsh realities of farm labor, and the success of the various boycotts was testament to their persuasiveness. In the same way, the undocumented immigrants who marched in 2006 left the shadows to publicly proclaim that the U.S. economy depended on them. They announced without apology that it was undocumented immigrants who worked in America's restaurants, cleaned America's buildings, cared for America's sick, and made much of the nation's food industry possible. The very sight of hundreds of thousands of Latino immigrants marching made a statement more powerful than any slogan on a banner. Not since UFW marches had the country seen a comparable type of protest event.

APRIL 2006: NATIONAL DAY OF ACTION

While the immigrant rights movement was doing its own "negotiating" by demonstrating support for legalization through mass marches across America, Eliseo Medina was in lengthy meetings with senators and their staffs. Following the first wave of protests in March and before the National Day of Action set for April 10, a deal was struck in the Senate to pass a compromise legalization measure that was said to have Bush's support. Under its terms, undocumented immigrants who had been in the country for at least five years would get a path to citizenship, but those who had lived here between two and five years would benefit little, and recent arrivals (those with less than two years' residence) would get nothing. The compromise followed the Senate's defeat of the Kennedy-McCain bill, which did not include the seniority provisions.

The proposed compromise legislation fell short of advocates' expectations. Medina had already faced dissent from immigrant rights activists and the AFL-CIO by agreeing to a guest worker component in Kennedy-McCain, but he had recognized that excluding such a provision was a deal-breaker for Bush and Senate Republicans. As he put it, "You can't simply get into that debate by saying nothing out there meets our expectations. Because then you can be sitting on the outside looking in without ever having any chance to solve the problem."[12]

But after many advocates agreed to some form of a guest worker plan—which opponents equated to the bracero program, which had effectively restricted farmworker power from the 1940s to the early 1960s—the new bill's plan to bar millions of immigrants from access to citizenship was unacceptable. What the media called a "breakthrough" was seen by immigrant rights activists as a reversal. Yet even this new bill, which passed the Senate Judiciary Committee, failed to get the sixty Senate votes necessary to cut off debate, and it subsequently died. The contrast between unprecedented numbers of people in the streets and Senate inaction spurred activists to send an even more powerful legalization message to Washington, D.C., in the rallies planned for Monday, April 10.[13]

The events of the weekend leading up to the National Day of Action signaled that anger about HR 4437 had not abated. A march in San Diego on Sunday, April 9, included crowds of between 50,000 (the *San Diego Tribune* estimate) and 150,000 (the Spanish-language media estimates). All agreed that it was the largest demonstration in the city's history. Again, many marchers carried American flags to show their desire to become citizens. In Dallas, police estimated that more than 350,000 marched, with many waving U.S. flags, in the city's largest protest event ever. Detroit's event drew an estimated 50,000 protesters. More than a dozen cities that historically lacked large Latino populations—including Birmingham; Boise; Lexington, Kentucky; Salt Lake City; and St. Paul, Minnesota—had crowds that numbered in the thousands. The St. Paul march had 30,000 participants.[14]

On April 10, more than 2 million protesters in over one hundred cities marched during the National Day of Action for Immigration Justice. Cardinal Theodore McCarrick gave the opening prayer at a rally of an estimated 200,000 protesters in the nation's capital, a short distance from where senators were still struggling to reach consensus on legislation. Crowd estimates ranged from 80,000 in Atlanta and 50,000 in Houston to more than 100,000 in New York City, 10,000 in Boston, and between 100,000 and 200,000 in Phoenix. There were over thirty marches in the South alone. Fort Myers, Florida, not known for its immigrant rights activism, had 75,000 protesters; the Atlanta march spanned two miles. In Omaha, Nebraska, also not viewed as an activist hotbed, 8,000 people marched.

In Fresno, located in California's Central Valley, 10,000 people marched in what police described as "by far the largest event we ever had in our city." Portland, Oregon, another city not known for a large Latino immigrant population, had several thousand marchers, and there were an estimated 25,000 to 50,000 protesters in Seattle. Immigrant ad-

Immigrant members of the New York Civic Participation Project wave U.S. flags at an April 10, 2006, march. Photo by Jeannine Briceno, NYCPP.

vocacy groups based in Nashville decided to forgo another rally in that city (they had had a successful event on March 29) and instead held protests in Memphis, Knoxville, and Jonesborough, in upper east Tennessee. In the little-known farming town of Garden City, Kansas, 3,000 people—10 percent of the town's population—took to the streets in an event whose chief organizer was UFW alumnus Mark Pitt, who was now with the United Steelworkers union. After leaving the UFW, Pitt had joined the J. P. Stevens boycott campaign (described in chapter 2) and embarked on a long career with UNITE.[15]

The size of the marches, and the huge number of Latino immigrant families participating, dominated the strongly favorable media coverage. But the impact of the April 10 events on Congress remained unclear. Bush said the April 10 rallies were "a sign that this is an important issue that people feel strongly about." Congressman Tom Tancredo, a Republican from Colorado and a leader of the anti-immigrant forces, saw the marches as demonstrating "how entrenched the illegal alien lobby had become." Congress was in recess for two weeks, and immigrant advocacy groups hoped that members would get feedback from their districts prior to the third planned nationwide event: the May 1 "Day without Immigrants."[16]

The May 1 marches were designed to show America that undocumented immigrants were so indispensable to the economy that if they did not show up to work for a day, business would grind to a halt. Some activists urged the immigrant rights movement to declare a one-day national boycott of economic activity to force Congress to overhaul the immigration system. But Medina, who had spent over a decade on the UFW boycott, disagreed. He argued that a boycott would "stain the sympathetic image immigrants have established with the public," turning "a positive approach into a negative one, creating confusion and resentment." What Medina was too polite to say was that the UFW boycotts succeeded because they had been connected to union and public organizing campaigns, while these latest calls for a boycott lacked these features and instead resembled the many ineffective paper boycotts that had left many cynical about the value of the tactic. The president of the San Antonio Hispanic Chamber of Commerce also noted that a boycott would most affect businesses that employed and served Latino communities.[17]

As plans proceeded for massive rallies on May 1 focused primarily on the indispensability of Latino workers, other groups of immigrants also raised their voices. Medina was among the leaders organizing a march of more than 4,000 protesters through the streets of Miami to denounce U.S. immigration policy toward Haitians. Medina, who had fought to improve working conditions for Florida's Haitians while working for the UFW in 1972, vowed "to fight to make sure there are no second-class citizens . . . Haitians will no longer go invisible!"[18]

MAY 1, 2006: A DAY WITHOUT IMMIGRANTS

It was hard to imagine that the immigrant rights movement could top its successful events in March and April. But the turnout of Latino immigrants on Monday, May 1, exceeded all expectations, as at least a million people walked through more than two hundred American cities in a truly dramatic display of "people power." Once again, Los Angeles led the way, with more than 650,000 marchers. The city's usually active port was almost completely closed. Cardinal Mahony had urged immigrants not to risk losing their jobs by skipping work and had asked children not to miss school; the Los Angeles march was held in the early evening to address these concerns. Crowd estimates in Chicago ranged from 450,000 to 700,000, with more than 75,000 in San Francisco and a similar number in Denver, where the event was described as the largest protest in the city's history. More impressive than the large turnouts in major strongholds was the extraordinary geographical breadth of the marches, which covered nearly all states and many small rural towns where national protest actions were rare. The thousands marching in places such as Omaha, Nebraska; Salem, Oregon; and Lumberton, North Carolina sent a powerful message that Latino immigrants now lived in and were inextricably linked with local economies well beyond the traditional areas of concentration in California, Florida, and the Southwest.[19]

A striking feature of the May 1 rallies was the thousands of signs that read TODAY WE MARCH, TOMORROW WE VOTE. Voting became a central issue for the movement. Republicans believed that Latino nonvoters could not hurt them politically and that supporting legalization would alienate their core voting base. The anti-immigrant Minuteman Project, an effort by "volunteers" to act as a vigilante "border patrol," responded to the May 1 rallies with its own plans for mobilizing voters. Stephen Eichler, the group's executive director, said, "Our power is not putting a million people on the street, our power is putting 10 million people at the voting box."[20] Opponents of immigrant rights disputed the assertion that most voters supported the protesters' cause and rolled the dice that the immigration issue would work in their favor in the November 2006 elections. Anti-immigrant positions had not hurt Republicans outside California in the past, and these forces did not believe that the immigrant rights movement could change this longstanding political calculus.

In the larger context, the anti-immigrant forces were also challenging the ability of immigrant rights activists to extend the UFW electoral model beyond California to other states with disproportionately low rates of Latino voting. To win this battle, immigrant advocacy groups in Arizona, Colorado, California, Illinois, and many other states launched voter registration and citizenship drives to boost Latino voting in November. Medina also announced that SEIU would sponsor citizenship forums in major cities and assist churches and activist groups in registering voters.[21]

The May 1 Day without Immigrants was like a social earthquake rumbling across the American landscape, leaving all to wonder what it really meant. Anti-legalization groups quickly weighed in. Mark Krikorian, head of the Center for Immigration Studies, believed that the marches "probably hardened the determination of the House not to give in to the threats of a mob." House Republicans soon confirmed Krikorian's blunt assessment. Republican representative Mary Bono of California asserted that the marches were "overwhelmingly polarizing people" and that they made it harder to get "thoughtful legislation passed." Sensenbrenner continued to insist that immigrant rights advocates had "misled people." He expressed no regrets for having sponsored HR 4437 and "dismissed suggestions" that House Republicans would soften their position as a result of the protests. Senator Mel Martinez of Florida, a sponsor of the Senate "compromise" bill, echoed the Republican argument that the mass protests had made passage of a bill more difficult: "Boycotts, walkouts or protests are not going to get this done. This is an issue that isn't going to get fixed on the streets. It's going to take thoughtful action by Congress."[22]

But Bono and the other Republicans who voted for HR 4437 were not worried about passing "thoughtful" legislation when they approved the criminalization of immigrants and later the construction of a seven-hundred-mile fence along the U.S.-Mexico border. In fact, both measures had been passed quickly after being introduced, avoiding any opportunity for a "thoughtful" public debate or a thorough legislative process. Given the draconian terms of the 2005 bill, it was hard to imagine how the marches could have hardened attitudes further.

Spokespersons for the immigrant rights movement had a quite different take on the impact of the May 1 rallies. Hilda Delgado of SEIU Local 1877 declared, "This is only the beginning. Now we have to reroute all of the energy and momentum and start registering to vote to send a clear message [for immigration reform] to the Senate and House in Washington." Teodoro Aguiluz of the Houston branch of the national Central American Resource Center echoed the views of many who praised immigrants for overcoming longstanding barriers to action: "The fact that so many of our people have gone out to the streets spontaneously shows that our people have been waiting for a chance to say 'Enough.' It's been accumulating for years."[23]

Newspapers quoted many legal immigrants who either had never become citizens or had never voted and who were now moved by the marches to take such actions. While Republican opponents of legalization seemed to assume that most marchers posed no political threat, they apparently did not realize that an estimated 8 million legal immigrants were eligible to apply for citizenship and that, of the 16 million Latino citizens eligible to vote, only 58 percent were registered. Between January and March 2006, citizenship applications had increased by 19 percent, and by the end of the year of mass marches the number had grown by 79 percent. In Los Angeles, the number of applications from January

2006 to 2007 rose a whopping 146 percent. In Chicago, a citizenship drive two days before the May 1 rallies brought nearly double the 1,000 people anticipated, a turnout attributed to fear generated by HR 4437.[24]

While Medina and other labor officials downplayed the role of unions in the marches, the *Los Angeles Times* described labor's involvement in the Los Angeles events as "instrumental." For the May 1 march and rally in Los Angeles, labor raised most of the $85,000 needed for portable toilets, first aid stations, and stages. A diverse group of unions played critical roles. Mike Garcia of SEIU Local 1877 and Jorge Rodriguez of AFSCME "managed the connections" between the many groups involved with the events. The Laborers Union handed out forty-five cases of bottled water and built the stage for the rally. The Communication Workers of America staffed media tables, the Teamsters joined with other unions in mapping out the marching routes and providing security, and Maria Elena Durazo, then interim executive secretary-treasurer of the county federation of labor, hosted the rally. The events foreshadowed how the AFL-CIO's shift in support of amnesty for undocumented immigrants at its 2000 convention would soon provide a dramatic boost for the nation's immigrant rights movement.[25]

The protests also made young people more eager to vote. Jessica Dominguez, who frequently spoke to student groups as head of the immigration section of the Los Angeles County Bar Association, noted, "My own 19-year-old son is so excited. He knows we are living through historic moments, and he can't wait." The major involvement of young people in the rallies was encouraging for the movement's future, as they used cell phones, e-mail, the Internet—including MySpace—and other twenty-first-century organizing techniques to organize school walkouts and boost attendance at rallies. Medina described the mass outpouring as "an incredible organic movement that's being born in this country. I have been organizing for 41 years, and I've never seen anything like it. Rather than organizers creating an activity, it's the activity creating the organization."[26]

The question on many minds, articulated by political scientist and longtime immigrant rights activist Armando Navarro, involved "the need to take this critical mass and organize it. . . . We need to harness this power." This desire led some to hope that a single umbrella organization or a "dynamic figurehead" like Cesar Chavez or Martin Luther King Jr. might emerge to lead the effort. But Medina, who had seen firsthand both the benefits and the downside of Chavez's charismatic leadership, described the successful events this way: "We are seeing hundreds of leaders coming together. Many of them are people nobody had ever heard of. This organic organization will outlive any one charismatic figure." Medina described the 2006 marches in a May 2 *Los Angeles Times* op-ed as "the birth of a national movement," but he was too modest to cite his own role in its creation.[27]

Medina was among the new generation of labor leaders who pushed unions to organize immigrants, and his success in Los Angeles became a national model. He had also led the fight to align the American labor movement with the cause of immigrant rights, which resulted in the AFL-CIO adopting a pro-immigrant policy for the first time in its history. In addition, Medina had created bonds of trust with Cardinal Mahony and the national religious community that resulted in the clergy's enthusiastic support for such activist events as the Immigrant Workers Freedom Ride and the protest marches of 2006. Many allies joined Medina in these struggles, but he clearly played the leading role in resurrecting the labor-clergy-community alliance that had brought success for the UFW in the past and that provided the vehicle for mass participation by Latino immigrants in 2006.

AFTER THE MARCHES: POLITICAL INACTION

Eliseo Medina's May 2 op-ed in the *Los Angeles Times* urged Congress to respond to the public protests by passing real immigration reform. But it was clear before the Senate returned from its recess the next week that no acceptable bill would pass the House. The immigrant rights movement continued to build public support for legalization, but its larger focus was on building Latino voting power for November 2006 and beyond. To help accomplish this, Medina worked with religious, community, and labor groups to launch the pro-legalization We Are America Alliance, which was composed of forty-one immigrant rights groups, unions, churches, day laborers, and Spanish-language deejays. According to Angelica Salas, executive director of the Coalition for Humane Immigrant Rights of Los Angeles, WAAA's civic action campaign would "continue building on the momentum of the marches by building political power." The coalition's May 17 kickoff began an ambitious campaign to register 1 million new voters, hand out citizenship applications, and distribute postcards for contacting members of Congress. Nearly fifty "democracy centers" were set up at churches, union halls, and community facilities in the region. Medina claimed that immigrants "are going to hear about citizenship at Mass, at union gatherings and at civic organization meetings."[28]

The post–May 1 actions also focused on registering the 4.9 million Latino eligible voters under the age of thirty. This age group represented the single largest untapped source of potential Latino voters. Maria Teresa Peterson, executive director of the New York–based Voto Latino, saw a dramatic increase in requests from young people wanting to volunteer on registration drives. Funded by actress Rosario Dawson and other Latino celebrities, Voto Latino produced public service announcements starring popular actress Cameron Diaz and organized "street teams" to create buzz about voting at youth events. Fernando Franco, an eighteen-year-old Latino, was quoted in the *Los Angeles Times* as saying that he would not miss the chance to cast his first ballot and that he had "never seen his friends this passionate about anything." Political scientist Ricardo Ramírez, a national expert on Latino voting patterns, noted that young Latinos were more likely to have directly observed the struggles of undocumented immigrants than their parents' generation and that "personal connection to immigrants can be used to motivate young people to vote."[29]

Although Bush gave a speech on May 15 that attempted to jump-start the process of compromise, the Republican-controlled House was not interested. Instead, the House leadership decided to hold hearings across America during the August recess to assess where people stood on the immigration issue. After returning to Washington in September, House Republicans passed a bill to require construction of a seven-hundred-mile fence along the Mexican border. This $2 billion expenditure was in addition to the $2.5 billion already allocated for "virtual fences" along the nation's northern and southern borders. The House also passed legislation deputizing state and local law enforcement officers to enforce federal immigration laws—in effect, requiring local police to arrest and detain suspected undocumented immigrants instead of focusing on fighting violent crime. Not content that these measures would do the job, the House also approved a bill requiring voters to show photo identification that demonstrated proof of citizenship in order to vote in federal elections. After sitting on the Senate's compromise legislation for months, the House essentially poked a finger in the eye of Bush and their fellow Republican senators by further enflaming the issue.

The AFL-CIO had criticized Medina, the Change to Win labor federation, and some immigrant rights activists for their willingness to go along with the weakened Senate bill. But after the House refused to act on the bill, Medina's strategy became clear. Rather than opposing a bill that he knew would not pass the House, Medina put the immigrant rights movement on the side of progress and cooperation. As a result, when House

Republicans killed any chance for real immigration reform in late September 2006, they took all the blame for Congress's failure to act on this pressing issue. An editorial in the *Washington Post* described House Republicans as engaging in a "cynical" endgame that was both "disappointing and dangerous." Many other papers, including those from normally pro-Republican areas, ran similar editorials, and criticism from conservative Republican senators such as Larry Craig of Idaho made the House action look even more extreme.[30]

"TODAY WE MARCH, TOMORROW WE VOTE"

According to a widely accepted report by the Woodrow Wilson International Center for Scholars, the cumulative turnout for the spring 2006 marches reached between 3.5 and 5 million.[31] But for all its success in holding mass marches, the immigrant rights movement knew that its political impact would be measured by the results of the November 2006 elections. House Republicans were not just talking about a voter backlash; they clearly believed that a silent majority of the electorate favored their extreme actions. This is why they returned from meetings with their constituents during the August recess more opposed than ever to addressing the protesters' concerns and quickly enacted even more punitive measures. Based on the example of California governor Pete Wilson, who had rebounded from a huge deficit in the polls to win easy reelection by riding the wave of Prop 187 in 1994, Republicans saw attacks on undocumented immigrants as a surefire strategy for galvanizing their political base. Would they be proven correct? Or would Latinos vote in increased numbers and engineer a political payback against backers of HR 4437?

While immigration was an issue in House and Senate races across America in November 2006, perhaps the best testing ground for evaluating the impact of the marches on congressional elections occurred in Colorado's 7th District, which surrounds Denver. Immigration was a "boiling issue" in the race, which pitted Republican Rick O'Donnell against Democrat Ed Perlmutter. Republican Bob Beauprez, who had previously held the seat, had strongly backed HR 4437 and was now running for governor on a tough anti-immigration platform. The 7th District was evenly split between Democrats, Republicans, and independents, with Latinos constituting 25 percent of the residents and potentially more than 10 percent of the electorate.

The media framed the race as a litmus test on the immigration debate. O'Donnell attacked Perlmutter for supporting "amnesty" for illegal immigrants and proposed a plan to send male high school seniors to serve as volunteer border guards. Republicans ran a thirty-second television spot linking Perlmutter to Senator Ted Kennedy, chief sponsor of the original Senate legalization bill. A voice stated: "Ted and Ed's plan? Illegal immigrants get handouts and amnesty. We get the bill." O'Donnell claimed that illegal immigration was the top concern of district voters, and he criticized Perlmutter for advocating in-state tuition for children of undocumented immigrants. Perlmutter expressed support for border security and workplace enforcement but argued, "We're not going to deport 12 million people. That's not right, and that's not where most Coloradans are." He criticized O'Donnell's plan to use high school volunteers as a "crazy idea" and sought to win Latino votes by running Spanish-language ads, having a "Perlmutter En Español" website, and walking Latino neighborhoods with politicians such as Congressman Xavier Becerra of Los Angeles.[32]

Before the furor sparked by HR 4437, Colorado Republicans had actively sought Latino votes. But the battle over immigration policy caused such efforts to "disintegrate," and even Robert Martinez, the Latino chair of the state Republican Party, bemoaned the fact that "we're throwing away tons of work we've put into Hispanic outreach just because of some people's attitudes." Nevertheless, a week before the election, Frank Tijerina Jr., the Republican state Hispanic Coalition director, was predicting that Republican O'Donnell would "win most of the Latino vote." In contrast, Democratic strategists saw Perlmutter winning 68 percent of Latino voters. The stakes in the election for Colorado's 7th District thus transcended the particular race to become a litmus test on voter attitudes toward undocumented immigrants.[33]

As election day neared, all evidence pointed to Latino voters making a critical difference in the race. On October 5, the Latino Policy Coalition released a poll of four key congressional districts whose Republican representatives had backed HR 4437, including Colorado's 7th District. Gary Segura of the University of Washington, a nationally recognized scholar of Latino voting, concluded that "strong pro-Democratic sentiment" among Latinos in these four districts represented an "ominous warning" to Republicans. The poll had Perlmutter 54 percentage points ahead of his Republican opponent among Latino voters. Segura saw the Mountain West, with its rapidly growing Latino population, as "the right location" for Democrats to make gains in former Republican strongholds. Latino voting expert Karthick Ramakrishnan of the University of California at Riverside saw Latino turnout as "likely proving crucial in the

Mountain West," where the numbers of Latino voters were large enough to provide the margin of victory. And in fact, after all the votes were counted in the 7th District, a race predicted to be a toss-up was easily won by Democrat Perlmutter, 54 to 42 percent.[34]

Simon Rosenberg of the New Democratic Network, which spent close to $2 million on Latino outreach during the November 2006 cycle, saw evidence of a "civic awakening" among Latino voters well before election day. Internal campaign polls showed that the immigration controversy made 54 percent of Latinos more likely to vote, which Rosenberg saw as a "significant shift." Polly Baca of the Latin American Research and Service Agency estimated that of the 50,000 to 75,000 protesters who attended Denver's March immigration rally, 70 to 80 percent were citizens, "and those are the people who registered to vote." Voter registration by Colorado Latinos had increased by 3.5 percent since 2005, a rise triple that of non-Latinos. Most of that increase occurred in the voter registration drives triggered by the We Are America Alliance, with individual groups such as Colorado ACORN, the Latina Initiative, and the Colorado Latino Voting Project bringing in more than 5,400 new registrations after July 1. Anna Sampaio, a political science professor at the University of Colorado at Denver, saw the growth in voter registration during a midterm election cycle as "a positive sign that Latino voters are in play." Her assessment was confirmed by an election eve analysis by the National Association of Latino Elected and Appointed Officials, which predicted a 38 percent rise in Latino voter turnout—45,000 additional voters—in Colorado over 2002.[35]

In its analysis of post-election polls for 2006, the Pew Hispanic Center concluded that 69 percent of Latino voters nationally voted Democratic, an increase of 11 percent over 2004 (white voters increased their Democratic vote by only 6 percent). Latino voter turnout rose 38 percent over the 2002 midterm election, representing an additional 1.8 million voters. In contrast, the number of white and African American voters decreased by 18 percent from 2002, making the huge rise in Latino voting even more significant. Pew's analysis found that Colorado's 7th District was one of four across the nation in which the Latino vote was high enough to have shifted the race. The impact of Latinos' national shift to Democrats in congressional contests was limited in 2006, since there were only seventy-five close races, with the Latino vote exceeding 10 percent of the electorate in only twelve of those. But there was broad agreement that those applying for citizenship as a result of the protest marches would swell this percentage in 2008 and beyond. Noting that

"Latino voters made it clear that immigration is a defining issue, and that those who adopt a hard line will be met with a hard response," the National Immigration Forum highlighted both the 7th District race and Democrat Bill Ritter's 56 to 41 percent victory over Bob Beauprez in the Colorado governor's race as confirmation.[36]

Medina and other immigrant rights leaders put the movement's political credibility on the line in November 2006, and they won big. The elections demonstrated the awakening of the long-slumbering Latino electoral giant and for the first time sent a national political message that attacking immigrants created serious political risks. Most Republicans who voted for HR 4437 did not represent districts where the Latino vote was large enough to make a difference and thus were easily reelected in 2006. But the geographical breadth of the protest marches showed that this dynamic was rapidly changing, particularly in the Mountain West. The huge Latino voter turnout in 2006 also coincided with the Democrats retaking control of the House of Representatives and the ascension of Nancy Pelosi, one of the immigrant rights movement's strongest congressional allies, to the powerful role of House Speaker.

2007 INTENSIFIES ANTI-LEGALIZATION BACKLASH

As 2007 began, immigrant rights supporters had reason for confidence. With Democrats now controlling both houses of Congress, and Nancy Pelosi, a strong backer of legalization, elected Speaker of the House of Representatives, the chief obstacle to passage of comprehensive immigrant rights reform had been removed. Further, Republicans had suffered the consequences of a Latino voter backlash in 2006, and party leaders would seemingly not be inclined to lose more congressional seats over the immigration issue in 2008.

But activists in the core Republican base, exemplified by right-wing talk show hosts and callers who admired the Minuteman Project and the Sensenbrenner bill, were not deterred by electoral realities. Instead of seeking to stop the shift of Latino voters to the Democratic Party, Republican activists devoted all their energies to reversing congressional progress toward legalization. Their efforts were bolstered by two factors. First, the president, who claimed to back legalization and should have been able to secure Republican support, was so politically weakened over Iraq and other failures that he could not keep even the more malleable Republican senators on board. Second, the political clout of core Republican voters was enhanced when the 2008 Republican presidential primary schedule was advanced so that the party nominee could be finalized as early as February 5, 2008. Instead of being a nonelection year in which passage of controversial legislation like immigration reform would have been facilitated, 2007 became the year for Republican presidential candidates to score points with primary voters by denouncing legalization. The impact of the early primary season became clear when Arizona's John McCain, the Senate Republican sponsor of the 2006 legalization bill, saw support for his presidential candidacy sharply decline as a result of his stance. Given his eagerness to secure conservative Republican support, McCain's enthusiasm for the measure began to wane. With "moderate" Senate Republicans running away from their "grand compromise" on legalization, no legalization bill could get the sixty Senate votes necessary to overcome a filibuster.

Another obstacle to progress in 2007 was the public split within the immigrant rights movement over the content of an acceptable legalization measure. This split pitted the AFL-CIO and many advocates against the Change to Win labor federation and its allies. The heart of this disagreement was over whether to accept any form of a guest worker policy as part of a final deal. The AFL-CIO and its allies adamantly opposed any such provision, while Eliseo Medina, who was a frequently quoted spokesperson for the pro-legalization side, argued that advocates should try to get a bill, however "imperfect," through the Senate and then work with Speaker Pelosi on a House version that everyone could support. The Senate's June refusal to cut off debate on the bill temporarily ended this tactical dispute and made it clear that enacting legalization legislation would require the election of a Democratic president and Congress in 2008.[37]

TOWARD THE FUTURE

Over the past years, Eliseo Medina and other UFW veterans such as Miguel Contreras, Steven Lerner, and Fred Ross Jr. joined with labor, religious, and immigrant activists in pursuing a vision that would boost labor power, enhance immigrant rights, and possibly transform America. The project had several tasks and aims:

- Focus on organizing immigrants into unions
- Realign the labor movement to support rather than oppose immigrant rights, and bring unions into an alliance with the religious community and immigrant rights groups

- Frame the right to legalization by emphasizing immigrants' role as workers and how indispensable they are to the nation's economy
- Build vehicles for fostering civic participation among undocumented immigrants, so that they feel empowered to improve their lives outside the workplace
- Engage in aggressive campaigns to encourage citizenship applications, voter registration, and then voter turnout
- Increase Latino voting so that the transformation of Los Angeles and much of California into pro-labor, pro-immigrant strongholds is mirrored in Arizona, Colorado, Florida, Nevada, Texas, and across America

The political impact of legalizing the 8 to 12 million undocumented Latino immigrants, along with increasing voter turnout among the estimated 8 million Latinos who do not vote but are eligible, could be dramatic. With 69 percent of Latinos now voting Democratic, the movement for legalization can easily be seen as the leading force for the progressive transformation of the United States. Medina and his UFW allies were not the only activists in the 1980s who had this vision for building an immigrant rights movement, but they played a central role in its implementation over the next two decades.

Despite setbacks at the federal level and increased anti-immigrant crackdowns by the Bush administration in 2007, the immigrant rights movement continued to grow. In December 2007, the National Immigration Forum released a summary of public opinion surveys taken throughout the year, which consistently showed that "a majority of Americans favored a realistic immigration policy solution that offered undocumented immigrants a path to citizenship." Ongoing anti-immigrant attacks and a steep hike in citizenship application fees set for August 1, 2007 (from $400 to $675, after costing only $95 as recently as 1998) led to a near doubling of citizenship applications compared to 2006. More than 1.4 million citizenship applications were filed between October 2006 and October 2007; in the Los Angeles region, applications were up 118 percent. New Latino voter registration continued to soar. A broad coalition of labor unions, churches, Spanish-language media, community organizations, and immigrant rights groups, working as part of the "Ya es Hora" (It's Time) campaign, was chiefly responsible for these sharp increases. This grassroots campaign became omnipresent in the nation's Latino communities. Its slogan "Ya es Hora! Ciudadania!" (It's Time! Citizenship!) was followed in November 2007 by the launch of a Latino voter registration/turnout drive urging "Ve y Vota!" (Go and Vote!). Eliseo Medina helped spearhead the Ya es Hora campaign, with SEIU and the Mi Familia Vota Education Fund joining with such organizations as the National Association of Latino Elected and Appointed Officials, Univision, ImpreMedia, the PICO network, and the National Council of La Raza.[38]

Virtually the entire immigrant rights movement has been involved in educating applicants on the citizenship process, effectively bringing the Active Citizenship Campaign to cities across America. The diversity of groups, whose working relationships have been strengthened by the emergence of more than 130 immigrant worker centers in recent years, reflects increasing activism in support of immigrant rights. Ironically, the net impact of their collective efforts to boost citizenship created a processing bottleneck at the U.S. Citizenship and Immigration Services (USCIS) not seen since the Active Citizenship Campaign. With backlogs for processing applications approaching eighteen months instead of the normal six, and applicants' ability to vote in the November 2008 election in doubt, the immigrant rights movement mobilized to demand action. Janet Murguía, president of the National Council of La Raza, called it "astonishing the government should be so unresponsive to immigrants who have enthusiastically taken all the steps to become Americans," and Medina denounced the "incompetence or the obstruction that might be going on." The UCSIS eventually responded to the widespread criticism by adding fifteen hundred new workers, claiming that it had not anticipated the "avalanche" of applications. But progress remained slow, and the Puerto Rican Legal Defense and Education Fund filed a federal class action lawsuit in March 2008 to force the UCSIS to complete applications in time for new citizens to vote in the November elections. Chung-Wha Hong, executive director of the New York Immigration Coalition, argued that the backlog "is excluding a whole segment of voters that will not be able to exercise their rights."[39]

All in all, just as the UFW of the 1960s and 1970s became the essential vehicle for activism in building a farmworkers movement, today's labor, community, religious, and worker advocacy groups have created multiple vehicles for building and expanding the movement for immigrant rights. As the number of such vehicles grows, and immigrant civic participation expands, enactment of a comprehensive legalization bill that the entire movement can support is only a matter of time.

10

THE DECLINE OF THE UFW

As previous chapters describe, UFW veterans have played key roles in strengthening the U.S. labor movement, boosting Latino political empowerment, and broadening the national movement for immigrant rights. Today's progressive movements have benefited immeasurably from the involvement of these individuals. But when California's Agricultural Labor Relations Act was enacted in 1975, most of the UFW's key leaders and volunteers fully expected to be working for the farmworkers union for the rest of their lives. In fact, this expectation of a long-term commitment to the UFW was commonly expressed in my interviews with key volunteers, even though most began working for the union in their teens or twenties. Nevertheless, by 1981, a mass exodus had occurred, with the UFW losing many of its best organizers and such talented leaders as Eliseo Medina, Miguel Contreras, Jessica Govea, and Marshall Ganz. Why did so many people who had made the UFW their life's work suddenly leave in the space of only a few years? And what role did the departure of these skilled activists play in the UFW's steady decline, which began in 1981, a time when the union was well positioned for its greatest expansion?

This chapter discusses the causes of the UFW's decline and why talented UFW activists left the farmworkers movement and took their skills beyond the fields. Chapter 11 then describes the specific paths taken by many of these activists in advancing struggles for social justice. Together, these two chapters confirm that the greatest legacy of Cesar Chavez and the farmworkers movement has been their impact on progressive campaigns of the twenty-first century, rather than their efforts toward a more powerful UFW or a once-dreamed-of nationwide union of farmworkers.

1976–1978: STRATEGIC ERRORS
AND INTERNAL CONFLICT EMERGE

1976: The Prop 14 Debacle

When California's historic Agricultural Labor Relations Act passed in 1975, providing farmworkers with the same union rights accorded other workers, it seemed that the biggest hurdles to the UFW's success had been overcome. No one expected growers to simply accede to UFW contract demands, but the union never doubted that it would win the vast majority of representation elections that followed enactment of the law—and that is what occurred. But trouble soon developed with the implementation of the ALRA. The five-member Agricultural Labor Relations Board that administered the law was strongly pro-UFW: Governor Jerry Brown had secured the appointment of former UFW insider LeRoy Chatfield; Bishop Roger Mahony, a close Chavez ally; Joseph Grodin, a prominent union labor attorney; and Joseph Ortega, a Latino activist—leaving only one seat for a grower representative. Outvoted, the large growers sought to use their legislative clout to deny necessary funding for the board in order to prevent it from certifying elections, enforcing workers' rights, and investigating violations.

In order to guarantee funding for the board, Chavez and the UFW made the savvy decision to prepare a statewide ballot initiative that would address the funding issue and other points of contention concerning the ALRB. After the union threatened to move forward with the ballot measure, the growers blinked. Fearing a repeat of their one-sided Prop 22 loss to the UFW in 1972, the growers caved in on virtually all the issues raised by the union. Meanwhile, the national Democratic Party convinced state Democratic legislators to address the UFW's concerns, fearing that if the initiative appeared on the ballot, it would mobilize pro-grower voters hostile to Jimmy Carter, the party's presidential candidate. This shift among Democratic legislators and growers represented a huge political victory for the UFW and ensured that the ALRB would have sufficient funds to certify elections, protect farmworkers from illegal firings, and carry out its other functions.[1]

But, in one of the first warning signs about the movement's future, Chavez refused to accept this victory. Instead, he pushed the UFW to proceed with the ballot measure. As chapter 6 describes, the union waged an intensive and costly campaign to pass the initiative. Instead of devoting UFW resources to winning more members and administering its existing labor contracts, Chavez redirected the union's money and virtually every volunteer and sympathizer to the Prop 14 battle. Despite this effort, Prop 14 suffered a landslide defeat in the November 1976 election. This loss was a political disaster for the UFW, one entirely self-inflicted.

Whereas the UFW's Prop 22 victory had enhanced Chavez's faith in the electorate, Prop 14's staggering defeat soured his belief in the power of grassroots politics. Despite his longstanding distrust of politicians, Chavez began after Prop 14 to steadily shift UFW resources from organizing workers to handing out campaign contributions to politicians. In the 1980s and 1990s, the UFW gave Democratic assembly Speaker Willie Brown alone more than $700,000 in political contributions. Defenders of the UFW's reliance on campaign contributions argue that this shift was necessary to combat the series of anti-UFW Republican governors who were elected in California between 1983 and 1998. But Chavez and the UFW had built the union's success on grassroots political organizing and had created a model of union political activism that was distinct from the AFL-CIO's standard approach of simply contributing money to politicians. Now it appeared that Chavez was moving the UFW into the type of financial relationship with politicians that had not served the labor movement well.[2]

1977: The "Game" and Increasing Authoritarianism

Despite Prop 14's defeat, the UFW entered 1977 in a very strong position. The ALRB was up and running, and on March 10, 1977, UFW general counsel Jerry Cohen completed negotiations to get the Teamsters out of the fields and end the strife between the two unions. As Eliseo Medina prepared for a major organizing drive in the citrus industry and Marshall Ganz envisioned a campaign to unionize vegetable and lettuce workers, Cohen's feeling was that "the table was now clear and we are going to run it." UFW leaders were slated to meet in La Paz to discuss the various organizing plans.[3]

Instead, Chavez decided in the spring of 1977 to bring the group to the Badger Pass headquarters of a cultish drug treatment program known as Synanon. Rather than discussing how the union could capitalize on the Teamsters' departure, Chavez subjected the UFW leadership to a group therapy exercise known as the "Game." The Game required the participants to "clear the air" by launching personal attacks against one another and even raising grievances against Chavez. While Chavez defended the ongoing exercise, it caused much anger and bitterness.

On the night of April 4, 1977, several once-trusted UFW volunteers were personally attacked in one of these sessions and terminated from the union for a variety of perceived wrongs. One volunteer said she had "never spent such a fearful night" and spoke of the "frenzied, hate-filled faces and voices of people who had been warm and friendly with me right through to the hour of the meeting." The Game began to create a cult-like atmosphere, perhaps not a surprising development given that it was borrowed not from an organization working for social change or from a religious group, but from Synanon. Charles Dederich, the founder and leader of Synanon, was a very controversial figure, who was eventually put on trial for conspiring to commit murder by putting a rattlesnake in the mailbox of an attorney who had sued the organization. Chavez's friendship with Dederich and his appreciation of Synanon's authoritarian methods were troubling. Jim Drake, who had begun working side by side with Chavez as a young migrant minister in 1962 and then devoted the next fifteen years to performing a variety of key roles for the farmworkers' cause, quit the union over the Game. Drake's departure clearly signaled that all was not well at the UFW.[4]

One of the most disconcerting effects of the Game was that it diverted energy from building the union. Exhausted activists who had worked seven days a week and at least ten hours a day on the statewide Prop 14 campaign now had to drive as long as five hours to reach the UFW's isolated headquarters in La Paz in the Sierra foothills to play the Game. After they had given every ounce of strength to the UFW cause, Chavez was now requiring them to let loose their inner feelings through a group encounter session that was not designed to build group solidarity.

That Chavez had suddenly decided to squander staffers' time playing psychological games in La Paz when there were representation elections to win, workers to organize, and UFW members to be served deepened suspicions about his judgment. It also raised concerns about his growing obsession with internal dissent. He began to accuse many longtime staff members and volunteers of disloyalty and often dispatched staffers to immediately terminate these individuals, severing their involvement with the union with no reasons given. Chavez even accused some veteran UFW staffers of being communists, a charge he had ridiculed when growers leveled it at him during the UFW's early years. As UFW volunteers saw their co-workers essentially kicked out of the movement, many decided to leave of their own accord.[5]

One of the great tragedies during this period was that Chavez was so trusted and so admired that otherwise rational and big-hearted union leaders justified the expulsions. These leaders, including Dolores Huerta and the Reverend Chris Hartmire, concluded that Chavez would never have forced people to leave the UFW without good cause; in fact, Huerta has never swayed from her view that Chavez was only trying to protect the union from internal attacks. Larry Tramutola was among those leading the denunciations of coworkers at the April 4, 1977, meeting and was regularly assigned by Chavez to fire staffers. Tramutola never doubted the legitimacy of his mission: he later observed that he and others felt that they were making such an impact in the world and that the movement was so vital that Chavez's actions could be rationalized as serving the greater good. Tramutola held this view until a day in 1980 when Chavez called him in and accused him of being a communist. Tramutola, who had won every UFW representation election he organized, then resigned from the cause to which he had dedicated the past eleven years of his life.[6]

Philip Vera Cruz, who was second vice president of the UFW and a member of its executive board from 1966 to 1978, believed that "Cesar was seen as so important, so indispensable, that he became idolized and even viewed by some followers as omnipotent. . . . If a union leader is built up as a symbol and he talks like he was God, then there is no way that you can have true democracy in the union because the members are just generally deprived of the right to reason for themselves." By all accounts, Chavez was devastated by the defeat of Prop 14. It is understandable that in seeking reasons for the loss he would reexamine the union's personnel and internal workings. But unfortunately for the UFW, he proceeded in an authoritarian way that drove out dedicated volunteers who did not feel comfortable in such an undemocratic environment. Even Gilbert Padilla, who had been one of the three original UFW organizers, along with Chavez and Huerta, sought to leave the union in 1977 over his differences with Chavez. (He stayed, under pressure, but subsequently left in 1980.)[7]

1977: Chavez Alienates Filipinos and Religious Leaders over Marcos

Further divisions emerged in August 1977 when Chavez was invited to visit the Philippines by the country's dictator, Ferdinand Marcos. Filipino farmworkers had played a central role in launching the Delano grape strike in 1965 (see chapter 1), and Filipino activist Philip Vera Cruz had been a top union officer since 1966. Like most Filipino American immigrants, Vera Cruz despised Marcos, who had imposed martial law and arrested and imprisoned thousands of activists without charges or benefit of trial. Chavez asked Vera Cruz whether he should accept Marcos's invitation, and Vera Cruz told him that he should not. Likewise, other longtime UFW allies in the religious community, who were also strongly opposed to the oppressive Marcos regime, pleaded with Chavez not to boost the dictator's credibility by visiting him.

But Chavez dismissed their concerns and went anyway. Worse, Vera Cruz heard that Chavez had been quoted as saying that "from what he had seen it looked like Marcos' martial law was really helping the people." Chavez then invited Marcos's labor minister, Blas Ople, to speak at the UFW's 1977 national convention. At the convention, Vera Cruz rose to respond to Ople's comments, but the UFW officer was denied the right to speak. Vera Cruz left the union that year and later wrote, "What Cesar did there in the Philippines is the saddest day in the history of the farmworkers movement in this country. It was a disgrace. Chavez was toasting Marcos with all those phony labor leaders appointed by Marcos at the presidential palace while, at the same time, on the other side of Manila, the real union leaders were in jail."[8]

From a strategic standpoint, perhaps the most surprising aspect of Chavez's alignment with Marcos was his willingness to alienate many of the UFW's staunchest supporters in the religious community. Father Eugene Boyle said that he and others in the Catholic community "deeply regretted" Chavez's decision to visit Marcos. Other Catholic activists felt that the church's relationship with the UFW "was never the same" after the visit; "we were deeply hurt." Declining support for the UFW from the Catholic Church was evident by 1979, when Catholic bishops did not publicly support the Salinas lettuce strike and boycott: the Catholic presence in an August 1979 march to Salinas was described as "thin," including only one priest. When a Catholic activist who had worked several times for the UFW wrote a letter to Monsignor George Higgins about her concern that Chavez saw himself as above criticism, the legendary labor priest wrote back acknowledging the problem but stating that he was reluctant either to confront the UFW leader or "to go public." The Cesar Chavez of the 1960s assiduously worked to build Catholic support and credited the religious community for boosting the farmworkers movement; by the late 1970s, however, Chavez instead gave the impression that faith-based activists were "outsiders" who had no right to get involved with the UFW's internal problems.[9]

1978: Eliseo Medina Leaves the UFW

Further signs of internal problems became clear when Eliseo Medina announced at the August 1978 executive board meeting that he was resigning as vice president and leaving the UFW. A Mexican immigrant who had entered fourth grade without speaking English and who went on to become a highly skilled organizer and boycott leader after working in the fields, Medina embodied the UFW's dream of farmworker empowerment. After learning the ropes from Fred Ross Sr. during the UFW's first representation election, Medina had led the campaign to defeat anti-farmworker legislation in Florida and was widely praised for his role during the Delano grape campaign as the Midwest boycott coordinator. During his first three months running the UFW's organizing department, the union won thirteen elections and gained 3,030 members. Medina's farmworker background, organizing and strategic expertise, and deeply spiritual feelings closely paralleled traits also identified with Cesar Chavez. Some assumed that Medina was Chavez's heir apparent, a notion that gained credence when Medina replaced Philip Vera Cruz in 1977 as the union's second vice president. But Medina began having serious policy conflicts with his mentor during the mid-1970s. This conflict reflected the growing tension between Chavez and many of his inner circle over the lack of worker input in setting the union's direction.

Medina later described his differences with Chavez by saying, "We were so close, and then it began to fall apart. . . . At the time we were having our greatest success, Cesar got sidetracked. Cesar was more interested in leading a social movement than a union per se." Philip Vera Cruz also made a distinction between the two types of organization, noting that it was "very dangerous" to use the "terms 'movement' and 'union' almost interchangeably." Vera Cruz saw movements as not necessarily democratic, whereas a union was a "democratically formed legal entity that has a very specific function." To Medina and others, the farmworkers movement had built a union, and it was now essential that this union be run democratically. Considering that Medina went on to devote the next three decades to empowering low-income workers and seeking to encourage their civic participation, his refusal to stay in an organization that he believed was not promoting these ideals was understandable.[10]

Medina's Mexican immigrant background, leadership skills, and successful organizing record likely made him the only UFW executive board member who could have seriously challenged Chavez over the UFW's di-

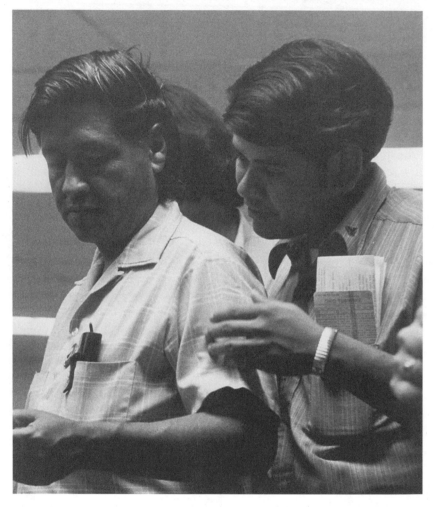

Cesar Chavez and Eliseo Medina confer in Columbus, Ohio, 1974. Photo by Mark Pitt.

rection. Ganz described Medina as "the one credible alternative to Cesar," whose departure "changed the dynamic" regarding the prospects of a shift in UFW control. But the prevailing view on the UFW's executive board was that Chavez was the one who had launched the farmworkers movement, that he was the charismatic leader who had inspired thousands to join, and that his vision of the union's future should prevail. Chavez was the most famous Latino in the country and had a powerful moral authority. As one veteran UFW organizer put it, Chavez's fame and stature put him on a "pedestal. It made it harder for him to listen, which is what he was best at." Chavez could have tried to address Medina's concerns in a way that would have kept the extraordinarily talented young organizer in the UFW, but he made no effort to do so. He instead made it clear that those who disagreed with his policies, including Medina, could leave if they did not like his plans; Medina, and many other veteran UFW organizers, then did so.[11]

Ganz, who argued that the board should not accept Medina's resignation, had written a private letter to Chavez in early 1978 expressing his own concerns about farmworkers' lack of involvement in UFW decision-making. Chavez brought up the letter at the executive board's March 25 meeting, which led Ganz to express dismay that "a lot of Cesar's attention seemed to be on the Game and on Synanon and on La Paz" at a time when the union faced critical strategic and policy decisions. Ganz felt that the UFW was not giving workers any real power or responsibilities in setting the union's direction: "We just seem to assume that whatever way we decide to go is automatically OK. It's not automatically OK." In addition, Chavez's decision that the UFW would not have geographically distinct "locals" left the union without the vehicles traditionally used by organized labor to obtain worker input. And the UFW's executive board in 1978 had no farmworker representation, leaving those working in the fields with no way to influence the UFW's direction.[12]

1978: The Legal Team Departs over Salaries

The year 1978 also brought to a head the serious question of union salaries. Throughout the 1960s and 1970s, the standard wage for a UFW staff member was $5 a week plus room and board. This compensation level was not a hard and fast rule, however; UFW attorneys, for example, were paid $600 per month. (It was later disclosed that some other UFW staff members were paid considerably higher salaries or were given other financial benefits that were not widely advertised.)[13] The UFW legal department was headed by Jerry Cohen, a graduate of Boalt Hall, the law school at the University of California at Berkeley. He was viewed by both allies and adversaries as a brilliant attorney whose intellectual acumen was combined with an understanding of community organizing; and idealistic young attorneys—and those seeking to become attorneys by apprenticing under Cohen—flocked to work under his tutelage.

Attorneys representing the UFW always faced an uphill task getting judges in California's Central Valley to follow the law (chapter 5 describes

Cohen's battle to get access to public records on pesticide use). Because growers felt that they could break the law with impunity, the union's legal staff was constantly dashing around the state putting out fires. A huge number of UFW cases ended up in the state courts of appeal, which meant additional work for the overburdened legal staff. Despite these difficulties, many saw the UFW legal staff as the union's not-so-secret weapon. Some of the nation's best and brightest young legal minds were out in the fields gathering declarations, fighting injunctions against picketing, defending Chavez from contempt charges, negotiating contracts, and engaging in about as wide a variety of tasks as the nature of the farmworker-grower struggle required. The growers could obtain the "best lawyers money could buy," but Jerry Cohen and his fellow UFW attorneys were not for sale.

The enactment of the ALRA in 1975 immersed the UFW legal staff in contract negotiations, lawsuits over claimed irregularities in representation elections, and the need to create all the legal documents involved with a formal union. As the law's passage appeared to indicate that the UFW was here to stay, the attorneys decided that they wanted to make a more long-term commitment to the union and requested a pay hike, to $1,000 a month, still much less than Legal Aid attorneys were earning at the time. Given Chavez's great reliance on Cohen over the years and the UFW leader's knowledge of the way the union's attorneys consistently outmaneuvered their better-paid (and much better dressed) adversaries, approval of the salary hike was expected to be a mere formality.[14]

But at the June executive board meeting, Chavez denounced the attorneys for being greedy. He saw the request for an extra $400 a month as undermining the union's history of reliance on essentially volunteer staff. Cohen, backed strongly by Ganz, warned Chavez that most of the legal staff would leave without the raise, which led Chavez to announce that he would quit the UFW if the board approved the raise. Despite this threat, when the board reconvened ten days later for a final vote, Chavez prevailed by only one vote, five to four. The split was entirely generational, with the younger group of Ganz, Medina, Jessica Govea, and Mack Lyons all favoring the raise. The attorneys indeed resigned, quickly disbanding one of the greatest legal teams ever assembled to work full time for a social change movement. The growers no longer had to fear that Cohen and his crew would somehow find a creative way to outfox them in court.

Why did Chavez make such a destructive decision? Cohen believes that it was primarily about control, not money. The same obsession with control that had led to the Game and the expulsion of veteran volunteers and staff also led Chavez to fear that even his trusted ally Jerry Cohen was trying to create an independent legal operation that would operate outside his control. While Cohen had never given Chavez reason to doubt his loyalty, Cohen had moved the legal team from La Paz to Salinas in 1974 to be nearer the courts. He had offered to resign as general counsel at the time if Chavez saw a problem with the move, but when the UFW leader urged him to retain his position, Cohen assumed that Chavez understood his decision to relocate the legal team. Cohen maintained this assumption until he learned in March 1977 through the Game that Chavez apparently felt "abandoned" by the relocation.[15]

In assessing why Chavez so cavalierly allowed the UFW's highly acclaimed legal team to leave over only $400 a month (money the union could have well afforded), Cohen has said that Chavez felt it would be easy to replace the existing legal staff with attorneys of equal caliber. But, as many of these attorneys demonstrated after leaving the UFW, they were an extraordinarily bright and capable group, whose intense experience with the UFW had given them litigation and negotiation skills that typically took decades to develop. Although the UFW recruited new attorneys as replacements, none had the stature or experience of Jerry Cohen, and few had the skill of his legal team. Chavez's insistence that he would quit the union if the executive board did not back him over the issue of attorney pay was a disturbing reflection of his priorities. Chavez got his way, and one of the UFW's key advantages over its adversaries—its high-quality legal team—was now gone.[16]

In the three years since Chavez and the UFW had fulfilled the "impossible dream" of winning the passage of the ALRA, providing the nation's first meaningful labor protections for farmworkers, the union was withering from within. Whether a UFW victory in the Prop 14 campaign in 1976 might have changed Chavez's post-election conduct cannot be known, but it is clear that within months of the staggering defeat he began viewing UFW staff and volunteers, rather than the growers who financed the No on 14 commercials, as the source of the union's problems. Chavez's introduction of the Game; the forced expulsion and voluntary departure of key organizers, volunteers, and legal staff; and Medina's exit left the UFW far weaker than it had been when the ALRA passed in 1975.

Chavez also terminated the UFW's boycott apparatus on May 5 (Cinco de Mayo) in 1978. This decision was understandable in light of the union's need to focus attention on winning and servicing contracts in the fields, but it eliminated the volunteer positions that had been critical entry points for training so many young organizers. The work of the boycott staff had also broadened the union's base, giving the UFW a closer relationship with the general public than other unions and organizations working for social change. The grape boycott's success at reducing consumer purchases of a targeted product had never been matched by later boycotts, but the other strengths that the boycott operation had brought to the union would be sorely missed in future years.

1979: LETTUCE STRIKE VICTORY
OFFERS THE PROSPECT OF A NEW DIRECTION

Despite the internal turmoil roiling the UFW from 1976 through 1978, workers were still being organized in the fields. When the Teamsters abandoned farmworker organizing in 1977, the UFW was left as the sole union representative, and rising membership provided financial resources the union had long lacked. With contracts in the Imperial Valley and the Salinas lettuce fields set to expire on January 1, 1979, the UFW saw a great opportunity to win impressive wage hikes and benefit gains in the new contracts. The lettuce industry was booming at the time, and, with fields owned by multinational corporations such as United Brands, the UFW argued that farmworkers should reap more of the benefits of this prosperity. Growers gave early signs that they wanted to avoid a nasty contract fight, but when these overtures proved illusory, the workers took matters into their own hands.

The 1979 lettuce strike began in Southern California's Imperial Valley and then expanded to include more than five thousand workers from the Arizona border to Salinas. Farmworkers walked out of the fields and traveled up the state as picketers, in a nearly year-long labor dispute that created unprecedented havoc in the state's lettuce and vegetable fields. Chavez declared that the strike made him "feel the way I have never felt before. We have thirty years of struggle behind us, but I am spirited and encouraged. I feel I can fight another hundred years." With Marshall Ganz and Jessica Govea playing central roles in building solidarity among workers on each ranch, the strike showed the ability of workers to maintain strike discipline and to take a greater role in shaping the union's future. Two of the key leaders among the workers were the brothers Mario and Salvador "Chava" Bustamante. Mario had long supported the UFW in the fields; Chava was less fiery, though he would later go on to become a leader in SEIU's Justice for Janitors movement in California.[17]

On February 10, a UFW striker named Rufino Contreras was shot and killed while in the fields trying to persuade strikebreakers to stop working. Four days later, seven thousand mourners followed Contreras's casket to his burial site. To address the anger over the murder, Chavez decided to call a special executive board meeting to play the Game, believing that this would be the best strategy to "clean ourselves up" in response to the murder. Even Chavez's brother Richard argued that the Game would not solve anything, but Cesar felt that those who rejected the Synanon tool might "be afraid of being told things they're guilty of."[18]

From the time of Contreras's death, Chavez sought to end the strike, whereas the workers and UFW organizers sought to expand it by drawing in additional workers. They made plans for creative work slowdowns by pickers who were still in the fields (having workers skip rows, for example) and for a massive rally in Salinas on the eve of the UFW's annual convention. More than six thousand farmworkers attended the August 11 rally, where both Governor Jerry Brown and Chavez gave rousing speeches that hinted of a general farmworker strike to support the lettuce workers. But Chavez's public support for the strike masked his private efforts to convince workers to end the work stoppage and instead launch a lettuce boycott. In a meeting with worker leaders on the night of the rally, he argued that the UFW had already spent $2.8 million on the strike and that a boycott was easier to win. The workers responded that they would lose their jobs if they left work to join a boycott, and the Bustamante brothers both emphasized that the workers' morale and faith in the UFW would be lost if the union abandoned the strike. To bridge the conflict, it was decided that the convention would endorse both a strike and a boycott. The number of workers going out on strike increased, although they did not receive strike benefits; meanwhile, Ganz refused to meet with Chavez to plan a boycott.[19]

Two weeks after the rally, the union won a total victory. The new UFW contracts raised starting wages for farmworkers by 40 percent, to $5.25 an hour (the federal minimum wage was $3.10 an hour in 1980). The UFW also won an improved medical plan, paid vacations, employer-paid union representatives to administer the labor contracts at the ranch level, a sharp increase in employer pension contributions, and the customary UFW restrictions on pesticide use. One of the contracts' most impressive features was the requirement that growers contribute to the medical plan for piece-rate workers, who worked only four or five hours a day; never before had these workers had such access to health care for their families.[20]

What made this dispute so significant was that UFW workers won the lettuce fight in the fields, using the most traditional of union strategies: the strike. When the Delano grape strike began in 1965, Chavez had known that farmworkers were not yet strong enough to prevail by using this strategy and that growers could easily get strikebreakers into the fields to pick grapes. This was why the UFW transformed what otherwise would have remained a Central Valley grape dispute into a national grassroots boycott campaign for social justice. The union's subsequent victories, including the enactment of the ALRA in 1975, were also a product of its boycott and political organizing prowess, not its ability to win a strike. But in 1979, this dynamic changed. The UFW overcame police and grower violence, the murder of a striking lettuce worker, and a national anti-UFW media campaign to beat the growers on their home turf. It was a strike won entirely by worker power.

After the UFW's lettuce victory, growers could no longer claim that forces outside the fields had defeated them; nor could they legitimately dispute that the UFW had a loyal, dedicated, and powerful base among the workers. Ganz believed that the 1979 strike "was the coming of age for us as a union," and UFW records showed that in that year the union had more than forty-five thousand members. The victory created the prospect that the UFW would overcome the internal problems of the past three years and that its progress would continue.[21]

But instead, the 1979 lettuce strike would represent the last high point in the UFW's history. The strike crystalized the increasing conflict between Chavez's desire to control the direction of the union and workers' demands for input. Although Chavez was thrilled to see lettuce workers mobilizing, this did not mean that he wanted to give them, or other workers, greater control over UFW decision-making. As workers empowered by the strike began to demand a greater voice in the union, it was only a matter of time before their demands started to conflict with Chavez's insistence on maintaining control. The clash soon intensified as a result of a key contract provision won in the strike: employers were required to pay the salaries of a dozen UFW workers, known as "paid reps," who would administer the contracts and address workers' issues at the ranch level. Ganz trained these reps to organize workers and to deal with more mundane service issues such as making sure that medical claims were paid and grievances properly handled. In many respects, the paid reps acted like union business agents. They were elected by fellow workers, and their popularity was clear. Many within the UFW were excited to see the paid reps building worker loyalty and empowering farmworkers on the ranches.

Unfortunately, there had been no formal reconciliation between Chavez and the Salinas strike leaders since their dispute over strategy on the night of the August rally. When the Salinas leaders decided to run their own slate of candidates for the executive board at the UFW's 1981 convention, the simmering conflict over issues of control broke out in public. It was at the convention that Chavez personally rebuffed efforts by seven Salinas worker representatives, who had been elected by their colleagues, to secure farmworker representation on the UFW executive board.

The top board candidate of the Salinas group was farmworker Rosario Pelayo. She had worked in the fields from the age of eight, had given birth to thirteen children, and had begun volunteering with the UFW in 1970. In 1977, she became president of the workers at her ranch. Even though Pelayo represented everything Chavez had worked for since 1962, and even though her election to the board would not have jeopardized Chavez's majority control, the UFW leader and Dolores Huerta opposed her. Both saw Pelayo's candidacy as part of a plot by Marshall Ganz to take over the union, even though Ganz had left the UFW earlier that year, having seen the writing on the wall. Despite Ganz's departure (and that of Cohen and Govea the same year), Chavez and Huerta insisted that Ganz had "manipulated" such longtime UFW activists as the Bustamante brothers and Sabino Lopez into running Pelayo. It was a condescending charge, implying that the Latino leaders could not decide on their own that the UFW needed farmworker representation on its board.[22]

Rather than turning a potential conflict into a positive by supporting Pelayo, Chavez used a procedural tactic to prevent the Salinas slate from even competing for votes. As a group of fifty Salinas workers walked out in protest, leaflets circulated accusing them of being communists. To send an even stronger message to workers who might consider similar moves, Chavez fired nine paid reps, including Mario Bustamante and Sabino Lopez. A court eventually ruled the firings illegal, but, in a further sign of the UFW's decline, the decision was issued after the lettuce contracts had expired, and by then the paid rep jobs had been lost.[23]

The controversies over the attorney salaries and the paid reps had a common feature other than Chavez's increasing desire for control: both involved the only groups within the union (other than those working in the fields) who were compensated for their services beyond a minimum stipend and room and board. Chavez himself lived a spartan life, never owning a house or earning more than $6,000 a year. His insistence on carefully reviewing UFW phone bills became an ongoing joke in the organization. But Chavez gave a little-known speech to a group of church people in La Paz in October 1971 that may have foreshadowed the union's future conflicts over financial issues.

The theme of the speech was the relationship between organizing and money. Chavez argued that unions that pay organizers are less successful than those (like the UFW at the time) that rely on individuals who are motivated solely by a desire to sacrifice for the cause. Explaining how the UFW beat the Teamsters in Delano, Chavez observed, "The Teamsters brought in a lot of organizers but after a while it was too expensive. All we needed was just enough to eat and a little gas. We don't have to worry about money. That's how things get done." He felt that "when you sacrifice, you force others to sacrifice," something they will not do if they "know that the other guys are getting a big fat salary." Chavez raised these ideas in the context of being "worried" about a request by some volunteers to raise the weekly stipend from $5 to $10 a week. Since he viewed even this small increase as potentially undermining the union, it is understandable that he would have seen the attorneys' request as "selfish." It may also help explain why he was uncomfortable with paid reps, even though these staffers earned only what they would have collected if they had been working in the fields.[24]

THE 1980S AND BEYOND

After 1981, Chavez and the UFW proceeded without most of the key people who had built the movement's success. No organization could suffer such a talent drain without adverse consequences. While the post-1981 UFW retained many committed staff members, the union's ability to secure new contracts, and to even maintain its existing ones, steadily declined. By 1984, the UFW had contracts with only fifteen of the seventy Delano grape growers; when Cesar Chavez died in 1993, the UFW had no table grape contracts. By 2007, the federal government reported that UFW membership had decreased to fewer than six thousand, though the union estimated that there were twenty-seven thousand who worked at least one day a year under a union contract.[25]

In 1995, the union launched a major campaign to organize an estimated 20,000 strawberry workers. In 1996, the newly revitalized AFL-CIO described the effort as its "absolute number one priority" and committed significant financial and organizing support to the campaign. These resources, sympathetic media coverage, and a "Five Cents for Fairness" campaign that won commitments from retailers and the general public to pay a nickel more for a package of strawberries to raise workers' wages, resulted in the most high-profile grassroots UFW campaign since the 1979 lettuce strike. But in two union elections in Watsonville, the UFW lost to a committee of workers hostile to the union. The UFW did sign a contract covering 750 strawberry workers in March 2001, but this was little to show for the millions of dollars that had been spent to organize an agricultural sector that employed 20,000. These defeats in the strawberry fields were a huge psychological blow to the UFW's hopes for rebuilding its membership. They also raised troubling questions about the union's ability to win support among the new generation of farmworkers. As the UFW steadily lost contracts, fewer farmworkers were protected from pesticide risks by contract provisions. Workers' health was also imperiled by the union's diminishing political influence during the 1980s and 1990s, which reduced pressures on state and local pesticide regulators for aggressive enforcement.[26]

Cesar Chavez justifiably became a national icon. But as typically happens to human beings who become symbols of larger ideals, Chavez's shortcomings, and his role in the union's post-1981 problems, have been minimized or even ignored. As a result, most accounts of the union's decline primarily blame external factors—chief among them California's election of a pro-grower Republican governor, George Deukmejian, in 1982. Deukmejian sought to stack the Agriculture Labor Relations Board against the UFW by appointing hostile commissioners and an anti-UFW ALRB general counsel. This new ALRB frequently delayed the certification of UFW election victories, thus preventing new union contracts from being signed and implemented, frustrating workers, and casting doubt on the union's ability to deliver. Another equally pro-grower Republican governor, Pete Wilson, followed Deukmejian in 1991; many link the sixteen years of Republican administrations, from 1983 to 1998, to the weakening of the UFW during this period.[27]

This oft-repeated view, which insulates Cesar Chavez from responsibility for the union's decline, actually undermines the great accomplishments of the farmworkers movement. It wrongly assumes that Chavez was powerful enough to continue building the UFW without most of his key allies, and it perpetuates the false idea that politicians can readily defeat progressive social movements. Such an analysis also conveys a message that grassroots movements are essentially powerless—after all, if the election of a Republican governor could reverse the progress of a movement that had grown steadily for two decades, why bother getting involved in such a fragile endeavor?

Cesar Chavez and the farmworkers movement won their landmark successes by organizing workers in the fields and winning over the general public in front of supermarkets, in churches, at their front doors, and in the streets. The UFW built the most powerful grassroots movement of its time, and it defies the historical record to imply that sympathetic politicians produced the union's success. Was it easier for the UFW to function under its ally Jerry Brown? Absolutely. But the farmworkers movement grew in the 1960s and early 1970s under the extremely hostile administration of Ronald Reagan, for whom defeating the farmworkers was a top priority. The UFW won the Delano grape boycott at a time when workers could be fired for union activity, growers could choose a union for their workers, and the rest of the worker protections later provided by the ALRA were lacking. The movement made its greatest strides despite strong opposition from a pro-grower president, Richard Nixon, and made a fool of California's Republican senator George Murphy when he tried to battle the UFW over pesticides.

Given the UFW's long history of overcoming political opposition, and the fact that pro-UFW Democrats controlled the California legislature during the Deukmejian years, the notion that the election of a Republican governor and the appointment of an unsympathetic ALRB doomed the union makes no sense. The UFW of the 1960s and 1970s knew how to surmount such political obstacles—but in the 1980s and beyond, these obstacles could not be overcome, in large part because of the massive loss of the skilled volunteers and workers who had been responsible for the union's earlier success.

Cesar Chavez did not build the UFW alone. To argue that the union could have continued to prosper after losing such key leaders as Eliseo Medina, Marshall Ganz, Philip Vera Cruz, Gilbert Padilla (these were four of the union's nine executive board members in 1977), Jerry Cohen, Jim Drake, and Jessica Govea, not to mention the huge number of incredibly dedicated organizers and attorneys, is to ignore the chief reason for the UFW's success. Regardless of California's governors in the 1980s and 1990s, the UFW was unable to grow, or even to sustain itself, without its most valuable asset: the remarkably talented activists who built the union.

While many veterans of the farmworkers movement view their days with the union as changing the course of their lives, some understandably maintain a residual bitterness. It is a sadness associated with lost opportunities and the acute disappointment that an institution they worked so hard to build reversed its progress at the height of its power. Many retain such a deep emotional connection to the union that debate still rages over the reasons for its decline. But Cesar Chavez and the UFW attracted an astonishing combination of activist talents, and, as the next chapter describes, many overcame their disappointment to continue the struggle for social justice beyond the fields.

11

HARVESTING JUSTICE
BEYOND THE FIELDS

The Ongoing Legacy of UFW Alumni

From 1965 to 1979, the UFW was an entry point to a lifetime of civic engagement for a generation of young activists. As earlier chapters describe, many went on to dedicate their lives to making a positive difference in the world. Some of these UFW veterans have been working for social justice for nearly forty years, with the farmworkers movement serving as a "bridge" to their future careers and commitments.

This chapter begins by updating the post-UFW careers of some of the activists previously discussed and then tells the life stories of some key alumni who were not highlighted in earlier chapters but whose contributions to progressive change are critical to understanding the UFW's impact beyond the fields. The accompanying table includes more than 220 individuals who went on to work for social justice and whom I was able to trace through personal contacts, interviews, and Internet research. Many of these individuals fit into several career categories, but I chose to list each person in only one. This does not imply a definitive assessment of the relative importance of their work in each category. In addition, there are no doubt some UFW alumni who deserve inclusion but whose post-UFW careers I either misinterpreted or was unable to discern.[1]

UFW VETERANS WORKING BEYOND THE FIELDS

Here is an update, in alphabetical order, on the post-UFW social justice efforts of some of the key activists discussed in previous chapters.

Salvador "Chava" Bustamante became the vice president of SEIU Local 1877, California's statewide janitors union. He has played a key role in building Strengthening Our Lives (SOL), the Latino voter outreach organization that began in California and has become a model for similar efforts in other states (see chapter 7).

THE STRUGGLE FOR JUSTICE BEYOND THE FIELDS

Labor Organizer/ Union Staff	SEIU/UNITE HERE	NGOs*/Academia/ Cultural Work
Bill Camp	Wren Bradley	David Averbuck
Joanne Carder	Chava Bustamonte	David Bacon
Ed Chiera	Mike Casey	Peter Baird
Guy Costello	Roberto De La Cruz	Bob Barber
Jessie De La Cruz	Jean Ellers	Bill Berkowitz
Susan Samuels Drake	Nancy Elliott	Jerry Brown
Alberto Escalante	Colin Gordon	Bob Datz
John Gardner	Bill Granfield	Elaine Elinson
Joel Glick	Gary Guthman	Rob Everts
Humberto Gomez	Khati Hendry	Peter Jones
John Govea	Nick Jones	Steve Jones
Marc Grossman	Stephen Lerner	Gretchen Laue
Fred Hirsch	Eliseo Medina	Raven Lidman
Bob Johnson	Kevin O'Connor	Augustin Lira
Michael Johnston	Liam O'Reilly	Victoria Lopez
Charles Keaton	Mark Pitt	Mary Mecartney
Carol Lambiase	Fred Ross Jr.	Meta Mendel-Reyes
Carlos LeGerrette	Susan Sachen	Oscar Mondragon
Linda LeGerrette	Mark Sharwood	Janis Peterson
Al Lucero	Mila Thomas	Jack Quigley
Maria Magnana	Scott Washburn	Mary Quinn
Artie Mendoza		Chris Schneider
George Nee		Hub Segur
Bob Purcell		Dave Smith
Jorge Rivera		Harriet Teller
Gilbert Rodriguez		Dan Thomas
Gloria Rodriguez		Luis Valdez
Virginia Rodriguez		Richard Ybarra
Jerry Ryan		Jane Yett
George Sheridan		
Ellen Starbird		
Marion Steeg		
Alice Sunshine		
Dan Thomas		
Lydia Villareal		
Dan Willett		

* Nongovernmental organizations

THE STRUGGLE FOR JUSTICE BEYOND THE FIELDS (cont'd.)

Religious Service	Politics	Community Organizers
Steve Burton	Tasha Doner	Gene Boutilier
Bonnie Chatfield	Larry Frank	Juanita Brown
Buckner Coe	Marshall Ganz	Nancy Grimley
Rosemary Cooperrider	Steven Hopcraft	Carleton
Verne Cooperrider	David Koehler	Patrick Deagen
David Havens	Esther Padilla	Sharon Delugach
Pat Hoffman	Gilbert Padilla	Jim Drake
Ken Irrgang	Steve Rivers	Alfredo Figueroa
Rosemary Matson	Richie Ross	Jessica Govea
Jose Murguia	Larry Tramutola	Chris Hartmire
Mary Sanchez	Deborah Vollmer	Andy Imutan
Christine Schenk Sr		Roberta Jaffe
Frances Smith		Julie Kerksick
Joe Tobin		Ken Leap
Dolores Velasco		Marco Lopez
		Georgiann Lyga
		Pearl McGivney
		Crosby Milne
		Paul Milne
		Ernie Powell
		Olga Reyna
		Maria Rifo
		Stephan Roberson
		Fred Ross Sr.
		Helen Serda
		Patty Teufel
		Philip Vera Cruz
		Dick Wiesenhahn
		Dan Willet

THE STRUGGLE FOR JUSTICE BEYOND THE FIELDS (cont'd.)

Social Change Activism/Government	UFW Progeny: Neighbor to Neighbor	Public Interest/ Labor Lawyers
Kevin Brown	John Adler	Dan Boone
Paul Carrillo	Greg Akili	Bill Carder
LeRoy Chatfield	Nick Allen	Aggie Rose Chavez
Kate Colwell	Jeannie Appleman	Jerry Cohen
Ida Cousino	Denise Bergez	Richard Cook
Eduard Cuellar	Pat Blumenthal	Tom Dalzell
Martha Diepenbrock	Mari Brennan	Ellen Eggers
Maria Fuentes	Mary Ann Buckley	Charles Farnsworth
Nancy Hickey Hughes	Donald Cohen	Ruth Friedman
Dolores Huerta	Ellie Cohen	David Grabill
Caren Jacobson	Marc Dohan	Ellen Greenstone
Sabino Lopez	Ed Dunn	Peter Haberfeld
Deborah Miller	Angie Fa	Linton Joaquin
Kate Munger	Alexis Gonzales	Ellen Lake
Kathleen Murguia	John Heffernan	Barbara Macri-Ortiz
Dan Murphy	Dana Hohn	Stephen Matchett
Margaret Murphy	Mary Hussman	Mary Mocine
Patty Park	Eli Lee	Bill Monning
Carolyn Purcell	Marion Magill	Sandy Nathan
Abby Flores Rivera	Lauren Martens	Barbara Rhine
Nancy Ryan	Shelley Moskowitz	Ramon Romero
Marc Sapir	Laura Mudd	Glenn Rothner
Pete Savin	Dennak Murphy	Jim Rutkowski
Ken Schroeder	Helen Schaub	Mario Salgado
	Glen Schneider	Alan Schlosser
	Terry Surguine	Chris Schneider
	Marcela Ureno	Carol Schoenbrunn
	Ken Weine	Jeff Sweetland
	Robin Weingarten	Bob Thompson
	Tracy Zeluff	Barry Winograd
		Danny Ybarra
		Kirsten Zerger

Miguel Contreras became a leading organizer and strategist for UNITE HERE and then the head of the Los Angeles County Federation of Labor. He played a central role in transforming the Los Angeles labor movement and in strengthening Latino political power in Los Angeles and statewide.

Susan Samuels Drake worked for the AFL-CIO Organizing Institute, recruiting young organizers.

Elaine Elinson spent more than two decades as information director for the American Civil Liberties Union in Northern California.

Marshall Ganz became a political strategist for campaigns ranging from Nancy Pelosi's initial 1987 congressional race to Howard Dean's 2004 presidential bid. Ganz also consulted for SEIU before joining the faculty of Harvard University as a lecturer in public policy at the Kennedy School of Government. He helped design the organizing strategy used in Barack Obama's 2008 presidential primary campaign and served as a trainer and advisor for its field program.

Jessica Govea became an electoral campaign organizer, a trainer of labor activists in El Salvador, and an instructor of immigrant workers at both Rutgers and Cornell University.

Bill Granfield became head of UNITE HERE's restaurant local in New York City, Local 100.

Gary Guthman is an organizer for SEIU in Los Angeles.

Nick Jones became an organizer for SEIU's Oakland-based health care workers union, Local 250.

Stephen Lerner founded Justice for Janitors and became building services director for SEIU. Lerner's December 2002 *Labor Notes* article, "Three Steps to Reorganizing and Rebuilding the Labor Movement," laid the groundwork for the decision by SEIU and other unions to break from the AFL-CIO in 2005 and form the new labor federation Change to Win. In 2007, Lerner became director of SEIU's Private Equity Project, which seeks to protect and benefit workers affected by corporate buyouts.

Eliseo Medina became an organizer for the Communication Workers of America and then headed SEIU's San Diego local. He went on to become international vice president of SEIU. He has been a leading figure in inspiring the labor movement to embrace the cause of immigrant rights and has played a major role in national efforts for progressive immigration reform.

Mark Pitt worked on the J. P. Stevens boycott, became an officer with UNITE, and then became a lead organizer for the United Steelworkers of America.

Bob Purcell played an important lobbying and organizing role in Neighbor to Neighbor. He has since spent nearly two decades with the Laborers International Union, for whom he is now director of public employees.

Fred Ross Sr. continued his life's work of training organizers by becoming involved with Neighbor to Neighbor.

Fred Ross Jr. founded Neighbor to Neighbor, worked full time to elect Nancy Pelosi to the House of Representatives in 1987, and helped lead the Active Citizenship Campaign. Ross is now training a new generation of organizers as a campaign strategist for SEIU and since 2007 has headed a statewide campaign in California to organize nearly ten thousand workers at nine hospitals affiliated with St. Joseph's Health Systems.

Susan Sachen worked on the J. P. Stevens boycott and on the first Justice for Janitors campaign in Denver in 1987. Sachen has worked for either SEIU or the California Labor Federation for more than twenty years.

Mark Sharwood has been a longtime organizer for SEIU Local 1877 in California and is currently its staff director in Northern California.

Larry Tramutola became one of California's leading campaign strategists, specializing in winning school bond campaigns.

Scott Washburn joined Ganz and Ross on the initial Pelosi campaign and has been involved in dozens of electoral and union campaigns. He became the head of SEIU's state council in Arizona, playing a key role in boosting Latino voter turnout in that state.

FAITH-BASED COMMUNITY ORGANIZERS

No person better embodies the role of UFW alumni as unsung heroes and mentors who have dedicated their lives to empowering others than Jim Drake. In 1962, Drake was a newly ordained United Church of Christ minister, who was sent to complete his training with the California Migrant Ministry in Delano. He spent the next sixteen years as one of the UFW's key organizers, working in California, Texas, and Arizona. Drake coordinated the UFW's nationwide grape boycott in the late 1960s and helped build religious support for the union during the critical early years when growers dominated Central Valley church congregations. But what is so impressive about Jim Drake is that he followed his sixteen-year UFW career with an equally impressive organizing career that lasted more than two decades.

In 1978, Drake was invited by the United Church of Christ to work with and help organize woodcutters in Mississippi. Timber was the largest agricultural crop in the region. International Paper, Georgia Pacific, and the other corporate mills treated the thousands of workers who cut and delivered the logs as independent contractors. This status meant that the woodcutters faced many of the same problems that California farmworkers had confronted when Drake first began working with them: they had no health insurance, no minimum wage, no health and safety laws to protect them. In an effort to escape from what approximated indentured servitude, some woodcutters in the early 1970s organized themselves into the Gulfcoast Pulpwood Association, which unfortunately was short-lived.

The United Church of Christ believed that Drake could apply what he had learned from the UFW to build a union among southern pulpwood cutters. Over the next few years, Drake did indeed unite the workers into the Mississippi Pulpwood Cutters Association. He helped them create a cooperative that enabled them to buy saws at much lower prices and a credit union that gave many workers access to credit for the first time. Drake developed a cadre of woodcutter leaders who built an activist organization modeled on the UFW, the United Woodcutters Association, which organized in more than thirty-five counties across rural Mississippi. The UWA stood up to the corporate timber companies, conducting strikes and winning a historic fair scaling law that prevented woodcutters from being underpaid for their piece-rate work.

Drake's success in Mississippi brought him a job offer from the Industrial Areas Foundation, which had funded Cesar Chavez's first organizing work with the Community Services Organization in the 1950s. Drake relocated to the Rio Grande Valley in South Texas, where he joined with Ernesto Cortes, the legendary founder of the Southwest IAF Network, in forming the Valley Interfaith Organization. (Cortes had worked on behalf of the UFW while a student in Texas, but his formative organizing training came from Ed Chambers at the IAF.) The group soon pressured the state into providing water and plumbing to the *colonias,* the shantytowns that proliferated along the Texas-Mexico border.

Drake was still working for the IAF when he was assigned to the South

Bronx in 1987, an area that had been devastated by arson and public ne-
glect. Drake's job was to organize the South Bronx Churches, a coalition
of more than forty churches that sought to improve the community's political clout. By 1990, Drake had helped build an organization so powerful that it won revamped control of the local hospital, new community
policing strategies, and the right to build affordable homes on twenty
acres of vacant city-owned land.

As was his custom wherever he worked, Drake proved to be a valuable mentor to the next generation of organizers. In this case, his pupil
was Lee Stuart, a young woman who became the group's lead organizer
in 1992. Stuart described Drake as "an essential mentor" in her life, who
helped her "learn how to bring diverse people and groups together, to
develop a strategy, to be unafraid of confrontation, and to maintain public relationships over long periods of time." Using the organizing prowess
of Drake and Stuart, the South Bronx Churches built more than 965
homes in a ten-year period and created a new public high school, the
Bronx Leadership Academy, which became a model for the small-school
reform movement in New York City.[2]

Hard as it may be to believe, Jim Drake was still not done improving
people's lives. While remaining involved in the South Bronx, Drake
moved on to help form the Greater Boston Interfaith Organization, a regional coalition of more than a hundred religious and community groups.
Drake saw the group as a vehicle to increase civic engagement, telling
the *Boston Globe* that "we are trying to get back to a more human element in politics," creating new interest among those who have dropped
out of a system in which the "person with the most money wins." One
of the group's goals was to build affordable housing; at the time of
Drake's death, in September 2001, the organization had raised its first
$5 million. Drake preached and practiced the empowerment of the dis-
enfranchised in a forty-year organizing career that spread social justice
and economic fairness well beyond the fields.[3]

Jean Eilers, born in 1940, joined the Sisters of the Holy Child convent
in 1959. She was teaching at an upper-income private Catholic high school
in 1972 when she first volunteered for the UFW, thinking that she should
"put some action into our words." Assigned to work on a letter-writing
project in Los Angeles supervised by Jessica Govea and Ruth Shy, Eilers
arrived at a shopping mall on her first day at 8:30 A.M.; at 10:00 P.M.
that night, she was still putting stamps on envelopes. Instead of being
deterred by this long workday, Eilers was inspired by the UFW's dedication. She proceeded to work for Fred Ross Jr. and Bob Purcell in the

UFW's No on Prop 22 campaign, building support among religious women, participating in human billboards, and even collecting bottles for money. As her involvement with the UFW increased, Eilers left her teaching post and began working with the union full time in 1976. She stayed until June 1981, when she also left the clergy.

For Eilers, becoming a nun had been one of the only routes available to Catholic women who wanted to serve society. But the UFW experience offered other options, and Eilers has devoted her post-UFW years to working in the labor movement. She began as an organizer for the American Federation of State, County, and Municipal Employees (AFSCME) and then went on to positions with the United Auto Workers and SEIU. In 1997, she became Oregon state director for the national AFL-CIO. In the fall of 2005, she left that post to become a community organizer for SEIU Local 49, covering Oregon and southwest Washington. Eilers remained involved in her local church and has helped boost religious support for labor causes. "Union people have a hunger and thirst for justice, in line with prophetic tradition," she says, noting the connection between religion and labor and adding that labor "has a lot to gain from the integrity of the church's stands."[4]

Like Jim Drake and Jean Eilers, David Koehler's involvement with the UFW began as a result of his religious background. Koehler was a minister with the United Church of Christ who worked for both the UFW and the National Farm Worker Ministry during the 1970s. He participated in the UFW's attempt to recall Arizona's governor in 1972. He was later sent to his denomination's general synod meeting, where he succeeded in getting ninety-five United Church of Christ delegates to go to Coachella to witness the farmworkers' struggle there. Koehler then worked on the boycott in Dayton, Ohio, and became the Cleveland boycott director in 1974 after Eliseo Medina, the previous director, was transferred to Chicago. It was Medina who told Koehler to purchase and wear a clerical collar: "We want people to know you are clergy when you are on the picket line." Koehler joined the rest of the boycott staff in California to work on the Prop 14 campaign in 1976, and Chavez sent him to direct the New York City boycott in 1977. Fred Ross Sr. was there to train the staff, and Koehler learned the techniques of holding house meetings and telling a story in a way that enabled the audience to truly "feel" the story.[5]

In 1978, Koehler and his wife, Nora Sullivan, also a UFW staffer, moved to Peoria, Illinois. Koehler became the community organizer/minister for Friendship House, a social services agency in a low-income neighborhood. In 1982, he was elected to a seat on the Peoria County Board.

He was reelected in 1986 and then ran for the city council, where he spent eight years. In 1985, Koehler became executive director of the Peoria Area Labor Management Council, a position he believes he obtained because of his UFW experience. He served until 2006, when he was elected as Peoria's representative to the Illinois state senate. Koehler has remained an ordained minister and is a pastor at a local church. He attributes his career path (and marriage) to the UFW and the National Farm Worker Ministry. He believes that the people he met during his UFW days helped to shape his life. As he notes, "One thing I learned in my time with the farmworkers and still hold dear is the ongoing spirit of 'sí se puede!'"[6]

CULTURAL CONTRIBUTORS

When the Delano grape strike began in September 1965, young people flocked to the fields to help the farmworkers' cause. Among this group was Luis Valdez, the son of Delano farmworkers, who had studied drama at San Jose State University and performed with the socially conscious San Francisco Mime Troupe. Valdez, who had visited Cuba in 1964 and was a staunch critic of the Vietnam war, strongly identified with the emerging movement for Chicano power. Valdez heard Cesar Chavez speak in San Francisco in the early weeks of the 1965 strike and soon got a chance to talk with him. Valdez proposed opening a street theater group that would use satire to address social issues, much as the Mime Troupe did, and that would cast farmworkers as performers in the skits. He had a vision of using theater to build unity among the strikers and to convey a pro-union message. Chavez was fine with the idea, though he cautioned Valdez, "There's no money, there's no actors, there's not time for you to rehearse even." Valdez jumped at this opportunity, and the legendary Teatro Campesino, which has continued for more than four decades, was born.[7]

El Teatro Campesino has been described as a cross "between Brecht and Cantinflas." Its use of Mexican folk humor in the service of a grassroots movement of the disenfranchised became a landmark contribution both to the farmworkers' struggle and to Chicano culture. The *Wall Street Journal* saw El Teatro as "proletarian pantomime," while young Chicano activists and theater critics saw Valdez's creation as representing "an historical link to Aztec-Christian-Mexican-Spanish theater of fiesta, rituals, morality, and Cinco de Mayo plays and processionals." Chicano intellectuals even touted El Teatro as "a key to a new historical consciousness." UFW members already had a newspaper, *El Malcriado,* which featured politically pointed, often ironic cartoons by artist Andy Zermeno. Valdez's live-action use of irony to convey serious messages about brutal foremen, greedy growers, and the often mundane day-to-day life on the picket line boosted strikers' spirits. At first, it was difficult to get farmworkers to appear in the skits. But when the workers realized that they would be acting out what they did in their own lives, Valdez's idea took hold.[8]

El Teatro followed the harvest and became the leading source of entertainment for those striking in the fields. During the day, the troupe would visit campuses and Latino neighborhoods to build support for the union and would also perform on a flatbed truck in the fields adjacent to picketing workers. At night, El Teatro performed in the fields on makeshift stages, before laughing and boisterous crowds, who watched performances illuminated by car headlights.

When Chavez and the farmworkers began their legendary march from Delano to Sacramento on March 17, 1966—with the theme of "Peregrinacion, Penitencia, and Revolución" (Pilgrimage, Penitence, and Revolution)—Valdez showed that his skill in fusing cultural and political symbols was not limited to El Teatro. He authored "El Plan de Delano," a farmworker manifesto that would become a landmark in UFW and Chicano history. The dominant theme of the Plan of Delano was "United we shall stand," and it combined religious imagery, themes from the Mexican revolution, and leftist social analysis. During the 1930s, Mexican muralists such as Diego Rivera, David Alfaro Siqueiros, and José Clemente Orozco also fused Mexican tradition and populist politics. But Valdez's Teatro and the Plan of Delano may have touched a deeper chord by resurrecting this fusion of culture and politics without the earlier generation's anti-religious sentiments. Valdez read "El Plan de Delano" to crowds in the towns where marchers stayed each night, broadening their understanding of the march's larger purpose.[9]

Valdez created a cultural center in Delano to teach farmworker children about their Mexican heritage through art, music, dance, and theater. In 1967, he moved El Teatro to the town of Del Rey and later, in 1971, to San Juan Bautista, where he established El Centro Campesino Cultural, with an art center and a professional production company. There, he began working in film. In 1981, he won widespread acclaim as the playwright and director of Zoot Suit, which told the nearly forgotten story of the sensationalist 1940s Sleepy Lagoon murder case in Los Angeles—in which Chicano youths were convicted of murder, despite a lack of evidence, thanks to denial of counsel and a biased judge—

and the city's "zoot suit riots" that followed, in which U.S. servicemen assaulted hundreds of Mexican and Chicano "zoot suiters." The Los Angeles police responded to this mob violence by arresting many of the victims; few of the white servicemen were ever charged or convicted. *Zoot Suit* epitomized the city's racial bias against Chicanos, and Valdez's play opened in Los Angeles to near universal acclaim. He then wrote the screenplay and directed the film version of *Zoot Suit,* which appeared in 1982. He went on to direct *La Bamba* (1987), a film biography of the Chicano rock-and-roll star Richie Valens.

Valdez put the struggles of the dispossessed and disenfranchised at the center of Chicano culture, encouraging future cultural workers to create socially conscious art. Valdez saw the farmworker as "the cultural root" of Chicano identity, and El Teatro Campesino unleashed some of the era's most powerful political art on behalf of the UFW. Chicano poet Max Benavides credits El Teatro with inspiring other artists to support the movement, including Antonio Bernal, Rupert Garcia, Carlos Almaraz (who painted signs for the UFW in Delano's grape fields), Carmen Lopez Garza, and Harry Gamboa Jr. In 1989, artist Barbara Carrasco's computer-animated billboard "Pesticides" ran for a month in New York City's Times Square to promote the union's anti-pesticide campaign.[10]

Despite being politically to the left of Chavez, Valdez remained his staunch ally to the end. At Chavez's funeral, Valdez and El Teatro appeared, following the eulogy, declaring, "You shall never die. The seed of your heart will keep on singing, keep on flowering, for the cause." Benavidez believes that "what Chicano art has ultimately become in all of its globally hip and often subtle permutations . . . owes a lot to Chavez and the labor movement." And to Luis Valdez, who took the opportunity Chavez and the UFW provided to inspire future generations and remake Chicano culture.[11]

UFW alumni Peter Jones and Steve Jones made their mark in a related field of cultural politics: labor-oriented songs. Singing was a central feature of UFW rallies. UFW veteran and Justice for Janitors organizer Mark Sharwood credits the movement with popularizing Spanish versions of traditional labor and civil rights songs, including "Solidarity Forever" and "We Shall Not Be Moved." Peter Jones joined the UFW in 1975 after graduating from college. A few weeks after joining the boycott staff in Washington, D.C., he brought out his guitar and started playing. Gilbert Padilla told Jones to bring the guitar to the next picket line. Jones knew only a few chords, but he gradually learned the union, civil rights, and farmworker songs that often accompanied UFW events.[12]

Although Peter Jones soon became burned out by the job and moved to Vermont, his brother Steve, inspired by Peter's example, began organizing for the UFW as part of the boycott staff in Washington, D.C., in 1976. Peter wrote five songs about the farmworkers that he sent to his brother, including "The Gallo Song," which became a UFW classic. A typical stanza went like this, with the name of the Gallo product changing in each subsequent stanza:

> I was lying in bed the other night talking with my friend Jane
> I brought out a bottle of baby oil and she brought out Andre Champagne.
> And I said . . . Andre Champagne is a Gallo wine—You got to take that bottle back
> And you cannot drink it until Gallo signs—You got to take that bottle back.

In April 1977, Peter joined Steve to work on the boycott in Los Angeles. The brothers started writing songs that were sung on picket lines and at rallies and staff meetings. After Peter was threatened with violence on a picket line, he came back and played Woody Guthrie's refrain, "Oh, you can't scare me, I'm sticking to the union." Peter and Steve returned to Washington, D.C., later that year and agreed to sing union songs every Monday night at a local café. They continued doing that for ten years, while also performing for labor and other progressive causes.[13]

In 1999, Peter became the executive director of the Labor Heritage Foundation, which works to expand the use of music and the arts in organizing campaigns. The LHF is a leading supplier of labor music, art, books, and video. In addition to exposing new generations to songs about Joe Hill, Mary "Mother" Jones, and other labor legends, the LHF runs an annual conference on creative organizing that trains activists to use cultural tools such as songs and art in their campaigns. The conference grew out of the Great Labor Arts Exchange, the long-running program that the LHF designed for union performers and artists. Jones believes that songs and skits that play off a company's slogan or a workplace issue can add energy to organizing campaigns, as El Teatro Campesino demonstrated for the UFW. Acknowledging that he "never would have gotten into the labor culture field without the UFW," Jones says that "organizing campaigns are often about dignity, solidarity, and social justice. Creative techniques help people showcase these aspects. They also help educate people, build morale, and bring people together."[14]

Steve Jones dropped out of music school at the University of Maryland to join the UFW boycott in 1976. He was exposed to music such as Daniel

Valdez's "Brown Eyed Children of the Sun" and often played his guitar as he led rallies in singing "Union Maid," "Hold the Fort," and other traditional labor classics adopted by the UFW. (Jones recalls that "De Colores" was a particular challenge: "I found that if you play it 1,000 times, you really get the hang of the chords.") Steve Jones became a professional musician and went on to create his own labor classic, writing the music and lyrics for a jazz opera, *Forgotten: The Murder at the Ford Rouge Plant*. The opera tells the story of one "forgotten" man, Lewis Bradford, to connect the audience with the lives of the thousands of workers who struggled to unionize the Ford Rouge plant and the eight million women and men who joined unions in the depths of the Great Depression. The opera opened in May 2003 to huge crowds and rave reviews in Washington, D.C., and played throughout the Midwest.[15]

David Bacon followed his UFW organizing career by becoming one of America's leading reporters and photojournalists covering farmworker and immigration issues. He is the author of numerous books on these topics, including *Communities without Borders: Images and Voices from the World of Migration* and *The Children of NAFTA: Labor Wars on the U.S./Mexico Border*. Bacon has been an associate editor with Pacific News Service and frequently writes about labor unions and immigrants for a wide spectrum of publications.[16]

SOCIAL ENTREPRENEURS

Dave Smith joined the UFW in 1968 and was assigned to design and implement a computerized system for the union's membership, credit union, and medical services. He also worked on the UFW's political campaigns. After leaving the UFW, Smith co-founded the garden store Smith & Hawken and then became a leader in the field of organic products. He helped to establish a natural food co-op and held leadership positions in a number of national organic businesses, including Seeds of Change. In 2004, Smith co-founded Organic Banquet, the first national organic flower company, and is involved in creating a chain of Organic To Go fast-food restaurants. In light of the UFW's long campaign against pesticides, it seems fitting that a UFW alumni should challenge the pesticide industry by offering organic alternatives.

Rob Everts left college in 1975 to join the UFW and worked there until 1982, when he became an organizer with the Hotel and Restaurant Workers Union. In 1987, he joined Neighbor to Neighbor (see chapter 2) and gained experience in the coffee industry when he helped lead the group's boycott. In 1997, Everts joined Equal Exchange, which sells organic gourmet coffee, tea, sugar, cocoa, and chocolate bars produced by democratically run farmer co-ops in Latin America, Africa, and Asia. After being hired to help design a grassroots organizing approach to building fair trade, Everts became co-executive director in 1999.

UFW PIONEERS

Philip Vera Cruz began organizing farmworkers in the 1950s, helped launch the 1965 Delano grape strike, and served as a UFW vice president and a member of the executive board from 1966 to 1977. After leaving the UFW to protest Chavez's visit to the Philippines to meet with dictator Ferdinand Marcos (see chapter 10), Vera Cruz remained active in the labor movement and outspoken on international issues for the rest of his life. He inspired Filipino workers, youth, and the entire community to oppose exploitation and oppression and to fight for social change. Vera Cruz's opposition to Marcos coincided with a national upsurge of radicalism among Filipino Americans, in particular the second- and third-generation youth, who were mobilized in the late 1960s and 1970s by the civil rights and antiwar movements. He saw these young people as the hope for a new future. Although Vera Cruz died in 1994, his stature in the Filipino American community remains high. In September 2001, labor, student, and community activists in the San Francisco Bay Area founded the Philip Vera Cruz Justice Project, which was organized to address the problems faced by undocumented Filipino immigrants and low-wage immigrant workers.[17]

After Cesar Chavez, Dolores Huerta is the person most identified with the UFW. She is also perhaps America's best-known Latina. While most of the UFW leaders from the 1960s had left the union by 1981, Dolores Huerta stayed with the UFW beyond Chavez's death in 1993. She has remained a steadfast defender of the former UFW leader against any and all criticism. After leaving her day-to-day work with the UFW during the 1990s, Huerta embraced two main causes: immigrant rights and the empowerment of women. In 2002, she was awarded the Puffin Foundation/Nation Institute Award for Creative Citizenship, which included a $100,000 grant. She used the money to establish an organization that had been her longtime dream, the Dolores Huerta Foundation's Organizer Institute. Dedicated to developing indigenous leadership through community organizing, the Dolores Huerta Foundation (www.doloreshuerta

.org) is a nonprofit organization whose mission is to "build active communities working for fair and equal access to healthcare, housing, education, jobs, civic participation and economic resources for disadvantaged communities with an emphasis on women and youth."

After leaving the UFW, Huerta traveled the country speaking about a wide variety of social justice and human rights struggles. She traveled to the University of Miami to help workers in their union organizing drive in the spring of 2006 (see chapter 4), using her fame as a labor and human rights leader to pressure university president Donna Shalala to resolve the dispute. During 2006 and 2007, Huerta frequently spoke out on the need for immigration reform and did not mince words about her feelings. For example, in April 2006, the seventy-six-year-old Huerta gave a speech at Tucson High School in which she encouraged students to march in protest of the anti-immigrant Sensenbrenner bill and twice stated that "Republicans hate Latinos." Long an outspoken feminist who never denied the sexism she experienced in the UFW, Huerta believes that "women are always at the front of every movement, [but] when history gets written, the women always get left out." She told an interviewer in 2007: "I really do believe that unless women get into positions of power, we will never end wars, we will never have peace, we will never end violence. I think part of the changes that we need in our world is for women to take power."[18]

While Huerta believes that she and other UFW women did not get their just credit during the union's heyday, her contributions have made her one of America's most honored women and clearly the most prominent female labor activist. In 1993, Huerta was inducted into the National Women's Hall of Fame. That same year, she received the American Civil Liberties Union Roger N. Baldwin Medal of Liberty Award, the Eugene V. Debs Foundation Outstanding American Award, and the Ellis Island Medal of Freedom. In 1998, she was designated one of three Women of the Year by *Ms* magazine and appeared on the list of the "100 Most Important Women of the 20th Century" compiled by the *Ladies Home Journal*. In 1998, Huerta received the Eleanor Roosevelt Award for Human Rights from President Bill Clinton.[19]

Gilbert Padilla began working with Cesar Chavez and Fred Ross Sr. in the 1950s with the Community Services Organization. Chavez became a CSO director in 1959, and he hired Padilla as a full-time organizer the next year. Padilla was among the small group who joined Chavez in launching the farmworkers union in 1962. In 1965, he and Jim Drake organized against the state's plan to raise rents in a labor camp in Tulare County. The two held the first successful rent strike against the state camps, building support for the farmworkers movement among the migrant workers there. In 1970, Padilla and his wife, Esther, were sent to Washington, D.C., to run the local boycott; Gilbert also served as the UFW's D.C. lobbyist. (In this capacity, Padilla was able to press for the 1972 congressional investigation that helped Eliseo Medina defeat anti-farmworker legislation in Florida, as described in chapter 6.)

By 1977, Padilla was sufficiently disenchanted with his longtime friend Cesar Chavez that he talked of quitting the UFW. At that time, he agreed to stay on, but he and his wife left in 1980. Padilla then worked in a variety of jobs before being appointed president of the Fresno Civil Service Commission in 1988. On the commission, he fought on behalf of African American police officers who had been consistently passed over for promotions by the city's white police leadership. After five months of hearings that became so heated that they had to be held in the local convention center to accommodate the crowds, Padilla led a three to two vote upholding the finding of racial discrimination against the officers. A number of the African American officers were subsequently promoted, and one became Fresno's deputy chief.

Padilla has worked on a number of local, state, and national political races and headed the absentee ballot campaign for Cruz Bustamante's first run for the California state assembly. Bustamante later became the state's lieutenant governor, at the time the highest-ranking elected Latino. In 1991, Esther Padilla became the first Latino elected to the Fresno city council. Best known within the UFW for her remarkable success at organizing meals for the five thousand attendees at the UFW conventions in 1973 and 1975, Esther Padilla had previously served as the local president of the Mexican American Political Association and later became Fresno's vice mayor.[20]

Humberto Gomez joined his father and brother working in the fields in 1965, at age fifteen. He soon got involved with the central San Joaquin Valley farmworkers support committee, which included Juan Contreras, father of Miguel. (Gomez still jokes that he was organized by Miguel's father, and then he organized the future L.A. labor leader.) Fred Ross Sr. called Gomez the "man behind the curtain" because Gomez did not like to take credit for his accomplishments, an attribute that may explain why someone who has organized thousands of workers into unions over the past four decades is largely unknown to the general public. Gomez was always loyal to Cesar Chavez and stayed at the UFW until 1989, long after many of his close friends and longtime allies, including UFW co-founder Gilbert Padilla, had left.[21]

After leaving the UFW, Gomez became a national organizer and strategist for the Laborers Union. He helped organize meatpacking plants in North Carolina and other states and was the union's leading expert on Latino organizing. When Gomez first signed on, many viewed the Laborers as controlled by organized crime. When Gomez succeeded in organizing workers, he would hear people attribute the victory to "the mafia." Gomez recalled that he did not mind being called a mafioso any more than he minded being called a "pinko" in his early days of organizing for the UFW.[22]

In the 1990s, Gomez found himself among many old-guard white union leaders who opposed organizing Latino workers. Although he was aware of this racial dynamic, he helped create and then became president of a new Laborers Local 882 in Los Angeles, whose members were primarily Latino construction workers. With his wife, Maria, he also helped to establish Local 550 in California's Central Valley, whose members were Latino janitors, packers, and recycling workers. His wife was Local 550's elected business manager and secretary-treasurer.

In 1997, Gomez spearheaded a drive to organize two thousand immigrant asbestos workers in the Los Angeles area. The goal was to organize the entire industry, much in the way SEIU's building services division under UFW alum Stephen Lerner has approached the nation's janitorial industry. While the Laborers campaign was not entirely successful, several hundred workers were organized, and the union overcame longstanding barriers to representing undocumented immigrants in the industry. In 1999, Gomez was in the San Joaquin Valley for Local 550, organizing the area's largest packing plant. He eventually served as director of organizing for the Southern California District Council of Laborers. In considering the difference between organizing for the Laborers and the UFW, Gomez believes that the state Agricultural Labor Relation Act's guarantee that elections would be held within thirty days of filing gave the UFW a huge edge; he sees the current National Labor Relations Act as allowing "endless" election delays, making it much harder for unions to win.[23]

After his arrival at the Laborers, the union's membership became increasingly Latino, many Spanish speakers became heads of locals, and the union began to target industries with concentrations of Latino workers. Gomez concludes, "It has been great for me at the Laborers. We've gotten rid of the corruption, played a major role in organizing the massive immigrants rights marches in Los Angeles in 2006, and are very involved in the community." He feels "blessed" to have worked for people who "trusted me to organize," and his track record of success for over forty years has certainly repaid that trust.[24]

POLITICAL ACTIVISTS

When Sharon Delugach was a fourteen-year-old girl living in the Silverlake neighborhood of Los Angeles, she went to the nearby Sav-On drugstore to buy a highlighter for her sister. In front of the store was Manuel Hernandez, a striking Gallo worker who was asking customers to boycott Sav-On because it was selling non-union Gallo wine. Delugach's family did not eat grapes or lettuce as a result of the UFW boycotts, so she was somewhat familiar with the union. When Hernandez approached her, she agreed to volunteer for the cause. Feeling guilty about patronizing Sav-On but needing to bring her sister a highlighter, Delugach resolved the conflict by stealing it from the store. She soon became a dedicated UFW volunteer and a boycott picket captain at age fifteen. After working full time for the UFW during the summer after tenth grade and living in a boycott house with the primarily college-age volunteers, Delugach quit school before eleventh grade began. She later graduated from an alternative high school that gave her academic credit for working for the farmworkers movement.

Delugach could not be a UFW organizer at the time, because she was too young to drive. She spent her days promoting the boycott in supermarket parking lots in South and East Los Angeles. She moved to Oakland for the Prop 14 campaign in 1976 and got her driver's license at age sixteen so that she could become a UFW organizer. Delugach "expected to spend my whole life building the farmworkers movement," but, like many others, she left the UFW when the Game and other internal conflicts emerged in 1977.[25]

Delugach became engaged in several community and labor organizing campaigns, often in coordination with Paul Milne, who had been her Oakland UFW supervisor. From 1983 to 1990, she worked for Jobs for Peace, a campaign to redirect military spending to human needs. After working briefly for Ron Carey's successful campaign for the presidency of the Teamsters Union, Delugach became chief of staff for progressive Los Angeles city council member Jackie Goldberg. In this position, she assisted in drafting and organizing support for the city's living wage ordinance in 1997. She later joined Goldberg's state assembly staff, where she helped enact legislation protecting the labor rights of car wash workers, a group some now see as ripe for union organizing.

Delugach later became policy director for newly elected Los Angeles council member Martin Ludlow. Ludlow had been recruited into organizing by UFW alum Scott Washburn and mentored by Washburn, Ganz, and Govea. An African American who had strong support from the Latino community and the labor movement in Los Angeles, Ludlow had a bright political future until it was derailed by a campaign financing scandal that forced his resignation. Delugach then joined the transition team for newly elected mayor Antonio Villaraigosa in 2005 and managed commission appointments for the mayor through 2006. In 2007, she joined the UCLA Labor Center as policy director. She credits the UFW with "changing the course of her life."[26]

Delugach is among many UFW veterans whose involvement in organizing caused them either to skip college altogether or to drop out and not return. Stephen Lerner, whose writings have charted the direction for SEIU and much of the labor movement, never attended college. Paul Milne dropped out of the University of California at Santa Cruz after his first year and never went back. Marshall Ganz left Harvard to work for the civil rights movement in Mississippi in 1964 and did not return to get his degree until 1989; he ended up getting his PhD and teaching organizing at Harvard. When you consider that Chavez, Medina, Contreras, and nearly all of the farmworkers who became UFW strategists and organizers also never attended college, it brings to mind John Adler's claim that he "learned more from Fred Ross Sr. in two weeks than he did at Yale in four years."[27]

LeRoy Chatfield left the UFW for family reasons after coordinating the union's successful 1972 statewide campaign against Prop 22. As chapter 3 noted, Chatfield had previously organized the support activities for Cesar Chavez's 1968 fast. Chatfield's organizational skills brought him to the attention of California Democratic gubernatorial candidate Jerry Brown, who hired Chatfield as a campaign advisor and strategist for the 1974 election. After Brown became governor, he appointed the close Chavez ally to the newly created Agricultural Labor Relations Board. Chatfield soon found himself caught between his desire to protect the farmworkers' interests and the requirement that the ALRB operate by procedures that the UFW deemed too slow and cumbersome. As pressure increased at the ALRB, Chatfield was looking to resign. Meanwhile, one of Brown's new pet programs, the California Conservation Corps, was foundering under weak leadership. In 1977, Brown appointed

Chatfield as director of the CCC, a workforce development program that provided young people with life skills training and hard work in environmental conservation, fire protection, and emergency response.[28]

Chatfield quickly revitalized the program, creating sixteen training centers around the state and increasing the number of participants from sixty to sixteen hundred. The image of inner-city youth fighting fires and preserving the environment was enormously popular with the public; by 2007, more than a hundred thousand young people had participated. Chatfield stayed at the CCC until 1979, when Brown appointed him to the California State Personnel Board. Chatfield also served for a brief time on California's Alcohol and Beverage Control Board (his fourth confirmation for office, which makes him perhaps the only person who has had to be approved for confirmation four times by the California state senate).

In 1987, Chatfield founded Loaves & Fishes, a remarkable comprehensive center for the homeless outside Sacramento. Chatfield's insistence on feeding the hungry, providing services, and advocating for homeless persons continually brought the group into conflict with local officials. He turned to UFW alumni Jerry Cohen and Chris Hartmire for both legal and strategic help and repeatedly succeeded in keeping the center open.[29]

After retiring from Loaves & Fishes, Chatfield created the Farmworker Movement Documentation Project (www.farmworkermovement.org), a website that is the leading source of information about the UFW during its heyday and includes often extremely frank essays from a broad array of UFW volunteers and staff. Chatfield's volunteer effort in soliciting essays, fostering discussion, and making the site such a vital historical resource is a testament to the UFW's impact on the remainder of his career.

After Larry Frank graduated from college, he decided to take a year off before entering Princeton Seminary. He had heard about a nonprofit group in Colorado involved with the issue of nutrition, and he drove there to volunteer. When Frank arrived, the nonprofit was no longer functioning, but he came across a dispute by cannery workers in Brighton, Colorado. Some of the white workers at the cannery were represented by the Teamsters Union, but the Latino workers were unrepresented. Frank began talking with these unrepresented workers and learned that Cesar Chavez and UFW staff members had visited them three years earlier to show support for their cause. Frank wanted to talk to the local UFW staff about the cannery workers' problems, but the union's Denver office was closed, since the entire staff had gone to California to work on the 1976 Prop 14 campaign. The office was empty, but Frank saw a single poster on the wall urging people to join the UFW and work for $5 a week plus room and board. It gave an address and phone number for an office in Los Angeles, and Frank, inspired to make a difference after speaking with the Latino workers, began driving to the coast.

Frank reached the UFW's Los Angeles office, where Larry Tramutola interviewed him. Tramutola had become a successful organizer after rigorous training from Fred Ross Sr., and Frank also got a chance to learn directly from the master when he began to hold house meetings. Frank spent four months in house meetings, and, according to him, Ross "kicked his butt" every day. But, as others had done before him, Frank came out of the process a highly skilled organizer.[30]

Frank stayed with the UFW until Chavez pulled the plug on the boycott operation on Cinco de Mayo in 1978. Frank then worked for the Amalgamated Clothing and Textile Workers on the J. P. Stevens boycott in Los Angeles before joining the national staff of the Communication Workers of America. He spent eight years on grassroots electoral work in Los Angeles before attending UCLA law school and then spent eleven years practicing labor law and criminal defense work. Bringing his career full circle, Frank returned to the labor movement as the staff and project director of the UCLA Center for Labor Research and Education. After Antonio Villaraigosa's election as Los Angeles mayor in 2005, Frank was selected deputy mayor of neighborhoods. He believes that not only was his UFW experience "pivotal" in his labor career but that the UFW "changed the course of my life."[31]

UFW ATTORNEYS

It would take a separate book to adequately discuss the UFW legal team's landmark achievements during the 1960s and 1970s. These capsule summaries give a small flavor of the attorneys' post-UFW careers.

In 1982, Governor Jerry Brown nominated longtime UFW general counsel Jerry Cohen to a judgeship in the Sixth District California Court of Appeal, which was just being created. Although the court was to be based in San Jose, its jurisdiction included the Salinas vegetable fields. Cohen's nomination triggered major opposition from right-wing growers, who urged attorney general and governor-elect George Deukmejian to block the appointment. Typically, such a nomination would be approved by a three-member panel made up of the attorney general, the chief justice of the California Supreme Court, and the presiding judge of the relevant Court of Appeal. Since the Sixth District would not exist until Cohen and two other Brown appointees were confirmed, only Attorney General Deukmejian and California Supreme Court justice Rose Bird were allowed to vote in this case.

Deukmejian denied Cohen's appointment and rejected all three appointees, who were defeated by a one to one vote. The *Los Angeles Times* described the governor-elect's action as "reprehensible" and noted that "never before in its history had the Commission on Judicial Appointments refused confirmation of a governor's appointee to the Court of Appeal." The *Oakland Tribune* castigated Deukmejian's "disgraceful performance" and observed that "many of the people who finance Deukmejian's campaigns cannot get used to the idea that farmworkers should have the same right to organize as all other citizens." Cohen went on to provide strategic and legal advice to UFW veterans in a wide variety of campaigns, serving as special counsel and a close advisor to Fred Ross Jr.'s Neighbor to Neighbor organization.[32]

These former UFW attorneys have played important roles representing labor unions:

Tom Dalzell joined the UFW in 1969 as a volunteer and became an attorney by apprenticing under Cohen. Dalzell was for many years the in-house counsel for the huge International Brotherhood of Electrical Workers (IBEW) Local 1245, which represents utility workers from California's Central Valley to the Oregon border. In 2006, he became the union's business manager/financial secretary, its top staff position.

Barbara Macri-Ortiz also joined the UFW in 1969 and became an attorney after working with Cohen. After Cohen's departure, Macri-Ortiz helped expand the union's legal apprenticeship program. After leaving the UFW in 1990, she became a legal services attorney.

Sandy Nathan, who was Cohen's top assistant at the UFW, has spent his post-UFW career as a partner in the San Francisco Bay Area's preeminent labor firms, representing a wide variety of California unions, including the Amalgamated Transit Union, the IBEW, and UNITE HERE. For many years, one of Nathan's law partners was Bill Carder, who had negotiated many of the UFW's labor contracts during the union's heyday.

Ramon Romero became an attorney for the California Teachers Association.

Glenn Rothner and Ellen Greenstone became partners in one of

Southern California's most successful firms representing unions and workers in civil rights and employment cases. In addition to working for unions such as the Laborers International, SEIU, and UNITE HERE, the firm was extensively involved in the successful court challenge to California's notoriously anti-immigrant Prop 187.

Jim Rutkowski and Dan Boone are both partners in the firm of Weinberg, Roger & Rosenfeld. Based in the San Francisco Bay Area, it is the nation's largest union-side labor law firm.

Carol Schoenbrunn has worked in Connecticut representing the United Electrical Workers for more than twenty-five years.

Jeff Sweetland is a partner in a Milwaukee, Wisconsin, law firm representing such labor unions as UNITE HERE, AFSCME, and the American Federation of Teachers–Wisconsin.

Kirsten Zerger became general counsel for the powerful statewide California Teachers Association.

Other former UFW attorneys served the public interest:

Aggie Rose Chavez represents low-income clients in Oakland.

Richard Cook is a private attorney specializing in political asylum cases.

Ellen Eggers, who fulfilled her dream of joining the UFW legal staff only to arrive after nearly all the legal team had left and Cohen was on his way out, has spent more than two decades as a public defender in Sacramento.

Charles "Chuck" Farnsworth spent a lengthy career representing workers in employment discrimination cases.

Ruth Friedman became an administrative law judge with California's Agricultural Labor Relations Board.

David Grabill represents low-income clients in Santa Rosa, California.

Peter Haberfeld became the executive director of a number of teachers unions throughout the San Francisco Bay Area. He then worked as a community organizer with parents and teachers to design and operate dozens of new small schools in Oakland.

Linton Joaquin is the longtime executive director and staff attorney for the National Immigration Law Center in Los Angeles, which has played a vital role in providing technical and legal support to the nation's immigrant rights movement.

Ellen Lake, who preceded her UFW legal career by participating in Freedom Summer in Mississippi in 1964, went on to work for the ACLU and California's Agricultural Labor Relations Board as well as in private practice representing "the underdog."

Stephen Matchett represents California prisoners on death row and others seeking judicial appeals of their criminal convictions.

Mary Mocine was a labor attorney who eventually changed careers to become a Buddhist nun.

Bill Monning specializes in nonviolent conflict resolution. In June 2008 he won the Democratic nomination for a California state assembly seat representing Monterey and Santa Cruz Counties, and is heavily favored to win in November.

Barbara Rhine's law practice focuses on children's issues and police misconduct.

Mario Salgado was director of public affairs for the progressive Vanguard Foundation and in 2007 was named executive director of the Legal Aid Foundation of Los Angeles.

Alan Schlosser, the only UFW attorney who was based outside California (in Boston), has spent his career as an ACLU–Northern California staff attorney.

Chris Schneider remained in California's Central Valley to head a nonprofit law firm that provides free legal services to low-income residents. Among his clients were sheepherders, who formed themselves into a union.

Bob Thompson, who also apprenticed under Cohen, spent his career with the California Public Employment Relations Board, where Barry Winograd was also an attorney.

Danny Ybarra has worked with disadvantaged youth and represented teenagers facing court proceedings as a result of drug problems.

UFW PROGENY

Neighbor to Neighbor

In 1986, when Fred Ross Jr. considered how to build a national organization to stop U.S. military aid to right-wing forces in Central America, he began by calling all the best organizers he knew. This included such ex-UFW organizers as Bob Purcell, Angie Fa, Paul Milne, and Rob Everts.

He also got his father, Fred Ross Sr., involved; Ross Sr. had already been training Central American peace activists, and Neighbor to Neighbor was his last major organizing campaign. This group then recruited and trained a collection of organizers who successfully built political pressure on Congress and later helped lead the Folgers coffee boycott that helped end El Salvador's civil war, a story that is told in chapter 2.

Like the UFW, Neighbor to Neighbor treated organizing as a discipline. The skills these young activists learned, and the group's success, likely contributed to the high percentage of Neighbor to Neighbor organizers who are working for justice two decades after their experience with the group began. Some became union organizers: John Adler, Mary Ann Buckley, Donald Cohen, Angie Fa, Alexis Gonzales, Dana Hohn, Lauren Martens, Dennak Murphy, Bob Purcell, Fred Ross Jr., and Tracy Zeluff. Others focused on community organizing: Greg Akili, Denise Bergez, Marc Dohan, Mary Hussman, Paul Milne, Laura Mudd, Helen Schaub, Glen Schneider, and Robin Weingarten. Jeannie Appleman, Pat Blumenthal, and Father Ed Dunn have worked to improve society through religious advocacy groups. Others, such as Mari Brennan, John Heffernan, Shelley Moskowitz, and Ken Weine, have used their talents in policy or human rights advocacy. Nick Allen, Eli Lee, and Terry Surguine have been involved in running political campaigns or raising money for progressive issues and candidates.[33]

Neighbor to Neighbor provided a critical training ground for young activists of the mid- to late 1980s, becoming another incubator for those seeking full-time careers working for justice. Many of these activists likely made their lifelong commitment as an outgrowth of the skills training, leadership development, and movement experience that the organization provided. Neighbor to Neighbor proved to be a sturdy branch off the UFW tree trunk, demonstrating the importance of creating similar vehicles for winning the diverse struggles for justice in the twenty-first century.

OTHERS INFLUENCED

In addition to the UFW activists included in this chapter and in the accompanying table, thousands of others were influenced by the farmworkers movement, even though their time with the union may have been brief. One example is Los Angeles mayor Antonio Villaraigosa, who got his first activist experience at age fifteen, when he volunteered for the UFW grape boycott. Another outstanding example is Willie Velasquez, whose life was tragically cut short by cancer at age forty-four in 1988.

Velasquez was headed for a diplomatic career in Washington, D.C., but he was "transformed" into a committed community activist after being exposed to a farm labor strike and the UFW in Texas in 1967. He became the San Antonio coordinator of a UFW-backed strike and boycott and not only was "thrilled" to be on the farmworkers' staff but also "wore his five dollar a week strike salary as a badge of honor." Velasquez was inspired by Cesar Chavez to create the Southwest Voter Registration and Education Project, which has conducted more than a thousand Latino voter registration drives and won more than eighty-five lawsuits enforcing Latino voting rights. The Texas-based William C. Velasquez Institute has been analyzing Latino voting patterns since 1988.[34]

CONCLUSION

FOSTERING SOCIAL JUSTICE
IN THE TWENTY-FIRST CENTURY

As this book has demonstrated, veterans of the farmworkers movement have made major contributions to the struggle for social justice. The UFW offered idealistic young people a political home and gave them the training and experience that led them to transform both themselves and those they organized. Most UFW alumni who have spoken or written on the subject believe that the UFW experience transformed their lives. When Eliseo Medina was asked by the great oral historian Studs Terkel where his life might have gone without the UFW, Medina replied, "If I had been lucky, I might be a foreman at a ranch. Otherwise, I'd probably still be picking grapes." For Medina, Miguel Contreras, Chava Bustamante, and so many of the farmworkers who became professional organizers, Cesar Chavez and the UFW clearly redirected their lives. While UFW organizers who had not come from the fields had more life options, most were not simply "children of the 1960s" who would have worked for social change in the UFW's absence. Yet many foreswore the career paths they were expected to pursue and dedicated their lives to promoting social justice. Some, like Mark Sharwood, gave up careers in entirely unrelated fields (geology, in his case) to work full time for $5 a week for the UFW.[1]

How did the UFW became such an effective "incubator" of activist talent? When we try to answer this question, it's important to look back—and in the process to also look at the present and the future. What if the UFW activists described in this book had been born fifteen or twenty years later? What options would they have had for developing organizing skills, leadership ability, and strategic thinking?

In looking back, several factors stand out. First, both the UFW and its progeny Neighbor to Neighbor instilled in young people a lifetime commitment to fostering progressive change and an understanding that such change would require a long-term struggle. New volunteers went through a training and education process that provided them with the skills and confidence they needed to build a lasting movement. A time line in the UFW meeting hall in Delano in 1968 reflected the UFW's emphasis on instilling a long-term view: its end point was not winning the grape boycott, or even passing a farm labor law; rather, it ended with the establishment of a nationwide union of farmworkers. A movement that inculcates participants with such a long-range perspective from the very beginning is sending a message that the struggle for social justice is a lifetime commitment.

Paul Milne, who worked for the UFW and Neighbor to Neighbor and has spent decades advising social change organizations, notes a second reason why the two groups developed so many lifelong activists. He observes that "both groups made a conscious effort to create a social movement that relied on people taking leadership within a structure, but gave them the opportunity to find their own way to achieve the movement's goals." In other words, both the UFW and Neighbor to Neighbor promoted a "sink or swim" mentality that gave young activists a chance to succeed and allowed them to use their own creativity in doing so.[2]

Creating opportunities for young people to assume leadership prevented the burnout that is often associated with grassroots organizing. It also meant that UFW volunteers and staff could continually build their skills and achieve meaningful goals. Eliseo Medina's explanation that his success with the Florida legislature in 1972 came from "finding the right button to push" is an example of the "freedom within structure" that was available to organizers. By prioritizing such creativity, both the UFW and Neighbor to Neighbor showed a respect for activists that encouraged ongoing involvement in the movement.

Both groups also prioritized the training of activists who would be fully capable of creating and leading efforts on their own. Eliseo Medina, Jessica Govea, and Miguel Contreras were all ex-farmworkers who, after receiving training from Cesar Chavez, Fred Ross Sr., and Marshall Ganz, passed on their experience and knowledge to others. It developed like a chain, with the people who had been organized then being trained to organize others, who in turn would be trained as organizers themselves. This process creates the broad social networks that help build social movements and continually multiplies the number of highly skilled organizers.

A third reason the UFW was able to attract and nurture young organizing talent was its ability to provide specific, concrete solutions to a profound moral crisis. The union drew widespread interest because its supporters felt that it was a moral imperative to improve farmworkers' lives. But people do not spend years working more than a hundred hours a week for $5 plus room and board unless they believe their efforts are making a difference. UFW leaders understood this, which is why volunteers and staff were required to report back on the number of signatures collected, bumper stickers handed out, doors knocked—these statistics demonstrated progress and showed how everyone's contribution made a difference. Since the UFW had a practical roadmap to victory—winning union contracts—activists knew the steps necessary to achieve this goal and could evaluate the impact of their labors. The union's steady growth from the mid-1960s through the late 1970s kept them in the movement, as it proved that their long hours were paying off; in later years, when the union's progress began to steadily reverse, so did the influx of idealistic young people into the movement.

Fourth, the UFW became a successful incubator of young activists because it aggressively recruited people to join its cause. From 1968 to the late 1970s, it was common to see UFW volunteers in front of supermarkets or on busy street corners recruiting supporters. As illustrated by the example of Gary Guthman (chapter 1), aggressive recruitment and prompt follow-up could transform an inquisitive observer into a full-time UFW activist in a matter of days. The UFW demonstrated that young people are looking to enlist in a cause larger than themselves—but they must be encouraged to join and then given meaningful assignments that inspire them to deepen their commitment. The UFW promoted recruitment and facilitated sustained involvement; too few organizations prioritize either.

A fifth factor involves the UFW's attitude toward money. Investing heavily in the training of young activists can be time consuming and expensive. But Cesar Chavez organized the UFW around his belief that money should never be an obstacle to movement building. He relied on a volunteer structure that paid only minimal wages precisely to ensure that a lack of funds would not deter organizing. Had the UFW of the 1960s been required to pay $15,000 a year for organizers, the U.S. and Canadian grape boycotts would never have happened; there was no money to support the hundreds of permanent boycott staff who carried out the work. The UFW's reliance on volunteers rather than on a traditionally funded organizing staff enabled it to become an ever-expanding entry point for new recruits, and the union could afford to retain these recruits even after they had become highly skilled organizers.

While today's dramatically increased living costs have made building a movement of volunteers earning $5 or even $100 a week less realistic, the rise of Internet fundraising lends credence to Chavez's mantra that lack of money need not be an obstacle to movement building. When one considers the tens of millions of dollars raised via the Internet in 2003 by an obscure Vermont governor named Howard Dean, or four years later by Barack Obama, or over the past several years by MoveOn.org, it is clear that a similar operation could easily fund multiple UFW-style grassroots social movements. When Internet fundraising is added to the enormous sums donated "offline" to progressive political candidates, it becomes even clearer that investing in new generations of activist leaders is a question of political priorities, not money.

UNITE HERE's Hotel Workers Rising movement has shown that groups can implement a successful multicity boycott while paying organizers a decent wage. SEIU and other unions also have the resources to invest heavily in organizer recruitment and training and are doing so. While the social movements of the twenty-first century rely less heavily than the UFW on long-term volunteers, progressive organizations that are not deterred by money can indeed develop and train young people seeking careers in social change.

Finally, Cesar Chavez's role as a charismatic leader cannot be overestimated as a reason people were attracted to La Causa. Chavez had a powerful aura of moral authority that led people of all ages and backgrounds to volunteer for the movement. Even Fred Ross Jr., who had grown up around Chavez and could have been expected to see him as a "regular" guy, was drawn to the UFW so that he could work with the magnetic leader. But, as the UFW's history shows, charisma can help build a movement, but it does not sustain one. Charismatic leaders are used to getting their way and often resist democratically imposed limits on their authority. Organizational dissent is either directly suppressed or forestalled by a reluctance to challenge the leader's decisions. It is not surprising that movements that emerged after the UFW, including the antinuclear movement of the 1970s, the Central American peace campaigns of the 1980s and early 1990s, and the more recent antiglobalization movement, responded to the troubling power dynamics of '60s-era movements by promoting nonhierarchical and even consensus-based decision-making. Chavez's role as a charismatic leader helped bring an unprecedented array of young talent into the UFW, but future movements are unlikely to be built through this style of leadership.

TWENTY-FIRST-CENTURY INCUBATORS

Although no single organization has produced the number and quality of career organizers and movement leaders that emerged from the UFW, many organizations across the United States currently offer activists full-time careers working for social change. These groups are involved in grassroots electoral work; campaigns for social justice at the local, state, and national levels; opposition to the Iraq war; and efforts to build support for immigrant rights. Among the leading groups seeking to fill this incubator role in the twenty-first century are the Associated Community Organizations for Reform Now (ACORN), the Public Interest Research Groups (PIRGs), and organized labor. Like the UFW of the 1960s and 1970s, these entities instill activists with a "movement" mentality, provide extensive entry points for those seeking full-time organizing careers, and offer essential skills training and leadership development.

ACORN

Founded in 1970, ACORN is the nation's largest community organization of low- and moderate-income families, working together for social justice and stronger communities. The organization has more than 350,000 member families, with chapters in more than a hundred cities. ACORN's rapid growth in recent years required the organization to aggressively recruit and train talented activists, some of whom are getting started as social change leaders in their thirties and forties, to run the new offices. These activists are not given quite as much freedom as UFW volunteers had, but they have far more strategic control of their campaigns than is typical of most social change organizations.[3]

Like many of the UFW members, ACORN members are low-income working people, primarily racial minorities. ACORN has historically prioritized campaigns that directly address its members' needs: ballot measures that raise the local or state minimum wage, legislative efforts to promote affordable housing and improved schools, and grassroots battles against unscrupulous mortgage lenders. Recruitment of members, often through door-to-door canvassing, is a top priority at ACORN. Like the UFW in its heyday, ACORN is looking for active members, not simply donations.

A major difference between ACORN and the UFW of the 1960s and 1970s is that ACORN does not run an overarching national or state campaign with a single theme that unifies all members and organizers. With no unifying campaign, ACORN's work in building movements around immigrant rights, the right to a living wage, and Latino political empowerment has not received the national acclaim and spotlight it deserves.

Despite ACORN's accomplishments in improving the lives of millions, the organization is not part of the broader public consciousness in the way the UFW once was; it is not seen as a chief destination for young activists seeking to make a difference in the world.

The PIRGs

The state PIRGs were also founded in 1970. By 2007, they employed close to four hundred organizers, policy analysts, scientists, and attorneys and were active in forty-seven states and Washington, D.C. The PIRGs decided in 2007 to split off their environmental activism into a new organization, Environment America, with chapters in twenty-three states. This new organization now joins the student PIRG chapters on campuses across the country as training centers for future generations of environmental and social justice activists.

Like ACORN and the UFW, the PIRGs emphasize recruitment of both members and staff, instilling the value of leadership development and the long-term nature of the group's agenda. They also view talented new volunteers as potential long-term staff, which means grooming skilled college sophomores and juniors to join the PIRG staff after graduation. U.S. PIRG has a national staff that focuses on federal issues, while the student chapters focus on both state and national campaigns. The state PIRGs hold annual regional meetings to create a sense of common purpose among students on the various campuses.[4]

The PIRGs have successfully recruited and trained young activists despite a funding model that requires college administrators—and often external boards appointed by the state's governor—to approve students' decision to allocate fees for PIRG chapters. During the 1990s, corporate polluters successfully pushed Republican governors in Ohio, Colorado, and other states to prevent expansion of the PIRGS, which they perceived as "breeding grounds" for effective activism. This political interference meant that the PIRGs were less able to capitalize on increasing student concerns about global warming and other environmental issues. In addition, rising college tuition, and the corresponding increase in the percentage of students who must hold paying jobs during the school year, has made recruiting more challenging. But changing political dynamics, which began with the 2006 elections, have enabled the PIRGs to increase expansion efforts, creating new opportunities for channeling idealistic young activists into full-time careers in the environmental and other social justice movements.

The Labor Movement

As this book describes, unions are increasingly training the next generation to assume strategic leadership for the labor movement. Both unions and institutions such as the Center for Labor Research and Education, at the University of California at Los Angeles, provide training and mentorship for young people interested in labor organizing. The transformation of Latino activists such as Javier Gonzalez of Strengthening Our Lives (SOL) from SEIU line workers to highly skilled activists and movement builders mirrors the process that took place in the farmworkers movement in the 1960s and 1970s. Increased civic participation by union members is laying the groundwork for the next generations of labor leadership. The immigrant rights marches of 2006 reflected the presence of highly skilled young labor activists throughout the nation. Most of the names of these young leaders are unknown to the general public, just as few knew the names of those organizing on the ground to win boycott support, representational elections, and political campaigns for the UFW.

THE TIMES THEY ARE A-CHANGIN'

Clearly, the nation's political mood over the past three decades has made it more difficult for any single group to replicate the UFW's success as an incubator for activists. The UFW's historic recruitment of young activists occurred in an era when optimism about overcoming social injustice was pervasive. The young people who flocked to join La Causa grew up in a social milieu that has not existed in the United States since the early 1970s. Some came of age during the civil rights and antiwar movements of the 1960s, while others entered adulthood in the early 1970s, when the nation's environmental movement began to take off and the women's movement was growing exponentially. In 1972, a grassroots campaign made Democrat George McGovern the most progressive presidential nominee since Franklin Roosevelt, and perhaps the most left-oriented major party candidate ever. The 1972 Democratic Convention featured state delegation leaders announcing on prime-time television their combined support for McGovern and the UFW lettuce boycott, a political context that those who came of age since the 1980s have never experienced and perhaps cannot even imagine. Additionally, it was an era when young people felt they had the opportunity to make history, and many saw college as a distraction, believing that participating in social movements provided a more relevant educational experience. By the 1980s, however, it was rare for young people to bypass a university education for a life of full-time activism.

Today, the pendulum is swinging away from nearly three decades of cynicism and retrenchment, and support is growing for a new progressive agenda. Voter turnout for the 2008 Democratic Party primary elections shattered all previous records, reflecting a pent-up demand to set the nation on a new direction. This passionate interest in changing the country's course is not confined to a particular region, ethnicity, income bracket, or age group, but crosses all demographic lines. Young people's participation in election campaigns has risen to a level not seen since the 1960s and early 1970s, and there is a palpable hunger among this new generation for the opportunity to make a full-time commitment to improving our world. To the extent that the spirit of the age led an earlier generation seeking social justice to join the UFW, a similar moment is upon us—the question is whether this momentum for change will be effectively harnessed and mobilized.

The movements and campaigns discussed in this book have a proven track record of successfully mobilizing for progressive change and have advanced even in the face of an inhospitable political climate. For example, Latino immigrants are playing important roles in social justice struggles, despite the obstacles of language and citizenship status and even the risk of deportation. Consider how many more Latinos would participate in the nation's civic life following the enactment of federal immigration reform that included a just and feasible path to legalization. Similarly, organized labor has increased its grassroots activism and political clout in the past decade despite having to struggle against outdated labor laws that deter unionization. Passage of a proposed federal law allowing a majority of workers to choose a union by signing cards rather than through elections that are easily delayed or manipulated by employers would dramatically increase union membership, allowing more working families to be involved in shaping national policies.

The incredible grassroots activism surrounding the 2008 presidential election means that tens of thousands of campaign volunteers may well be seeking ways to continue working for social justice after the November election. This represents a tremendous pool of activists to be recruited into existing groups and creates opportunities for new mobilizing vehicles to emerge. One is hard-pressed to think of any progressive organization or movement that will not benefit from the rising tide of hope for a new future that is sweeping the United States. And, whereas the UFW of the 1960s and 1970s depended on flyers, campus appearances by Chavez, and personal contacts to attract volunteers, today's movements can recruit through e-mail, cell phones, Web 2.0, and websites, including social networking venues such as MySpace and FaceBook. These twenty-first-century recruiting techniques will make it easier to build new and stronger social movements pushing for social and economic justice.

When Cesar Chavez decided in 1968 to make "*sí se puede*" the rallying cry of the farmworkers movement, he could not have suspected that forty years later that chant, and the anglicized "yes we can," would become the theme of a major presidential campaign and reverberate across the nation's political landscape. The ongoing potency of the spirit of "*sí se puede*" is a tribute both to Chavez and to the vast majority of UFW alumni who have spent decades improving people's lives without seeking the limelight. These activists have measured their impact by the number of workers organized and campaigns won, not by the amount of press clippings they have accumulated or the number of times their names appear in a Google search. This book has tried to rectify this lack of public credit. It also reminds readers of the widespread and deeply felt influence of these UFW veterans, who have fought for social and economic justice for all these years. All who care about this struggle owe them thanks.

NOTES

INTRODUCTION

1. Jacques E. Levy, *Cesar Chavez: Autobiography of La Causa* (New York: W. W. Norton, 1975), pp. 40–72, 66, 75. Levy's work is the best primary source on Chavez and proved extremely helpful in the writing of this book.

2. Chavez's early organization, the National Farm Workers Association (NFWA) merged with the AFL-CIO–backed Agricultural Workers Organizing Committee (AWOC) and became the United Farm Workers Organizing Committee (UFWOC) in 1966. After formally affiliating with the AFL-CIO in 1972, the group became the United Farm Workers of America (UFW). Unless otherwise noted, the text identifies the farmworkers movement launched by Cesar Chavez as the UFW.

3. This widely accepted membership figure is cited in Dick Meister and Anne Loftis, *A Long Time Coming: The Struggle to Unionize America's Farm Workers* (New York: Macmillan, 1977), p. 190; Linda C. Majka and Theo J. Majka, *Farm Workers, Agribusiness, and the State* (Philadelphia: Temple University Press, 1982), p. 223; and Ronald Taylor, *Chavez and the Farm Workers* (Boston: Beacon, 1975), p. 13. UFW membership numbers often diverge because of difficulties in recordkeeping and the high percentage of migrant workers who paid membership dues only while actually working in the fields.

4. Susan Ferriss and Ricardo Sandoval, *The Fight in the Fields: Cesar Chavez and the Farmworkers Movement* (Orlando: Harcourt Brace, 1998), pp. 221–22.

5. UNITE HERE was formed in 2004 from the merger of the Union of Needletrades, Industrial, and Textile Employees (UNITE) and the Hotel and Restaurant Employees International Union (HERE). HERE was the union that included many UFW alumni, but to avoid confusion I have referred to the entity as UNITE HERE throughout the book.

1. CESAR CHAVEZ AND THE UFW

1. Chavez's youth and early family life are described in Jacques E. Levy, *Cesar Chavez: Autobiography of La Causa* (New York: W. W. Norton, 1975), pp. 73–77.

2. Ibid., pp. 78–79; F. Arturo Rosales, ed., *Testimonio: A Documentary History of the Mexican American Struggle for Civil Rights* (Houston: Arte Público Press, 2000), p. 276.

3. The Roosevelt administration official is quoted in Dick Meister and Anne Loftis, *A Long Time Coming: The Struggle to Unionize America's Farm Workers* (New York: Macmillan, 1977), p. 34; these authors also cite the U.S. Senate report (pp. 46–47). See also ibid., pp. 10–14; and Susan Ferriss and Ricardo Sandoval, *The Fight in the Fields: Cesar Chavez and the Farmworkers Movement* (Orlando: Harcourt Brace, 1998), p. 5.

4. Meister and Loftis, *A Long Time Coming*, pp. 82–83.

5. Levy, *Cesar Chavez*, p. 175; Ferriss and Sandoval, *The Fight in the Fields*, p. 74; Marshall Ganz, "David Conquered Goliath with Five Smooth Stones: So It Was with the Farm Workers," in *The New Rank and File*, ed. Staughton Lynd and Alice Lynd (Ithaca, N.Y.: Cornell University Press, 2000).

6. Levy, *Cesar Chavez*, pp. 160–61; Fred Ross Jr., e-mail to author, July 19, 2007; Richard J. Jensen and John C. Hammerback, eds., *The Words of César Chávez* (College Station: Texas A&M University Press, 2002), p. 179.

7. Phillip L. Martin, *Promises to Keep: Collective Bargaining in California Agriculture* (Ames: Iowa State University Press, 1996), p. 86; Levy, *Cesar Chavez*, p. 183; John Gregory Dunne, *Delano: The Story of the California Grape Strike* (New York: Farrar, Straus and Giroux, 1967), pp. 170–71.

8. Ganz, "David Conquered Goliath," p. 19; Levy, *Cesar Chavez*, pp. 201, 202.

9. Levy, *Cesar Chavez*, p. 292. On the origin of the term "boycott," see http://en.wikipedia.org/wiki/boycott.

10. Levy, *Cesar Chavez*, pp. 201, 202.

11. Ibid., p. 306; Marshall Ganz, "Why David Sometimes Wins," manuscript, p. 297. (Ganz's book *Why David Sometimes Wins: Strategy, Leadership, and the California Agricultural Movement*, based on this manuscript, is forthcoming from Oxford University Press.)

12. Ganz, "David Conquered Goliath," pp. 296, 303; Ferriss and Sandoval, *The Fight in the Fields*, pp. 114, 127.

13. Marshall Ganz, interview with author.

14. Eliseo Medina, interview with Marshall Ganz, cited in Ganz, "David Conquered Goliath," p. 303.

15. Ferriss and Sandoval, *The Fight in the Fields*, pp. 131–32.

16. Ibid.; Sam Kushner, *The Long Road to Delano* (New York: International Publishers, 1975), p. 190.

17. Eliseo Medina, Democratic Socialists of America 2001 Convention, keynote address, www.dsausa.org/convention2k1/eliseo.html; Levy, *Cesar Chavez*, pp. 268, 196.

18. Ganz, "David Conquered Goliath," pp. 307, 315, quoting Levy, *Cesar Chavez*, pp. 196–97.

19. "Gary Guthman 1976–1978," essay, Farmworker Movement Documentation Project, www.farmworkermovement.org/essays/essays/178%20Guthman_Gary.pdf.

20. "Lilli Sprintz 1969–1974," essay, Farmworker Movement Documentation Project, www.farmworkermovement.org/essays/essays/064%20Lilli%20Sprintz%20Essay.pdf.

21. Harriet Teller, interview with author, April 10, 2006.

22. Ganz is quoted in Kim Fellner, "In Search of the Movement," in *Union*

Voices: Labor's Response to Crisis, ed. Glenn Adler and Doris Suarez (Albany: State University of New York Press, 1993), p. 225. Fellner's analysis comes from personal experience in the labor movement and is unusually compelling.

23. Ibid.

24. Levy, *Cesar Chavez,* pp. 196–97.

25. Kushner, *The Long Road to Delano,* p. 215.

26. Fellner, "In Search of the Movement," p. 225; Robert H. Zieger, "George Meany: Labor's Organization Man," in *Labor Leaders in America,* ed. Melvyn Dubofsky and Warren Van Tine (Urbana: University of Illinois Press, 1987), pp. 343–44; Linda C. Majka and Theo J. Majka, *Farm Workers, Agribusiness, and the State* (Philadelphia: Temple University Press, 1982), pp. 227–29, citing an interview with the late Jim Drake, September 1, 1974.

27. Zieger, "George Meany," pp. 343–44; Drake quoted in Majka and Majka, *Farm Workers,* 227–29.

28. Fellner, "In Search of the Movement," p. 225; Susan Sachen, interview with author, June 16, 2006; Margaret Eleanor Rose, "Women in the United Farm Workers: A Study of Chicana and Mexicana Participation in a Labor Union, 1950–1980," PhD diss., University of California at Los Angeles, Department of History, 1988, p. 71.

29. Rose, "Women in the United Farm Workers," p. 83, quoting a letter from Huerta to "Vicious Boycotters," January 27, 1969, United Farm Workers Organizing Committee, New York Boycott.

30. Ferriss and Sandoval, *The Fight in the Fields,* pp. 149, 152; Rose, "Women in the United Farm Workers," pp. 216–18.

31. Ferriss and Sandoval, *The Fight in the Fields,* p. 152; Rosales, *Testimonio,* p. 296; Rose, "Women in the United Farm Workers," pp. 216–18.

32. Rose, "Women in the United Farm Workers," p. 222, quoting *El Malcriado,* August 1, 1970.

33. Ibid., pp. 226, 230.

34. "Maria Saludado Magana 1965–1980," essay, Farmworker Movement Documentation Project, www.farmworkermovement.org/essays/essays/019%20 Saludado_Maria%20Magana.pdf.

35. "Wendy Brooks 1963–1967," essay, Farmworker Movement Documentation Project, www.farmworkermovement.org/essays/essays/007%20Brooks_ Wendy.pdf.

36. "Hope Lopez Fierro 1966–1974," essay, Farmworker Movement Documentation Project, www.farmworkermovement.org/essays/essays/031%20Lopez_ Hope.pdf.

37. Rose, "Women in the United Farm Workers," p. 95, citing Huerta interview, *San Francisco Examiner and Chronicle,* February 6, 1983, and an interview with Mary Ethel Byers Lopez, May 1, 1984.

38. "Susan Samuels Drake 1962–1973," essay, Farmworker Movement Documentation Project, www.farmworkermovement.org/essays/essays/003%20 Drake_Susan.pdf.

39. Ibid.

40. Elaine Elinson, interview with author, December 12, 2006.

41. Rose, "Women in the United Farm Workers," p. 95, citing Huerta inter-

view, *San Francisco Examiner and Chronicle*, February 6, 1983. Rose's invaluable dissertation notes that in Washington, D.C., and other cities a "family model" of the boycott emerged. Although this model appeared to reinforce traditional gender roles, Rose observes that the UFW may also have "inadvertently laid the foundation for the emergence of a feminist consciousness among Mexicanas and Chicanas" (pp. 170–71, 191).

42. Susan Eaton, "Women in Trade Union Leadership: How More Women Can Become Leaders of Today's and Tomorrow's Unions," in Adler and Suarez, *Union Voices*, p. 176; Rose, "Women in the United Farm Workers," p. 165, citing "California Table Grape Industry: Study of Boycott Effect, 1968–69 Season, March 1970, New York City, Montreal, Philadelphia, Vancouver (Pam Smith), Cleveland (Dixie Lee Fisher)." While UFW conventions featured women delegates and focused on union issues, the AFL-CIO's annual events featured scantily clad showgirls as late as 1989 (Fellner, "In Search of the Movement," p. 221).

43. Craig J. Jenkins, *The Politics of Insurgency: The Farm Worker Movement and the Politics of the 1960s* (New York: Columbia University Press, 1985), p. 170.

44. Lens is quoted in Kim Moody, *An Injury to All: The Decline of American Unionism* (London: Verso, 1988), p. 60.

45. Ganz, "David Conquered Goliath," p. 304; "religious crusade" comment from Jerry B. Brown, "The United Farm Workers Grape Strike and Boycott, 1965–1970: An Evaluation of the Culture of Poverty Theory" (PhD dissertation, Cornell University, 1972), p. 168; Jenkins, *The Politics of Insurgency*, p. 155.

46. "Nancy Grimley Carleton 1975–1976," essay, Farmworker Movement Documentation Project, www.farmworkermovement.org/essays/essays/166%20Carleton_Nancy.pdf.

47. Ganz, "David Conquered Goliath," p. 18. Tramutola has related this story to the author on multiple occasions since 2003.

48. Ronald Taylor, *Chavez and the Farm Workers* (Boston: Beacon Press, 1975), pp. 230–33.

49. Marshall Ganz, e-mail to author, September 8, 2007.

50. Mark Sharwood, interview with author, June 25, 2006.

51. Industry trade publications are quoted in Peter Matthiessen, *Sal Si Puedes! Cesar Chavez and the New American Revolution* (New York: Random House, 1969), p. 41; Grant is quoted in Taylor, *Chavez and the Farm Workers*, pp. 234–35.

52. Rose, "Women in the United Farm Workers," p. 80; Majka and Majka, *Farm Workers*, p. 207; Levy, *Cesar Chavez*, p. 302.

53. Jenkins, *The Politics of Insurgency*, p. 170.

54. Tiffany Anne Dyer, "Pesticides and the United Farm Workers: An Extension of the Struggle for Social Justice," senior thesis, University of Puget Sound, Fall 2004, www2.ups.edu/faculty/dsackman/400papers/fall2004/dyer.htm; Jenkins, *The Politics of Insurgency*, p. 171, cites *U.S. News and World Report*; and Steinberg is quoted in Levy, *Cesar Chavez*, p. 296. See also Kushner, *The Long Road to Delano*, pp. 172–73.

55. Levy, *Cesar Chavez*, pp. 301–3, 309; Ganz, "David Conquered Goliath," p. 24; Martin, *Promises to Keep*, p. 88; Meister and Loftis, *A Long Time Coming*, pp. ix, x.

56. Giumarra is quoted in Meister and Loftis, *A Long Time Coming*, p. 190; Department of Agriculture statistics are cited in Martin, *Promises to Keep*, p. 88. See also Majka and Majka, *Farm Workers*, p. 223; Taylor, *Chavez and the Farm Workers*, p. 13.

57. Accounts by Matthiessen and Dunne, originally published in magazines, later appeared as books. See Matthiessen, *Sal Si Puedes!*; Dunne, *Delano*; Joan London and Henry Anderson, *So Shall Ye Reap: The Story of Cesar Chavez and the Farm Workers Movement* (New York: Crowell, 1970).

58. Meister and Loftis, *A Long Time Coming*, p. 190.

59. Fred Ross Jr., interview with author, July 25, 2006; Ferriss and Sandoval, *The Fight in the Fields*, p. 192.

60. Ross interview.

61. Ibid.; Ferriss and Sandoval, *The Fight in the Fields*, pp. 191–95.

62. Ferriss and Sandoval, *The Fight in the Fields*, pp. 191–95.

63. Bernstein is quoted in Majka and Majka, *Farm Workers*, pp. 263, 265; "Nick Jones 1966–1976," essay, Farmworker Movement Documentation Project, www.farmworkermovement.org/essays/essays/036%20Jones_Nick.pdf.

64. Levy, *Cesar Chavez*, p. 332.

2. THE UFW BOYCOTT TRANSFORMED

1. Craig J. Jenkins, *The Politics of Insurgency: The Farm Worker Movement and the Politics of the 1960s* (New York: Columbia University Press, 1985), p. 141.

2. Sarah Douglass, *Labor's New Voice: Unions and the Mass Media* (Norwood, N.J.: Ablex, 1986), p. 249.

3. Paul Milne, interview with author, May 21, 2007.

4. Susan Ferriss and Ricardo Sandoval, *The Fight in the Fields: Cesar Chavez and the Farmworkers Movement* (Orlando: Harcourt Brace, 1998), p. 267; W. K. Barger and Ernesto M. Reza, *The Farm Labor Movement in the Midwest: Social Change and Adaptation among Migrant Farmworkers* (Austin: University of Texas Press, 1994), p. 136.

5. Ferriss and Sandoval, *The Fight in the Fields*, pp. 265–67; Barger and Reza, *The Farm Labor Movement in the Midwest*, pp. 70, 80, 136, 148.

6. Mike Casey, interview with author, October 11, 2006.

7. Milne interview.

8. Kevin Danaher, e-mail to author, June 5, 2006. His writings include, for example, Kevin Danaher and Jason Mark, *Insurrection: Citizen Challenges to Corporate Power* (New York: Routledge, 2003).

9. Milne interview.

10. Fred Ross Jr., interview with author, July 25, 2006.

11. Ibid.

12. Miguel A. Salaverria, "Salvadoran Coffee Boycott Does Harm," letter to the editor, *New York Times*, January 14, 1990.

13. Fred Ross Jr., e-mail to author, July 19, 2007.

14. Ibid.

15. Ross interview; Anthony Ramirez, "Procter & Gamble Pulls Some TV Ads over Slur to Coffee," *New York Times*, May 12, 1990.

16. John Greenwald, "Bitter Cup of Protest," *Time*, May 28, 1990, www.time .com/time/magazine/article/0,9171,970198,00.html; Daniel F. Cuff, "P&G Heir Leads Effort for Salvadoran Boycott," *New York Times*, September 21, 1990.

17. Ross interview. Greenwald ("Bitter Cup of Protest") notes that the coffee boycott reduced El Salvador's export earnings by at least 30 percent.

18. Ross e-mail.

19. John Adler, interview with author, September 13, 2006.

20. San Francisco statistics from "Hotel Workers Rising Community Briefing" packet, February 2, 2006; based on data provided by the State of California. Nationally, in 2006, the average full-time hotel housekeeper earned $17,340 annually, whereas unionized hotel workers averaged approximately $26,000 (Harold Meyerson, "Taking on the Hotels," *Washington Post*, January 18, 2006, www.washingtonpost.com/wp-dyn/content/article/2006/01/17/AR2006011700936.html).

21. Dave Glaser, interview with author, October 25, 2006; Lisa Jaicks, interview with author, October 12, 2006.

22. Casey interview; Local 2 newsletter, "Two Victories," November 2002.

23. Casey interview.

24. Glaser interview.

25. Sam Pullen, e-mail to author, September 18, 2007. The PowerPoint presentation was e-mailed to the author and is not available to the public.

26. Glaser interview.

27. Pullen e-mail.

28. Ibid; boycott flyer prepared by Ben Mantle, UNITE HERE Local 8, Seattle.

29. See *Edward J. DeBartolo Corp. v. Florida Gulf Coast Building and Construction Trades Council*, 485 U.S. 568, 108 S. Ct. 1392, 99 L. Ed. 2d 645 (1988). Matt Ross contributed to my understanding of this case. As this book goes to press, cases are pending involving efforts to expand or contract the less than "bright" line between coercive (and therefore illegal) tactics and noncoercive (and therefore protected) speech urging secondary boycotts.

30. Pullen e-mail.

31. Glaser interview; Jaicks interview.

32. A copy of Lawson's letter was given to the author.

33. UNITE HERE flyers prepared by Jim McNeil.

34. Jim McNeil, interview with author, December 5, 2006.

35. Ibid.

36. Tom Witkowski, "Tactics at Condo Site Display More Aggressive Union Efforts," *Boston Business Journal*, September 30, 2005.

37. Ibid.; McNeil interview.

38. Rev. Teran Loeppke, interview with author, December 8, 2006; flyers prepared by Loeppke.

39. Ibid. During the struggle, the union maintained a website that posted complaints from guests who had the unfortunate experience of staying at the Congress; see www.congresshotelstrike.info.

40. Sam Pullen, interview with author, September 16, 2007; Mischa Gaus, "After Years of Struggle, California Hotel Workers Make Gains," www.labor notes.org/node/1784.

41. Alicia Ortiz, e-mail to author, September 14, 2007.
42. Glaser interview.
43. Ibid.; see www.inmex.org.
44. Glaser interview.
45. Ibid.
46. Ryan Ellis, "Unions Use Smear Tactics in 'Corporate Campaigns,'" HumanEvents.com, April 23, 2007, www.humanevents.com/article.php?id=20366.

3. BUILDING THE CLERGY-LABOR ALLIANCE

1. Richard J. Jensen and John C. Hammerback, eds., *The Words of César Chávez* (College Station: Texas A&M University Press, 2002), p. xix; Susan Ferriss and Ricardo Sandoval, *The Fight in the Fields: Cesar Chavez and the Farmworkers Movement* (Orlando: Harcourt Brace, 1998), p. 46.
2. Sydney D. Smith, *Grapes of Conflict,* with foreword by Cesar Chavez (Pasadena, Calif.: Hope Publishing, 1987), p. 39.
3. Ann McGregor, Cindy Wathen, and George Elfie Ballis, *Remembering Cesar: The Legacy of Cesar Chavez* (Clovis, Calif.: Quill Driver Books, 2000), p. 20.
4. Ibid.
5. Jensen and Hammerback, *The Words of César Chávez,* pp. 139, 140, 143; Francisco A. Rosales, *Chicano! The History of the Mexican American Civil Rights Movement* (Houston: Arte Público Press, 1997), p. 134.
6. Cesar Chavez, foreword to Smith, *Grapes of Conflict,* p. 1.
7. George G. Higgins with William Bole, *Organized Labor and the Church: Reflections of a "Labor Priest"* (New York: Paulist Press, 1993), pp. 63, 64.
8. Patrick J. Sullivan, *Blue Collar–Roman Collar–White Collar: U.S. Catholic Involvement in Labor-Management Controversies, 1960–1980* (Lanham, Md.: University Press of America, 1987), p. 39.
9. Ibid., pp. 42, 44, 45.
10. Ibid., pp. 46, 47.
11. Ibid., pp. 51, 52.
12. Ibid., p. 65.
13. Ibid., p. 66.
14. Ibid.
15. Ferriss and Sandoval, *The Fight in the Fields,* p. 120. The text of the Plan of Delano is available online; see, for example, http://chavez.cde.ca.gov/Model-Curriculum/Teachers/Lessons/Resources/Documents/plan_of_Delano.pdf.
16. Craig J. Jenkins, *The Politics of Insurgency: The Farm Worker Movement and the Politics of the 1960s* (New York: Columbia University Press, 1985), p. 154; Jacques E. Levy, *Cesar Chavez: Autobiography of La Causa* (New York: W. W. Norton, 1975), pp. 213–14.
17. Ronald Taylor, *Chavez and the Farm Workers* (Boston: Beacon Press, 1975), p. 180; Levy, *Cesar Chavez,* pp. 206–8.
18. Higgins, *Organized Labor and the Church,* p. 64.
19. Ibid., pp. 64, 72; Anthony Stevens-Arroyo, "From Barrios to Barricades: Religion and Religiosity in Latino Life," in *The Columbia History of Latinos in*

the United States since 1960, ed. David Gregory Gutiérrez (New York: Columbia University Press, 2004), p. 323; Levy, *Cesar Chavez,* pp. 282–83.

20. Higgins, *Organized Labor and the Church,* p. 72.

21. Dick Meister and Anne Loftis, *A Long Time Coming: The Struggle to Unionize America's Farm Workers* (New York: Macmillan, 1977), p. 152.

22. Levy, *Cesar Chavez,* p. 273.

23. Ibid., pp. 269, 273; Peter Matthiessen, *Sal Si Puedes: Cesar Chavez and the New American Revolution* (New York: Random House, 1969), pp. 186–87; Smith, *Grapes of Conflict,* p. 98.

24. Levy, *Cesar Chavez,* p. 277; LeRoy Chatfield, interview with author, August 22, 2006; Ferriss and Sandoval, *The Fight in the Fields,* p. 143.

25. Levy, *Cesar Chavez,* pp. 277, 279, 280.

26. Ferriss and Sandoval, *The Fight in the Fields,* p. 143; Meister and Loftis, *A Long Time Coming,* p. 153.

27. Matthiessen, *Sal Si Puedes,* pp. 186–87.

28. Chatfield interview; Matthiessen, *Sal Si Puedes,* pp. 183, 185.

29. Chatfield interview; Matthiessen, *Sal Si Puedes,* pp. 183, 185.

30. Chatfield interview; Matthiessen, *Sal Si Puedes,* pp. 183, 185.

31. Levy, *Cesar Chavez,* pp. 280–81.

32. Ibid., p. 281.

33. Ibid., p. 283.

34. Ibid., pp. 284, 285.

35. Meister and Loftis, *A Long Time Coming,* p. 153.

36. Levy, *Cesar Chavez,* p. 286.

37. Ibid., pp. 277–78.

38. Chavez provided this account of the origins of *"sí se puede!"* recounted in Levy, *Cesar Chavez,* p. 464. Scott Washburn, who was present when the slogan emerged, said that Chavez, not Huerta, had initially spoken the now famous words (interview with author, June 23, 2006). Washburn's account is consistent with that provided by longtime Chavez aide Marc Grossman in Ferriss and Sandoval, *The Fight in the Fields,* p. 197. Here, I rely on Chavez's own account of the event.

39. Ferriss and Sandoval, *The Fight in the Fields,* p. 246; see www.imahero .com/is/bios/cesarchavez.html.

40. Steven Greenhouse, "Going Hungry to Make a Point," *New York Times,* March 31, 2000.

41. Essay on Maria Elena Durazo, in Ruth Milkman and Kent Wong, *Voices from the Front Lines: Organizing Immigrant Workers in Los Angeles,* trans. Luis Escala Rabadán (Los Angeles: Center for Labor Research and Education, University of California, 2000), pp. 11–22.

42. Cynthia Cuza, "Victory at USC Is Victory for Student Activism," Change links.org, November 1999. See also Mike Davis, "Trojan Fortress," *L.A. Weekly,* December 1, 1995.

43. Cuza, "Victory at USC."

44. Chatfield interview; LeRoy Chatfield, "A Public Fast," www.leroychatfield .us/pdf_documents/A%20Public%20Fast.pdf.

45. Ibid.

4. YES WE CANE

The chapter epigraph is taken from the author's interview with Stephen Lerner, September 26, 2006.

1. For a discussion of BSEIU's history and the deunionization drive, see Ruth Milkman, *L.A. Story: Immigrant Workers and the Future of the U.S. Labor Movement* (New York: Russell Sage Foundation, 2006), pp. 62–33, 101–4.

2. Lerner interview.

3. Ibid.

4. Ibid.

5. Ibid.

6. Noah Bierman, "Union Boosters," *Miami Herald*, December 20, 2005; Forrest Norman, "Donna vs. Donna: The UM President Talks out of Both Sides of Her Mouth," *Miami New Times*, November 24, 2005, http://miaminewtimes.com/2005-11-24/news/donna-vs-donna.

7. Bierman, "Union Boosters"; Niala Boodhoo, "Janitors' Strike Is Over, but Union Efforts Continue," *Miami Herald*, May 7, 2006.

8. Alexandra Alter, "Coalition of Clergy Embraces UM Strikers," *Miami Herald*, April 25, 2006; Kim Bobo, interview with author, July 28, 2006.

9. Rev. C. J. Hawking, interview with author, October 4, 2006.

10. Bierman, "Union Boosters."

11. Eric Brakken, interview with author, October 10, 2006.

12. Father Frank Corbishley, interview with author, October 19, 2006.

13. Anjali Athavaley, "Janitors at University of Miami Protest Wages, No Health Benefits," *Miami Herald*, October 7, 2005; Jay Rooney, "Living Wages Campaign Faces New Obstacles," *Miami Hurricane*, October 11, 2005, http://media.www.thehurricaneonline.com/media/storage/paper479/news/2005/10/11/News/Living.Wages.Campaign.Faces.New.Obstacles-1015992.shtml.

14. Norman, "Donna vs. Donna."

15. Bierman, "Union Boosters"; Brakken interview.

16. Jacob Coker-Dukowitz, "Corporate Interest vs. Workers' Interest," letter to the editor, *Miami Herald*, January 8, 2006; Jay Rooney, "STAND Continues Fight for UNICCO: Administration's Role Questioned amid New Developments in Worker Dispute," *Miami Hurricane*, February 10, 2006, http://media.www.thehurricaneonline.com/media/storage/paper479/news/2006/02/10/News/Stand.Continues.Fight.For.Unicco-1607875.shtml.

17. Hawking interview.

18. Edward Lewine, "An Academic Retreat," *New York Times Magazine*, February 12, 2006.

19. Amy Argetsinger and Roxanne Roberts, "For Donna Shalala, Nice Digs, Lousy Timing," *Washington Post*, February 22, 2006; "Donna Shalala: Let Them Eat Mangoes," http://wonkette.com, February 17, 2006.

20. Niala Boodhoo and Noah Bierman, "UM to Review Worker Wages, Perks," *Miami Herald*, February 24, 2006.

21. Niala Boodhoo and Noah Bierman, "UM Janitors Vote to Strike," *Miami Herald*, February 27, 2006.

22. Michael Newall, "Backed by Church, Janitors Push for Union," *National Catholic Reporter*, May 19, 2006.

23. Lerner is quoted in Jessica Gresko, "UM Janitors' Strike Highlights Battle of Immigrants, Employers," Associated Press, HeraldToday.com, Bradenton, Fla., March 1, 2006. Zoila Garcia's situation is described in Ana Menendez, "While Shalala Lives in Luxury, Janitors Struggle," *Miami Herald*, March 1, 2006.

24. Menendez, "While Shalala Lives in Luxury, Janitors Struggle."

25. Rev. C. J. Hawking, "Report on Miami Janitors' Strike," May 2006, South Florida Interfaith Committee for Worker Justice; Hawking, interview with author.

26. Benjamin L. Weintraub, "Workers Protest at University of Miami," *Harvard Crimson* online edition, March 8, 2006, www.thecrimson.com/article.aspx?ref=511905.

27. Niala Boodhoo, "Strike at Airport Delayed," *Miami Herald*, March 10, 2006.

28. Niala Boodhoo, "UM to Raise Wages of Janitors, Groundskeepers by at Least 25 Percent," *Miami Herald*, March 16, 2006; *CBS 4 News*, Miami, March 16, 2006.

29. March 16, 2006, broadcasts by *CBS 4 News*, Miami; *Local 10 News*, ABC, Miami; *7 News*, WSVN-TV, Fox News, Miami.

30. "Cleaners across the Tri-State Area Stand Up in Solidarity against UNICCO," *SEIU 32BJ News*, March 15, 2006.

31. Niala Boodhoo, "Nova Enters Janitor Pay Controversy," *Miami Herald*, March 22, 2006.

32. Frank J. Corbishley, "UM Janitors," letter to the editor, *Miami Herald*, March 23, 2006; Corbishley interview.

33. Jennifer Kay, "Miami Students Hold Sit-in to Support Striking Janitors," Boston.com, March 29, 2006; Annie Fox, "Janitors, Students Force U of Miami to Talk," *People's Weekly World*, March 30, 2006; Hawking, "Report on Miami Janitors' Strike"; Jacob Coker-Dukowitz, interview with author, March 8, 2007.

34. Ana Menendez, "Striking UM Janitors Invisible No Longer," *Miami Herald*, March 29, 2006.

35. Hawking, "Report on Miami Janitors' Strike"; Yes, We Cane, SEIU press release, "Janitors at University of Miami Enter 6th Day of No Food," April 10, 2006.

36. Hawking, "Report on Miami Janitors' Strike"; Yes, We Cane, SEIU, April 10, 2006 press release.

37. Stephen Lerner, "Let's Get Moving! Organizing for the '90s," *Labor Research Review*, no. 18 (Fall 1991): 7. See, for example, Scott Van Voorhis, "Union: Skip Lunch to Aid Striking Janitors," *Boston Herald*, April 11, 2006; Benjamin L. Weintraub, "Janitors Ask for SLAM's Help," *Harvard Crimson* online edition, April 10, 2006, www.thecrimson.com/article.aspx?ref=512583.

38. Jay Rooney, "No End in Sight as Hunger Strike Continues," *Miami Hurricane*, April 14, 2006, http://media.www.thehurricaneonline.com/media/storage/paper479/news/2006/04/14/News/No.End.In.Sight.As.Hunger.Strike.Continues-1851658.shtml.

39. Ibid.; Charles Rabin, "UM Protests Strike Pressure Tactics," *Miami Herald*, April 13, 2006.

40. Josh Gerstein, "Ex-Aide to Clinton Is at the Center of Labor Dispute," *New York Sun,* April 14, 2006; William Glanz, "Shalala Pressed on Labor Dispute," *Washington Times,* April 14, 2006.

41. Sebastian del Marmol, "Student Hunger Striker Rushed to Hospital," *Coral Gables Gazette,* April 20–26, 2006.

42. Clara Vargas is quoted in an article by Yes We Cane: "Day 18: UM Hunger Strike Ends; Solidarity Fast Begun by Union, Students, Others," April 22, 2006, available through the Miami Independent Media Center, http://miami.indymedia.org/news/2006/04/4378.php.

43. Brakken interview.

44. Ihosvani Rodriguez, "Union, Strikers Swap Spots," *South Florida Sun Sentinel,* April 22, 2006; Sebastian del Marmol, "Student Hunger Striker Rushed to Hospital"; Yes We Cane, SEIU press release, "National SEIU Leaders Join Hunger Strike as Chorus Grows Calling on Shalala to Intervene," April 21, 2006; Lerner interview.

45. Rev. Wayne C. "Chris" Hartmire, interview with author, August 23, 2006.

46. Ibid.; Corbishley interview.

47. Tony Winton, "Edwards, Hoffa Join Fla. University Strike," Associated Press, *Washington Post,* April 25, 2006; Yes, We Cane, SEIU press release, "Farmworkers' Union Co-Founder Dolores Huerta Joining Fast in Support of Striking UNICCO Janitors," April 26, 2006; Glanz, "Shalala Pressed on Labor Dispute."

48. Stephen Lerner, "Three Steps to Reorganizing and Rebuilding the Labor Movement," *Labor Notes,* December 2002, http://labornotes.org/node/575; "Global Labor Leaders Ask University President Donna Shalala to Intervene," *Picketline: Social Justice and Democracy in Miami,* April 27, 2006, http://picketline.blogspot.com/2006/04/all-over-world-tonight.html.

49. Newall, "Backed by Church."

50. Hawking interview; Lerner interview.

51. Jessica Gresko, "UM Janitors Reach Agreement with Employer and Will End Strike," Associated Press, May 1, 2006; Niala Boodhoo, "UM Janitors End 2-month Strike," *Miami Herald,* May 2, 2006.

52. Medina is quoted in both Boodhoo, "UM Janitors End 2-month Strike," and Steven Greenhouse, "Walkout Ends at University of Miami as Janitors' Pact Is Reached," *New York Times,* May 2, 2006. The UM spokesperson is quoted in Gresko, "UM Janitors Reach Agreement." Hurd is quoted in Boodhoo, "UM Janitors End 2-month Strike."

53. Boodhoo, "Janitors' Strike Is Over."

54. Boodhoo, "UM Janitors End 2-month Strike"; Ana Menendez, "Janitors Head Back to Work at a Changed UM," *Miami Herald,* May 7, 2006.

55. Stern is quoted in Carl Lipscombe, "Victory at U. Miami," hrnetnews, May 2, 2006 (article in the author's possession); Mewelau Hall, interview with author, March 8, 2007; Rev. C. J. Hawking, *Interfaith Worker Justice Newsletter,* May 2006.

56. Coker-Dukowitz interview.

57. Niala Boodhoo, "Strength in Numbers," *Miami Herald,* June 16, 2006; Menendez, "Janitors Head Back to Work."

5. THE UFW BATTLES PESTICIDES

1. "Tribute to Jessica Govea," statement read by Jerry Cohen at the memorial service for Jessica Govea Thorbourne, April 9, 2005.

2. Rachel Carson, *Silent Spring* (New York: Houghton Mifflin, 1962), cited in Kirkpatrick Sale, *The Green Revolution: The American Environmental Movement, 1962–1992* (New York: Hill and Wang, 1993), pp. 3–5.

3. Statement of Elijah Boone, U.S. Senate Committee on Labor and Public Welfare, Subcommittee on Migratory Labor, *Migrant and Seasonal Farmworker Powerlessness,* June 9 and 10, 1969, 91st Cong., 1st and 2nd sess., pt. 1 (Washington, D.C.: U.S. Government Printing Office, 1970).

4. Robert Gordon, "Poisons in the Fields: The United Farm Workers, Pesticides, and Environmental Politics," *Pacific Historical Review* 68, no. 1 (February 1999): 56. Gordon cites folder 4, box 7, Office of the President, UFW Collection, Walter P. Reuther Library of Labor and Urban Affairs, Wayne State University, Detroit; and *El Malcriado,* January 15, 1969, p. 3. See also Laura Pulido, *Environmentalism and Economic Justice: Two Chicano Struggles in the Southwest* (Tucson: University of Arizona Press, 1996), p. 73.

5. Gordon, "Poisons in the Fields," p. 57, citing both Marion Moses, "Farmworkers and Pesticides," in *Confronting Environmental Racism: Voices from the Grassroots,* ed. Robert D. Bullard (Boston: South End Press, 1993), p. 14; and U.S. Congress, *Congressional Record,* August 1, 1969, p. 21892.

6. Whitten is quoted in Ruth Harmer, *Unfit for Human Consumption* (Englewood Cliffs, N.J.: Prentice-Hall, 1971), p. 6, citing the Conservation Foundation Letters, May 5, 1969. See also "Help Stymied for Poison Victims," *Los Angeles Times,* August 25, 1963, cited in ibid., p. 285, fn. 7.

7. Harmer, *Unfit for Human Consumption,* pp. 103, 104.

8. Ibid., pp. 107–10.

9. Ibid., p. 110.

10. Ibid., p. 253; "Boy Made Ill by Pesticide Wins Claim," *Los Angeles Times,* February 1, 1969. On the emergence of organophosphates, see Gordon, "Poisons in the Fields," p. 57.

11. Gordon, "Poisons in the Field," p. 58; Peter Matthiessen, *Sal Si Puedes: Cesar Chavez and the New American Revolution* (New York: Random House, 1969), p. 352.

12. Joan London and Henry Anderson, *So Shall Ye Reap: The Story of Cesar Chavez and the Farm Workers Movement* (New York: Thomas Y. Crowell, 1970), pp. 161–62; "UFWOC Demands Ban on Dangerous Pesticides," *El Malcriado,* July 15–31, 1969; Harmer, *Unfit for Human Consumption,* p. 255.

13. Statement of Jerry Cohen, General Counsel, United Farm Workers Organizing Committee, before the U.S. Senate Subcommittee on Migratory Labor, August 1, 1969, *Congressional Record,* p. 3034; Jerry Cohen, interview with author, March 21, 2007; Prepared Statement of Jerry Cohen, General Counsel, United Farm Workers Organizing Committee, Delano, Calif., *Congressional Record,* pp. 3009–26.

14. Thomas J. Foley, "Murphy Retracts Accusations against Union on Pesticides," *Los Angeles Times,* October 1, 1969.

15. Ibid.; Michael Green, "Witnesses Disprove Murphy," *Sacramento Bee,* September 30, 1969.

16. Green, "Witnesses Disprove Murphy."

17. Ibid.; Foley, "Murphy Retracts Accusations."

18. Green, "Witnesses Disprove Murphy."

19. Matthiessen, *Sal Si Puedes,* p. 352.

20. London and Anderson, *So Shall Ye Reap,* p. 162. For more information on organophosphates, see T. Christian Miller, "California Company a Place Old Pesticides Go to Find New Sales, Not Die," *Los Angeles Times,* reprinted in the *Seattle Times,* April 22, 2007; Tom Philpott, "Chemically Dependent: Decades after *Silent Spring,* Pesticides Remain a Menace—Especially to Farmworkers," *Grist,* October 18, 2006, www.grist.org/comments/food/2006/10/18/pesticides/index.html. In 1993, the National Academy of Sciences began a ten-year research project into the impact of organophosphates on children's neurological development. In 2006, the Environmental Protection Agency angered scientists by approving thirty-two organophosphates despite their known dangers.

21. Harmer, *Unfit for Human Consumption,* p. 110.

22. Tiffany Anne Dyer, "Pesticides and the United Farm Workers: An Extension of the Struggle for Social Justice," senior thesis, University of Puget Sound, Fall 2004, www2.ups.edu/faculty/dsackman/400papers/fall2004/dyer.htm. Dyer cites the following flyers: "It Doesn't Matter If You're Man or Mouse," November 25, 1969, distributed by the United Farm Workers of California at the San Francisco Moratorium march; "Pesticides and Grapes," 1969; "Warning: Eating Grapes May Be Hazardous to Your Health," October 9, 1969, distributed by the United Farm Workers Organizing Committee at the University of California at Berkeley (all three found in the Social Protest Collection, 1960–1982, BANC MSS 86/157c, Bancroft Library, University of California at Berkeley); and "A Peligro de Muerte!" 1969, Paul Schuster Taylor Papers, BANC MSS 84/38c, Bancroft Library, University of California at Berkeley.

23. Harmer, *Unfit for Human Consumption,* p. 255.

24. Moses, "Farmworkers and Pesticides," pp. 166, 172; Susan Ferriss and Ricardo Sandoval, *The Fight in the Fields: Cesar Chavez and the Farmworkers Movement* (Orlando: Harcourt Brace, 1998), p. 156. On the number of table grape workers covered by the 1970 contracts, see Philip L. Martin, *Promises to Keep: Collective Bargaining in California Agriculture* (Ames: Iowa State University Press, 1996), p. 88.

25. Gordon, "Poisons in the Fields," pp. 66, 64, citing *El Malcriado,* March 9, 1973, pp. 8–9; and Info/Research-Pesticides 1974 folder, box 11, UFW Collection, Walter P. Reuther Library of Labor and Urban Affairs.

26. Gordon, "Poisons in the Fields," p. 53, citing folder 15, box 178, Sierra Club Records, vol. 1, Sierra Club Collection, Bancroft Library, University of California at Berkeley. This article by Gordon is the best analysis of the relationship between the UFW and environmental groups.

27. Gordon, "Poisons in the Fields," pp. 67–69.

28. Robert Gordon, "Shell No! OCAW and the Labor-Environmental Alliance," *Environmental History* 3, no. 4 (October 1998): 460–87, www.findarticles.com/p/

articles/mi_qa3854/is_199810/ai_n8808857/pg_1; Gordon, "Poisons in the Fields," p. 68.

29. Les Leopold, *The Man Who Hated Work and Loved Labor: The Life and Times of Tony Mazzocchi* (White River Junction, Vt.: Chelsea Green, 2007), pp. 302–3; Gordon, "Poisons in the Fields," p. 72.

30. Gordon, "Poisons in the Fields," pp. 68–70.

31. Jerry Cohen, interview with author, April 20, 2007.

32. Ferriss and Sandoval, *The Fight in the Fields,* pp. 234, 237.

33. Ibid., pp. 235–38.

34. Ibid., p. 238; Cohen interview.

35. Ferriss and Sandoval, *The Fight in the Fields,* pp. 245–46.

36. Address to Nader environmental conference, October 27, 1991, cited in ibid., p. 250.

37. Leopold, *The Man Who Hated Work and Loved Labor,* pp. 308, 309.

38. Cohen, "Tribute to Jessica Govea"; Elaine Woo, "Jessica Govea Thorbourne," 58; "Organizer for UFW Sounded Alarm on Pesticides," *Los Angeles Times,* February 2, 2005.

39. "Cornell Helps New York's Chinese Home-Care Workers Lower Language Barrier to Union Leadership Training," press release, *Cornell News,* August 29, 2002.

6. THE UFW GRASSROOTS POLITICAL MODEL

The chapter epigraph, a comment from Eliseo Medina, is taken from Jacques E. Levy, *Cesar Chavez: Autobiography of La Causa* (New York: W. W. Norton, 1975), p. 462.

1. On Roybal's 1949 campaign, see Kenneth C. Burt, "Edward Roybal's Election to the LA City Council Marked the Birth of Latino Politics in California," Institute of Governmental Studies, University of California at Berkeley, *Public Affairs Report* 43, no. 1 (Spring 2002), http://igs.berkeley.edu/publications/par/spring2002/roybal.htm. This article was excerpted from Kenneth C. Burt, "The Power of a Mobilized Citizenry and Coalition Politics: The 1949 Election of Edward R. Roybal to the Los Angeles City Council," *Southern California Quarterly* 85, no. 4 (Winter 2003): 413–38.

2. Levy, *Cesar Chavez,* p. 218.

3. Susan Ferriss and Ricardo Sandoval, *The Fight in the Fields: Cesar Chavez and the Farmworkers Movement* (Orlando: Harcourt Brace, 1998), p. 122.

4. Levy, *Cesar Chavez,* p. 288.

5. Marshall Ganz, interview with author, February 28, 2007; Sam Kushner, *The Long Road to Delano* (New York: International Publishers, 1975), p. 167.

6. Schrade is quoted in Kushner, *Long Road to Delano,* pp. 167, 168. Kushner also cites the three journalists, who wrote a book about the campaign: Lewis Chester, Godfrey Hodgson, and Bruce Page, *An American Melodrama: The Presidential Campaign of 1968* (New York: Viking Press, 1969).

7. Levy, *Cesar Chavez,* p. 450.

8. Fred Ross Jr., e-mail to author, July 19, 2007.

9. Medina later estimated that the campaign had spent $500, all raised from

donations. See Levy, *Cesar Chavez*, pp. 454, 462; Linda C. Majka and Theo J. Majka, *Farm Workers, Agribusiness, and the State* (Philadelphia: Temple University Press, 1982), pp. 208–9.

10. Levy, *Cesar Chavez*, p. 455.

11. See Levy's discussion in ibid., pp. 458–62.

12. Ibid.

13. Ibid.

14. Ibid., p. 464.

15. Ibid., p. 468; Dick Meister and Anne Loftis, *A Long Time Coming: The Struggle to Unionize America's Farm Workers* (New York: Macmillan, 1977), p. 180. Levy reports that 168,000 signatures were gathered; Meister and Loftis place the figure at 175,000.

16. Meister and Loftis, *A Long Time Coming*, p. 180; Levy, *Cesar Chavez*, pp. 463–68.

17. Meister and Loftis, *A Long Time Coming*, p. 182.

18. "Ellen Eggers 1972–1987," essay, Farmworker Movement Documentation Project, www.farmworkermovement.org/essays/essays/128%20Eggers_Ellen .pdf. Eggers's essay is among the most insightful in this collection and is highly recommended.

19. Ibid.

20. Ibid.

21. Meister and Loftis, *A Long Time Coming*, p. 182.

22. Majka and Majka, *Farm Workers, Agribusiness, and the State*, pp. 210–11.

23. Ibid., p. 236; J. D. Lorenz, *Jerry Brown: The Man on the White Horse* (Boston: Houghton Mifflin, 1978), p. 75.

24. Lorenz, *Jerry Brown*, pp. 136–39; Sandy Nathan, interview with author, May 8, 2007. Other accounts erroneously have this sit-in occurring in Los Angeles.

25. Lorenz, *Jerry Brown*, pp. 75–78; Nathan interview.

26. Lorenz, *Jerry Brown*, pp. 136–39. I am aware that Lorenz felt betrayed by Brown and saw his book as a form of "payback." But the specific accounts cited above are consistent with other sources.

27. Ibid.

28. Ferriss and Sandoval, *The Fight in the Fields*, p. 208.

29. Larry Tramutola, interview with author, February 28, 2007; Mark Sharwood, interview with author, June 25, 2006.

30. Elaine Woo, "Harry Kubo, 84; Farm Leader Was Defender of Private Property Rights," *Los Angeles Times*, December 16, 2006.

31. Herbert B. Asher, Eric S. Heberlig, Randall B. Ripley, and Karen Snyder, *American Labor Unions in the Electoral Arena* (Lanham, Md.: Rowman & Littlefield, 2001), pp. 85, 86. The authors observe that from the 1950s through 1994, Democrats controlled the House of Representatives and many state legislatures across America, and unions did not believe that they had to aggressively mobilize for elections; they assumed that, by relying on campaign contributions and insider lobbying rather than grassroots activism, they could devote more of their resources to member services. Even the Democratic Party's failure to deliver for labor after winning control of the White House and Congress in 1977 did not move labor toward the UFW's grassroots electoral approach. Instead, as long-

time labor journalist Kim Moody has noted, organized labor doubled its campaign donations from 1978 to 1982 and increased its number of Washington lobbyists from 185 to 287 (Kim Moody, *An Injury to All: The Decline of American Unionism* [New York: W. W. Norton, 1988], p. 148). It was not until UFW alumni assumed important roles in mainstream labor organizations that the AFL-CIO began adopting the grassroots activist electoral strategy that Cesar Chavez and the UFW had pioneered decades earlier.

32. Fred Ross Jr., interview with author, July 25, 2006.

33. Ganz interview; Ross interview; Tramutola interview; Scott Washburn, interview with author, June 23, 2006.

34. Ganz interview.

35. Ibid.

36. Harold Meyerson, "Indentured Public Servant," *American Prospect* 12, no. 3 (February 12, 2001), www.prospect.org/cs/articles?article=indentured_public_servant; Ganz interview.

37. Ganz interview; Washburn interview; Meyerson, "Indentured Public Servant."

38. Mark Barabak, "Times Profile: Nancy Pelosi," January 26, 2003, www.latimes.com/news/politics/la-me-pelosi012603,1.2568548.story; John Burton, interview with author, March 9, 2007.

39. Ross interview.

40. Barabak, "Times Profile: Nancy Pelosi." The campaign fostered a close relationship between Pelosi and Ross, which led the UFW alum to join her staff in the late 1990s.

41. Richie Ross used his UFW background to become a leading political consultant in California, usually working for the more conservative candidate in Democratic primaries. Many UFW alumni blamed him for his role in convincing Cesar Chavez that the UFW could run a consumer boycott by relying on direct-mail appeals rather than on the union's traditional grassroots boycott model. Ross's big-money approach to elections and the moneyed interests he often represents have made him widely unpopular among the many UFW veterans with whom I spoke about him.

42. I worked on the Art Agnos for Mayor campaign in 1987 from its earliest days, and these facts come from my experience.

7. THE LABOR-LATINO ALLIANCE

1. Aurelio Rojas, "From Farm Laborer to Potentate in Capitol," *Sacramento Bee,* May 19, 2002, http://latinovoterguide.org/spotlight.html.

2. Marshall Ganz, interview with author, February 28, 2007.

3. Ibid.; Larry Tramutola, interview with author, June 25, 2006.

4. Ganz interview.

5. Ibid.; Rojas, "From Farm Laborer to Potentate in Capitol."

6. Ganz interview. For the study on the next generation of labor leaders, see Marshall Ganz, Kim Voss, and George Strauss, "Why Lead Labor? Project and Pathways in California Unions, 1984–2001," Institute for Research on Labor and Employment, Working Paper Series, Paper iirwps–093–03, University of

California at Berkeley, June 19, 2003, http://repositories.cdlib.org/iir/iirwps/iir-wps-093-03.

7. Ganz interview; Ruth Milkman and Kent Wong, *Voices from the Front Lines: Organizing Immigrant Workers in Los Angeles,* trans. Luis Escala Rabadán (Los Angeles: Center for Labor Research and Education, University of California, 2000), pp. 17–21.

8. Harold Meyerson, "The Architect: Miguel Contreras, 1952–2005," Power lines, *LA Weekly,* May 12, 2005, www.laweekly.com/news/powerlines/the-architect/8547/; Kent Wong, interview with author, November 17, 2006. Meyerson's columns on Contreras and the Los Angeles labor scene were invaluable in preparing this book. Meyerson's analysis is consistent with that of Larry Frank, Ruth Milkman, Kent Wong, and other insightful scholars from the UCLA Center for Labor Research and Education. Many of the citations that accompany this chapter reflect conclusions, analysis, and factual findings from the writings of all four authors as well as those of labor activist and author Peter Dreier.

9. Meyerson, "The Architect."

10. Larry Frank and Kent Wong, "Intense Political Mobilization: The Los Angeles County Federation of Labor," *Working USA: The Journal of Labor and Society* 8, no. 2 (2004): 155–81; Kent Wong, interview with author, February 13, 2008. The Frank and Wong article is an essential resource on Contreras's leadership in transforming the Los Angeles labor movement. All page numbers are from the online version of the article, available at www.community-wealth.org/_pdfs/articles-publications/state-local-new/paper-frank1.pdf.

11. Frank and Wong, "Intense Political Mobilization," p. 5; Ruth Milkman and Kent Wong, "L.A. Confidential: An Interview with Miguel Contreras," *New Labor Forum* 10 (Spring/Summer 2002): 52, 61. In "L.A. Confidential," Contreras specifically notes his goal of taking the seats necessary to restore Democratic control of the assembly (p. 61).

12. Meyerson, "The Architect."

13. Peter Dreier and Kelly Candaele, "Labor Warrior," *AlterNet,* May 13, 2005, www.alternet.org/story/21989.

14. Frank and Wong, "Intense Political Mobilization."

15. Ibid., p. 7.

16. Ruth Milkman, *L.A. Story: Immigrant Workers and the Future of the U.S. Labor Movement* (New York: Russell Sage Foundation, 2006), p. 129.

17. Harold Meyerson, "A Clean Sweep," *American Prospect* 11, no. 15 (June 19–July 3, 2000), www.prospect.org/cs/articles?article=a_clean_sweep, quoting Garcia; Meyerson, "The Architect."

18. Frank and Wong, "Intense Political Mobilization"; Meyerson, "The Architect."

19. Frank and Wong, "Intense Political Mobilization."

20. Milkman and Wong, "L.A. Confidential," pp. 59–60.

21. Ben Monterroso, interview with author, February 14, 2007.

22. Frank and Wong, "Intense Political Mobilization," p. 9.

23. Ibid., p. 8.

24. Ibid.

25. Milkman and Wong, "L.A. Confidential," p. 60.

26. Dreier and Candaele, "Labor Warrior"; Meyerson, "The Architect."
27. Meyerson, "The Architect."
28. Ibid.
29. Ibid.
30. Javier Gonzalez, interview with author, December 19, 2006.
31. Ibid.
32. Ibid.
33. Blanca Perez, interview with author, December 20, 2006; Gonzalez interview.
34. Perez interview; Gonzalez interview.
35. Gonzalez interview; Mark Gomez, interview with author, April 17, 2007. SOL election statistics are available online at http://sol-california.com/facts.html.
36. Gonzalez interview; Gomez interview.
37. Gonzalez interview.
38. Chava Bustamante, interview with author, June 22, 2006.
39. Ibid.; Gomez interview.
40. Adrian Pantoja, Ricardo Ramírez, and Gary Segura, "Citizens by Choice, Voters by Necessity: Patterns in Political Mobilization by Naturalized Latinos," *Political Research Quarterly* 54, no. 4 (2001): 729–70. These researchers found that California's Latino turnout increased far more among those who became citizens between 1992 and 1996 than it did among similarly situated newly naturalized Latinos in Florida and Texas, states that lacked such threatening initiatives. Pantoja, a leading scholar on Latino voting, told me in an April 9, 2006, e-mail that he believes labor unions are playing a critical role in boosting Latino turnout but that he is unaware of any research that has focused on the impact of unions' voter outreach efforts. There have been studies on the role of voter mobilization efforts by Latino organizations in increasing turnout, but neither of the two groups involved in such efforts—the National Association of Latino Elected and Appointed Officials (NALEO) and the Southwest Voter Registration Education Project (SVREP)—has anything near the resources or electoral operation of California's labor movement. A study by Stephen Nuño ("Latino Mobilization and Vote Choice in the 2000 Presidential Election," *American Politics Research* 35, no. 2 [2007]: 273–93) found that Latinos are best persuaded to vote by fellow Latinos, which is organized labor's approach.
41. Luis Ricardo Fraga, Ricardo Ramírez, and Gary M. Segura, "Unquestioned Influence: Latinos and the 2000 Elections in California," in *Muted Voices: Latinos and the 2000 Elections,* ed. Rodolfo de la Garza and Louis DeSipio (Lanham, Md.: Rowman & Littlefield, 2005), p. 175; Joe Mathews, "Voting Like It's Manana," *Los Angeles Times,* February 24, 2008. Statistics from the New Democratic Network show Latino voters as 29 percent of the total voter turnout in California's 2008 presidential primary; see http://ndn.org/hispanic/2008-latino-turnout-statistics-1–1.jpg.
42. Mike Madden, "Groups Push to Register 1 Mil Voters," *Arizona Republic,* May 11, 2006.
43. Henry Flores, interview with author, May 10, 2006.
44. Fraga, Ramírez, and Segura, "Unquestioned Influence," p. 181.
45. William C. Velasquez Institute, "California Latino Voter Statistics," citing

U.S. Census Bureau, *Current Population Reports: Voting and Registration in the Election of November 1992–2002*, www.wcvi.org/latino_voter_research/latino_voter_statistics/ca_lv.html; Matt Barreto, "Latino Immigrants at the Polls: Foreign-born Voter Turnout in the 2002 Election," *Political Research Quarterly* 58, no. 1 (March 2005): 79–86.

46. Fraga, Ramírez, and Segura, "Unquestioned Influence," p. 192.

47. Velasquez Institute, "California Latino Voter Statistics."

48. Ricardo Ramírez, "Giving Voice to Latino Voters: A Field Experiment on the Effectiveness of a National Nonpartisan Mobilization Effort," *Annals of the American Academy of Political and Social Science* 601, no. 1 (2005): 80.

49. Pantoja, Ramírez, and Segura, "Citizens by Choice, Voters by Necessity." For two valuable analyses of California's Latino voting increase in 1996, see Meyerson, "The Architect"; and Matt Barreto, Ricardo Ramírez, and Nathan Woods, "Are Naturalized Voters Driving the California Latino Electorate? Measuring the Effect of IRCA Citizens on Latino Voting," *Social Science Quarterly* 86, no. 4 (December 2005): 792–811.

50. S. Karthick Ramakrishnan, *Democracy in Immigrant America: Changing Demographics and Political Participation* (Stanford, Calif.: Stanford University Press, 2005), p. 123.

51. William C. Velasquez Institute, "2006 WCVI Turnout Results," http://wcvi.org/latino_voter_research/polls/national/2006/2006turnout.htm. WCVI's turnout data based on 2002 and 2006 WCVI exit polls, California Secretary of State election results, and an analysis of 2006 national exit polls from CNN, AP, and the *Los Angeles Times*.

52. Ibid. WCVI exit polls had Florida declining by only 9.1 percent.

53. "*Texas Monthly*'s Paul Burka on Tejano Politics," Tejano Insider, December 15, 2006, http://tejanoinsider.blogspot.com/2006_12_01_archive.html, citing a writer for the South Texas Chisme blog on the number of block walkers and quoting Aaron Peña.

54. Paul Hogarth, "Latino Voters Bring Victory to Texas Democrats," BeyondChron, December 14, 2006, www.beyondchron.org/news/index.php?itemid=4016; also see Markos Moulitsas Zúniga, "TX-23: Post-mortem," Daily Kos, December 13, 2006, www.dailykos.com/storyonly/2006/12/13/12224/230, citing The Hotline On Call, http://hotlineblog.nationaljournal.com/archives/2006/12/tx_23_dems_pull.html.

55. Charles S. Bullock III and Ronald Keith Gaddie, "An Assessment of Voting Rights Progress in Arizona," prepared for the Project on Fair Representation, American Enterprise Institute, www.aei.org/view.asp?docRecNo=7301&docType=0, tables 1 and 2, citing U.S. Census Bureau data. On Latino support for Prop 200, see CNN, "Ballot Measures/Arizona Proposition 200/Exit Poll," www.cnn.com/ELECTION/2004/pages/results/states/AZ/I/01/epolls.0.html.

56. Scott Washburn, interview with author, February 22, 2007; Martin Manteca, interview with author, February 20, 2007.

57. Washburn interview; Manteca interview; Arizona turnout data from Jose Quinonez, BlueLatinos.org.

58. Lauren Martens, interview with author, January 17, 2007.

59. Peter W. Wielhouwer, "Political Parties and Participation Inequality in

2004," paper presented at the 2005 State of the Parties conference, Bliss Institute of Applied Politics, University of Akron, October 5–7, 2005, p. 23; see www.uakron.edu/bliss/docs/wielhouwer.pdf.

8. BUILDING THE IMMIGRANT RIGHTS MOVEMENT

1. Jacques E. Levy, *Cesar Chavez: Autobiography of La Causa* (New York: W. W. Norton, 1975), p. 118.

2. Dick Meister and Anne Loftis, *A Long Time Coming: The Struggle to Unionize America's Farm Workers* (New York: Macmillan, 1977), pp. 75–76; Levy, *Cesar Chavez*, pp. 129, 130.

3. Levy, *Cesar Chavez,* pp. 143, 144.

4. Richard Griswold del Castillo and Richard Garcia, *César Chávez: A Triumph of Spirit* (Norman: University of Oklahoma Press, 1995), pp. 159, 160.

5. Ibid., p. 162.

6. Ibid., pp. 159, 160, 167, 168.

7. Ibid., p. 162.

8. Ibid.

9. Ibid., pp. 167, 170.

10. Ibid., p. 168; Steven Lerner, interview with author, September 26, 2006.

11. Griswold del Castillo and Garcia, *César Chávez,* pp. 168–69.

12. Luz Villarreal, "Group Seeks to Join INS Outreach Effort," *Los Angeles Daily News,* June 30, 1995.

13. Douglas S. Massey, Jorge Durand, and Nolan J. Malone, *Beyond Smoke and Mirrors: Mexican Immigration in an Era of Economic Integration* (New York: Russell Sage Foundation, 2002), p. 90; Villarreal, "Group Seeks to Join INS Outreach Effort"; Matt Barreto, Ricardo Ramírez, and Nathan Woods, "Are Naturalized Voters Driving the California Latino Electorate? Measuring the Effect of IRCA Citizens on Latino Voting," *Social Science Quarterly* 86, no. 4 (December 2005): 797, 798.

14. Villarreal, "Group Seeks to Join INS Outreach Effort."

15. Ron Kaye, interview with author, January 22, 2007. The other IAF groups were the United Neighborhoods Organization, the Southern California Organizing Committee, and the East Valleys Organization.

16. Cecilia Barragan, interview with author, January 21, 2007.

17. Ibid.; Consuelo Valdez, interview with author, January 22, 2007; Villarreal, "Group Seeks to Join INS Outreach Effort."

18. See David Schippers, "Gore Pressured INS to Win in '96," www.american-patrol.com/INDUSTRIAL-AREAS-FOUNDATION/SchippersGoreCitUSA000 828.html. This article is excerpted from Schippers's book *Sellout: The Inside Story of President Clinton's Impeachment* (Washington, D.C.: Regnery, 2000). See also Thomas McArdle, "Al Gore's Voter Mill," *National Review,* March 24, 1997.

19. Ibid.; Father Vega is quoted in Dick Kirschten, "The Politics of Citizenship," GovernmentExecutive.com, January 1, 1997, http://govexec.com/features/0197s4.htm.

20. Schippers, "Gore Pressured INS"; Schippers's article links to the full

memo, which is available at www.americanpatrol.com/INDUSTRIAL-AREAS-FOUNDATION/IAFMemo0001105Show.html.

21. Fred Ross Jr., interview with author, July 25, 2006; Kirschten, "The Politics of Citizenship."

22. Luz Villarreal, "Activists Stage Protest," *Los Angeles Daily News,* February 28, 1996.

23. Rick Orlov, "INS Sets Goal for Processing Applications," *Los Angeles Daily News,* May 2, 1996; Schippers, "Gore Pressured INS," p. 3.

24. Orlov, "INS Sets Goal."

25. Luz Villareal, "Activist Groups Plan Convention to Get Out Vote," *Los Angeles Daily News,* July 13, 1996.

26. Eliseo Medina, interview with author, February 13, 2007; Barragan interview.

27. Luz Villarreal, "Volunteers Hit Streets to Register New Voters," *Los Angeles Daily News,* October 6, 1996.

28. Dennis Love, "Latinos Look to Build on Record Vote," *Los Angeles Daily News,* November 11, 1996; Yvette Cabrera, "60,800 Naturalized in L.A. in One Month," *Los Angeles Daily News,* August 19, 1996; Luz Villarreal, "Registering Their Power," *Los Angeles Daily News,* November 17, 1996.

29. Love, "Latinos Look to Build on Record Vote."

30. Kaye interview; Valdez interview; Barragan interview.

31. Kirschten, "The Politics of Citizenship."

32. Ibid.

33. Gore's responses to the Office of the Inspector General's questions are available online at www.usdoj.gov/oig/special/0007/dappendix.htm.

34. Schippers, "Gore Pressured INS"; Schippers, *Sellout.*

35. Ross interview.

36. Ibid.

37. Vernon M. Briggs Jr., "Immigration Policy and American Unionism: A Reality Check," *Briggs Papers and Speeches,* Vernon M. Briggs Jr. Collection, Kheel Center for Labor-Management Documentation and Archives, School of Industrial Relations, Cornell University, 2004, vol. 4, p. 16. This paper is available for downloading at http://digitalcommons.ilr.cornell.edu/briggsIV/13.

38. Ibid., pp. 17, 18.

39. Ibid., p. 19.

40. Eliseo Medina, "On Hope and Activism," in Studs Terkel, *Hope Dies Last: Keeping the Faith in Difficult Times* (New York: New Press, 2003), www.commondreams.org/scriptfiles/views03/1111-09.htm.

41. Medina interview; Marshall Ganz, interview with author, February 28, 2007.

42. Medina interview; Ganz interview.

43. Medina interview.

44. Ben Monterroso, interview with author, February 14, 2007.

45. Medina interview.

46. Ibid.

47. James Parks, "Recognizing Our Common Bonds," www.aflcio.org/aboutus/thisistheaflcio/publications/magazine/commonbonds.cfm.

48. On the AFL-CIO's new policy, see "A Nation of Immigrants," 2001 AFL-CIO Convention Resolution, www.aflcio.org/aboutus/thisistheaflcio/convention/resolutions_ecstatements.cfm#immigration. The text of the 2000 resolution is not available online.

49. Medina interview.

50. Ibid. Contreras is quoted in Lloyd Billingsley, "Union Card for Green Card: The Radical Vanguard in the Los Angeles Labor Movement," August 2000, www.americanpatrol.com/RECONQUISTA/NUNEZ-FABIAN/UnionCdGreen Cd000800Nunez.html. Billingsley is militantly anti-immigrant, and his article reflects this.

51. Mario Garcia, *Memories of Chicano History: The Life and Narrative of Bert Corona* (Berkeley: University of California Press, 1995), pp. 246, 247.

52. Ibid., pp. 249–50, 290–91.

53. Billingsley, "Union Card for Green Card."

54. Medina interview.

55. Ibid.; Arthur Jones, "Catholic Hospital Organization Signs Accord with Union," *National Catholic Reporter,* April 20, 2001.

56. Luis Alonso Lugo, "Remittances Are Mexico's Biggest Source of Income, Says Fox," Associated Press, September 24, 2003, *San Diego Union-Tribune,* www.signonsandiego.com/news/mexico/20030924-2051-us-mexico.html; Susan Ferriss, "Surprising Allies on Immigration," *Sacramento Bee,* May 8, 2006. On the composition and recommendations of the Carnegie panel, see U.S.-Mexico Migration Panel, "Mexico-U.S. Migration: A Shared Responsibility," Carnegie Endowment Report, February 14, 2001, www.carnegieendowment.org/publications/index.cfm?fa=view&id=623&prog=zgp.

57. Eliseo Medina, keynote address, Democratic Socialists of America convention, November 9, 2001, www.dsausa.org/convention2k1/eliseo.html.

58. Medina interview.

59. Ibid.; Bill Carder, interview with author, February 15, 2007; e-mail from Marshall Ganz, February 17, 2007; Daniel Weintraub, "A Union's New Focus Is on Immigrants and Voting," *Sacramento Bee,* November 14, 2002.

60. Michael Denney, "Participant Citizenship in a Marginal Group: Union Mobilization of California Farm Workers," *American Journal of Political Science* 23, no. 2 (May 1979): 330–37; Weintraub, "A Union's New Focus."

61. Medina interview; "Roberto De La Cruz 1971–1991" interview by Anamaría De La Cruz, Farmworker Movement Documentation Project, www.farmworkermovement.org/essays/essays/109%20De%20La%20Cruz_Roberto.pdf.

62. Gouri Sadhwani, interview with author, February 12, 2007; Hilary Russ, "Making Change: Union Schmooze," *City Limits* magazine, February 2003.

63. See "Election Day 2006," www.seiu32BJ.org.

64. James Parks, "Immigrant Workers Freedom Ride," www.aflcio.org/aboutus/thisistheaflcio/publications/magazine/0903_iwfr.cfm. Parks provides an invaluable account of the IWFR.

65. Ibid.

66. Ibid.

67. Ibid.

68. Ibid.

69. Ibid.; Victor Narro and Dan Gregor, "People's Lawyering on the Bus: How a Small Band of NLG Members Became the Legal Vanguard for Immigrant Freedom Riders," *Guild Practitioner* 63, no. 2 (Spring 2006): 65–72; Steven Greenhouse, "Immigrants Rally in City, Seeking Rights," *New York Times*, October 5, 2003, http://query.nytimes.com/gst/fullpage.html?res=9D06E5D6123CF 936A35753C1A9659C8B63.

70. Narro and Gregor, "People's Lawyering on the Bus."

71. Roy Van Dyke, *The Immigrant's Journal,* www.immigrantjournal.com; Parks, "Immigrant Workers Freedom Ride"; Maya Raquel Anderson, "Immigrant Workers' Freedom Ride: 'Somos Uno, We Are One,'" *Peacework* magazine, November 2003, www.peaceworkmagazine.org/pwork/0311/031106.htm.

72. Judith Le Blanc, "Immigrant Workers Freedom Ride: A New Movement Is Born," *People's Weekly World,* October 11, 2003, www.pww.org/article/view/ 4206/1/184.

73. Ibid.; Greenhouse, "Immigrants Rally in City, Seeking Rights."

74. Greenhouse, "Immigrants Rally in City, Seeking Rights."

9. THE IMMIGRANT RIGHTS MOVEMENT EXPLODES

1. John M. Broder, "Bush Provided Spark for Immigration Furor," *New York Times,* May 21, 2006.

2. Rachel L. Swarns, "Bill on Illegal Immigrant Aid Draws Fire," *New York Times,* December 30, 2005; White House, Office of the Press Secretary, "President Applauds House for Passing Immigration Reform Bill," December 16, 2005, www .whitehouse.gov/news/releases/2005/12/20051216–13.html; U.S. Congress, *Congressional Record,* House, December 16, 2005, H11952.

3. Swarns, "Bill on Illegal Immigrant Aid"; Eliseo Medina, "The Birth of a National Movement," *Los Angeles Times,* May 2, 2006.

4. "The Gospel vs. H.R. 4437," editorial, *New York Times,* March 3, 2006; Sensenbrenner quoted in Broder, "Bush Provided Spark."

5. Niraj Warikoo, "Latinos Voice Opposition: Thousands Protest Immigration Proposal," *Detroit Free Press,* March 28, 2006; Myung Oak Kim, "Service Workers Demand Their Voice Be Heard," *Rocky Mountain News,* June 5, 2006, www.rockymountainnews.com/drmn/local/article/0,1299,DRMN_15_4750959 ,00.html.

The crowd estimates used in this chapter are based primarily on two sources. The first is data compiled by Xóchitl Bada, Jonathan Fox, Elvia Zazueta, and Ingrid García Ruíz and included in Xóchitl Bada, Jonathan Fox, and Andrew Selee, eds., *Invisible No More: Mexican Migrant Civic Participation in the United States* (Washington, D.C.: Woodrow Wilson International Center for Scholars, 2006), p. 36, table 8.1, www.wilsoncenter.org/news/docs/Invisible%20No%20More1.pdf. The second source is a list compiled by Clare Bayard: "A Catalogue of Resistance: Immigrant-Led Human Rights Mobilizations, Spring 2006," www.deletetheborder .org/node/1126. I have used official police or fire department estimates whenever possible, which are typically lower than those offered by participants.

6. Teresa Watanabe and Hector Becerra, "How DJs Put 500,000 Marchers in Motion," *Los Angeles Times,* March 28, 2006.

7. Martin Manteca, interview with author, February 27, 2007.

8. Amy Goodman and Juan Gonzalez, "Immigrant Rights Protests Rock the Country: Up to 2 Million Take to the Streets in the Largest Wave of Demonstrations in U.S. History," *Democracy Now,* April 11, 2006, www.democracynow.org/article.pl?sid=06/04/11/1426231.

9. Marshall Ganz, interview with author, February 28, 2007.

10. Goodman and Gonzalez, "Immigrant Rights Protests Rock the Country"; Scott Gold, "Student Protests Echo the '60s, but with a High-Tech Buzz," *Los Angeles Times,* March 31, 2006; Harold Meyerson, "The Smartest Movement," *LA Weekly,* April 12, 2006; Watanabe and Becerra, "How DJs Put 500,000 Marchers in Motion"; Teresa Watanabe and Nicole Gaouette, "Next: Converting the Energy of Protest to Political Clout," *Los Angeles Times,* May 2, 2006.

11. Elliot Spagat, "Veterans Drawn into Immigration Debate," Associated Press, *Washington Post,* April 24, 2006, www.washingtonpost.com/wp-dyn/content/article/2006/04/24/AR2006042400746_pf.html.

12. Rachel L. Swarns, "Union Leader Supporting Guest Worker Proposal," *New York Times,* February 23, 2006.

13. Ibid.; William Branigin and Jonathan Weisman, "Immigration Legislation Compromise Announced," *Washington Post,* April 6, 2006.

14. For crowd estimates in this and the following two paragraphs, see Bada, Fox, and Selee, *Invisible No More;* Bayard, "A Catalogue of Resistance"; Goodman and Gonzalez, "Immigrant Rights Protests Rock the Country."

15. Tennessean.com, "Immigrants Regroup, Resume Protests after Bill Stalls," Tennessean News Services, www.tnimmigrant.org/TN_Coalition/Press/Tennessean—2006Apr10thRallies.htm; Goodman and Gonzalez, "Immigrant Rights Protests Rock the Country"; Mark Pitt, interview with author, May 24, 2006.

16. "Rallies across U.S. Call for Illegal Immigrant Rights," CNN.com, April 10, 2006, www.cnn.com/2006/POLITICS/04/10/immigration/index.html?iref=newssearch.

17. Hernan Rozemberg, "Advocates Divided on Boycott by Immigrants," *San Antonio Express-News,* April 30, 2006.

18. Peter Bailey, "Thousands March for Haitian Rights," *Miami Herald,* April 24, 2006.

19. Bada, Fox, and Selee, *Invisible No More;* Bayard, "A Catalogue of Resistance."

20. Mike Colias, "Immigrant Rally Chiefs Ponder What's Next," *Seattle Post-Intelligencer,* May 2, 2006.

21. Ibid.

22. Ibid.; Watanabe and Gaouette, "Next."

23. Watanabe and Gaouette, "Next"; Dudley Althaus and Cynthia Leonor Garza, "Dreams of Many Ride on Boycott," *Houston Chronicle,* May 1, 2006.

24. Peter Prengaman, "More Legal Immigrants Seek Citizenship," *Seattle Post-Intelligencer*, May 10, 2006; Anna Gorman and Jennifer Delson, "Citizenship Requests Soar before Big Changes," *Los Angeles Times,* February 25, 2007.

25. Teresa Watanabe and Joe Mathews, "Unions Helped to Organize 'Day without Immigrants,'" *Los Angeles Times,* May 3, 2006.

26. Althaus and Garza, "Dreams of Many Ride on Boycott"; Watanabe and Gaouette, "Next."

27. Colias, "Immigrant Rally Chiefs Ponder What's Next"; Medina, "Birth of a National Movement."

28. Teresa Watanabe, "Latinos Urged to Head for the Polls," *Los Angeles Times,* May 17, 2006; Prengaman, "More Legal Immigrants Seek Citizenship"; Darryl Fears, "Immigrant Supporters to Counter Bush Speech," *Washington Post,* May 15, 2006.

29. Teresa Watanabe, "Hispanics Embrace U.S. Citizenship to Cast Votes," *Los Angeles Times,* May 16, 2006.

30. See the following editorials: "Immigration Ugliness," *Washington Post,* September 22, 2006; "House Fumbles Reforms," *Arizona Republic,* September 22, 2006; "Immigration: Failure Looms Once Again," *Lincoln (Nebraska) Journal-Star,* September 20, 2006; "U.S. Immigration Needs Real Reform," *Denver Post,* September 22, 2006; "Stall Game," *Orlando Sentinel,* September 17, 2006; "Border Fence More Stunt Than Solution," *Waco (Texas) Tribune,* September 18, 2006; "Immigration's Lost Year," *New York Times,* September 19, 2006. Reactions even in the fiercely pro-Republican *Wall Street Journal* ("The Great Wall of America," September 21, 2006) ranged from scathing to disappointed in the House Republican actions.

31. Bada, Fox, and Seles, *Invisible No More.*

32. Nicole Gaouette, "Immigration Galvanizes Latino Voters," *Los Angeles Times,* October 27, 2006.

33. Ibid.

34. Latino Policy Coalition, "Latinos Voting for Change in Key Republican Held Congressional Districts, Non-Partisan Survey Finds," press release, October 5, 2006, www.latinopolicycoalition.org/LPC_telemundo_poll_final.htm, which quotes Segura and Ramakrishnan.

35. Rosenberg is quoted in Gaouette, "Immigration Galvanizes Latino Voters." Polly Baca and the analysis by the National Association of Latino Elected and Appointed Officials are cited in Ann Imse and Hector Gutierrez, "Hispanic Vote Sprouting Muscles," *Rocky Mountain News,* November 2, 2006. Sampaio's remarks are found in Elizabeth Aguilera, "Latino Registration Logs 3.5% Bump," *Denver Post,* November 2, 2006. See also National Immigration Forum, "The Surprise Winner in This Year's Election Is . . . Comprehensive Immigration Reform," press release, November 9, 2006, www.immigrationforum.org/Desktop Default.aspx?tabid=856.

36. The William C. Velasquez Institute exit polls differed from Pew by finding that only 6 percent of Latinos shifted to the Democrats, based on WCVI's statistics that showed a higher Latino percentage for Democrats in 2004. But the end result of both polls is a 40 percent margin in the Latino Democratic vote, an astonishing disparity for a constituency considered "up for grabs" as recently as the 2000 presidential race. See "Latinos and the 2006 Mid-term Election," fact sheet, Pew Hispanic Center, November 27, 2006, http://pewhispanic .org/files/factsheets/26.pdf; National Immigration Forum, "The Surprise Winner"; Aguilera, "Latino Registration Logs 3.5% Bump"; Elizabeth Aguilera, "Dems Won Over Latino Voters, Study Says," *Denver Post,* November 28, 2006.

Turnout figures are reported from CNN exit polls; see www.bluelatinos.org/node/497.

37. Eliseo Medina, "Keep Working on Immigration," TomPaine.common sense, June 8, 2007, www.tompaine.com/articles/2007/06/08/keep_working_on_immigration.php.

38. National Immigration Forum, "While Debate Rages, the Public Continues to Support Realistic Immigration Solutions," December 10, 2007, www.immigrationforum.org/documents/PressRoom/PublicOpinion/2007/Polling-Summary0407.pdf; National Council of La Raza, "National Coalition Unveils Unprecedented Campaign to Increase the Latino Vote in 2008 Presidential Election," press release, November 14, 2007, www.nclr.org/content/news/detail/49451; Susan Ferriss, "Lining Up for Citizenship," *Sacramento Bee,* January 15, 2008; Pico National Network, L.A. Voice, "Ya es Hora Ciudadania! Campaign Gains Strength in Los Angeles," November 10, 2007, www.piconetwork.org/news/ya-es-hora-ciudadania-campaign-gains-strength-in-los-angeles.html.

39. Ferriss, "Lining Up for Citizenship"; Julia Preston, "Latinos Seek Citizenship in Time for Voting," *New York Times,* March 7, 2008; Miriam Jordan, "Paper Jam May Curb Latino Vote," *Wall Street Journal,* January 18, 2008, p. 4; Albor Ruiz, "One Million More Wait to Answer Call," *New York Daily News,* January 10, 2008. Jennifer Gordon (*Suburban Sweatshops: The Fight for Immigrant Rights* [Cambridge, Mass.: Harvard University Press, 2005], p. 281) reports that there were more than 130 immigrant worker centers in 2005.

10. THE DECLINE OF THE UFW

1. On the issue of the Carter campaign's role, see Marshall Ganz e-mail, May 9, 2004; Farmworker Movement Documentation Project, www.farmworkermovement.org/disc/May%5B1%5D%5B2%5D.pdf.

2. Susan Ferriss and Ricardo Sandoval, *The Fight in the Fields: Cesar Chavez and the Farmworkers Movement* (Orlando: Harcourt Brace, 1998), p. 227. For the most thorough (and controversial) detailing of the UFW's decline, see Miriam Pawel's four-part *Los Angeles Times* series, "UFW: A Broken Contract," January 8, 9, 10, 11, 2006. Pawel's series was controversial primarily for its criticism of current UFW projects rather than her account of the union's decline after 1980.

3. Jerry Cohen, interview with author, May 22, 2007.

4. Miriam Pawel, "Decisions of Long Ago Shape the Union Today," *Los Angeles Times,* January 10, 2006, p. 3, quoting the volunteer; Ferriss and Sandoval, *The Fight in the Fields,* p. 213.

5. A review of essays at the Farmworker Movement Documentation Project, www.farmworkermovement.org, confirms that most left the movement voluntarily.

6. Pawel, "Decisions of Long Ago." I have had multiple conversations with Larry Tramutola over the course of several years about his termination.

7. Craig Scharlin and Lilia V. Villanueva, *Philip Vera Cruz: A Personal History of Filipino Immigrants and the Farmworkers Movement* (Seattle: University of Washington Press, 2000), pp. 115–16, 125.

8. Ibid., pp. 134–35.

9. Patrick J. Sullivan, *Blue Collar–Roman Collar–White Collar: U.S. Catholic*

Involvement in Labor-Management Controversies, 1960–1980 (Lanham, Md.: University Press of America, 1987), pp. 159–62.

10. Ibid., p. 122; Pawel, "Decisions of Long Ago"; Scharlin and Villanueva, *Philip Vera Cruz*, p. 122.

11. Pawel, "Decisions of Long Ago"; Ferriss and Sandoval, *The Fight in the Fields*, p. 225, quoting Doug Adair.

12. Pawel, "Decisions of Long Ago."

13. For example, Cohen learned that the cook at La Paz earned well above the standard rate (Jerry Cohen, interviews with author, April 21, 2007, and May 18, 21, 2007).

14. Ibid.

15. Ibid.; Ferriss and Sandoval, *The Fight in the Fields*, pp. 212–13. On the five to four board vote, see Marshall Ganz, "David Conquered Goliath with Five Smooth Stones: So It Was with the Farm Workers," in *The New Rank and File*, ed. Staughton Lynd and Alice Lynd (Ithaca, N.Y.: Cornell University Press, 2000), p. 30.

16. Cohen interviews.

17. Ferriss and Sandoval, *The Fight in the Fields*, p. 216; Pawel, "Decisions of Long Ago."

18. Pawel, "Decisions of Long Ago."

19. Ibid.

20. Philip L. Martin, *Promises to Keep: Collective Bargaining in California Agriculture* (Ames: Iowa State University Press, 1996), p. 91; Pawel, "Decisions of Long Ago"; Ferriss and Sandoval, *The Fight in the Fields*, p. 221.

21. Ferriss and Sandoval, *The Fight in the Fields*, pp. 216, 221.

22. Ibid., pp. 228, 229; Pawel, "Decisions of Long Ago."

23. Pawel, "Decisions of Long Ago."

24. "Cesar Chavez on Money and Organizing, October 4, 1971," in *The Words of César Chávez*, ed. Richard J. Jensen and John C. Hammerback (College Station: Texas A&M Press, 2002), pp. 65–71.

25. Richard Griswold del Castillo and Richard Garcia, *César Chávez: A Triumph of Spirit* (Norman: University of Oklahoma Press, 1995), p. 134; Martin, *Promises to Keep*, pp. 91, 96; James Rainey, "Clinton Gets Warm Welcome from Latinos," *Los Angeles Times*, January 23, 2008. Miriam Pawel ("Farmworkers Reap Little as Union Strays from Its Roots," *Los Angeles Times*, January 8, 2006) estimated UFW membership in 2006 as fewer than seven thousand.

26. The AFL-CIO is quoted in William Claiborne, "Labor Picks Strawberry Fields as Organizing Battleground," *Washington Post*, May 11, 1997. See also Eric Brazil, "UFW, Strawberry Growers Sign Historic Labor Contracts," *San Francisco Chronicle*, March 9, 2001; Todd Purdum, "A Setback for United Farmworkers," *New York Times*, May 28, 1999.

27. *The Fight in the Fields*, the excellent account by Susan Ferriss and Ricardo Sandoval, is typical of sources that highlight Deukmejian's election and the resulting shift in the ALRB. A leading academic study of California farmworkers noted the union's internal problems as a factor in its decline but particularly emphasized such reasons as the changing structure of farm employment, especially the rise of farm labor contractors and increased legal and illegal im-

migration (see Martin, *Promises to Keep*). But because the power of the UFW had largely driven labor contractors out of the fields in the 1960s, and since immigration was always an issue in any period, these factors were not as decisive in the union's decline as the massive talent drain.

11. HARVESTING JUSTICE BEYOND THE FIELDS

1. To compile the list, I assessed every name in the Essays section of LeRoy Chatfield's Farmworker Movement Documentation Project website, www.farm workermovement.org. I then added the names of other individuals I had come across through researching this book.

I already had information about many post-UFW careers; for the rest, I questioned interviewees and conducted Internet searches. As I was primarily interested in careers that furthered the struggle for social justice, I began to narrow down the list. The biggest challenge was characterizing certain jobs. For example, teachers, social workers, and health care workers perform very important functions in society, and UFW experience may have led some to choose those careers. In the end, the connection between these jobs and the role of a UFW activist seemed too tenuous, and I judged that including these and similar career paths risked diminishing the table's role in representing the specific impact of the UFW experience.

2. Stuart is quoted in "Lee Stuart's Commitment to Social Justice Leads to a Fulfilling but Unexpected Life," *Alumni: Desert Stars*, Prescott College, Prescott, Arizona, http://prescott.edu/alumni/desertstars.html.

3. Drake's comments to the *Boston Globe* are quoted in A. V. Krebs, "Social Justice, Farmworker Activists Mourn Deaths of Drake, Brown," *Agribusiness Examiner*, no. 130 (October 22, 2001), www.electricarrow.com/CARP/agbiz/130.htm.

4. Ed Langloi, "Catholics Seek Links with Unions," *Catholic Sentinel*, March 26, 2004, www.sentinel.org/node/1073.

5. "David Koehler 1974–1978," essay, Farmworker Movement Documentation Project, www.farmworkermovement.us/essays/essays/158%20Koehler_David.pdf.

6. Molly Parker, "Koehler Earns Democratic Nod," *Peoria Journal Star*, March 22, 2006; "David Koehler 1974–1978," essay.

7. Richard Griswold del Castillo and Richard Garcia, *César Chávez: A Triumph of Spirit* (Norman: University of Oklahoma Press, 1995), p. 48; Susan Ferriss and Ricardo Sandoval, *The Fight in the Fields: Cesar Chavez and the Farmworkers Movement* (Orlando: Harcourt Brace, 1998), pp. 108, 109, 111.

8. Griswold del Castillo and Garcia, *César Chávez*, p. 152; Ferriss and Sandoval, *The Fight in the Fields*, pp. 110–12.

9. Griswold del Castillo and Garcia, *César Chávez*, p. 58; Ferriss and Sandoval, *The Fight in the Fields*, p. 120.

10. Ferriss and Sandoval, *The Fight in the Fields*, pp. 258, 259.

11. Ibid.; Griswold Del Castillo and Garcia, *César Chávez*, p. 174.

12. Peter Jones, interview with author, May 30, 2007; "Mark Sharwood 1976–1982," essay, Farmworker Movement Documentation Project, www.farmworkermovement.org/essays/essays/104%20Sharwood_Mark.pdf.

13. "Peter Jones 1975–1977," essay, Farmworker Movement Documentation

Project, www.farmworkermovement.org/essays/essays/169%20Jones_Peter.pdf; "Steve Jones 1976–1977, 1979–1980," essay, www.farmworkermovement.org/essays/essays/181%20Jones_Steve.pdf.

14. "Peter Jones 1975–1977," essay; Peter Jones interview.

15. "Steve Jones 1976–1977, 1979–1980," essay. The soundtrack to *Forgotten: The Murder at the Ford Rouge Plant* is available at www.laborheritage.org/forgotten.htm.

16. David Bacon, *Communities without Borders: Images and Voices from the World of Migration* (Ithaca, N.Y.: Cornell University Press, 2006); David Bacon, *The Children of NAFTA: Labor Wars on the U.S./Mexico Border* (Berkeley: University of California Press, 2004). A sample of Bacon's photos and stories is available at http://dbacon.igc.org.

17. Vera Cruz's writings have been assembled in Craig Scharlin and Lilia V. Villanueva, *Philip Vera Cruz: A Personal History of Filipino Immigrants and the Farmworkers Movement* (Seattle: University of Washington Press, 2000); the information outlined here is based on pp. 115–16, 125. In September 2002, PVCJ was established as the community-based organization FOCUS, continuing Vera Cruz's commitment to social justice into the future.

18. Eric Sagara, " 'Hate-Speak' at School Draws Scrutiny," *Tucson Citizen,* April 13, 2006, www.tucsoncitizen.com/daily/local/9256; Ray Estrada, "Mother of 11 with a Cause," *Vida en el Valle,* May 13, 2007, http://news.newamericamedia.org/news/view_article.html?article_id=7261d803a816658da4e0f8672ff83dfo; Chelsea Ross, "Rebel for the Cause: United Farm Worker Pioneer Leads Immigrant Rights Struggle," *In These Times,* May 11, 2007, www.inthesetimes.com/article/3125.

19. See "Dolores Huerta Biography," www.doloreshuerta.org/dolores_huerta_foundation.htm.

20. Gilbert Padilla, interview with author, May 30, 2007.

21. Humberto Gomez, interview with author, May 24, 2007; "Humberto Gomez 1965–1989," essay, Farmworker Movement Documentation Project, www.farmworkermovement.us/essays/essays/023%20Gomez_Humberto.pdf.

22. Gomez interview.

23. Ibid.

24. Ibid.

25. Sharon Delugach, interview with author, May 24, 2007.

26. Ibid.

27. Stephen Lerner, interview with author, September 26, 2006; Paul Milne, interview with author, May 21, 2007; John Adler, interview with author, September 13, 2006.

28. LeRoy Chatfield, interview with author, May 19, 2007.

29. Ibid.

30. Larry Frank, interview with author, May 26, 2007.

31. Ibid.

32. "Shabby Show," *Los Angeles Times,* December 31, 1982; "A Disgraceful Performance," *Oakland Tribune,* December 30, 1982. Also see Frank del Olmo, "Deukmejian Gets a Bad Start with California's Latinos," *Los Angeles Times,* January 13, 1983.

33. Information on the later work of Neighbor to Neighbor veterans was obtained from Internet searches and from information graciously provided to the author by John Adler and Fred Ross Jr.

34. Deborah White, "Immigration Marches May Rise on Cesar Chavez Holiday," About.com: US Liberal Politics, March 29, 2006, http://usliberals.about.com/b/a/2006_03_29.htm; Juan Sepulveda Jr., *The Life and Times of Willie Velásquez* (Houston: Arte Público Press, 2003), p. 164; Juan Sepulveda Jr., interview with author, March 20, 2006.

CONCLUSION

1. Eliseo Medina, "On Hope and Activism," in Studs Terkel, *Hope Dies Last: Keeping the Faith in Difficult Times* (New York: New Press, 2003), p. 124, www.commondreams.org/scriptfiles/views03/1111-09.htm. In a study by Marshall Ganz, Kim Voss, and George Strauss ("Why Lead Labor? Project and Pathways in California Unions, 1984–2001," Institute for Research on Labor and Employment, Working Paper Series, University of California at Berkeley, 2003, http://econpapers.repec.org/paper/cdlindrel/1091.htm), the UFW is described as a "bridging organization," where activists who viewed unions as "undemocratic upholders of the status quo and the war effort" learned that unions could be vehicles for social change.

2. Paul Milne, interview with author, May 21, 2007.

3. For more information about ACORN, see www.acorn.org.

4. For more information about the PIRGs, see www.uspirg.org.

INDEX

Cousino, Ida, 271
Craig, Larry, 242
Cranston, Alan, 130, 160
Cuellar, Edward, 271

D'Alesandro, Tommy, 163
Dalzell, Tom, 271, 290
Danaher, Kevin, 54, 309n8
Datz, Bob, 269
Davis, Gray, 172, 176
Dawson, Rosario, 241
Day, Mark, 66
DDT, 122, 127–28, 131–32
De Colores, 81, 281
De La Cruz, Jessie, 269
De La Cruz, Roberto, 269, 326
Deagen, Patrick, 270
Delgado, Hilda, 238
Delugach, Sharon, 38, 270; joins UFW, 286; political activist, 286–87
Democratic National Convention, 145, 153, 185, 230
Denver Labor Federation, 191
Deukmejian, George, 138, 265, 289
Diaz, Cameron, 241
Diepenhrock, Martha, 271
DiGiorgio Farms, 20, 21
DiMarzio, Nicholas, 225
Dohan, Marc, 271, 293
Dole, Robert, 153
Dominguez, Jessica, 239
Doner, Tasha, 270
Donohoe, Hugh A., 79
Drake, Jim: 1968 fast, 91, 276, 307; as early Chavez ally, 76–77; as key UFW leader, 266; on George Meany, 27; post-UFW career, 270, 273–75; quits UFW over the "Game," 252
Drake, Susan Samuels, 34, 269, 272, 307
Dukakis, Michael, 161
Dunn, Ed, 271
Dunne, John Gregory, 306
Durazo, Maria Elena: background, 93–94; Cranston campaign, 160–61; develops SOL, 179; forms OLAW, 173–77; heads LACFL, 239; HERE Local 11 and, 94; immigrant rights marker, 239; meets Miguel Contreras, 168; National Chair of IWFR, 221, 225; seeks labor religious immigrant unity, 212; USC rolling fast and, 93–95; USC, 179; works on 1986 Cranston campaign, 160–61

Eagle Hospitality, 70–71
Edwards, John, 116
Egan, Cardinal Edward M., 225

Eggers, Ellen, 151, 271, 291, 319n18
Ehrenreich, Barbara, 111
Eilers, Jean, 269, 275–76
El Malcriado (Voice of the Farm Worker), 32, 35, 40, 307, 316
"El Plan de Delano," 81, 278
El Teatro Campesino, 277–79
Elinson, Elaine, 35, 269, 272, 307
Elliott, Nancy, 269
Environmental justice, 134–37
Environmental Protection Agency: bans DDT, 133
Episcopal Student Center, 104, 119–20
Equal Exchange, 59
Escalante, Alberto, 269
Estefan, Gloria, 109
Estevez, Emilio, 83
Estevez, Felipe, 108
Everts, Rob, 269

Fa, Angie, 271
Faces of War, 55
Farm Labor Organizing Committee (FLOC): Campbell Soup boycott, 52; UFW influence, 52, 53
Farmworker Justice Center, 140
Farmworkers: in 1930s, 9; organizing history, 14, 15; strikes, 15. See also United Farm Workers
Farm Worker Service Center, 121
Farnsworth, Charles, 132, 271
Fast for Life, 92
Fasting: as organizing tool, 87–92; adopted by progressive movements, 93–96. See also Chavez, Cesar
Feinstein, Dianne, and recall campaign, 159–60
Fellner, Kim, 28, 306
Ferriss, Susan, xi, 331n27
Fielder, Octavia, 34
Fight in the Fields, The, xi, 331n27
Figueroa, Alfredo, 270
Figueroa, Hector, 220
Filipinos, 18, 253
Fishman, Mike, 109. See also Service Employees International Union
"Five Cents for Fairness," 264–65
Flores Rivera, Abby, 271
Flores, Henry, 184
Frade, Bishop Leo, 110
Franco, Carolina, 24, 33
Frank, Larry, 94, 270, 288, 321n10
Fuentes, Maria, 271

Gallo Wine, UFW boycott of, 32, 47–49
Gamble, James, 58
"Game," the, 251–53

stein recall and 168, 176, 190–
91, 269, 211, on "sí se puede,"
312n38
Washington Post, 106, 116, 242, 310,
313, 315, 328, 329, 331
We Are America Alliance, 244
Weine, Ken, 271
Weingarten, Robin, 271
Weisenhahn, Dick, 270
Welfare reform: immigrants and, 208–9
Whitten, Jamie, 123, 316
Wielhouwer, Peter, 191
Wilhelm, John, 168; calls for national
hotel workers campaign, 62; Durazo
and, 94; IWFR and, 222
Willet, Dan, 269, 270
William C. Velasquez Institute, 294,
329n36
Williams, Jack, 149
Williamson, Steve, 222

Willinger, Aloysius, 81
Willis, Joaquin, 106
Wilson, Pete, 183, 242
Winograd, Barry, 271
Wong, Kent, 81, 321n10
Wonkette, 106
Woo, Mike, 169
Woodrow Wilson International Center
for Scholars, 327n9
Working Families Party, 302
Wrath of Grapes, The, 139

Ybarra, Danny, 271
Ybarra, Richard, 269
Yett, Jane, 269

Zapata, Emiliano, 82
Zeliff, William, 207
Zeluff, Tracy, 59, 174, 179, 271, 293
Zerger, Kirsten, 271

Text: 10/13 Sabon
Display: Franklin Gothic Demi, Sabon
Compositor: Integrated Composition Systems
Printer and binder: Thomson-Shore, Inc.